Norm Clasen

Elizabeth Obediente

L. Hunter Lovins and Boyd Cohen

The Way Out

L. Hunter Lovins, named a *Time* magazine Hero of the Planet and called by *Newsweek* "the green business icon," is president and founder of Natural Capitalism Solutions, whose clients include Bank of America, Walmart, PG&E, the Pentagon, the city and county of Los Angeles, and Boulder, Colorado, to name just a few. Boyd Cohen is CEO of CO2IMPACT and a former professor of sustainable entrepreneurship in Spain, Costa Rica, and Canada.

Also by L. Hunter Lovins

Transforming Industry in Asia

Climate Protection Manual for Cities

LASER Guide to Community Development (with Gwendolyn Hallsmith et al.)

*The Natural Advantage of Nations: Business Opportunities,
Innovation and Governance in the 21st Century*
(eds. Karlson "Charlie" Hargroves and Michael H. Smith)

Natural Capitalism: The Next Industrial Revolution
(with Paul Hawken and Amory B. Lovins)

Green Development: Integrating Ecology and Real Estate
(with Alex Wilson et al.)

Factor Four: Doubling Wealth, Halving Resource Use
(with Amory B. Lovins and Ernst von Weizsäcker)

Energy Unbound: A Fable for America's Future
(with Amory B. Lovins and Seth Zuckerman)

The First Nuclear World War (with Amory B. Lovins and
Patrick O'Heffernan)

Brittle Power: Energy Strategy for National Security (with Amory B. Lovins)

Least-Cost Energy: Solving the CO_2 Problem (with Amory B. Lovins,
Florentin Krause, and Wilfrid Bach)

Energy/War: Breaking the Nuclear Link (with Amory B. Lovins)

The
Way Out

The Way Out

Kick-starting

Capitalism

to Save

Our Economic Ass

L. Hunter Lovins and Boyd Cohen

Hill and Wang

A division of Farrar, Straus and Giroux   New York

HILL AND WANG
A division of Farrar, Straus and Giroux
18 West 18th Street, New York 10011

Distributed in Canada by D&M Publishers, Inc.
Printed in the United States of America
Originally published in 2011 by Hill and Wang as *Climate Capitalism:*
Capitalism in the Age of Climate Change
First paperback edition, 2012

Interior spot photographs copyright © iStockphoto.com

The graph on page 254 is from *From Risk to Opportunity: Insurer Responses to Climate*
Change by Evan Mills, Ph.D., report for Ceres, April 2009. Reprinted with permission.

Library of Congress Cataloging-in-Publication Data
Lovins, L. Hunter, 1950–
   [Climate capitalism.]
   The way out : kick-starting capitalism to save our economic ass / L. Hunter Lovins and
Boyd Cohen. — 1st pbk. ed.
     p. cm.
   "Originally published in 2011 by Hill and Wang as Climate Capitalism: Capitalism in
the Age of Climate Change."
   Includes bibliographical references and index.
   ISBN 978-0-8090-3469-7 (alk. paper)
   1. Sustainable development—Environmental aspects.   2. Entrepreneurship—
Environmental aspects.   3. Capitalism—Environmental aspects.   4. Climatic changes—
Economic aspects.   5. Environmental policy—Economic aspects.   I. Cohen, Boyd.
II. Title.

HC79.E5 L67 2012
338.9'27—dc23

2011050956

Designed by Abby Kagan

www.fsgbooks.com

1 3 5 7 9 10 8 6 4 2

This book is dedicated to
the memory of
Dr. Stephen Schneider,
a true pioneer
who gave his life
protecting the climate.

Contents

1. Entrepreneuring the Solutions: The Business Case for
   Climate Protection   3
2. Energy Efficiency: Low-Hanging Fruit That Grows Back   28
3. Both Are Better: Energy Efficiency and Renewable Energy
   Unleash the New Energy Economy   57
4. Green Buildings, Green Neighborhoods: Where Climate
   Capitalism Lives   95
5. Moving On   123
6. World Without Oil   147
7. Growing a Better World   178
8. Carbon Markets: Indulgences, Hot Air, or the New Currency? 220
9. Adapting to Climate Chaos   249
10. A Future That Works   272

   Appendix: How to Calculate and Offset Your Carbon Emissions 309
   Notes   311
   Acknowledgments   367
   Index   371

The
Way Out

Entrepreneuring the Solutions: The Business Case for Climate Protection

Entrepreneurs, companies, and countries are prospering from climate protection even in challenging times. This book describes how you, your family, your community, your company, and the world can profit from Climate Capitalism. The chapters present the good news about how you can become a part of the solution. They show that intelligent use of market mechanisms can solve the climate crisis not at a cost but as an investment, delivering enhanced profitability and a stronger economy as well as a better future for the planet. The best and fastest way to protect the climate is to reduce the unnecessary use of fossil energy. It is also the fastest way to an immediate return on investment. Cutting waste saves money, whether you are a business leader or head of a household.

The case stories that follow demonstrate that entrepreneurship is alive and well. Which is good: without it no solution to climate change makes any sense. It is good for another reason. Entrepreneurs discover opportunity even in the midst of financial crisis. Throughout history, the nations that have innovated to meet human needs have ruled the world, economically, politically, and militarily. How we respond to the twin crises defining our generation—economic collapse and climate change—will very likely determine the world future generations will live in.

The current economic crisis is extremely fluid. It could go in any of several directions. Commitments by global leaders to unleashing the green economy could turn the world around. Conversely, delay in implementing sustainable measures could deepen the current depression, now recognized as the worst since the 1930s.[1]

Change *will* occur because past best practices are no longer sufficient to deal with the challenges facing the world. Businesses and industrial policy *will* implement the measures described in this book, or the world will face crises far exceeding what this young century has already brought.[2]

The choices you make this year and next will determine whether you, your community, and ultimately your country come out of the economic collapse prosperous and in a position to secure the future you want, or whether life will become an unending reaction to emergencies that batter our ability to cope.[3] Recent American history suggests there is reason for hope. The Architecture 2030 project points out:

> During the 1970s oil crisis (an 11-year period from 1973 to 1983), this country, drawing on American determination and ingenuity, increased its real GDP by over one trillion dollars (in Year 2000 dollars) and added 30 billion square feet of new buildings and 35 million new vehicles, while decreasing total US energy consumption and CO_2 emissions. This was accomplished with increased efficiency and with cost-effective, readily available, off-the-shelf materials, equipment and technology.[4]

A new reality, now recognized as "the sustainability imperative," is inexorably driving companies to implement practices that are more responsible to people and the planet because they are more profitable.[5] When the likes of Goldman Sachs and Deloitte report that companies leading in environmental, social, and good governance policies have 25 percent higher stock values, change is clearly under way.[6] Or when an industry giant such as Walmart begins to require its sixty to ninety thousand suppliers to answer a sustainability scorecard tracking their carbon footprint, their impact on water and other resources, and their engagement with local communities, it is clear that behaving in more sustainable ways has moved from a chic niche position to a business imperative.[7]

Melting Capital and the Warming Climate

Two words define the current era: "climate" and "capitalism."

People raised on images of limitless possibilities, muscle cars, Western superiority in world markets, and a rising standard of living watched in shock as General Motors, the iconic American business, melted into bankruptcy in 2008. For many the magnitude of that collapse has yet to sink in. Nor has the recognition that Toyota became the world's largest car company—subsequently supplanted by Volkswagen in the top spot— by riding to preeminence on the success of fuel-efficient vehicles that seem an affront to everything that made America great. GM's reemergence from bankruptcy is similarly based on a small electric hybrid. The economic collapse of 2008 devastated communities and families, leaving more than 15 million people out of work, and sent unemployment over 25 percent in Detroit and other cities.[8] It made economic recovery almost everyone's top priority.

Another meltdown, however, poses an even greater threat. In the fall of 2009, the United Nations warned that even if the nations of the world deliver on existing promises to cut emissions of greenhouse gases (GHGs), the globe will still warm beyond levels ever experienced by humankind by the end of the century, perhaps sooner. In his introduction to the film *An Inconvenient Truth*, Al Gore called climate change "a moral issue." But at heart it is neither a moral nor an environmental issue. It is a crisis of capitalism. What is little recognized is that the twin threats, to the climate and to the economy, are linked in both cause and cure. Unless nations move aggressively to implement energy efficiency and renewable energy, key elements of the transition away from fossil fuels and necessary to save the climate, it is difficult to see how our economy can lift itself from recession or avoid further crises. Solving the climate crisis IS THE WAY OUT of the economic crisis.

Capitalism to the Rescue

Critics argue that the science is uncertain. Absolutely. The goal of science isn't infallibility or unanimity. Scientists don't know how bad it's going to be, or how fast climate chaos will proceed. If anything, the science is conservative in its predictions: for example, the observed reality of climate change is outrunning the scientific models, happening faster even than the most alarmed scientists predicted that it would.[9]

But with all due respect to the great climate scientists, let's assume that the skeptics are correct. They are not, and you would be a fool to go to Vegas on the odds that they might be, but in a sense, the science is irrelevant. For purposes of argument, let's assume for a moment that the skeptics are right. If all you are is a profit-maximizing capitalist, you'll do exactly the same thing you'd do if you were scared to death about climate change because smart companies are recognizing that you don't have to believe in climate change to believe in its solutions. We know how to solve this problem at a profit: through Climate Capitalism. DuPont was among the early climate capitalists. About a decade ago the company's leaders pledged to cut its carbon emissions 65 percent below their 1990 levels, and to do it by 2010. That's a bit more ambitious than the United States, which still refuses to ratify the Kyoto Protocol, a pledge to cut emissions 7 percent below 1990 levels by 2010, will accept.

Has DuPont joined Greenpeace?

No. The company made its announcement in the name of increasing shareholder value.

And it has delivered on its promise. The value of DuPont stock increased 340 percent while the company reduced its global emissions 67 percent. DuPont's program had by 2007 reduced the company's emissions 80 percent below 1990 levels. Doing this created a financial savings for the company of $3 billion between 2000 and 2005.[10] The company's climate protection program showed it costs less to implement energy savings measures than it does to buy and burn fuel. In short, DuPont was solving the problem at a profit. In 1999, DuPont estimated that every ton of carbon it no longer emitted saved its shareholders $6. By 2007, Du-

Pont's efforts to squeeze out waste were saving the company $2.2 billion a year. The company's profits that year? $2.2 billion.[11]

DuPont became a company that's profitable because it's protecting the climate. DuPont is not the edge of the envelope. Back in the 1990s, STMicroelectronics, a manufacturer of computer chips, set what Jim Collins, the business author, calls a BHAG: a big hairy audacious goal. STMicroelectronics pledged to achieve zero net CO_2 emissions, becoming carbon neutral, by 2010 while increasing production forty-fold. When the company made this pledge it had no earthly idea how to achieve it, but figuring it out drove corporate innovation, taking STMicroelectronics from the number-twelve chip maker in the world to number six. Along with winning awards, ST reckoned that by the time it had reached its goal, it would have saved about a billion dollars.[12]

Natural Capitalism Solutions (www.natcapsolutions.org) and other sustainability consultants work with such companies to help them cut waste, transform how they make products, and implement more sustainable ways of doing business. One company with which NCS worked had a practice of leaving its 6,300 computers and monitors turned on 24/7. Various urban myths about shortening the life of the computer by turning it off, or claims that the IT department required them to be left on, had led the company to waste energy and money. NCS consultants pointed out that simply issuing a policy that employees turn computers off when no one is in front of them would save $700,000 the first year alone.[13] In the United States $2.8 billion a year is wasted simply because computers are left on when no one is using them. Such IT costs can represent a quarter of the cost of running a modern office building.[14] In March 2010, Ford Motor Company announced that it would save $1 million each year by shutting off unused computers.[15]

A team from NCS worked with a large distribution center, a 7-million-square-foot warehouse, in which five-hundred-watt lightbulbs shone down on the tops of boxes stacked floor to ceiling. The workers below used task lighting so they could see where they were going. Simply flipping a switch would save $650,000 dollars a year.[16] Nationally we waste $5 billion to $10 billion each year leaving unnecessary or redundant lights on.[17]

The savings from eliminating this waste are free—or better than free. And they exist throughout American businesses.

Even where achieving energy savings that will protect the climate requires an up-front investment of money, it is one of the best investments a company can make. Diversey, a Wisconsin-based global provider of commercial cleaning, sanitation, and hygiene solutions, projects 160 percent return on its investments to cut its carbon footprint by saving energy.[18] That is a just a bit better than you're going to get on your 401(k).

In Europe and Asia, adherence to the Kyoto Protocol is driving competitiveness. Given how much energy was saved in the examples just recounted, it should come as little surprise that in 2008 American businesses, most of which have not implemented aggressive efficiency programs, used twice as much energy to produce a unit of GNP as their European and Asian competitors. The American Council for an Energy-Efficient Economy estimates that the U.S. economy wastes 87 percent of the energy it consumes.[19] Far from constraining innovation, signatories to the Kyoto Protocol, which obliges them to save energy to cut carbon emissions, have signed on for innovation, saving money in the process.

Risk Management in a World of Climate Chaos

Smart companies now recognize that tolerating wasteful energy use and higher carbon emissions is a high-risk strategy. Geopolitical volatility, the unpredictability of energy supplies, price increases, threats to business from extreme weather events, and the risk of liability claims for failing to manage carbon output all make carbon reduction a good business strategy. The FTSE Index, the British equivalent of the Dow Jones Industrial Average, put it succinctly: "The impact of climate change is likely to have an increasing influence on the economic value of companies, both directly, and through new regulatory frameworks. Investors, governments and society in general expect companies to identify and reduce their climate change risks and impacts, and also to identify and develop related business opportunities."[20]

In 2007 Oxfam International released a report showing that natural disasters had increased from an average of 120 a year in the early 1980s to as many as 500 a year.[21] Flood and windstorm disasters rose six-fold, from about 60 in 1980 to 240 in 2006. From the mid-1980s to the mid-1990s, 174 million people were affected annually by disasters of all types. From 1995 to 2004 this number rose to 254 million a year. The 2007 floods in Asia alone affected 250 million people. The International Federation of Red Cross and Red Crescent Societies agreed, estimating that natural disasters of all types now kill more than 120,000 people per year, double the toll in the 1990s.[22]

These numbers represent not only a humanitarian disaster but also a business risk. In 2003 *The Wall Street Journal* reported that the second-largest reinsurance firm, Swiss Re, "announced that it is considering denying coverage, starting with directors and officers liability policies, to companies it decided aren't managing their output of greenhouse gases."[23] The prescience of this statement came clear as claims from weather-related disasters rose twice as fast as those from all other mishaps.[24] The year 2008 was the third-worst year on record for loss-producing events, with losses jumping from $82 billion in 2007 to over $200 billion, and more than 220,000 lives lost. The all-time record remains 2005, with $232 billion in insured losses. Costs are now growing ten times faster than premiums, the population, or economic growth.[25]

"Nervous investors have begun asking similar questions of the insurers," *The Washington Post* reported in 2007. "At a meeting of the National Association of Insurance Commissioners, Andrew Logan, insurance director of the investor coalition, representing $4 trillion in market capital, warned that 'insurance as we know it is threatened by a perfect storm of rising weather losses, rising global temperatures and more Americans living in harm's way.'"[26] John Dutton, dean emeritus of Penn State's College of Earth and Mineral Sciences, estimated that $2.7 trillion of the $10-trillion-a-year American economy is susceptible to weather-related loss of revenue, increasing companies' off-balance-sheet risks.[27]

Not surprisingly, investors are banding together to influence how companies deal with climate change. Large institutional investors are conducting shareholder campaigns urging companies to disclose climate risk and implement mitigation programs.[28]

The Investor Network on Climate Risk comprises over eighty institutional investors collectively managing more than $8 trillion in assets. Launched in 2003, the network announced a ten-point action plan that calls on investors, leading financial institutions, businesses, and governments to address climate risk and seize investment opportunities. American companies, Wall Street firms, and the Securities and Exchange Commission (SEC) were asked to provide investors with comprehensive analysis and disclosure about the financial risks presented by climate change. The group pledged to invest $1 billion in prudent business opportunities emerging from the drive to reduce GHG emissions.

On January 27, 2010, they succeeded, as the SEC issued an "interpretive guidance" advising that public companies should warn investors of any serious risks that global warming might pose to their businesses. Mary Shapiro, chair of the SEC, stated:

> It is neither surprising nor especially remarkable for us to conclude that of course a company must consider whether potential legislation—whether that legislation concerns climate change or new licensing requirements—is likely to occur. Similarly, a company must disclose the significant risks that it faces, whether those risks are due to increased competition or severe weather. These principles of materiality form the bedrock of our disclosure framework.[29]

Indeed, even before this ruling, the Sarbanes-Oxley Act, the American corporate ethics law, made it a criminal offense for managers of a company to fail to disclose information, including such environmental liabilities as carbon emissions, that could alter a reasonable investor's view of the organization.[30] In France, the Netherlands, Germany, and Norway, companies are already required to report their GHG emissions.[31]

Companies that fail to manage their carbon footprint face other risks as well. Since 2002, a British NGO, the Carbon Disclosure Project, has surveyed the Financial Times 500, the five hundred biggest companies in the world. Initially, only 10 percent of the companies that the CDP requested reports from answered. After all, who died and named the CDP God? In 2005, however, 60 percent of the surveyed companies replied. Such corporate giants as Chevron, Cinergy, DTE Energy, Duke Energy, First Energy, Ford Motor Company, General Electric, JP Morgan Chase, and Progress Energy made public commitments supporting mandatory limits on greenhouse gases, voluntarily reducing their emissions, or disclosing climate risk information to investors as a result of the CDP questionnaire.[32]

Why the change? The threat of Sarbanes-Oxley played a role, but perhaps more proximately, the CDP represents 534 institutional investors with over $64 trillion in assets, almost a third of all global institutional investor assets. Any company interested in the capital markets would be advised to answer CDP's questions. CDP now receives annual corporate carbon footprint reports from almost 80 percent of the *Financial Times* 1,800. Institutional investors use the CDP database to make investment decisions based on a company's greenhouse gas emissions, emission reduction goals, and strategies to combat climate change. Companies that do not responsibly manage their carbon footprint are deemed not worthy of investment.

The 2007 CDP report found that the world's major companies are increasingly focused on climate change and that many see it as an opportunity for profit. Nearly 80 percent of respondents around the world considered climate change a commercial risk, citing extreme weather events and tightening government regulations. Some 82 percent said that they recognized commercial opportunities for existing or new products, such as investments in renewable energy. Globally, 76 percent of the companies said they had instituted targets and plans to reduce emissions, yet only 29 percent of American respondents had implemented greenhouse gas reduction programs with timelines and specific targets.[33]

In 2008, companies got another reason to report their environmental profile. Walmart did more than respond to CDP's survey—it hired the CDP to go to China and survey its suppliers there, and to notify them that if they wished to remain suppliers to the world's largest retailer, they would report their carbon footprints.[34]

Walmart: Capitalism's 800-Pound Gorilla

The new wisdom that cutting a company's carbon footprint is simply better business is perhaps most convincingly demonstrated by the commitment of Walmart to implement more sustainable practices. In 2005 Walmart pledged:

- To be supplied 100 percent by renewable energy
- To create zero waste
- To sell products that sustain resources and the environment

Lee Scott, then Walmart's CEO, announced goals to reduce energy use at Walmart stores by 30 percent over three years, double the efficiency of its vehicle fleet, and build hybrid-electric long-haul trucks.[35] The company projects that this will save $300 million each year by 2015. Installing a device that limits truck idling is already saving Walmart $25 million each year.[36]

In 2006 Walmart realized that replacing the incandescent bulbs in its own ceiling fan displays with compact fluorescent bulbs throughout its 3,230 stores (ten models of ceiling fans on display, each with four bulbs) could save the company $7 million a year. Chuck Kerby, the employee who did the math, reflected, "That, for me, was an 'I got it' moment."[37] Walmart realized that the same logic would benefit its customers, helping retain its image as the low-cost store. It set out to sell 100 million CFLs (compact fluorescent lightbulbs) in 2007—which would save its customers $3 billion on their electric bills.[38] This also saved enough electricity to run the city of Philadelphia.[39]

Recognizing that lighting in its stores represented about a third of its electricity costs, Walmart formed a partnership with General Electric to innovate lower costs for light-emitting diodes (LEDs). LEDs last longer, produce less heat, contain no mercury, and use significantly less energy than other types of lights. Over a three-year period Walmart invested about $17 million in developing an LED lighting system for its refrigerator cases. Installing these bulbs in its coolers in more than five hundred

Walmart stores cut refrigerator energy use three-quarters, saved about $3.8 million per year, and reduced carbon dioxide emissions by 65 million pounds.

The real gain for the company, though, Lee Scott stated, "is in creating a new market for LED lighting. Tens of thousands of grocery stores and other retailers will be able to take advantage of this new technology . . . So multiply the cost savings. Multiply the savings in carbon dioxide emissions. And just think about the impact on our economy and the environment."[40]

Walmart is not implementing such practices out of the goodness of its heart. When he announced the sustainability initiative, Scott observed that a corporate focus on reducing greenhouse gases as quickly as possible was just a good business strategy, stating, "It will save money for our customers, make us a more efficient business, and help position us to compete effectively in a carbon-constrained world."[41] In the two years after Walmart began its waste-reduction program, cutting unnecessary packaging by just 5 percent saved the company $11 billion globally.[42] Walmart's goal of reducing overall packaging 5 percent by 2013 would be equal to removing 213,000 trucks from the road, saving about 324,000 tons of coal and 77 million gallons of diesel fuel per year.[43]

In October 2008, Walmart—which if it were a country would be the twentieth largest in the world—called its thousand largest Chinese suppliers to a meeting with representatives of the Chinese government, the Carbon Disclosure Project, and others. Walmart executives described the aggressive goals the company had established to build a more environmentally and socially responsible global supply chain. They announced that these requirements would be phased in for all of its suppliers in China in 2009, and expanded to suppliers around the world by 2011.[44]

The criteria required that the top two hundred factories from which Walmart sources its materials achieve a 20 percent improvement in energy efficiency by 2012. By that date, the company stated, it would source 95 percent of its production from factories with the highest ratings in audits for environmental and social practices. It further revealed that Walmart China will design and open a new store prototype using 40 percent less energy.

Walmart was one of only two companies in the Dow Jones Industrial Average whose stock price rose in 2008—by 18 percent; its sustainability efforts are credited in part for this performance.[45] In 2009, Reuters quoted the company's new CEO, Mike Duke, as saying that he wants to accelerate Walmart's sustainability efforts: "I am very serious about it. This is not optional. It's not something of the past. This is all about the future."[46]

True to Duke's word, in July 2009 Walmart rolled out to its several thousand largest suppliers worldwide a comprehensive environmental and social scorecard, covering product packaging and waste reduction to improve product design and delivery.[47] Globally, Walmart has sixty thousand to ninety thousand suppliers, all of whom are now on notice that they too will have to comply. In early 2010, Walmart set a goal of cutting 20 million metric tons of greenhouse gas emissions (one and a half times the company's estimated global carbon footprint growth over the next five years) from its global supply chain by the end of 2015. Duke commented, "Energy efficiency and carbon reduction are central issues in the world today. We've been working to make a difference in these areas, both in our own footprint and our supply chain. We know that we have an opportunity to do more and the capacity to do more."[48]

If you sell to Walmart, you had better get a copy of its scorecard and begin figuring out how to answer its questions. Be warned: The first asks if you are measuring your carbon footprint. The second asks whether you are reporting it to the Carbon Disclosure Project.

Walmart is not the only company now requiring its supply chain to document more environmentally responsible practices. Hundreds of major European and American companies are establishing supplier codes of conduct and hiring third-party verifiers to audit their factories to ensure compliance with social and environmental standards. Along with Walmart, such companies recognize that their survival depends on behaving in more sustainable ways, and consequently they are changing how the world does business.

Buildings: A Good Place to Start

For Walmart suppliers and everyone else, one of the best places to start saving energy is in buildings. As described in detail in chapter 4, American buildings are responsible for a lot of energy use and greenhouse gas emissions. The architect Ed Mazria, founder of the Architecture 2030 project, states, "Seventy-six percent of the energy produced in this country goes just to operating buildings."[49] For all of this waste, buildings generally have indoor air quality that's worse than the outdoor air America claims to regulate. Yet it is possible to take virtually any existing building and make it three to four times as efficient as it is now, and new ones ten times as efficient as they would be with conventional construction technology. What is more, efficient buildings cost less to maintain and can even cost less to build.[50]

Green building practices promote greater labor productivity.[51] That is one of the reasons that Walmart is going green. About a decade ago the company conducted an inadvertent controlled experiment. Setting out to build a green building, they got halfway through, lost interest, and wound up with a building half green and half not so green. Surprise: the green side posted 40 percent higher retail sales and all the associates wanted to work there.[52] Walmart now has an excellent green building department. Pacific Gas and Electric, the largest utility on the North American continent, also found that introducing green design features such as daylight into schools resulted in higher test scores.[53]

These measures represent the greatest return on investment (ROI) hiding in plain sight. For example, changing out inefficient incandescent bulbs with high-quality compact fluorescents delivers greater than 40 percent annual ROI. The return on investment for common stocks might achieve 1.5 percent; by late 2010 you were lucky to get even that on a money market account.[54] Even the lowest ROI energy efficiency investments, such as increasing wall or attic insulation, bring twice the return as that on a thirty-year bond.[55] Saving energy is simply the best investment you can make. If you have money and you are not investing in increasing the efficiency of your home, your office, or the buildings in your community, you are throwing money down the drain.

The Impact on Communities

Climate protection investments improve the overall well-being of communities as well. At least a fifth of a typical community's gross income is spent to buy imported energy. Given that four-fifths of those dollars never return, this is reverse economic development.[56]

This is in part why well over a thousand American mayors pledged their cities to meet the goals set forth in the Kyoto Protocol to reduce their emissions of greenhouse gases by at least 7 percent by 2012.[57] Some local governments have already met even more aggressive targets over the same time frame, ranging from a 20 percent reduction by Portland, Oregon, to a 42 percent reduction by Sebastopol, California.[58] Communities that are implementing climate protection programs are finding that smart, comprehensive approaches to climate planning make them more competitive and put hundreds of billions of dollars back into the economy from savings.

Programs to help buildings use less energy and to encourage the use of efficient cars, appliances, and machines stimulate new manufacturing ventures, increase farm income, and generate increased community income. A local government commissioner from Portland, Oregon, stated, "We've found that our climate change policies have been the best economic development strategy we've ever had. Not only are we saving billions of dollars on energy, we are also generating hundreds of new sustainable enterprises as a result."

A 2003 study of the impact of energy efficiency and renewables in Oregon found that conserving 1 megawatt (1 million watts) of energy has the following impacts on the state's economy:

- An increase of $2,230,572 in annual economic output
- An increase of $684,536 in wage income

- An increase of $125,882 in business income
- Creation of twenty-two new jobs in Oregon

The study found that more than 12 megawatts were saved as a result of Energy Trust of Oregon's activities to increase energy efficiency in 2002. By 2006 that number grew to 125 megawatts.[59]

Similar results are achieved wherever climate protection programs are implemented. In 2008, over a seven-month period, the city of San Francisco created 180 new jobs by enabling 640 residents and enterprises to install small rooftop solar electric systems that generate 2 megawatts. Workforce trainees filled more than four-fifths of the jobs. The City's SF Energy Watch helped 1,500 businesses and multifamily properties save more than $5.7 million in energy bills by delivering 6 megawatts of energy efficiency savings.[60]

Add It Up: The Impact on the States

Studies have assessed the broader economic impact. In Florida, the Republican governor commissioned a Republican task force to look at what it would cost the state to implement measures to cut greenhouse gas emissions. Perhaps he'd been reading the *Sports Illustrated* swimsuit edition that depicted a Marlins baseball player standing up to his waist in water. Recognizing that under even the most optimistic projections of climate change, much of Florida will flood, Governor Charlie Crist wanted to know what it would cost to prevent this.

The answer? Not a dime. Governor Crist was surprised to find that implementing aggressive measures to reduce Florida's carbon footprint would *add* $28 billion to the state economy between now and 2025.[61]

In the world's eighth largest economy, Californians have held their energy consumption to zero growth since 1974 while national per capita energy consumption grew 50 percent. This has enabled the average Californian family to pay about $800 less for energy each year than it would if the state had not pursued energy efficiency.[62] In 2004, California ranked twelfth in the nation in energy prices, but only forty-fifth in energy costs per person.[63] A 2008 study by the University of California found that California's programs to reduce energy dependence and increase energy productivity three decades ago directed a greater percentage of its consumption to in-state, employment-intensive goods and services whose supply chains largely reside within California. This created a strong "multiplier" effect on job creation, generating 1.5 million full-time-equivalency jobs with a total payroll of more than $45 billion, and saving California consumers more than $56 billion in energy costs. Going forward, fully implementing California's Republican-sponsored cap on greenhouse gas emissions (reducing carbon emissions 80 percent by 2050) would increase the gross state product by $76 billion, increase real household incomes by $48 million, and create as many as 403,000 new efficiency and climate action jobs.[64]

It is now well established that protecting the climate creates, rather than costs, jobs. Chapter 4 describes how smart climate protection efforts are restoring Braddock, Pennsylvania, a Rust Belt town outside Pittsburgh whose population went from twenty thousand to two thousand. Its mayor declared, "We're not going to die, we're going to go green."[65]

In Colorado over the last ten years, more new jobs have been created in the clean-tech sector than all other sectors in the state combined.[66] In 2008 green industries generated 8.5 million jobs nationwide and more than a trillion dollars in revenues. By 2030, this is predicted to rise to at least 40 million jobs.[67]

In contrast, jobs in the fossil fuel industry have been steadily declining for reasons that "have little to do with environmental regulation." Mechanization and mergers have meant that although U.S. coal production increased 32 percent between 1980 and 1999, coal-mining employment decreased 66 percent, from 242,000 workers to 83,000. The clean-energy sector, on the other hand, produces ten times more jobs per megawatt of power installed, per unit of energy produced, and per dollar of investment, than the fossil fuel sector. In short, there could be a net gain in employment from shutting down the coal industry and investing instead in climate protection, particularly if governments implement sensible policy interventions aimed at minimizing the impact of the ongoing transition.[68]

More than twenty U.S. states, representing more than two thirds of the United States economy and population, are implementing comprehensive multisector greenhouse gas reduction plans. Such programs will expand employment, income, and investment, and contribute to national economic recovery while generating as many as 2.5 million new jobs and $134 billion in economic activity in the United States. The programs will also deliver such side benefits as energy independence, cleaner air and water, and environmental protection.[69]

No capitalist likes regulation, and you may not, either. But if you are intellectually honest you recognize that the status quo represents massive and uneconomic government intervention in the market in favor of the incumbent fossil-based industries. As described in chapter 10, the fossil fuel industry is the recipient of at least $550 billion a year in direct financial subsidies, primarily to make energy look cheaper than it is. All that climate capitalists ask for is a level playing field. We'd prefer elimination of all subsidies, but absent the establishment of a true free market, let's at least ensure that the pricing and regulatory signals approximate the outcomes that full cost accounting and honest economics would deliver. In chapter 3 we describe such measures as feed-in tariffs—a policy that requires regional or national electric grid utilities to buy renewable electricity from all eligible participants—now used in Germany to unleash the new energy economy, create jobs, and drive prosperity.

Energy policy is not a partisan red or blue issue for Americans. R. James Woolsey, previously head of the CIA, describes how American energy policy forces us to pay for both sides of the war on terror: paying for our guys to fight it and buying oil from the guys who pay our enemies to fight us. Woolsey, most assuredly not a liberal, drives a 100-miles-per-gallon plug-in hybrid car he powers from the solar panels on his roof, with a bumper sticker on the back that says, "Osama Bin Laden hates my car." He rightly sees energy as a national security issue.

This opinion was supported by the study "National Security and the Threat of Climate Change," in which eleven retired three-star and four-star admirals and generals offer advice, expertise, and perspective on the impact of climate change.[70] They found that projected climate change poses a serious threat to America's national security, acting as a threat multiplier for instability in some of the most volatile regions of the world. The study concluded that climate change will add to tensions even in stable regions of the world. The report made the following recommendations:

- Fully integrate the national security consequences of climate change into national security and national defense strategies.
- The United States should commit to a stronger national and international role to help stabilize climate change at levels that will avoid significant disruption to global security and stability.
- The United States should help less-developed nations build the capacity and resiliency to better manage climate impacts.
- The Department of Defense should accelerate the adoption of innovative technologies that deliver improved U.S. combat power through energy efficiency.
- Conduct an assessment of the impact on U.S. military installations worldwide of rising sea levels, extreme weather events, and other possible climate change impacts over the next thirty to forty years.

New Energy Supply

The transition away from fossil fuels to the energy systems of the future can take place rapidly. In the next chapter we describe how to take advantage of massive improvements in energy efficiency that are currently available and cost-effective. In chapter 3 we describe how, after we've implemented greater energy productivity, renewable forms of energy can deliver all the power that a dynamic industrial society requires, and why the marginal investments in clean energy are better buys than any of the sunset industries like coal or nuclear.

In 2008, the wind industry added 27 gigawatts (1 gigawatt = 1 billion watts, or the output of a typical nuclear power station) of new wind-power generating capacity around the world.[71] In 2009, the world added another 37 gigawatts of wind-power generating capacity. Had that amount of power instead come from sixty-four new nuclear plants, you might have noticed. In good sites, wind power actually costs less than just running an existing coal plant. Almost any decent site will deliver wind power at far lower cost than building a new coal plant. Which is why utilities have canceled well over one hundred proposed new coal plants across the United States. Some utility commissions have officially ruled that coal plants can no longer compete with the cheapest power, wind.[72]

Solar power is now the world's fastest-growing energy source, nearing cost-competitiveness with coal, and is already cheaper than nuclear power.[73] Southern California's independent power producers were building a megawatt of solar power per week, prior to the economic collapse. Southern California Edison (SCE) built a 250 megawatt power plant on roofs spread around the region at a price of about $875 million—close to the price of a coal plant recently canceled in Montana projected to cost $800 million.[74] SCE's action leveraged the implementation of another 250 MW of solar brought on by private investors.[75] This means that solar electricity, one of the more expensive of the renewable sources of energy, is coming very close to "grid parity"—the point at which alternative means of generating electricity is equal in cost to or cheaper than grid power—beating the cost of producing energy using dirty, dangerous coal.

Innovation for Security

Business success and national stature in a time of technological transformation demands innovation. People in the business community talk a lot about innovation, but a great deal more than shareholder equity rests on successful innovation. Since the First Industrial Revolution (ca. 1760)[76], there have been at least six waves of innovation, each shifting the technologies underpinning global economic prosperity, political influence, and military ascendancy. In the late 1700s water power drove the mechanization of textiles and iron mongering, and enabled modern commerce to develop in Britain. The second wave of innovation, starting in 1850, also in Britain, introduced steam power, trains, and steel.

The British Navy ruled the waves, and the sun never set on the British empire.

In the mid-1880s oil was discovered in the United States. By the 1900s, electricity, chemicals, and cars came to dominate, and America came to rule the world, militarily, politically and economically. German and Japanese industrial machines sought to challenge American dominance, but Yankee resources and ingenuity prevailed.

By the middle of the twentieth century petrochemicals and the space race, along with electronics, drove American prosperity. The Soviets challenged American economic hegemony, but American innovation and entrepreneurial excellence dominated. The most recent wave of innovation led to the advent of computers, iPods, and digital information.

The next wave of innovation is already centering on clean technology, the transition to more sustainable ways of manufacturing products, and on delivering the services that humans desire in ways that will enable the planet to survive. As the early Industrial Revolutions play out and economies move to cloud-computing and biomimicry, older industries are suffering dislocations. There's nothing new about this. These industries' choice is the one faced by DuPont when it began shifting from gunpowder to chemicals, back in 1912. Now DuPont is leading the increasing number of companies implementing the array of sustainable technologies that will make up the next wave of innovation.[77]

A 2010 report by Nick Robins for the HSBC bank, "Sizing the Climate Economy," predicted that by 2020 annual capital investment in the green economy will grow from an annualized $460 billion in 2010 to at least $1.5 trillion.[78] Citing mounting pressure on land, water, and energy as a result of growth in emerging economies and world population that will add momentum toward a more efficient "climate economy," the report states that the green economy would more likely triple to $2.2 trillion, implying global annual market growth of 7 to 11 percent between 2009 and 2020. Renewable energy is the biggest low-carbon sector now, and revenues would grow at 9.4 percent annually to a market size of more than $500 billion by 2020 but still lag transport efficiency at nearly $700 billion in ten years' time after 18 percent annual growth.[79]

The United States is losing global leadership by lagging in the new green gold rush. The Senate's failure to pass climate legislation has consigned America to playing catch-up behind China and South Korea, Germany and the United Kingdom—countries that have already required power companies and others to generate more electricity from renewable sources and are investing hundreds of billions of dollars to make themselves green energy superpowers (see chapter 3).[80] The China Greentech Initiative reported in September 2009 that China's market for energy efficiency, renewable energy, and other green technology could become a trillion-dollar market by 2013. The report cites "the fast pace of renewables growth as one example—wind capacity has doubled every year for the last four years to reach 12.2 gigawatts in 2008 and one in 10 households has a solar water heater installed. The government has a target of deriving 20 percent of energy from renewable sources by 2020."[81]

China broke ground in 2009 on what will be the world's largest and cheapest wind farm. Delivering 5 gigawatts by 2010, the facility will reach 20 gigawatts by 2020; another six wind farms are planned, each on a similar scale.[82] China surpassed the United States as a wind power in 2009, and could well have 30 gigawatts of wind power installed by the end of 2010. The Chinese project investments of $440 to $660 billion in solar and wind power over the next ten years. [83]

Thomas Friedman, the author and *New York Times* op-ed writer, in article after article warns of the loss of American competitiveness if we let China take over this leadership. In a September 2009 article, he noted that China's rulers aren't bothering to waste time arguing about global warming, but focus instead on positioning China to meet the growing demand for clean, renewable power:

China is going clean-tech. The view of China in the U.S. Congress—that China is going to try to leapfrog us by out-polluting us—is out of date. It's going to try to out-green us. Right now, China is focused on low-cost manufacturing of solar, wind and batteries and building the world's biggest market for these products.

"If they invest in twenty-first-century technologies and we invest in 20th-century technologies, they'll win," says David Sandalow, the assistant secretary of energy for policy. "If we both invest in twenty-first-century technologies, challenging each other, we all win."

Unfortunately, we're still not racing. It's like Sputnik went up and we think it's just a shooting star. Instead of a strategic response, too many of our politicians are still trapped in their own dumb-as-we-wanna-be bubble, where we're always No. 1, and where the U.S. Chamber of Commerce, having sold its soul to the old coal and oil industries, uses its influence to prevent Congress from passing legislation to really spur renewables.[84]

In a prior article titled "Have a Nice Day," Friedman lamented that the solar panel fabrication manufacturer Applied Materials, a U.S. company, is opening fourteen new panel manufacturing plants, none in America. Friedman writes, "Let's see: five are in Germany, four are in China, one is in Spain, one is in India, one is in Italy, one is in Taiwan and one is even in Abu Dhabi. I suggested a new company motto for Applied Materials' solar business: "Invented here, sold there." He continues:

O.K., so you don't believe global warming is real. I do, but let's assume it's not. Here is what is indisputable: The world is on track to add another 2.5 billion people by 2050, and many will be aspiring to live American-like, high-energy lifestyles. In such a world, renewable energy—where the variable cost of your fuel, sun or wind, is zero—will be in huge demand.

China now understands that. It no longer believes it can pollute its way to prosperity because it would choke to death. That is the most important shift in the world in the last 18 months. China has decided that clean-tech is going to be the next great global industry and is now creating a massive domestic market for solar and wind, which will give it a great export platform.

In October, Applied will be opening the world's largest solar research center—in Xian, China. Gotta go where the customers are. So, if you like importing oil from Saudi Arabia, you're going to love importing solar panels from China.

Have a nice day.[85]

The Business Case: The Integrated Bottom Line

Then you get the inevitable question: "Ah, but is there a business case . . . ?"

Yes. In fact, the business case for acting to protect the climate, to make the transition to more sustainable business, is now so robust that you ignore it at your peril.

Companies around the world are recognizing that drivers of change such as global warming will require that they shift how they do business. They are also recognizing that companies that behave more responsibly to people and to the planet are a better investment risk and enhance all aspects of shareholder value. Over the past decade, more than twenty studies have shown that companies that focus on and implement sustainability programs achieve greater profitability than their industry's average. A company's actions to make it more sustainable also make it less exposed to value erosion, and strengthen every aspect of business value.

Shareholder value is enhanced when a company cuts its costs, as DuPont did, maintaining profitability because it committed itself to squeezing out waste. A company that grows its top-line sales through innovation, as STMicroelectronics did, captures superior market advantage. As the Investor Network on Climate Risk showed, responsible management of a company's carbon footprint enables it to secure better access to capital from the socially responsible investment community, and to better manage its risks. Cutting carbon emissions in buildings enhances labor productivity, increases a company's ability to attract and retain the best talent, and improves creativity and morale in the workplace.

A corporate commitment to use energy more efficiently, to cut its carbon footprint, and to act to protect the climate strengthens every aspect of core business value and shareholder equity. Called the Integrated Bottom Line, this approach shows that companies that implement sustainability programs not only reduce expenses now, but also position themselves for better long-term performance and better manage their supply chains and stakeholders.[86] Such businesses enjoy enhanced government relations, reputations, and brand equity. Over time, a commitment to behave more sustainably enhances core business value by delivering sector performance leadership and first-mover advantage. The companies that get it right will be first to the future; we're talking about the billionaires of tomorrow.[87]

As noted earlier, these conclusions are borne out by a 2007 report from those wild-eyed environmentalists at Goldman Sachs showing that companies that are leaders in environmental, social, and good governance policies have outperformed the MSCI world index of stocks by 25 percent since 2005.[88] Seventy-two percent of the companies on the list outperformed their industry peers, were financially healthier, and achieved enduring value.[89] From 2006 through 2007 companies on the Dow Jones Sustainability World Index performed ten points above the S&P 500.[90] A study by the Economist Intelligence Unit confirmed these findings and found, further, that the worst-performing companies in the economy were most likely to have nobody in charge of sustainability.

In 2009, the management consultancy A. T. Kearney released the findings of their report "Green Winners," which compared the economic performance of companies with a commitment to sustainability to companies in the same industry without such a commitment.[91] The report tracked the stock price performance over six months prior to November 2008 of ninety-nine firms on the Dow Jones Sustainability Index and the Goldman Sachs list of green companies. The results showed that in sixteen out of the eighteen industries evaluated, businesses deemed "sustainability focused" outperformed industry peers over three- and six-month periods and were "well protected from value erosion." In the study period of three months the differential between the companies with and without a commitment to sustainability was 10 percent, and over six months the differential was 15 percent. "This performance differential translates to an average of $650 million in market capitalization per company," the report stated.[92]

A 2009 study of European companies by Atos Consulting put the point bluntly: "Companies with more mature sustainability programs enjoy higher profit."[93]

The Bottom Line

Companies will implement more sustainable processes and procedures or they will lose competitiveness in a world that can no longer tolerate unsustainable behavior. A 2009 article in *Harvard Business Review* concluded, "Sustainability isn't the burden on bottom lines that many executives believe it to be. In fact, becoming environment-friendly can lower your costs and increase your revenues. That's why sustainability should be a touchstone for all innovation. In the future, only companies that make sustainability a goal will achieve competitive advantage. That means rethinking business models as well as products, technologies and processes."[94]

Acting to protect the climate will unleash a new energy economy and create the greatest prosperity in history.

If we fail to act, it will be the greatest market failure ever in history.[95]

Business-as-usual is changing. The economic collapse of 2008–2009 had many causes, but at root it stemmed from the fundamental unsustainability not only of the global financial system but of the way business is conducted around the globe. If the massive stimulus packages rushed to the market prove "successful," and the global economy returns to the boom days of the early twenty-first century, the challenge of climate change will inexorably force the system into the next collapse. Overcoming the financial crisis, avoiding the next collapse, and creating a society in which all people can prosper will require rethinking how business is conducted. Businesses and governments can either drive change in ways that allow companies and economies to flourish, or they will be forced to respond to a cascade of crises and to hope for the best.

The global collapse of 2008–2009 showed the folly of that approach. The challenges facing modern industry go far beyond the usual task of ensuring sufficient cash flow to stay in business. They pose systemic challenges that will fundamentally alter how everything is made and delivered. Nothing will go untouched by this transformation.

This book describes how businesses are prospering as they make the transition to genuine sustainability.

Will you join them?

2

Energy Efficiency: Low-Hanging Fruit That Grows Back

Climate Capitalism represents the best and most certain way to make a large amount of money, and a very large difference. Businesses that work to protect the climate are and will continue to be sources of untold wealth across the planet. There are many opportunities, from services that implement more efficient ways to use energy to investments in the growing market for clean-energy technologies (described in chapter 3) to trading what are called carbon credits in the already $100-billion-a-year carbon market (carbon markets are discussed in greater detail in chapter 8).[1]

The 2009 year-end review and 2010 forecast by *Progressive Investor* declared, "The genie has finally escaped the bottle, ushering in a clean-tech renaissance. In 2010, spending on clean-energy technologies will rise 50 percent to $200 billion, topping the 2008 high of $155 billion." There is no going back. Corporations, utilities, and governments are too far along and investment for strategic and economic value will drive the field forward. For example, American Electric Power (AEP), one of the dirtiest, most coal-dependent utilities (and one of the biggest spenders lobbying against climate legislation), plans to buy 2,000 megawatts of wind power by the end of 2011. This doubling of its original target is animated by something more than the company's need to meet the various renewable-energy requirements in the southern and midwestern states it serves. As AEP's senior vice president Bruce Braine told Bloomberg, "You're paying a premium relative to alternatives like coal or gas, but once you get them in place, particularly for wind or solar, the nice thing is that the energy is almost free."[2]

The new energy economy is driven by several factors: the fact that more-efficient use of energy is the cheapest way to meet our need for energy services; the growing number of regulations meant to encourage greater efficiency; customer demand for low-carbon and carbon-free products; and the prospect of making a lot of money. This chapter will describe some of the forces driving these changes and opportunities in energy efficiency, including ways to grab your share.

Market Demand

Concern over the climate is all well and good, but what really motivates a business is the chance to make money. In mid-2010, a partnership formed between the Environmental Defense Fund and a private equity firm, Kohlberg Kravis Roberts & Co. L.P. (KKR), to help companies cut energy waste and carbon emissions announced that the eight companies within KKR's portfolio saved $160 million in reduced operating costs and avoided 345,000 metric tons of CO_2, 8,500 tons of paper, and 1.2 million tons of waste.[3]

As described in chapter 1, demands of business leaders such as Walmart and organizations such as the Carbon Disclosure Project are forcing companies that are suppliers to these big retailers to measure and manage their carbon footprint, regardless of regulations.

More basic economic challenges are also driving change. "Rattling Supply Chains," a report by A. T. Kearney and the World Resources Institute, describes how commodity shortages and rising prices are cutting profits at companies that do not implement more efficient practices. The report concludes:

Based on our scenario of more stringent climate change regulations, enhanced and enforceable forest policies, growing water scarcity in key agricultural regions, informed biofuel policies, and a greater consumer demand for green products, we estimated a reduction of 13 to 31 percent in earnings before interest and taxes (EBIT) by 2013 and 19 to 47 percent in 2018 for FMCG [fast moving consumer goods] companies that do not develop strategies to mitigate the risks posed by environmental pressures.[4]

The net effect is that it does not matter whether you believe in climate change or not. The companies that are innovating to reduce their energy use and carbon emissions are profiting and prospering.

Efficiency: The Foundation of Prosperity

No climate protection program, national energy strategy, or economic policy makes sense unless it is based on a dramatic increase in the efficiency with which all energy is used. Using fewer fossil fuels, the form of energy responsible for emitting 56.6 percent of the greenhouse gases, saves money, cuts the cost of doing business, and forms the foundation of climate protection and economic prosperity. As Walmart has shown, cutting waste is just better business.

Executives everywhere have begun to realize that energy efficiency has become big business for multinational companies seeking ways to cut costs. Johnson Controls, a company that sells products and services to optimize energy, conducts an annual survey of more than one thousand North American executives with respect to their attitudes and actions toward efficiency. Johnson Controls' 2009 report, "Energy Efficiency Indicator," found that 71 percent of the respondents (mostly CEOs and senior executives) were paying more attention to energy efficiency than in 2008; 58 percent said that energy management was either very important or extremely important.

Why, then, aren't more companies acting? Actually, as this chapter will show, a lot—58 percent of those surveyed—are. But 42 percent of the companies that responded are hindered by limited capital availability, the report found. They feel that paybacks for energy efficiency longer than three years are unacceptable. Despite this, 85 percent of respondents believe that significant legislation mandating energy efficiency and/or carbon reduction is likely within two years and 44 percent said that government and utility incentives will help convince them to implement energy efficiency.[5]

Pay attention, legislators! Every competent analysis going back to the early end-use studies in the 1970s has shown that energy efficiency costs far less than providing new energy supply. By 1998 researchers from the U.S. Department of Energy, Oak Ridge National Laboratory, and Lawrence Berkeley National Laboratory had documented this conclusion. A report from these laboratories analyzed results from four engineering-economic studies of the potential for energy technologies to reduce greenhouse gas emissions. The study found that large carbon reductions are possible at marginal costs lower than the value of the energy saved. That is to say that the decarbonization is better than free.

The report, which included a sector-by-sector assessment of specific technology opportunities and their costs, as estimated by the national laboratories, the Tellus Institute, the National Academy of Sciences, and the Office of Technology Assessment, concluded that energy efficiency remains underused in every sector of the economy and is by far the cheapest "source" of energy. New renewable supply, it found, has a net cost, but when combined with efficiency, it can deliver climate protection at a profit. "In combination," the study concluded, "large carbon reductions are possible at incremental costs that are less than the value of the energy saved." The study called for an aggressive national commitment to carbon reduction, stating that "some combination of targeted tax incentives, emissions trading, and non-price policies is needed to exploit these carbon reduction opportunities."[6]

A 2007 study by McKinsey & Company evaluating the costs and effectiveness of carbon mitigation strategies reinforced this conclusion.[7] The study observed that many programs focus on manufacturing, but cautioned that this sector can deliver less than one half of the low-cost greenhouse gas emission reductions that can be achieved. The report concluded that more attention should be paid to encouraging efficiency improvements in transportation, buildings, forestry, and agriculture. The study found that almost a quarter of possible emission reductions could result from measures, such as better insulation in buildings, that far more than pay for themselves over their lifetime—in effect, they come for free. Most (70 percent) of the identified low-cost emissions-reduction measures do not require any major new technology developments. The study also pointed out that about a quarter of the low-cost abatement measures require no lifestyle changes and can be achieved simply by eliminating the many barriers that keep the market from working efficiently.

Many market imperfections are obvious. The 1997 report "Climate: Making Sense and Making Money" detailed eight categories of market imperfections, including the fact that companies (and the rest of us) lack adequate information and education about what the opportunities are, what efficiency measures make sense, and how to implement them. The market lacks appropriate financing measures, and access to capital is inequitable. Utilities that build power plants have access to cheap financing, but we pay MasterCard interest rates on home efficiency improvements. Most efforts to install efficiency measures face opaque codes and standards, and, well, doing things differently is a hassle.[8] There also exist an array of obsolete organizational practices. In New York City unions at first insisted on being required to screw in a compact fluorescent lightbulb (having an electronic ballast, they were claimed to be an electronic device, requiring a union member to install).[9] Happily this silliness has since been resolved, but hundreds of barriers remain to be locally identified and cleared. As a result, implementing efficiency is seen by many managers as just not worth the hassle.

A 2007 McKinsey study of the energy efficiency potential in the United States supported this, finding energy-saving opportunities worth $130 billion annually that remained unrealized due to these various market barriers. McKinsey's research shows that the U.S. economy has the potential to reduce annual nontransportation energy consumption by roughly 23 percent by 2020, eliminating more than $1.2 trillion in waste—well eclipsing the $520 billion up-front investment that would be required. The reduction in energy use would also deliver a reduction of 1.1 gigatons of greenhouse gas emissions annually—the equivalent of taking the entire U.S. fleet of passenger vehicles and light trucks off the road.[10] Verified utility programs to install a set of ten efficiency measures such as replacing incandescent bulbs with compact fluorescent bulbs (which use just a quarter as much electricity and last ten times as long) cost under a cent per kilowatt-hour for the energy saved.[11] This electricity cost is dramatically less than the four to six cents per kilowatt-hour it costs just to operate a coal plant, or the roughly ten cents per kilowatt-hour it would cost to construct a new one.

Obviously, something is preventing efficiency from sweeping the market. Given all this, the real surprise is how many companies are not waiting for government regulation to help overcome the barriers but are going ahead all on their own. Google, for example, is on a mission to reduce the energy consumption used by its servers and data center facilities. Striving for carbon neutrality, Google reduced energy costs as a percentage of overhead costs of their data centers from the industry average of 96 percent to just 19 percent.[12] Similarly, in March 2010 Hewlett Packard cut the ribbon on a data center in the United Kingdom that will use 40 percent less energy and be cooled entirely by wind blowing off the North Sea. Given that by 2011 HP expects equivalent data centers to spend $15.33 million per year on cooling systems, its scheme is quite cost-effective, as well.[13] In Finland, waste heat from a data center in a cave beneath the capital city of Helsinki is being used to heat water for the city's district heating system. "It is perfectly feasible that a quite considerable proportion of the heating in the capital city could be produced from thermal energy generated by computer halls," said Juha Sipila, project manager at Helsingin Energia.[14]

In late 2009 Google applied to the Federal Energy Regulatory Commission (FERC) for permission to buy and sell electricity on a wholesale basis, so that it could better manage its energy supplies and gain better access to renewable power.[15] Claiming that it had become a power marketer simply to supply renewable power to its voracious data centers and to leverage its Carbon Mercantile Exchange and Green Carbon Bank (its greenhouse gas offset programs), Google did little to quell fears that it plans to sell its energy management service and speculate in energy markets.[16] Granted marketing authority by FERC in early 2010, Google began moving in ways that are worrying various utilities. It now appears that the giant intelligence company may indeed intend to enter the smart grid market. Google has already introduced Power Meter, a smart meter that enables consumers to know how much energy their devices are using, as well as free software to enable customers to pull data from these smart meters and repackage it in user-friendly charts and graphs on the customer's Google account. Google has partnered with Energy Inc., the maker of The Energy Detective (T.E.D.), a leader in the smart meter field.[17]

Google is not alone in making such a move. In 2007, Walmart created Texas Retail Energy to buy power for its Texas stores and warehouses. Similarly freaking out the utilities, Walmart refused to rule out selling electricity to customers, but has so far contented itself with saving about $15 million a year from more efficiently matching its energy supplies to its energy loads.[18]

While enhancing energy efficiency in corporate operations gets the most attention, significant opportunities exist for companies to transform the products they make so that their customers can save energy, too. As energy costs rise, consumers will increasingly seek out or be required to buy more efficient products.

Philips, the Dutch electronics company, was one of the first global companies to embrace energy efficiency, introducing the first compact fluorescent lightbulbs in the 1980s. Philips has continued to innovate, introducing substantial operations and product changes designed to reduce energy consumption and emissions from its operations and the use of their products. Under its EcoVision 4 program Philips pledged to meet the following targets by 2012:

- Generate a third of total revenues from green products (up from 15 percent in 2006)
- Double investment in green innovations to €1 billion
- Further increase the energy efficiency of operations by a quarter[19]

An early proponent of saving energy to cut carbon emissions, the World Business Council for Sustainable Development is a CEO-led network of more than two hundred of the world's largest companies. The WBCSD coined the term "eco-efficiency" before the UN 1992 Earth Summit in Rio de Janeiro. It encompasses:

- A reduction in the material intensity of goods or services
- A reduction in the energy intensity of goods or services
- Reduced dispersion of toxic materials
- Improved recyclability
- Maximum use of renewable resources
- Greater durability of products
- Increased service intensity of goods and services

The WBCSD promotes market-oriented approaches to achieve enhanced resource productivity, especially measures that cut carbon emissions. The Council helps members share knowledge, experiences, and best practices on energy and climate, but also raises issues of development, ecosystem protection, and the role of business in society. The Council helps companies develop sustainable value chains, build sustainability capacity, decrease energy and water use in buildings, and more. It also conducts sector-specific studies to help companies reduce resource use in such areas as cement, electric utilities, mining and minerals, mobility, tires, and forestry. WBCSD's executive committee includes leaders of General Motors, DuPont, 3M, Deutsche Bank, Coca-Cola, Sony, Oracle, BP (formerly British Petroleum), and Royal Dutch Shell.

The WBCSD's website is one of the best global databases of case studies of efficiency measures, featuring improvements that its member-companies have implemented. For example, the global mining corporation AngloAmerican increased the production capacity of a Mondi-owned pulp mill in South Africa by 25 percent, accommodating a 40 percent increase in timber supply from more than 2,800 small growers, while increasing the efficiency of using waste wood to power the plant, decreasing the use of bleach chemicals, reducing the use of coal from 562 metric

tons per day to 234 tons, significantly cutting its costs, and cutting greenhouse gas emissions, including:

- 2,177 tons of sulfur dioxide (SO_2), a 50 percent reduction
- 509 tons of nitrogen oxide (NOx), a 35 percent reduction
- 297,121 tons of carbon dioxide (CO_2), a 50 percent reduction
- 60 percent reduction in total sulfur (TRS) emissions

Efficiency technologies also cut water consumption and purchased
energy. These enabled the mill to cut energy purchases in 2005 almost
in half compared with 2003, the baseline year. During 2005, the mill
also enabled the town in which it was located, Richards Bay, South Africa, to reduce its energy and water costs by more than a quarter.

Sometimes such measures do not even require a capital expenditure.
The T. K. Chemical Complex Ltd., a privately owned, medium-size paper mill located in Chor Khyderpur near Chittagong in Bangladesh,
produces office paper for the Bangladeshi market. It was able to cut energy and water use simply by implementing better management policies. The mill had previously raised steam for indirect heating in the
paper machine cylinders and for the drying process. Much of the condensate was not recovered because it drained off during electrical failures and shutdowns, pouring into the sewer. This wasted not only water
but also furnace oil because new steam then had to be raised in the
boiler when the plant powered back up. Eliminating power failures and
timing the stoppages enabled the mill to better manage its steam and
increase condensate recovery from 70 percent to 90 percent. Achieving
these savings required no investment costs, only better management,
and delivered annual savings of $8,620. Twelve kiloliters of fuel oil are
now saved every year, reducing thirty-two tons of CO_2 emissions, and
water is also saved, as less fresh input water is now required.[20]

Even if implementing efficiency has an up-front cost, such measures
deliver higher rates of return than any other investment in the facility.
ITC Limited's Paperboards and Specialty Paper Division (PSPD) is the
largest single-location mill in India. An integrated paperboard company
located at Bhadrachalam in South India, the mill produces 210,000 tons

of papers and boards per year. Beginning in 2003, PSPD identified and implemented thirty-six options to reduce energy and other materials and wastes. Measures implemented in 2003 delivered over $550,000 in savings with a six-month payback. After being used to pay back the investment, the money saved was invested into even greater efficiency measures. These subsequent measures then saved over 15 tons of coal, for a net reduction in greenhouse gases of more than 23,000 tons a year.

In 2004 the program of waste reduction required an investment of almost $300,000 but resulted in savings of more than $725,000, for a simple payback of five months. It cut over 23,000 tons of greenhouse gases, the need for about 12,639 tons of coal each year, and saved 3,722,720 kilowatt-hours of electricity. It also eliminated the need for almost a million cubic meters of water each year.

Cumulatively, an investment of a bit above $530,000 over several years created savings of more than $1.2 million, all with a simple payback of five months. The investment eliminated the need for 28,120 tons of coal and 3,525,120 kilowatt-hours of electricity, resulting in a 3.5 percent reduction in the GHG emissions of the company.[21]

Table 2.1			
Options Implemented by PSPD[22]			
Focus Area/ Option	Action Taken	Financial Feasibility	Environmental Benefits
FBC Boiler Reduction of unburned coal and coal fines in boiler by installing fines separation mechanism and low-speed crusher	Production process or equipment modification	Investment: $149,989 Cost savings: $94,640/yr Payback period: 19 months	GHG emissions reduction: 4,159 tons CO_2/ year Coal savings: 2,713 tons/year

(cont.)

Focus Area/ Option	Action Taken	Financial Feasibility	Environmental Benefits
Flash Steam Recovery Flash steam recovery from boiler blowdown and steam air heat condensate	On-site recovery and reuse	Investment: $35,000 Cost savings: $45,349/year Payback: 9 months	GHG emissions reduction: 1,909 tons CO_2/ year Coal savings: 1,248 tons
Increase in Heat Transfer Area Increase of heat transfer area in the blow heat recovery system to improve heat recovery	Production process or equipment modification	Investment: $46,512 Cost savings: $400,186/year Payback: 2 months	GHG emissions reduction: 17,200 tons CO_2/year Coal savings: 11,520 tons/year Increased electricity consumption: 472,000 kWh/ year
Replacement of Vacuum Fans Replacement of inefficient vacuum fans with more efficient and higher-capacity vacuum fans at former machines	New technology or equipment	Investment: $8,957 Cost savings: $10,657/year Payback: 10 months	GHG emissions reduction: 245 tons CO_2/ year Electricity savings: 274,400 kWh/ year

(cont.)

Focus Area/ Option	Action Taken	Financial Feasibility	Environmental Benefits
Lighting Improvements Fluorescent lights with electric chokes, metal halide lamps, automatic timers, lighting transformers	New technology or equipment	Investment: $32,540 Cost savings: $24,564 Payback: 16 months	Electricity savings: 632485 kWh/year GHG emission reductions: 565 tons CO_2/year

Small Businesses Prosper from Efficiency, Too

Much of the innovation in energy efficiency has been made by multinationals with deep pockets, global brands, and vast distribution channels, but small companies as well have been and will continue to be innovators in energy efficiency.

Small businesses are the economic engine of any country, in North America generating more than half of non-farm private gross domestic product. They represent 99.7 percent of all employer firms, employing nearly 60 million workers, or about half of all private-sector employees. For the past decade they have generated 60 to 80 percent of net new jobs each year.[23] They confront correspondingly promising opportunities and bear significant responsibility for global sustainability.

Energy efficiency remains one of the best investments that a small business owner can make. Ripe, a five-person graphic design company in Washington, D.C., replaced incandescent lights with compact fluorescent bulbs and held its meetings in rooms lit by natural light. Employees now turn off computers and lights when they aren't in operation by using power strips so the equipment draws no power at all. Ripe's energy efficiency and phantom load–killing efforts cut the company's electricity bill from $220 a month to $90.[24] (Many appliances actually continue to suck electricity even when they are switched off, a phenomenon called phantom load. Americans spend more money powering DVD players when they are turned off than when they are actually in use.)[25]

A ReMax real estate office in Florida implemented a weatherization program, caulking windows and weather-stripping doors. These simple measures cut their need for air-conditioning and put $7,900 of savings into their pocket the first year. Such measures as installing more efficient lightbulbs and sealing leaky ducts have a 40 percent or greater return on investment. Programmable thermostats return 30 percent per year in savings.[26]

Alice Celebre, the owner of Basil Bandwagon Natural Market in Flemington, New Jersey, wanted to make sure that her 6,000-square-foot store was as efficient as possible. Built in 2006, the store incorporated daylighting with solar tubes, T-8 lighting (more-efficient fluorescent bulbs that give the same light but use less energy than the ubiquitous fat T-12s), high-efficiency air circulation, and other efficiency measures, including LED exit signs. The store's annual savings are $7,800.[27]

The New York State Energy Research and Development Authority office in Albany, New York, is a 54,000-square-foot building with two floors that are occupied by approximately two hundred full-time employees. The authority purchased Energy Star (EPA-certified energy-efficient) office equipment with electricity management features. The office used simple timers on coffee makers and water coolers, and installed occupancy sensors on vending machines. The measures cut the authority's plug-load by 38 percent, saving $9,330 a year.[28]

BusinessWeek noted that such measures not only cut direct energy use but also drive prosperity throughout the economy: "Reducing energy waste in U.S. homes, shops, offices, and other buildings must, of necessity, rely on tens of thousands of small concerns that design, make, sell, install, and service energy-efficient appliances, lighting products, heating, air-conditioning, and other equipment. Small businesses can also save as much as 20–30 percent on their own energy bills by making their own workplace more energy-efficient."[29]

Small businesses consume half the electricity in the country, yet despite proven cost-effective opportunities to reduce energy use, only about a third have invested anything in energy efficiency. For example, less than half of small business owners surveyed are aware that the EPA's Energy Star program could help them lower energy usage. But then that EPA program has only two staff positions and expends just $1 million to get information to 25 million small businesses.[30] Small and medium enterprises operate on very tight budgets. Any push for change can feel like a shove. This is unfortunate. Major industries around the world are hiring sustainability consultants to enable them to implement measures to cut their wastes and costs and are joining such organizations as the World Business Council for Sustainable Development, the United Nations Global Compact, and other organizations promoting more efficient use of resources. But although a growing body of information on efficiency opportunities is flooding the Web, small-business owners and cash-strapped entrepreneurs cannot afford to hire outside experts to help, and even motivated small-business owners have little time to read through the advice offered them on how to implement cost-cutting efficiency measures. Without appropriate tools, busy entrepreneurs focus on maintaining short-term cash flow, which always seems to be a higher priority than making investments in efficiency improvements or more aggressive sustainability measures that would, in the longer term, put even greater profit in their pockets.

Those tools are now available. In partnership with Cogbooks, an inventive Scottish company specializing in online training, Natural Capitalism Solutions developed "Solutions at the Speed of Business," a Web-based implementation tool to help busy entrepreneurs cut their costs and increase sales to bigger businesses that are demanding that their suppliers have emissions reduction programs in place. It offers pragmatic measures that save money and enhance brand image. The tool guides small-business owners to develop an individual action plan; it provides the information, advice, and instructions that suit each small-business user's unique circumstances and learning style. It is now being used by Natural Capitalism, Inc., a separate for-profit company that convenes learning circles of business leaders, helping them implement energy efficiency profitably (for more information on this approach see www.natcapinc.com). NCI's initial use of this powerful tool has enabled Hero Arts, a small manufacturing business in California, to save $45,000 on its heating, ventilating, and air-conditioning system. Another company, Give Something Back Office Products, used the lighting module to develop a plan to save $7,350 a year retrofitting its lights. The retrofit cost $6,000, but delivered to the owners a 106 percent return on their investment. Mi Rancho Tortilla Factory in San Leandro, California, implemented NCI's recommendations to save $35,000 on electricity that they would otherwise spend to run inefficient lights, and another $140,000 eliminating unnecessary packaging and waste. This approach speeds the adoption of sustainable practices by the small-business sector, the lifeblood of most nations' economies.[31] Obviously, many of the energy efficiency measures offer a higher return on money than putting it in a bank.[32]

The New Energy Economy: The Dance Between Opportunity and Regulation

Smart money is moving rapidly into clean-energy technologies. This is in part because it is such a good place to invest money, but also because players in the energy market see regulations looming. From the local to the global level, businesses have essentially no choice: climate regulation is here and more is coming. Despite the persistent claims by climate change deniers that climate regulation will destroy prosperity, most companies recognize that a rules-based system is needed to establish a predictable and level playing field. Business associations representing more than six thousand members have called for national carbon legislation to provide a consistent investment environment for all businesses.[33] They know that companies that correctly anticipate looming regulations and get ahead of them will reap exceptional opportunities for innovation and profit. General Electric's CEO, Jeffrey Immelt, and the venture capitalist John Doerr both agree: businesses need a price on carbon, and setting one is essential to solving the climate crisis and enhancing their profits.[34]

Industries have faced similar situations before. In the last decades of the twentieth century, the American auto industry correctly bet that its lobbying strength would defeat safety regulations and fuel efficiency requirements. Rather than innovate and lead their sector, most car companies waited until they were forced to act. The strategy resulted in the bankruptcy of much of the American auto industry (with the exception of Ford Motor Company, which recast itself as a "green" car company) as Toyota innovated and became the world's largest car company.

Similarly, in the late twentieth century many American electronics manufacturers dragged their feet, putting off their obligations to meet the broadly announced European regulations governing the use of toxic materials. Almost 60 percent of global electronics companies innovated, removing lead and other hazardous compounds from their products, proving that it was possible. However, a survey of the industry conducted a few months before the regulations went into force found that almost 40 percent of electronics companies were unprepared to meet them. The survey observed, "The 'train wreck' now facing the electronics industry—owing to many companies' failure to keep up with increasing global requirements for environmental performance—was completely avoidable. It raises concerns about the level of fiduciary duty exercised by business leaders who should have done a better job of seeing it coming, and of preventing it."[35]

That same train wreck faces companies choosing whether to resist climate legislation or to innovate and leapfrog their competition. The European Union's High Level Group on Competitiveness, Energy and Environment stated in 2007, "European leaders have made clear that Europe intends to lead the move to a global low carbon economy. The opportunity is to be technology leader and therefore technology supplier in the future. Taking action now can give European businesses an advantage over others, so they manufacture the safest and cleanest products, which the world is waiting for."[36] The report focuses on greater competitiveness and market share. Safeguarding a habitable environment is not a bad ancillary benefit.

The scientific consensus that human-induced global warming represents the greatest challenge our species faces has driven politicians to implement local, regional, national and international regulations, all impacting how business is done. Despite efforts by climate change deniers to discredit the science, countries responsible for the bulk of global carbon emissions met the January 2010 deadline to submit national emission goals under the Copenhagen Accord.[37]

The European Union reinforced its carbon markets. The 2009 decision by the United States Environmental Protection Agency to declare carbon dioxide a hazardous pollutant, together with the SEC ruling in early 2010 that companies must disclose their carbon risks, made companies subject to a new era of carbon regulation.

In the absence of comprehensive U.S. federal legislation, regulations are being issued at various levels of local government. The town of Babylon, New York, declared energy waste, including CO_2, to be a "solid waste," subject to programs aimed at reducing it.[38] Boulder, Colorado, and San Francisco joined Finland, Sweden, Denmark, Great Britain, New Zealand, Quebec, and British Columbia in taxing carbon emissions. The Regional Greenhouse Gas Initiative (RGGI), implemented in 2008 by the six New England and four mid-Atlantic states, was a forerunner of the now-implemented California system.[39] A midwestern carbon trading system may also emerge. Variations among these regulatory systems will annoy companies and may spur demand for the creation of one system of overarching federal greenhouse gas regulations.

Utility Programs to Promote Efficiency

Although it is in everyone's interests to pursue efficiency first, few utility programs deliver this service. Until recently, public utilities implemented only as much efficiency as regulators required them to do.

To prompt utilities to show more interest in promoting efficiency, various states have experimented with regulations that force utilities to meet customers' needs in the cheapest way. Programs such as Integrated Resource Planning require utilities to compare the cost of building any new capacity with the opportunities of meeting customers' needs through energy efficiency instead. Such programs have sought to level the playing field between conservation and building new capacity. Both are sources of energy, but because most utilities are paid according to how much power they sell, their incentive has continued to be to construct new power plants.[40]

Some publicly owned utilities (also called municipal utilities, or munis) have pioneered smarter ways to meet their customers' needs through favoring energy efficiency. Wes Birdsall was the general manager of the Osage Iowa Municipal Utility in the late 1970s. Facing the prospect of having to build a new coal plant, Birdsall ran the numbers and realized that it would be cheaper to help his customers use less of his product by helping them plug energy leaks in their houses. He understood that his customers had no direct use for what most electric utilities believe they are in business to produce: kilowatt-hours of electricity. Birdsall knew that his customers were using electricity to obtain the energy "services" of comfort in their homes, productive machines in factories, light so that they could see, and all the outcomes that they really wanted: cold beer, hot showers, and industrial shaft power.

Building a new coal plant, the conventional utility way to meet increasing customer demands, would raise his costs and force him to increase the rates that his customers would have to pay. He reasoned that his customers would jump at the opportunity if he could help them get the same or improved service more cheaply through efficiency. By doing this, Birdsall began one of the most remarkable economic development—and climate protection—stories in rural America.

The Osage program reduced electric bills to half the state average and unemployment to half the national average, because lower electricity rates attracted new factories. Osage's new factories increased demand, so Birdsall implemented more efficiency, holding electric growth level for years. Birdsall's work saved over a million dollars a year in a town of 3,800 people, and generated over one hundred new jobs; not surprisingly the program was profiled in *The Wall Street Journal* and replicated by other utilities. According to a U.S. Department of Agriculture study of Osage, "The local business people calculated that every $1 spent on ordinary consumer goods in local stores generated $1.90 of economic activity in the town's economy. By comparison, petroleum products generated a multiplier of \$1.51; utility services, \$1.66; and energy efficiency, \$2.23. Moreover, the town was able to attract desirable industries because of the reduced energy operating costs resulting from efficiency measures put in place."[41] A report on the program stated, "Industries are expanding and choosing to remain in Osage because they can make money through employees who are highly productive and through utility rates that are considerably lower than [those of] neighboring cities."[42] The coal plant remained unbuilt and so never emitted CO_2 into the atmosphere.

In 1989, the voters in Sacramento, California, took matters into their own hands when they voted to shut down the city utility's 1,000-megawatt nuclear power plant. Rather than invest in a centralized fossil fuel plant, the Sacramento Municipal Utility District, the local utility, met its citizens' needs through energy efficiency and renewable energy, including wind, solar, and biofuels. It also invested in more efficient fossil-powered distributed technologies such as co-generation (generating industrial heat in a way that also produces electricity). In 2000, an econometric study showed that the program had increased the regional economic health by over \$180 million, compared to just running the existing nuclear plant.[43] The utility was able to hold rates level for a decade and to retain two thousand factory jobs that would have been lost under the 80 percent rate increase that operating the power plant would have caused. The program generated 880 new jobs, and enabled the utility to pay off all of its debt.[44]

BC Hydro, the public utility serving British Columbia, Canada, has launched numerous campaigns offering its customers free and discounted compact fluorescent lightbulbs and providing rebates to encourage customers to buy energy-efficient appliances. It subsidized corporate and industrial customers to acquire energy-efficient devices and provided incentives for construction companies to adopt low-energy design practices. It created a DVD training program for high school students to enable them to audit their school and their homes for energy efficiency. The students gained training as they cut their energy costs.

Perhaps the most aggressive energy efficiency program run by a utility is offered by ENMAX, the publicly owned utility serving Calgary,

Canada. ENMAX's visionary CEO Gary Holden is committed to energy efficiency and climate protection. Calling his program Utility 2.0, Holden arranged for the utility to partner with Cisco to create a smart grid that would allow users to specify how much energy their homes, devices, and businesses would use at what time to control energy use and cost. ENMAX's vision includes reduction of commercial and residential energy usage, energy management of buildings, residential energy management, cogeneration, district heating, data center efficiency, system security, and renewable-energy optimization.[45]

Why would utilities that make money from selling electricity spend money trying to reduce consumption? Because smart utility managers like Wes Birdsall and Gary Holden recognize that energy efficiency is a better business to be in than electricity generation. Because the Osage utility, the Sacramento utility, BC Hydro, and ENMAX are all publicly owned utilities, they find it easier to focus on what best serves their customers.

In contrast, investor-owned utilities, because they focus on paying dividends to their shareholders from money they make by charging their customers for the power that they sell, generally require state or federal legislation to prompt them to see the wisdom of enabling customers to cut their bills by implementing efficiency. To ensure that they do not charge more than a fair price, these "regulated monopolies" are overseen by Public Utility Commissions, state government entities that regulate utilities. Charged with protecting the public interest, they establish the rates that utilities can charge, and seek to ensure that utility programs benefit the public. Before the 1970s, when building more new power plants actually reduced the costs of each one, utilities gave customers incentives to use more electricity—it seemed to make good economic sense for everyone. In the era of the "all-electric home," regulatory commissions allowed utilities to offer what are called "declining block rates": the more you use, the less you pay for each unit of electricity. Utilities were allowed to charge enough to recover their costs and ensure an attractive rate of return for their shareholders. In return they were required to keep the lights on and ensure abundant supplies of energy.

But as the economies of scale relating to the building of power plants shifted, as new efficiency technologies entered the market, and as the cost of renewable energy came down, public utility commissions began to impose what are called "inverted rates": the more you use, the *more* per unit of electricity you pay. This is just good market economics, and signals to actors in the market that wasteful use of electricity has real costs to the utility and to society. But good economics and good politics do not always coincide. Higher rates are never popular, especially to large preexisting industries that are used to paying for cheap energy via the older rate structure.

Recognizing that energy efficiency is a better deal for customers than paying to build more coal or natural gas power plants, at least a dozen state regulatory commissions implemented a program known as "decoupling." Decoupling separates the profit that a utility makes from the amount of electricity it sells. These utilities are no longer rewarded in the rate structure for selling more electricity nor penalized for selling less. In theory, the utility then does not care whether it generates and sells kilowatt-hours, or whether it helps its customers meet their needs through efficiency. But in practice, utilities still very much want to build more power plants. There is something less "manly" about efficiency that some utility executives find distasteful.

At least two states, California and Idaho, have gone even further, actively rewarding utilities for cutting their customers' bills through efficiency, by giving the utilities a share of the efficiency savings that the utility helps its customers achieve to pass on to their shareholders. This helps overcome any lingering desire to build that one last plant and is the best way to ensure that customers get the lowest-cost options; it is inspiring several more states to consider adopting similar statutes.

In 1991, when California first implemented this plan (called the Batinovich plan, after California's public utility commissioner, Robert Batinovich, who first developed it), Pacific Gas and Electric, the country's biggest private utility, spent $150 million to help its customers become more efficient. It kept 15 percent of the resulting savings, boosting its profits that year by $40 million to $50 million. Consumer advocates squeaked that the utility was creaming off savings that ought to go to the customers. More observant policy advocates pointed out that by incentivizing the program, the commission had encouraged the utility to act in a way that saved its customers nine times as much as the utility made, and that 85 percent of a positive number is a whole lot better than 100 percent of zero, which is the amount of savings that the customers would have gotten if the utility had not had an incentive to promote efficiency. The public utility commission found that between 1990 and 1993, utility-driven efficiency measures saved customers a net present value of almost $2 billion.[46]

A variety of market-based experiments have helped utilities deliver better value to their customers. In the early 1990s eight states implemented programs to allow vendors to compete in open auctions on ways to make or save electricity. Such auctions would typically open bidding to all companies who could make or save electricity. The bidding would start at, say, one cent per kilowatt-hour. The utilities would then sign contracts for any bids received, typically all from increased efficiency. If the utility still needed to gain more capacity, it would then reopen bidding for efficiency or energy supply at two cents per kilowatt-hour. The utility would sign a new round of contracts at that level. If it still needed more capacity it would reopen bidding at three cents. The utility would typically meet all of its anticipated needs for increased capacity to meet its customers' desires for comfort in buildings, illumination, and industrial shaft power at costs as low as two to three cents per kilowatt-hour, most obtained from energy savings. This dramatically lowers costs for everyone in the system as compared to building a new fossil-fired plant, and keeps more carbon from being emitted.[47]

The approach contrasts sharply with conventional utility practice, in which it is assumed that demand for electricity is going to grow simply because it has in the past, and that therefore the utility will have to build more power plants, typically fossil fuel plants, and maybe, if required by a government program, purchase some renewable-energy supply. Energy efficiency is relegated to the status of "good housekeeping," not serious utility strategy.[48]

Happily, this attitude is changing. Delaware recently created an energy efficiency utility, the Sustainable Energy Utility (SEU), which aims to improve the efficiency of all fuel consumption in the residential, business, and transportation sectors by one third by 2015. The state will fund the

SEU through a thirty-six-cent surcharge on each utility bill each month, as well as a $30 million private bond issue. This "sustainable energy" bond, rather than being guaranteed by the full faith and credit of the state, which would tie the risk of any negative impacts to the cost of borrowing or to Delaware's credit standing, will be repaid by sharing a portion of each dollar of energy savings achieved by residents. When a resident purchases an efficient appliance or a hybrid car or installs energy-efficient measures in their home, the SEU will pay the difference up front and will collect 35 percent of the customer's energy savings for the first five years. To complement this incentive program, Delaware plans to boost its renewable-energy production to 300 megawatts by 2019.[49]

Such measures make brilliant economic sense while they also protect the climate. This was demonstrated by the Energy Trust of Oregon, an energy efficiency utility organized by the Oregon Public Utility Commission and dedicated to reducing demand. The Energy Trust is funded by a 3 percent "public purpose charge" on utility bills from the two largest investor-owned utilities in Oregon. Since its formation in 2002, the Energy Trust has saved customers of Portland General Electric, Pacific Power, NW Natural, and Cascade Natural Gas a total of $440 million. In 2008 alone the trust saved customers $144 million and, according to the trust, "Since 2002, our investments created more than 1,800 Oregon jobs, and stimulated $60 million in wages and $9.1 million in new business income."

Most entrepreneurs balk at rules, taxes, mandates, and bureaucracy. But when regulations are smartly designed and employed, they can unleash entrepreneurial opportunity. The World Resources Institute has observed, "A well-designed climate policy framework will create huge opportunities for innovative companies to flourish as new markets are created and demand shifts to more efficient, more advanced and higher-value-added products and services."[50]

If projections that demand for electricity will rise are real—the U.S. Energy Information Administration predicts a 30 percent growth in demand by 2030—utilities face the enormous costs of building new power plants. As Birdsall found, this will raise rates for everyone. The construction of a typical 300-megawatt power plant costs in excess of $1 billion.[51]

If the plants are fossil-fueled, it will also lead to further environmental and climate impacts. If energy efficiency, which can cost as little as a third of a cent per kilowatt-hour saved, and demand-side management can delay or even prevent the construction of new power plants, utilities and their customers both benefit.[52] As utilities around the world prepare for regulation of their carbon emissions, deferring new power plant construction reduces the risk of future costs for purchasing carbon offsets.

Smart Meters

Many utilities have found that just educating customers to understand their bills and tie them to rate structures can elicit dramatic savings.

Energy Aware, the winner of British Columbia's "Most Promising Startup" prize in 2009, has developed real-time energy-monitoring devices. Known as Power Tab, the technology connects the homeowner to information from the utility in real time.[53] A study by Natural Resources Canada showed that enabling customers to see their energy usage as it is happening led to an average 20 percent reduction in energy consumption. Making people aware of their energy consumption habits as they occur helps users become motivated to save energy.[54]

At West Coast Green, the world's leading interactive conference on green innovation for the built environment, Intel vice president Doug Davis announced Intel's efforts in corporate responsibility, the impact of Intel technology on the energy efficiency of homes and offices, and Intel's various plans for involvement in smart grid technology.[55] But as all of the corporate announcements unfolded, it became apparent that a tiny company, Powerzoa, also exhibiting at the show, actually had a far smarter, customer-ready way to enable citizens to analyze and control their power usage, while Intel's device is yet an empty shell.[56] Powerzoa, called "the plug-and-play energy saver," is a small cube into which a user plugs any device he wishes to monitor; it is a low-cost, high-intelligence way to achieve the same result, but user-friendly. The cube measures the energy use of the chosen appliance, sending that information to a personalized website on your computer, allowing you to schedule when you want your energy-using devices to turn on and off. Created as a student project while its developers were MBA students of Hunter Lovins, Powerzoa is now contending with the big boys.

Another start-up, I'm In Control, has developed sophisticated software to allow homeowners to interface with and control all of their energy-using devices. Working with smart grid vendors, utilities, and service providers, all these smart meter technologies give residents much greater and more user-friendly control over their electric bills than most utility-based smart grid programs.

As described in greater detail in chapter 3, smart grids offer the opportunity to dramatically improve the efficiency with which we use electricity. The current electrical system is, well, dumb, able to send electrons in your direction but unable to know whether you want them at that moment or would prefer to have fewer now and more later. A smart grid can communicate with your house, office, car, and many other energy-using devices via a modern network that allows utilities and consumers to make choices together in ways that will revolutionize how we create and consume energy. Smart grids deliver electricity from suppliers to consumers and, if there is distributed generation, back again, using digital technology to save energy, reduce cost, and increase reliability. Many countries are implementing smarter electricity networks to cut energy waste and reduce climate change. The U.S. Department of Energy has estimated that if the grid were just 5 percent more efficient, it would be the climate protection equivalent of removing 53 million cars from the road.

Such information technologies are gaining investor interest. In 2009, five major Silicon Valley venture capital firms vied to fund Silver Spring, a smart meter company. Foundation Capital, Silver Spring's initial investor, chose Kleiner Perkins Caufield and Byers, perhaps the best-known green-tech investor, to join the company. Two of Kleiner's partners, John Doerr and Al Gore, took positions on Silver Spring's advisory board. Silver Spring provides hardware, software, and services that connect every device on the grid, creating a wireless communications network allowing meters, load management controllers, and plug-in vehicles all to communicate with one another and with the utility. This improves energy efficiency, empowers customers, and ensures reliable delivery of least-cost services.

Foundation Capital has also invested in Enernoc, a company that monitors energy use in office buildings, grocery stores, and hospitals and helps managers move power where it is needed from locations where it isn't needed. Enernoc went public in May 2007, five years after its first round of venture capital investment. It raised $98 million in its public offering on annual revenues of $106 million, with expectations of significant growth.[57]

Getting Ahead of the Game

In his landmark work *The Next Sustainability Wave*, Bob Willard, a former IBM executive, described the stages that a company can evolve through as it moves from resisting regulation to innovating to get out ahead of it as the smart grid players are doing.[58]

In Stage 1, "pre-compliance," the company feels no obligation to do anything but generate profits. Rather than seek opportunities to cut its costs by increased efficiency, it cuts corners and tries not to get caught. BP's oil spill is an example of just such a management strategy. The decision to avoid spending $500,000 for a part to prevent a blowout and to avoid taking more care with the cement composition cost BP at least $10 billion in cleanup, forced them to set aside $20 billion for compensation claims, and drove a 50 percent loss of share value.[59]

In Willard's Stage 2, companies manage their liabilities by "compliance," obeying environmental, health, and safety regulations. They reactively do what they legally have to do. Regulations such as climate protection measures impose costs undertaken as end-of-pipe retrofits. Most companies that think of themselves as good corporate citizens are at this stage. It is this mentality, however, that has given rise to the mythology that climate protection is costly and imposes a burden on companies.

"Beyond compliance," or Stage 3, companies are those that have moved from defense to offense, realizing that they can save expenses by implementing efficiency measures proactively, using cleaner processes, and implementing better waste management. These companies recognize that investing in their communities and engaging in authentic social marketing minimizes uncertainty, enhances their reputations, and enhances shareholder value. Still, at this stage initiatives are assigned to specialized departments—tacked on as "green housekeeping."

By Stage 4, or "integrated strategy," the firm is transforming and rebranding itself. It is committed to climate protection and is integrating sustainability into key business strategies. It captures added value by implementing breakthrough initiatives that benefit all stakeholders, and understands that enhanced sustainability is the route to profitable investments and opportunities, not an imposition of costs and risks. It makes cleaner products, applies eco-effectiveness and life-cycle stewardship, and captures competitive advantages from its sustainability initiatives.

The real winners, Willard claims, however, are the companies that have reached Stage 5, the "purpose and passion"–driven companies. Governed by a values-based commitment to improving the well-being of the business, the society, and the environment, the company is building a better world because it is the right thing to do.

Aggregating just seven aspects of the concept introduced in chapter 1 (the Integrated Bottom Line) that implementing more sustainable practices enhances every aspect of shareholder value, Willard calculates that embracing such measures as energy efficiency and a commitment to cut carbon emissions can together contribute up to 38 percent greater profit to a sustainable business. These measures include:

- Easier hiring of the best talent
- Higher retention of top talent
- Increased employee productivity
- Reduced expenses for manufacturing
- Reduced expenses at commercial sales
- Increased revenue and market share
- Reduced risk, easier financing[60]

This means that companies that implement climate protection pro-actively will establish a competitive advantage, an advantage that will only strengthen as the climate crisis worsens. On his website, Willard offers spreadsheets that enable a company to insert its own metrics and determine the enhanced profitability that it can achieve through more sustainable behavior.

Conclusion: Seizing the Entrepreneurial Imperative

The efficiency revolution has only begun. It is technically possible and economically attractive to save at least half (and maybe three quarters) of all of the energy now used at prices well below the cost of just running a fossil power plant. Entrepreneurial opportunities exist to implement efficiency in every home, office, and industry. Opportunities exist to create new businesses, new efficiency devices, and new business models.

This chapter has described some of the ways to make money by cutting waste in energy use. The next chapter shows how similar opportunities abound in renewable energy. In both areas, entrepreneurs are creating prosperity while meeting our needs for energy services and ample and affordable supplies. This new energy economy offers unparalleled opportunities. The British economist Sir Nicholas Stern, in a 2006 study commissioned by the UK government on the economics of climate action, estimated that by midcentury, the global market for low-carbon technologies could deliver up to $2.5 trillion a year in economic benefits. *The Stern Review* put the 2010 value of the global environmental market at $700 billion.[61]

General Electric's CEO, Jeffrey Immelt, and the World Resources Institute's executive director, Jonathan Lash, in "The Courage to Develop Clean Energy," concluded that the growing corporate commitments to protect the climate, even on the part of former climate-change skeptics, are an explicit message that companies and communities that are not following suit will fall behind the curve. Such companies and communities are ceding ground, perhaps irrevocably, to those demonstrating visionary leadership, responsible action, and the ability to capture public goodwill and patronage. This is one arena in which the business and advocacy communities agree.[62]

Climate Capitalism is an opportunity for businesses and communities to reinvent themselves for the twenty-first century, thereby reinvigorating the economy and workforce, creating millions of new, local jobs, and reasserting leadership in knowledge, ingenuity, and technological innovation.

3

Both Are Better: Energy Efficiency and Renewable Energy Unleash the New Energy Economy

The most effective way to reduce greenhouse gas emissions, to increase money in your pocket, and to drive prosperity is to invest in energy efficiency. But efficiency alone, although it is the foundation of any intelligent energy policy, is only the beginning. Combining efficiency programs with renewable-energy supply enables communities and companies to achieve energy security, enhance their economies, and reduce carbon emissions as rapidly as scientists are telling us is necessary.

And it's happening. In 2006, renewables accounted for 18 percent of global electricity generation. By the end of 2015 they are poised to overtake natural gas as the second-largest source of electricity behind coal.[1] The European Union has committed itself to renewables in order to meet its environmental goals, reduce its collective greenhouse gas emissions, and reduce its dependence on foreign oil. The EU sees improved energy efficiency and use of renewables as essential to competitive advantage in the twenty-first century.[2] The Energy Intelligent Europe Initiative, signed by parliamentarians from all fifteen member countries, calls for the integration of energy efficiency and renewable energy as the basis for

European competitiveness and high quality of life in the twenty-first century.[3] The EU is seeking to source 22 percent of its electricity and 10 percent of its energy from clean sources such as wind by 2020.[4] Doing this is expected to provide up to 2.8 million jobs and add 1 percent to the GDP. To ensure that member countries meet their goals, the European Union set "indicative trajectories"—intermediate targets—for each member state. The EU energy commissioner, Andris Piebalgs, stated, "Benefits of renewables in terms of security of supply and fighting climate change can go hand in hand with economic benefits."[5] As described below, individual EU countries are going much further than the EU targets already.

The combination of efficiency and renewable power is also unleashing a new energy economy of clean manufacturing and good jobs in the United States.[6] Over 43,000 U.S. firms today are manufacturing and assembling renewable-energy technologies. A 2006 analysis of that market's potential, "Renewable Energy Demand: A Study of California," found that a nationwide program to develop renewable energy would create over 850,000 new high-tech manufacturing jobs. It would also drive over $160 billion in investment into manufacturing companies.[7]

Consistent support for renewable energy could deliver far greater benefits to the economy, however. According to estimates by researchers at the University of California–Berkeley, comprehensive clean-energy and climate protection legislation could create up to 1.9 million new jobs.[8] Similarly, the Center for Climate Strategies found that if the twenty-three core actions that individual states have taken in their climate action plans were extended to the whole country through federal regulations, it would reduce emissions nationally by 16 to 25 percent below 1990 levels, save $350 billion, and generate 2 million jobs.[9] But a report in late 2010 observed that spending for renewables was declining following the failure of the United States to pass climate legislation. The absence of an international accord and lack of consistent policy support are undercutting spending on clean energy. Douglas Lloyd of VB Research Taylor stated that investment by venture capital and private equity firms had fallen from €4.3 billion to €3.5 billion ($5.5 billion) since the second quarter of 2010. In Europe investment in renewable energy fell by a third.[10]

Renewables Across the Globe

Despite the heel-dragging by the United States, renewable-energy technologies are the fastest-growing form of energy supply, outpacing all new coal, oil and nuclear plants.[11] In early 2007, renewable sources accounted for 9.89 percent of domestic energy production; by mid-2008 that portion was 10.2 percent. Renewable energy sources delivered 11.18 percent of net U.S. electrical generation for the first six months of 2009, compared to 9.9 percent for the first half of 2008; and in June 2010, the most recent month for which data are available as of this writing, biofuels, biomass, geothermal, hydroelectric, solar, and wind provided 11.37 percent of domestic U.S. energy production.[12] In comparison, nuclear power increased only fractionally, while American fossil fuel extraction dropped by almost one percentage point. The consumption of all fossil fuels, including imports, declined almost 8 percent.

In some cases, renewable sources are cheaper than conventional supply. Wind turbines in good sites are cost-competitive with the four to six cents per kilowatt-hour it costs just to run an existing coal plant.[13] Running an existing gas plant typically costs five to six cents per kilowatt-hour. The average price of electricity from the grid in the United States is at least nine cents per kilowatt-hour, and often far higher. The cost of building a new nuclear plant can be as much as twenty-five cents per kilowatt-hour.[14] And these numbers do not begin to reflect the costs that coal or gas plants actually impose on us all by emitting carbon, mercury, and other air pollutants and threatening the climate. As a result, public utility commissions are increasingly denying utilities' applications to build new coal plants, reminding the executives that wind is cheaper.[15]

The world's "green energy superpower" is China.[16] Already the global leader in wind-power generation, in 2010 China committed the equivalent of another $14.6 billion to expand its leadership in renewable energy.[17]

China, now the world's biggest emitter of greenhouse gases, committed to invest $220 billion in renewable energy by 2012, increasing its wind-power capacity to 100 gigawatts by 2020, eight times the current level.[18] Investing heavily in solar as well, China reportedly committed to spend over a half trillion dollars to promote clean-energy industries by 2020.[19] The international bank HSBC predicts that China will invest more money in renewable energy and nuclear power between now and 2020 than in coal- and oil-fired electricity.[20]

China's embrace of renewable energy is due to many forces. Shi Li-shan, deputy director of renewable energy at the Chinese National Energy Administration, has said, "Wind power is 'vital' as it is the cheapest form of renewable energy." Perhaps the most powerful reason for China's green energy policy, however, is that China has little choice but to go green. As Thomas Friedman pointed out, it's choking on its pollution. The thirty years since Deng Xiaoping launched China on its course of market-oriented growth have lifted hundreds of millions of Chinese from poverty and made China the world's leading producer and consumer of consumer goods,[21] but the choice to achieve this miracle using the technologies of the First Industrial Revolution has left China with sixteen of the world's twenty most polluted cities. Only 1 percent of the country's 560 million city dwellers breathe air considered safe by the European Union. Wang Jinnan, a Chinese environmental researcher, states, "It is a very awkward situation for the country, because our greatest achievement is also our biggest burden."[22]

A recent report in *The Guardian* agreed that the political calculus is particularly challenging for the Communist Party. Cutting pollution is essential, but rising prosperity placates the public, satisfies well-connected officials, and forestalls demands for political change. "A major slow-down," the article concluded, "could incite social unrest, alienate business interests and threaten the party's rule."[23] In 2007, the *Financial Times* reported that Chinese officials convinced World Bank researchers to remove from the Bank's annual report the fact that 750,000 Chinese are dying each year from pollution.[24]

The ancient Chinese city of Baoding is showing how to resolve this. It is now the world's first "carbon-reducing" city: the carbon saved by the renewable-energy technologies it manufactures and exports exceeds what Baoding itself emits. Baoding set out to earn that distinction after the pollution from several hundred factories killed thousands of fish in its nearby lake in 2009. Its newly elected young mayor, Yu Quin, a former college math teacher, had to cope with the problem. He acted swiftly, closing the polluting factories down, even though that lost his economy two percentage points in annual economic growth. But Mr. Yu was determined to transform the economy of his town. "We chose renewable energy to replace traditional industry," Yu said, observing, "Polluting first and cleaning up later is very expensive."

Writing in the *Christian Science Monitor*, Peter Ford reported that in three years, Baoding transformed itself from a town manufacturing cars and textiles into "the fastest-growing hub of solar, wind, and biomass energy equipment makers in China. Baoding now has the highest growth rate of any city in Hebei Province. Its 'Electricity Valley' industrial cluster—consciously modeled on Silicon Valley—has quadrupled its business."[25]

The rest of Asia is not standing by passively. Japan is investing to achieve a twenty-fold expansion of installed solar energy production by 2020.[26] Japan—the home of the city of Kyoto, where the world's nations agreed to limit carbon emissions with the Kyoto Protocol—is now gearing up to export the city of the future, based on renewable energy. The Japanese Combined Exhibition of Advanced Technologies, Ceatec for short, devoted one area of the show floor to selling a vision of urban life in 2020 and beyond called "smart city." Ceatec envisions high-quality life in a post–fossil fuel world. Scheduled for implementation first in Yokohama, the scheme would enable the city to distribute renewable power to buildings, homes, and electric cars connected to each other through smart grids, monitoring supply and demand throughout the network to maximize efficiency. "The goal is to drastically cut carbon emissions—ideally to zero," wrote Tomoko Hosaka at the *Huffington Post*. The bigger dream is for the smart city to become Japan's next big export, fueling new growth and ambition at a time when the country finds itself in an economic rut and eclipsed by China as the world's second-largest economy (the United States is in first place)."[27] Japan also expects sales of hybrid vehicles in the United States to rise from 6 percent of vehicles sold in 2005 to 20 percent by 2012.[28]

The government of India acknowledges that its nation is now the third-largest emitter of carbon after China and the United States. Currently India has little solar generation, but the government has announced plans to invest $20 billion to build a solar market and an Indian solar photovoltaic industry.[29] This includes producing 20 gigawatts of solar energy by 2020 with a total of 200 gigawatts of solar generation by 2050. By 2012 it expects to be generating a gigawatt of solar power from solar panels installed on the rooftops of public-sector buildings and in local solar manufacturing parks.

South Korea is devoting $85 billion, or 2 percent of its GDP, to green industries and technologies over the five years until 2015, implementing carbon trading in 2011.[30] In January 2009 the government of South Korea passed a plan, called the Green New Deal, to invest in energy conservation, recycling, carbon reduction, and other environmental projects. The goal is to lift the economy out of the current recession while creating nearly a million jobs.[31] "We are in an unprecedented global economic crisis," South Korea's prime minister, Han Seung-soo, stated when he announced the new initiative. "We must respond to the situation in an urgent manner." South Korea's response of embracing the green economy will position it as a global leader in the years to come.

Renewable energy and energy efficiency are lifting the American economy as well, generating over a trillion dollars in sales and creating over 9 million jobs in 2007. This is more than the combined 2007 sales—$905 billion—of the three largest U.S. corporations, Walmart, Exxon-Mobil, and GM. If the proposed federal energy policies are implemented, the clean-tech industries could generate over 37 million jobs per year in the United States by 2030.[32]

In 2009 the Pew Charitable Trusts released a report of the first ever "hard count of green jobs created across the 50 states"; it showed that in the United States between 1998 and 2007, "the clean energy economy grew at a national rate of 9.1 percent, while traditional jobs grew by only 3.7 percent . . . Despite a lack of sustained government support [for renewable energy] in the past decade, by 2007, more than 68,200 businesses across all 50 states and the District of Columbia accounted for about 770,000 jobs." In contrast, the report stated, "The well-established fossil-fuel sector—including utilities, coal mining and oil and gas extraction, industries that have received significant government investment—comprised about 1.27 million workers in 2007."[33]

The American Recovery and Reinvestment Act of 2009 was billed as a start at reversing decades of lopsided investments, and to some extent it worked. The largest amount of funding under the act, by sector, went to clean energy: $46 billion of federal spending leveraged $107 billion in spending by the private sector, resulting in over $150 billion in total investments in energy efficiency, renewable generation, research, and other areas. Smart-grid programs received $4.5 billion in funding under the act, encouraging the private sector to invest an additional $6 billion in smart grid projects, bringing total investment to over $10 billion.[34]

However, America was projected to invest only $10 billion annually in a clean-energy economy, even had the American Clean Energy and Security bill passed. It died in the Senate. In the end, the renewables industries only narrowly extended the Treasury grant program for one more year.[35]

This represents a missed opportunity. A study of the potential impact of the legislation in Ohio, conducted by the Public Economy Research Institute, found that it would create between 41,063 and 52,214 new jobs across the state:[36] "PERI's analysis finds that investing in the retooling and conversion of small and medium-sized manufacturing firms in Ohio would create a robust engine of job growth for the state," said Heidi Garrett-Peltier, the economist who conducted the analysis of IMPACT (Investment for Manufacturing Progress and Clean Technology). The Ohio-based program to establish state-level revolving loan funds to support new investment in industry could create more than 52,000 new jobs in Ohio over ten years. "We find that the investments from IMPACT would not only retain current jobs, but they would also create new jobs that utilize the skills of the workers of Ohio. These investments are a potentially powerful way to revitalize the manufacturing sector in the state."[37] The implications are even more profound for the nation. Various observers believe that unless the United States enters the race to transform its economy using energy efficiency and renewable energy in a serious way, Asia will capture this manufacturing sector.[38]

This result would be consistent with several decades of American energy policy that has ceded leadership in renewable power to others. For years the dominant solar country has been not the United States, with its sunny Southwest, but cold, overcast Germany, where the renewables industry added more jobs than all other German industries combined. Led by the visionary parliamentarian Hermann Scheer, the Germans implemented a national "feed-in tariff" policy that paid anyone who produced renewable energy an attractive and predictable price for the power they generated. Because of this sensible policy, Germany, even at its far north latitude, has been producing half the solar energy generated worldwide.[39]

Wind turbines line the approach from the airport to Munich, whole villages have become entirely powered by renewable energy, and the German solar market continues to grow at over 25 percent a year. Renewable energy now delivers over 12 percent of Germany's electricity.[40] The first nation to power its parliament building with renewable energy now plans to become the world's first industrial power to use 100 percent renewable energy. At current rates it could reach that green goal by 2050, generating 800,000 to 900,000 new clean-tech jobs by 2030 in the process.[41]

Given German leadership in renewables, it is no surprise that there is a German town that gets 100 percent of its energy from renewable sources: Dardesheim has become "Germany's Renewable Energy Town." By focusing on solar, wind, and biomass, the eighty thousand residents of Dardesheim, in Sachsen-Anhalt, are reducing their dependence on fossil fuels, reducing their carbon emissions, and leveraging their focus on renewables to grow their economy. What is more, the community's investment in renewables has become a development engine for the entire region. All the investment from the project stays in the region, encouraging local job creation. The renewable supply company, Enercon, in nearby Madgeburg, employs three thousand and has become the largest industrial employer in the state of Sachsen-Anhalt.

The project leases land for wind turbines, paying royalties of typically 3 to 5 percent of gross project revenues. Not only the landowner on whose land a wind turbine stands but also nearby landowners are paid in this way. The Dardesheim projects set aside 1 percent of the royalty for the nearest villages to support community groups, sports halls, and other projects. Half of the 4 percent remaining is paid to the landowner and half is distributed among surrounding landowners. In this way, everyone benefits.[42]

The Germans are not alone in boosting the percentage of energy use that comes from renewables. Denmark aims to get 60 percent or more of its energy from renewables within a few years. At the Copenhagen global climate summit in late 2009, DONG (Danish Oil and Natural Gas) Energy announced a goal of flipping its ratio of renewables to fossil supplies from 15 percent renewables and 85 percent fossil to 85 percent renewables by 2025.[43]

Communities around the world, particularly in Europe, are encouraging the use of renewables. Samsø Island, a two-hour ferry ride from the coast of Denmark, has a population of just around 4,300. Famous for its potatoes and its beaches, Samsø Island is also one of the first modern communities to be powered by 100 percent renewable energy. Samsø harnessed its plentiful wind, selling shares in the turbines to local islanders so the machines produce local power and local profits. Locally grown straw, fed into central boilers, produces super hot water that is pumped through underground pipes to provide carbon-neutral heat for homes. Samsø Island, now titled "Denmark's Renewable Energy Island," has been so successful in generating renewable energy that it sells its excess supply back to mainland Denmark.[44]

Globally, investment in the renewable-energy projects market could reach $50 billion by 2011, with double-digit annual growth rates.[45] The United Nations described "a gold rush of new investment into renewable power," concluding that clean energy could provide almost a quarter of the world's electricity by 2030.[46] The European Renewable Energy Council was even more optimistic, claiming that 50 percent of the world's energy supply can come from renewable energy sources by 2040.[47]

Renewable Technologies

Solar Thermal

Solar thermal, using the sun's heat to warm buildings or water, is an ancient technology. Cliff dwellers in the American Southwest used solar heat to keep their homes comfortable even in freezing temperatures. It emerged as a commercial way to heat water in 1891, and by the early 1900s solar water heaters were being used in one third of Pasadena, California, homes.[48] Today, less than 1 percent of the world's solar water-heating energy is produced in the United States. To reverse this, the California Public Utilities Commission has recommended the establishment of a $300 million incentive program to encourage homeowners to install solar water heaters.[49]

Companies are ready to sell the units. Over five thousand Chinese solar manufacturers already compete to deliver their solar thermal products to domestic and export markets. In Rizhao, China, a city of almost 3 million people, 99 percent of homes have solar-heated hot water. This is not uncommon in China, where the government encourages low-carbon technologies in order to enable industries to scale up for export. Rizhao's solar systems cost only $220 but are sized for the Chinese market, which, on average, uses only half as much hot water per capita as Americans. "The market is huge, but the competition is fearsome," said Bi Bangquan, president of Rizhao Gold Giant Solar Power, one of 150 manufacturers based in Rizhao hoping to export to the United States.[50]

Europe has embraced solar thermal, with 15 percent of detached homes in Austria using the technology for space and water heating. The European Solar Thermal Industry Federation action plan, supported by the Intelligent Energy–Europe program of the European Commission, states: "In a few decades, wasting gas, oil or electricity for low temperature uses such as space heating will no longer be an option. There will be strong competition for limited biomass resources. For heating and cooling, solar will be the main outstanding alternative, combined with geothermal where available."[51]

The European action plan calls for installing a square meter of solar collector per person by 2020—an annual growth rate of 31 percent. This growth rate may sound like a lot, but 2 million EU families have already installed this amount of solar systems at this growth rate, which is less than what Europeans achieved in 2006 and only 7 percent above the 2002–2006 average rate of growth. If this level of deployment is maintained, by 2020 Europe would have 320 gigawatts of thermal energy, and the hundreds of thousands of jobs that go with creating such a success.[52] Remember, a gigawatt is roughly the electrical output of a nuclear plant. It's a lot of energy.

Solar thermal can also assist in cooling buildings, providing heat for industrial processes, and producing electricity. In 2007 Google invested in the start-up company eSolar, whose motto is "Harnessing the power of the sun 20,000 times over." Gregory Miller, managing director of investments for Google.org, announced the investment as part of a new Google.org initiative, RE<C, stating, "Today Google launched a major R&D effort and set a lofty goal of generating a gigawatt of renewable electricity at a cost below electricity from coal-fired power plants. Google.org will be a partner in this ambitious endeavor by providing funding for companies and projects with promising, scalable, and potentially breakthrough energy technologies."[53]

The new venture eSolar seeks to multiply the power of the sun by using fields of mirrors that reflect the sun's energy onto a boiler on a tower. The boiler generates steam that powers a turbine and sends electricity into the power grid. eSolar's units can be scaled from 25 megawatts to over 500 megawatts at energy prices competitive with those of traditional fossil fuels. Early in 2010, Google and Oak Investment Partners added more than $130 million to eSolar, and the company won a contract from the Chinese government to install 2 gigawatts of solar thermal electricity production in China.[54] Partnering with Shandong Penglai Electric Power Equipment Manufacturing, eSolar will develop solar thermal farms valued at $5 billion.

"eSolar's mission is to beat the price of fossil fuels without relying on subsidies," says Bill Gross, founder and chairman of eSolar. "Our technology is modular, scalable and so efficient that my dream to power the whole planet with solar energy can become a reality."[55] Governor Arnold Schwarzenegger of California praised the company, saying, "eSolar is proving that California's energy and environmental leadership are advancing carbon-free, cost-effective energy that can be used around the world."[56] eSolar, which built its first plant in California in less than twelve months, is actively seeking licensing agreements around the world.

A particularly innovative solar thermal was installed in New York City's Transit Complex on Coney Island in 2010. Most solar water heaters operate at temperatures below boiling. The Coney Island system uses vacuum insulation to achieve very high temperatures and keep the system from freezing during cold weather. The first of its kind to be installed in the United States, the system, which replaces an electric boiler, will save $94,000 and cut 86 tons of carbon dioxide emissions each year.[57]

In September 2010, the California Energy Commission cleared the way for construction of the world's largest solar thermal array, a $6 billion gigawatt-scale plant in the southeastern desert of California.[58] Such plants use troughs of giant mirrors to focus the sun's energy on tubes through which a liquid is pumped, running an electric generator. This plant will produce as much electricity as a nuclear plant, but with free fuel and no waste.

Wind

Modern wind turbines may come in second to solar thermal collectors in terms of generating capacity already installed, but the capacity is growing faster and overtaking the various solar technologies. Despite shortages of capital, in 2009 global wind capacity grew at 31 percent, outpacing 2008's 29 percent growth, which brought global wind output to 120 gigawatts. Some market studies estimate the size of the wind energy market at nearly $63 billion per year.[59] Wind power's growth in 2009 added an additional 37.5 gigawatts of energy supply, employed half a million people, and reflected an industry growing at seven times the rate that nuclear power grew even at the peak of its popularity.[60] It is expected that by 2020, global installed wind-power capacity will reach over 1,000 gigawatts.[61]

In good sites, wind can deliver electricity cheaper than existing coal or gas plants can.[62] The costs of wind turbine construction declined 10 percent in 2009, faster than construction costs for any other energy supply, as lower turbine and tower costs drove the decline.[63]

China surpassed the United States in 2009 as the world's largest "wind-power power," doubling its installed capacity every year from 2006 on. In early 2008 the Chinese government aimed to have 5 gigawatts of wind power installed by 2011. In 2009, however, it broke ground on the first of six huge wind-power projects, each with more capacity than sixteen big coal-fired power plants. One array, the world's largest and cheapest, is projected to deliver at least 20 gigawatts and perhaps twice that.[64] Critics point out that even this massive amount of wind is a small contribution to China's overall energy demand, and pales in comparison to China's practice of building one coal-fired plant a week (down from two such plants a week in 2009). It becomes more significant, however, given that coal construction has halved, and wind targets are being increased exponentially.

In Europe, DONG Energy teamed up with Siemens to construct five hundred offshore wind turbines in 2010, supplying 1.8 gigawatts. This agreement, the world's largest of its sort, is a major step toward making offshore wind production commonplace. Both parties expect the agreement to be expanded to more gigawatts. Wolfgang Dehen, CEO of Siemens Energy Sector USA, said that the agreement "supports our goal to grow faster than the market in order to become one of the top 3 suppliers worldwide in the wind power market by 2012."[65] He went on to note, "In fiscal 2009, Siemens' Environmental Portfolio delivered about 23 billion euros in revenue, making Siemens the world's largest supplier of eco-friendly technologies. In the same period, our products and solutions enabled customers to reduce their CO_2 emissions by 210 million tons."

This deal will only strengthen the offshore wind sector in Europe. Globally, that industry is expected to install nearly 43 gigawatts of wind energy by 2020. Existing orders through 2013 exceed 6 gigawatts, and the $10 billion industry is predicted to grow to $30 billion in the next decade. Europe is set to lead this expansion with around 76 percent of global offshore wind installed between 2009 and 2020.[66]

Iberdrola, based in Bilbao, Spain, now the world's largest wind provider, has evolved to become the second-largest utility in Spain. Founded in 1901, the utility is also the second-largest generator of wind power in the United States. Its renewable-energy unit, Iberdrola Renewables, has an installed base of 10 gigawatts of wind in twenty-three countries and, at 55 gigawatts, the largest combined renewable asset base and pipeline in the world.[67] This may slow significantly in 2011, however, as Spain, as part of its austerity campaign, has cut the compensatory subsidies for renewable energy. The plan may save €100 million, but it will lose Spain EU subsidies worth €1 billion and slow the country's ability to achieve energy independence.[68]

The only energy company in North America with more installed wind capacity than Iberdrola is Florida Power and Light, a Florida-based electric utility. FPL Group's renewable-energy division, Nextera, now boasts nearly one hundred projects operating in twenty-five states and Canada. Income from Nextera grew from $82 million in 2000 to $915 million in 2008, surpassing the $789 million from FPL Group's traditional utility business. Lewis Hay III, chairman and CEO of FPL Group, remarked, "Imagine what the energy company of tomorrow will look like: it will be heavily invested in renewable sources of electricity, it will have a low emissions profile to succeed in a carbon-constrained world, and it will be financially strong enough to withstand disruptions to the economy. In short, the energy company of tomorrow will look surprisingly like FPL Group today." With more than 7,000 megawatts of new wind energy coming on line in the United States in 2009 alone, he's looking to be proved right.[69]

Most wind farms supply power into the electric grid, but increasingly, individuals and even communities are purchasing wind power to ensure access to lower-priced, reliable energy. The community of Radnor Township in Pennsylvania is one example. After voting to support the use of renewable energy, in January 2007 the township purchased ninety-eight wind blocks per month from its local utility (a wind block is 100 kilowatt-hours of power). Energy from wind represented 6 percent of the township's electricity supplies, saving 129,021 pounds of carbon dioxide, 293 pounds of nitrogen oxide (NOx), and .004245 lbs of mercury. This equals the greenhouse gas savings that would be achieved by planting 8,777 trees, taking 9.33 cars off the road, or eliminating 111,940 miles of driving. In January 2008, the township purchased another ninety-eight wind blocks per month, doubling power from wind to 12 percent of the township's electricity load.[70]

Siemens, Iberdrola, FPL Group, and many others are building multi-megawatt wind machines, but companies are prospering from manufacturing and selling home-sized units as well. Bergey Windpower has led the small-wind-power industry for years, with installations in all fifty states and over ninety countries. Bergey designs and develops some of the most reliable systems anywhere, providing electricity to the Panjshir Valley in Afghanistan, and to UN missions in East Timor. The Bergey BWC XL.1, a 1 kilowatt machine, provides direct-current output at a cost of a bit under $6,000; the Bergey Excel, a 10 kilowatt turbine designed for grid-tie or off-grid installations, ranges from $24,000 to $30,000.[71]

Even smaller are the urban turbines manufactured by Aerotecture. Designed to fit on building rooftops and bring wind power to urban dwellers, the helical designs grace various Chicago buildings, and have even been installed on and power the Hornblower Hybrid cruise boat in San Francisco Bay, providing the only emission-free cruise on the bay. The turbines are designed to be installed on building roofs, delivering power where people need it without massive transmission lines; they can be coupled with solar panels to deliver even greater reliability. Made of plastic and metal struts, the devices look like tubular artwork that moves. Very reliable, able to operate at low wind speeds, and able to be mounted horizontally on a roof, or stacked into wind towers, these are the perfect urban power source. [72]

Photovoltaics: Electricity from the Sun

After wind, the fastest-growing technology to produce electricity from renewable sources is solar electric. If the world decided to get off fossil fuels with wartime urgency, solar may be the only technology that could scale fast enough and deliver massive amounts of energy quickly. To give an indication of the solar potential, the U.S. Department of Energy calculated that the electric power demand of the United States could be met entirely just by covering 9 percent of the state of Nevada (roughly 92 square miles) with photovoltaic panels (panels that transform the heat energy of the sun into direct-current electricity). Intriguing, but a stupid way to meet our needs, because the sun shines on every state and the persistent utility tendency to remake inherently distributed renewable power over in the image of big centralized fossil plants is neither economical nor smart. Why pay for big, capital-intensive centralized power plants that cover vast tracts of farmland with solar panels, then pay for massive transmission lines to bring the power to the cities of flat roofs where it is needed, when it is far easier and cheaper to capture the energy on those roofs and in the cities? Nor is there any reason to install solar only in the sunniest regions. Germany has already shown that modern solar panels work well in cloudy, far northern environments. The Bering Straits Native Corporation in Nome, Alaska, has even put solar panels on its building.[73]

Growing at 51 percent over 2008, solar electric production in 2009 topped 10.7 gigawatts, with 16 gigawatts projected for 2010. Though slower than the industry's 89 percent growth in 2008, it is still pretty impressive for an industry that only reached 1 megawatt in 2004.[74]

Companies are installing photovoltaic panels on their roofs to cut their electricity costs and their carbon emissions. Toyota's Torrance, California, office complex, completed in 2003, combines such energy-efficiency strategies as an advanced building automation system, an Energy Star cool roof system, and thermally insulated, double-paned glazing with photovoltaic solar electricity. The campus, over 600,000 square feet, is 24 percent more efficient than California's stringent energy-efficiency requirements but cost the same to build as a conventional office complex.[75]

Until recently, the largest solar array, on a corporate campus producing 1.6 megawatts, was at Google's headquarters in Mountain View, California, where it covers 20 percent of the campus's needs. In a marvelous YouTube video, Google chairman Eric Schmidt describes how he came to approve its construction. After attending an environmentalist meeting on climate change at which he was told, "We're all gonna die," he began reflecting on what Google could do to reduce its use of energy in buildings. He asked his facilities people, and was told that there were many efficiency actions that they could implement. Putting on his best "Republican, CEO tough-guy tone," he asked what all of this was going to cost, only to be told that it would save the company money.

"Really?" he asked. "Why haven't you done it?"

"You never asked," came the reply. This, he observed drolly, was a true story.

"Well, go do it. Come back when you need more money," Schmidt directed. And shortly obtained millions of dollars in savings for Google's shareholders. It also inspired his engineers. They came back with a new idea: to mount what was then the world's largest private solar generating array on Google's campus buildings.

"What will that cost?"

"Oh, not that much," came the reply, "and with rising electricity prices, and solar tax credits, it will save us money."

Emboldened, Schmidt then set out to solve "every known problem at once" at a cost of only one trillion dollars. He and Gregory Miller, managing director of Google.org, created the Google 2030 project to meet America's needs for abundant affordable energy, create jobs, eliminate dependence on foreign oil (and the wars that incites), enhance American security, and, oh, by the way, solve the climate crisis. The project laid out a sophisticated plan for energy efficiency, decentralized renewable supply, smart grids, electric vehicles, green buildings, and much more—all of which, his analysts told him, could be done for $1 trillion. But then a funny thing happened: Google learned that it would not cost $1 trillion—it would actually *make* that amount! "It's pretty neat," says Schmidt with a chuckle. "It doesn't get better than this, guys. Here I am with my businessman hat on making a trillion dollars, which everyone can use, plus we're gonna solve every known problem at once."[76]

This sort of logic appeals to smart utilities across the country. In late 2010, the Jacksonville, Florida, utility, JEA, flipped the switch on a 15-megawatt solar array, the third largest in the country. Featuring 200,000 solar panels, the array was constructed by Juwi Solar GmbH, a German-based developer of turnkey solar projects that is owned by

PSEG Solar Source, LLC, which will sell the electricity to the city. The venture created 240 jobs and provided workforce training for hundreds of new solar installers, will keep 22,430 tons of carbon out of the atmosphere each year, will generate power for 1,450 homes, and the solar array will be removable should the land become more valuable for a different purpose at another time. Site work was careful to use low-impact construction techniques and to preserve the topsoil so that the land can be returned to farming.[77]

Solar power offers a wealth of entrepreneurial opportunities for small companies, too. Dan Leary was serving in Iraq when he determined to create a clean-energy company that specializes in solar installation. Perhaps not surprisingly, Leary feels that "one of the most important topics of our generation is national security—all the energy we can produce here is less energy we can import from elsewhere." Leary's company, Nexamp, founded in 2006, has grown from its initial six employees to over forty-five, and in 2010 won one of the largest solar contracts awarded in Massachusetts. Nexamp is now installing 4.1 megawatts of solar energy at twelve municipal and regional public water and wastewater treatment facilities.[78] The project will save Massachusetts $650,000 in energy costs per year, even at current prices.

Carmanah Technologies, based in Victoria, Canada, has been innovating solar-powered products since 1996. The company offers solar electricity for a range of target markets, including outdoor lighting, traffic lights, aviation and marine lighting, and larger projects to deliver power to the electric grid. Their products are particularly well suited for remote, off-grid locations such as military airports and rural communities. But Carmanah's best-known product is the i-Stop, a solar-powered lighting solution for transit stops. The i-Stop provides a flashing beacon to prevent accidentally failing to pick up a waiting passenger, gives enhanced security for transit passengers, and provides illuminated bus schedules. And because it is solar powered, there is no need to dig up sidewalks or run installation to connect a bus shelter to the electrical grid. Communities from London, England, to Orange County, California, have chosen this route to safer, more useful bus stops.

Opportunities abound for vendors who supply the companies making solar panels, as well. Voltaix is a twenty-four-year-old company that is on the ground floor of the solar gold rush. It is the world leader in the manufacture of chemicals such as germane, diborane, trisilane, and trimethyl boron, needed to make electronics products, including photovoltaic cells. Voltaix products enable solar cells to absorb a broader portion of the solar spectrum, and improve manufacturability by minimizing defect formation. In 2009, Voltaix ranked number 276 on the Technology Fast 500, Deloitte LLP's ranking of five hundred of the fastest-growing technology, media, telecommunications, life sciences, and clean-technology companies in North America. Voltaix grew 465 percent between 2004 and 2008. In 2010 the company obtained $10 million in equity financing from MissionPoint Capital Partners, a private investment firm providing growth capital to companies focused on clean-energy solutions.[79]

Energy from the Earth

The sun and the wind have the potential to meet most of the planet's energy needs, but there are many other natural energy sources as well. Geothermal energy derived from the earth's heat can supply baseload power to complement energy delivered from wind and solar installations. Geothermal can be cost-effective wherever on the earth hot rock and water are within a few miles of the planet's surface, and more than fifty countries now use it. Iceland, which already gets as much as 50 percent of its energy from geothermal sources, is now betting its economy on this technology. As air travelers discovered to their dismay in 2010,

The island is basically one big volcano, formed over millions of years as molten rock bubbled up from the seafloor. The porous rock under its treeless plains sponges up hundreds of inches of rain every year and heats it belowground. Using this energy is simply a matter of digging a well, drawing the hot fluid to the surface, and sticking a power plant on top. Then, as power plants go, it's business as usual: Steam spins a turbine that drives a generator, and electricity comes out the other end.[80]

Iceland is the highest per capita producer of geothermal power and is fourteenth in the world in total capacity. Geothermal electricity makes up about 25 percent of the country's power consumption, and meets nearly 90 percent of the nation's demand for heat and hot water. But it could do even more.

In October 2008 Iceland's economy collapsed as its bid to be Europe's banker fell victim to the financial crisis. The country is now staking its economic future on geothermal facilities to create electricity that can be sold to Europe via undersea cables. Iceland's geothermal facilities now operate at 20 percent capacity. If fully exploited, these existing facilities could produce about the same energy output as three nuclear reactors. To expand that, the Tyr geothermal drilling rig, the largest in Iceland, is drilling a two-mile-deep geothermal well into an active volcano. If this and several other efforts are successful, Iceland, the size of Kentucky, could produce five times more geothermal electricity output than all of the United States, now the world's largest producer of geothermal electricity.[81]

In the United States, geothermal facilities operate in California, Nevada, Alaska, Hawaii, New Mexico, Colorado, Wyoming, and Utah. These facilities deliver about two nuclear reactors' worth of energy each year, or 0.33 percent of U.S. electricity consumption.[82] Existing resources could, however, produce the electricity output of twenty nuclear reactors. The U.S. Department of Energy projects that with approximately $1 billion invested in research and development, the United States could derive 100 gigawatts of energy from geothermal facilities, but there are some obstacles.[83] In December 2009, the Department of Energy suspended a project undertaken by Altarock that it sponsored near the already functioning Geysers project in Northern California because of "seismic abnormalities," but another Altarock project, in Oregon, is continuing. This Enhanced Geothermal System (fracturing the hot rock and passing water through it to heat it enough to run a boiler) will, when complete, produce enough power for a small town.[84] EGS got its start with investments of over $10 million from Google.org.[85] The Energy Department followed suit, now sponsoring more than 120 additional geothermal energy projects in several states.[86] By mid-2010 the federal government already had put more than $300 million into geothermal energy projects.[87] In November 2010 the SMU Geothermal Laboratory, another of Google.org's projects, as it updated the 2004 American Association of Petroleum Geologists Geothermal map of North America, discovered that the highest-grade geothermal resources east of the Mississippi are in West Virginia.[88] SMU estimates that less than 2 percent of these resources could deliver almost 19 gigawatts of electricity, giving West Virginia coal miners a whole new line of work and freeing this resource colony from the tyranny of King Coal.[89]

Wave Power

Companies have sought for decades to commercialize technologies to derive energy from the oceans. During the past several years these dreams have become reality. In 2007 the Scottish first minister, Alex Salmond, delivering the keynote address to the World Renewable Energy Congress, held in Glasgow, announced Scotland's commitment to move to 100 percent renewable energy.[90] He observed that Scotland was blessed with wind and flowing water, but especially with a capacity to tap massive tidal and wave energy. Pelamis Wave Power, founded in 1998, has its headquarters in Edinburgh, Scotland. A leading player in the development of wave power technologies, Pelamis technology consists of semi-submerged, articulated structures linking cylindrical sections with hinged joints. Waves flowing across the structure drive an undulating motion that is resisted by hydraulic rams. The rams pump high-pressure fluid through hydraulic motors, which drive electrical generators to produce electricity. Power from all the devices flows down cables linked to the shore. This technology is now being used in the Aguçadoura wave farm off the northern coast of Portugal, the world's first commercial wave farm. The project started at 2.25 megawatts, but plans to expand to 20 megawatts. The power of the waves coming in from the Atlantic, could, by 2050, enable wave power to represent 30 percent of the energy generated in Portugal (www.power-technology.com/projects/pelamis).

In late 2009, First Minister Salmond threw the switch at the European Marine Energy Centre (EMEC) in the Orkney Islands to start the Oyster, which combines wave power and hydroelectric generation. Developed by the Scottish wave energy company Aquamarine Power, the Oyster consists of a hinged flap connected to the seabed about thirty feet below the surface. Each wave moves the flap, which drives a hydraulic piston that delivers high-pressure water to an onshore turbine, which then generates electricity.[91] Six months earlier, the official start-up of a new wind farm gave Salmond the chance to state, "Our potential for electricity generation from renewables is up to 60GW—more than ten times our peak demand." He noted that Scotland had already hit its interim target of meeting 31 percent of the country's electricity demand from renewables by 2011.[92]

In early 2010 ScottishPower Renewables, a part of Iberdrola Renewables, partnered with the UK subsidiary of the Norwegian tidal power developer Hammerfest Strom AS, to test a 1 megawatt tidal power device at the European Marine Energy Centre. This tidal turbine is expected to be fully operational by 2011. Funded by a £3.9 million grant from the Carbon Trust for the construction, the companies have plans to install a 10 megawatt tidal power array in the Sound of Islay by 2012, the largest tidal power project in the world. If successful it will put ScottishPower Renewables at the forefront of global tidal power developers.[93]

Hydroelectric

From the earliest times, dams have delivered clean, renewable power by using falling water to power mills and turn turbines. Primitive water mills ground grain, powered sawmills, and carried out other heavy tasks. By the mid-1700s the French had harnessed falling water to drive a water wheel that drove a generator to create electricity, and by 1800 water power was providing electricity for street lighting in Michigan. Soon the growing desire for electric power ushered in the era of big dams, but at the cost of losing most free-flowing rivers throughout the world. The construction of these dams and the lakes that back up behind them created substantial destruction of wildlife habitat, ecosystem loss, and displacement of human settlements. Native peoples from Northern Canada to India are still fighting proposals to flood their lands. As water gathers now behind the massive Three Gorges Dam across the Yangtze River, Chinese officials are belatedly admitting that the $24 billion, 18 gigawatt project, the world's largest, could be an environmental disaster, altering whole ecosystems and endangering the lives and livelihoods of millions of people. Some critics doubt that the project will ever be completed.[94]

That history should not obscure the fact that smaller, less harmful, and less capital-intensive hydroelectric and run-of-the-river projects (run-of-the-river means using the natural flow and elevation drop of a river to generate electricity without a dam) have been introduced around the world, and at appropriate sites can be important local sources of power.[95]

A particularly clever and practical small hydro application was introduced in 2010 by the start-up company Lucid Energy Technologies. Their patented small turbine fits into existing water pipes, replacing pressure reducers and reclaiming some of the energy that it took to pump the water through the pipe in the first place. Water utilities use huge amounts of pumping energy to move water—in California, the State Water Project is the single largest user of electricity in the state. Lucid's simple, cost-effective, and low-impact turbine reclaims some of that energy. The concept has thousands of applications, from water pipes to wind turbines. Lucid was formed by Tim Braun, a young MBA student of Hunter Lovins. Tim had previously run a manufacturing firm in Goshen, Indiana, supplying the recreational vehicle industry. In 2008 he joined forces with the inventor, investors, and tech team that developed the Gorlov Helical Turbine (GHT).[96] A helical turbine is a vertical axis turbine with blades modeled after birds' wings. The first incarnation, developed in 1931 by the French engineer Georges Jean Marie Darrieus, tended to snap under pressure. In 1944 the Russian engineer Alexander Gorlov twisted the Darrieus blades into a helical shape, strengthening the system and eliminating destructive vibrations. Despite tests at the University of Michigan in the late nineties showing that the Gorlov Helical Turbine worked in water moving as slowly as two knots and could capture about 35 percent of the kinetic energy of the current, Gorlov was unable to commercialize the idea until Braun, tired of telling stories about the potential of renewable energy, made the leap and six months later was on his way as a climate capitalist. Two months later, Lucid signed a development agreement with Northwest Pipe Company to design and build an in-conduit hydropower system based on the Gorlov technology.

At a kickoff meeting with Northwest Pipe in October 2008, the team developed what became the foundation for its success. After spending just a few hours batting design ideas back and forth, they put the technology in a pipe. The in-conduit hydropower technology, marketed as Northwest PowerPipe, generates electricity from excess water pressure in the pipes, present in any gravity-fed, water-transmission lines. "There is a tremendous amount of power in moving water," explains Lucid's website. The key difference between Lucid's device and other hydropower devices is its ability to generate electricity from small pressure reductions with minimal impact on pipeline operation—without disrupting the water flow. The device can be shut down to increase volumetric flow, where other devices further reduce or completely cut flow off when shut down. This option allows utilities to manage pressure levels in the pipeline in concert with electricity generation.

The first beta system was installed in the Gage Canal pipeline in Riverside, California, in 2010. Its electricity output is small but the installation was successful. Subsequent installations produced much higher output, and, funded by a million-dollar grant from the Department of Energy, Lucid launched a fully commercial unit in early 2011.[97]

Powering Cities with the Sun

Many cities are rising to the climate challenge faster than the governments of the countries in which they are located. The 2009 UN Climate Change Conference of the Parties in Copenhagen (COP15) made stark the widening gap between the world's nation-states and its cities. As nations dithered, cities seized the initiative to develop and implement policies to prepare for climate change. Mayors, city councils, universities, and local businesspeople are able to enact change faster at a local level than are presidents, prime ministers, national legislatures, and parliaments. "Leaders of cities and towns around the world who support and promote local renewable-energy projects can blaze the trail towards greenhouse gas mitigation, energy security, sustainable development and social benefits for their citizens," said Nobuo Tanaka, the executive director of the International Energy Agency (IEA).[98]

In the United States, frustrated by the inaction on energy security and climate change, a handful of mayors, led by Greg Nickels, a former Seattle mayor, had already taken matters into their own hands. They launched the U.S. Conference of Mayors Climate Protection Agreement to provide tools, resources, and action on climate change at the city level. More than a thousand mayors of small and large cities around the United States have committed their cities to meeting the carbon reduction goals of the Kyoto Protocol, cutting their emissions by 7 percent, to at least 93 percent of their 1990 levels by 2012. Houston, Texas, not normally thought of as a green leader, was highlighted in 2009 for its comprehensive renewable-energy program. The goal, set by Houston's Mayor Bill White, is to source 80 megawatts of renewable energy to fill 50 percent of the city's total energy consumption. In 2008, the City of Houston purchased 30 megawatts of renewable energy, the second-highest total of any city in the United States.[99]

CPS Energy, the San Antonio, Texas, utility, buys wind-generated electricity wholesale from the Desert Sky wind farm near Iraan, Texas, and the Cottonwood Creek wind farm near Sweetwater, Texas. It transmits the wind energy via the state's electric grid to the CPS Energy distribution system, helping businesses in San Antonio and neighboring communities to become 100 percent renewably powered. CPS Energy has set the goal of meeting 15 percent of its customers' peak electrical demand with renewable sources such as wind by 2020.[100] Nearby Helotes, Texas, has committed to buying 100 percent "windricity."[101]

Cities are also helping their citizens get the money to implement renewable energy. A city clerk in Berkeley realized that the city frequently provided favorable loans to businesses that wanted to clean up an alley or put utility wires underground. The recipients then repaid the loans by means of a slight increase in their property taxes. The clerk asked, "Why don't we do this for renewable energy?" In November 2008, the

city introduced Berkeley First, providing loans to enable citizens to install solar panels on their roofs. The first million-dollar offering sold out
in nine minutes.[102]

In July 2008, California passed Assembly Bill 811, which allows local
officials in California to authorize cities to create financing districts for
energy improvements and authorizes cities to issue tax-assessment-
based loans. Palm Desert then started up a $4 million renewable loan
program. Boulder County, Colorado, implemented a $40 million version.
Sonoma County's version has worked so well that in the first nine
months of 2009 the construction industry grew by 8.4 percent, attribut-
able to loan-driven improvements, while in neighboring Napa County,
where no such program was in place, the industry was down 3 percent.
Because of the program several solar companies have set up shop in
Sonoma, bringing even more jobs to the local economy.[103] By late 2009,
the county had contracted more than $18 million in new clean-energy
jobs. A study by the chair of the economics department at Sonoma State
University estimated that if the program reached $1 billion in cumula-
tive spending by September 2012, 11,270 new jobs would be created; if
the program reached $500 million, 5,635 would be created; at $100 million, there would be 1,127 new jobs.[104]

The spread of this innovation (now called PACE, for Property Assessed Clean Energy) across the country was undercut in 2010 when
the bankrupt mortgage giants Fannie Mae and Freddie Mac intervened
to kill the program. Pleas by cities, counties, states, and policy advocates
fell on deaf federal ears. Undeterred, Sonoma has gone ahead with its
program, but many municipal programs are on hold, and many pio-
neers in the program have seen their mortgages altered to front-load
the tax payments.[105]

The Palm Desert website states:

> Rolling out PACE across our nation accelerated Freddie Mac and Fan-
> nie Mae's recognition of this highly Consumer-centric finance program
> and the death knell was rung.
>
> Without understanding the myriad of positive effects of AB811 /
> PACE, and living in constant fear of a repeat of the implosion that we

are experiencing as a result of the "Era of Unbridled Housing Leverage" that helped bring our country into this Not So Great Depression, the Federal Housing Finance Agency (FHFA) has stepped forward (July 9, 2010) in their role as Moderator and halted all lending through these programs.

The crux of the problem, in the eyes of Fannie and Freddie, is that the loan is senior to the home mortgage. In a foreclosure process, the energy efficient loan is paid off before the mortgage lender gets their money back . . . The financing structure was implemented with other types of specialty property taxes in mind. Other property tax assessments for municipal improvements . . . are senior to home mortgages and have not raised red flags from mortgage lenders in the past.

The application process here in Palm Desert began showing strangulation of the spirit of the program as we entered this last lending phase. We see clearly now that our local program was actually just preparing to go lock step with what the requirements that the Fed's [*sic*] were hinting at to allow the PACE to flourish nationwide. And since the US Treasury Department is the true Overseer of PACE they called the halt of such programs until the FHFA could structure the rules. And the rules that we operate by in Palm Desert are nearly identical to the rules that the FHFA are hinting at making standard in the PACE. As stated earlier, strangulation.

When the smoke clears there will be a nationwide program (PACE) founded on the principles of first and foremost protecting quasi-governmental lending agencies and not promoting the financing of energy efficiency and renewable energy integration. Three years from now banks will begin to finance the PACE to generate revenue on their private capital.

In Morris County, New Jersey, a different approach was tried. Schools and agencies were offered the chance to sign up for solar energy at a fixed rate of 10.6 cents per kilowatt-hour for solar-produced power versus a current average of more than 15 cents for traditional energy sources. County officials announced that those involved in the renewable-energy project would save an average of 35 percent on their energy bills, and

more than 40 percent by the end of the initial fifteen years of the program. As of 2010, solar panels were being installed on fourteen public
schools and some county government buildings. Christine Johnson, the
superintendent of the Morris County school district, expects to save
$16,000 and cut energy consumption in her district by 36 percent. She
expects savings to reach $25,000 a year by the fifteenth year. "Anything
we can do to show the community we are trying to save money and reduce energy is worthwhile," Johnson told a local reporter. The program
will also be integrated into the district's curriculum.[106]

Nuclear Power: The Nonsolution

Some advocates claim that nuclear power is necessary to quickly displace
coal-fueled power plants and slow global warming. They forget a few facts
about nuclear power plants. First, they represent an uneconomic answer.
A recent study by Craig Severance, a utility commission analyst, found
that new nuclear plants will cost twenty-five cents per kilowatt-hour of
power produced. Changing out inefficient lightbulbs costs half a cent per
kilowatt-hour or less.[107] Wind in good sites can cost as little as three cents
per kilowatt-hour, solar as little as twelve cents. Power from new nuclear
power plants at twice that price is simply too expensive.[108]

Nuclear is also too slow. If Dr. James Hansen of NASA is right, reductions in carbon emissions must be undertaken aggressively in the
next couple of years. It takes ten years or more to bring a nuclear plant
on line, once all of the permits have been secured. The Chinese can do
it in four, but in the United States the only plants now under construction have already cost over $17 billion and are well behind schedule.[109]

And let us not forget: nuclear power plants remain dangerous. There
are good reasons you don't want one in your backyard. For that matter,
you don't really want them in anyone else's backyard, either. Replacing
all of the coal plants around the world with nuclear would make it impossible to prevent any country or motivated subnational group that
wanted raw material for making a nuclear bomb from obtaining it. Not
a nice prospect.[110]

Nuclear plants waste water. They require large amounts of water for cooling. Climate change will mean that droughts are going to become more common. Water shortages have already forced nuclear plants to shut down.

Nuclear plants produce dangerous waste materials. There is no technical solution for safely disposing of the radioactive waste.

Perhaps most disturbing is that nuclear power, because it is so dangerous, requires a technological priesthood to keep it running safely. This threatens basic democratic principles.

In sum, the prospect of more nuclear power plants is most unattractive to free marketers like us. Utility executives are understandably reluctant to put their shareholders' money into an industry in which a nuclear accident anywhere in the world can threaten to shut down every other plant. So they now demand your and my tax dollars to create the "nuclear renaissance." This is not Climate Capitalism; it is socialism for some very wealthy companies who won't put their own money where their fast talk is, so they want yours.

This litany of problems is not very encouraging for a technology that has already cost taxpayers well over $150 billion in the United States alone, and taxpayers in France, the UK, China, India, Pakistan, Israel, etcetera many times that—more than the Vietnam War and the space program combined—for a technology that now delivers to us about as much energy as wood.[111]

Capital Markets for New Energy Ventures

Renewable-energy companies need money to innovate, scale up, and deliver commercially relevant amounts of product. Traditionally, established companies led most energy initiatives, buying promising start-ups but often failing to bring the new technologies to market. The clean-tech revolution, however, is a field made for climate capitalists large and small. If they can get the capital. There are many ways for innovators to get the money they need to flourish. Many conferences, websites, and books are devoted to funding energy ventures. It is beyond the scope of this chapter to cover the whole field, but here are some of the more innovative approaches.

Perhaps the best way to capitalize investments in clean energy is to pay for them out of prior efficiency measures. At a symposium put on by Clean Air, Cool Planet, Gary Hirshberg, the CEO of Stonyfield Farms, stated that his company's efficiency measures had been uniformly profitable and called them "our venture capital." He praised energy reductions of any size, quipping, "Anyone who thinks they are too small to make a difference has never been in bed with a mosquito."[112]

In recent years, new private equity funds dedicated to renewable and clean-technology solutions have enabled new ventures in all sectors of the low-carbon economy. Despite the worsening economy in 2009 and the lack of a federal or international policy, clean-tech investments valued at $5.6 billion were made by the venture capital markets in North America, Europe, India, and China.[113] Capital-intensive new energy ventures would not get out of the starting gates without access to large amounts of high-risk venture capital. The funds that have emerged around the world provide a lifeline for innovative clean-tech ventures. As with most innovation, many entrepreneurs get their start using capital from "friends and family." Increasingly, however, angel investors are seeking new renewable-energy companies. Government loan programs are beginning to be made available for renewable-energy start-ups. Still, many aspiring companies will find themselves in the grasp of what has been called "vulture capital."

The big venture capital funds are household names: Vinod Khosla, a native of India who was one of the founders of Sun Microsystems, began his venture capitalist career at Kleiner Perkins Caufield and Byers, one of the preeminent venture capital funds on Sand Hill Road, the Menlo Park, California, street known for its concentration of venture capital companies. He launched Khosla Ventures in 2004, and by 2009 he announced the creation of a billion-dollar fund for new clean-tech investments. Known for attracting big-name investors, Khosla recently brought Bill Gates into the business of low-carbon investments.

Richard Branson, the charismatic billionaire business titan behind Virgin Records, Virgin Atlantic, Virgin Galactic, Virgin Mobile, and other

companies in the Virgin Group, who has been using capitalism to promote social and environmental solutions far longer than Khosla, is serious about Climate Capitalism. In 2008 he launched a new nonprofit, the
Carbon War Room, to convince venture capitalists, private equity investors, and U.S. industrial giants that cutting greenhouse gas emissions
can drive long- and short-term profits and is good for the U.S. economy.
The group stated: "This is our Great War. Our global industrial and energy systems are built on carbon-based technologies and unsustainable
resource demands that threaten to destroy our society and our planet.
Massive loss of wealth, expanding poverty and suffering, disastrous climate change, water scarcity, and deforestation are the end results of this
broken system."[114]

Noting that shipping and airlines, as well as cities and housing offer
opportunities to make money while cutting carbon, Branson and Carbon War Room staff have created partnerships with companies including Maersk, the global tanker operator, to cut some of the pollutants
and carbon dioxide emissions that come with shipping goods across the
ocean. The War Room has initiated programs with Portland, Oregon;
Babylon, New York; Burlington, Vermont; Birmingham, UK; Charles-
ton, South Carolina; Chicago; Copenhagen; Gainesville, Florida; London; New York City; San Francisco; Washington, D.C.; Toronto; and
Vancouver as part of the Green Capital Global Challenge to bring private investors to fund public-sector sustainability projects. It issued its
initial investments by the end of 2010.[115]

The Carbon War Room's director, Jigar Shah, who made his money
as the founder of SunEdison, a company providing solar electricity, has
said, "We realized that over 50 percent of carbon emissions globally
have profitable technologies that exist today that can offset the offend-
ing technology. So the question is, what the hell are people waiting for?"[116]
He states, "This business-as-usual system represents the greatest threat
to the security and prosperity of humanity—a threat that transcends
race, ethnicity, national borders, and ideology. We need new thinking,
new leadership, and innovation to create a post-carbon economy. Our
goal is not to undo industry, but to remake it into a force for sustainable
wealth generation." [117]

Venture-capital funds increasingly are specializing in clean tech. California-based Firelake Capital is one of the most competent and successful such firms. Featuring a team of managing directors with personal experience in energy efficiency, clean energy, and Climate Capitalism, the firm helps promising entrepreneurs gain funding, intellectual property protection, and management expertise to ensure that their ideas grow into prosperous companies. Martin Lagod, one of the founders of Firelake Capital, serves on the boards of directors of many of the clean-tech companies in which he invests. Firelake Capital is responsible for the success of the exciting Climate Capitalist firm EOS Climate (described in chapter 8).[118]

The United States has long been the most important center for venture-capital funding, but London is an increasingly important hub of Climate Capitalism. Among the rapidly growing number of firms specializing in bringing finance to companies that are solving the climate crisis is E+Co, which makes clean-energy investments in developing countries and provides opportunities for high returns and poverty alleviation while mitigating or adapting to climate change. E+Co makes small investments, ranging from a $20,000 microcredit loan to a Bolivian manufacturer of solar-powered cook stoves to a $500,000 investment in a distributor of cleaner-burning liquefied natural gas in Mali and a $225,000 investment in a photovoltaic panel distributor in Bangalore. This sort of midlevel capital investment is crucial if firms in developing countries—which often have the most cost-effective investment opportunities to displace carbon with sustainable technologies, but are unable to get funding—are to enter the world of Climate Capitalism.

Also based in the UK, Low Carbon Accelerator Ltd. invests in clean energy, cleaner fuels, energy efficiency, and buildings in Europe and North America that will deliver immediate reductions in carbon dioxide emissions. In 2006 Low Carbon Accelerator launched on the Alternative Investment Market of the London Stock Exchange, raising £44.5 million. Low Carbon Accelerator expects an internal rate of return of at least 30 percent within three to five years of investment; it has invested £6.65 million in such companies as Proven Energy, a small wind turbine manufacturer with over three thousand wind machines operating in over sixty countries.

Environmental Technologies Fund is another London-based firm that supports entrepreneurs throughout Europe to enable clean-tech ideas to achieve rapid growth. ETF seeks to create economic value and a more sustainable environment for future generations by coming in as a lead investor, active on a company's board. Focusing primarily on European companies that already have some revenue and have great growth prospects, ETF has the ability to invest both at an earlier and at a later stage of development. Typically it supports a business through more than one investment round, committing €5 million ($12 million).[119]

Traditional financing will always be an important part of Climate Capitalism, but there are better ways than traditional financing to ensure that everyone can get a share of these new opportunities. Perhaps the best way to fund renewable energy is to require that the utility that receives clean energy from independent power producers—including home owners, businesses, and others with small-scale installations—pay those producers a fair rate for the power. As described earlier, this concept, called feed-in tariff, creates a stable, long-term investment climate in which installers of solar, wind, wave, or any other renewable power can be confident that they will recover their investment and make money. A recent study by Deutsche Bank concluded that the use of feed-in tariffs was what gave Germany the lead in renewable-energy production. In the four years following, introduction of the tariffs created 300,000 new jobs and cut the unit cost of solar panels 30 percent in 2009 alone—enough so that the installations could pay for themselves within five to seven years and reach grid parity (provide electricity at the same cost as grid electricity) by 2013.[120] The tariffs also became a powerful driver of the German economic regeneration, enabling Germany to pay its own citizens to produce, install, and maintain their own renewable-energy systems, instead of buying imported fossil fuels.[121] The program added a cost of two to three euros per month to electricity bills in Germany.

Some might feel that adding roughly $50 to customers' electricity bills each year is too high a price to pay, and from 2004 to 2006, the feed-in tariff cost Germans a total of €8.6 billion. Another study by Deutsche Bank found, however, that the savings made by the scheme outstripped the total cost of payments made by households. Had customers bought their electricity from conventional generation and paid the costs of fossil fuel generation, Germans would have had to fork over €9.4 billion but would not have gained the jobs or the stronger economy.[122]

Deutsche Bank analyzed renewable policies now prevalent in the United States. It found them to be complex, fragmented, and lacking the transparency, longevity and certainty that investors require before they will bring capital to a field. The report warned that the U.S. preference for renewable portfolio standards (regulations obliging utilities to get a certain percentage of their power from renewables) and renewable-energy certificates (payments by utilities or others to investors or others who install renewable energy), coupled with a morass of federal and local incentives, will deliver results only if long-term hedgeable renewable-energy credit markets emerge as federal incentives also start expiring in 2010.

Some advocates favor Renewable Portfolio Standards, now in place in thirty-three states, because they mandate utilities and other jurisdictions to bring a certain percentage of renewable power into their energy mix by a given date.[123] For example, in 2010 the state of Colorado increased its renewable portfolio standard to require that the utilities get 30 percent of their power from renewables by 2020. A 2009 report by the U.S. Department of Energy analyzed the impacts of Colorado's RPS on the state's economic health. It found that the state's first 1,000 megawatts of wind-power development (generating enough electricity to power nearly 250,000 homes), resulted in the addition of 1,700 full-time jobs during construction with a total payroll of more than $70 million and would support about 300 permanent jobs with a total annual payroll of more than $14 million. The wind program generates $35 million in annual local economic activities, more than $4 million in annual property taxes, and more than $2.5 million annually in extra income for farmers and ranchers who lease their land to developers.[124]

There's nothing wrong with Renewable Portfolio Standards, but by themselves they will prove inadequate. The Deutsche Bank report argued that feed-in tariffs should be integrated with such policy measures as RPS and REC markets. The feed-in tariff would set a floor price to ensure that investors would recover their costs. If renewable-energy contracts then became standardized, investors would see the transparency they seek. This could then become the basis for constructing power purchase agreements in the United States.[125]

In early 2009, Gainesville (Florida) Regional Utilities, at the unanimous direction of the city council, became the first entity in the United States to implement a feed-in tariff. The utility's assistant general manager, Ed Regan, visited Germany to study the system before proposing the use of it for his city. "The feed-in tariff is more attractive to solar investors than traditional solar rebate programs because it guarantees that the utility will buy all of the electricity produced by the PV system at a fixed rate for 20 years," he explained. "It offers investors a reliable and predictable source of income."[126] Groups like the FiT Coalition are working to get feed-in tariffs in place in California and elsewhere, but until they do, solar entrepreneurs face a tough market.

Dr. Murray Cameron, vice president of the European Photovoltaic Industry Association, believes that the United States could become the "largest market for solar on the planet. In the difficult economic times that we are going through now, there are few safer havens for a stable return on investment than solar."[127] But without good policy that brings the transparency, longevity, and certainty that the Deutsche Bank report identified as necessary to launch a new industry, this is not going to happen. Many solar companies that had a solid product, seemingly solid financing, and good management and thus should have prospered instead found themselves forced out of business in the 2008 financial crisis. Of course the worst such crisis since the Great Depression wiped out many businesses, but renewable promoters faced an especially cruel situation. Some observers have pointed out that every time renewable energy has been about to gain real market share, something has occurred that killed the industry: in the 1930s it was cheap oil; the solar subsidies proposed by the Carter administration were delayed so long that the industry was wiped out as customers waited on the tax credits; in 2008, soaring—then crashing—oil prices blew the bottom out of the

renewables market. What's it going to take to get the renewables industry off the ground, they wonder? In late December 2010, the UK answered this by proposing to abandon its RPS and implement a feed-in
tariff.[128]

Feed-in tariffs certainly eliminate the uncertainty and the "valley of
death" that renewable energy has seemed trapped within for decades.
But until advocates can organize the political will to implement the tariffs, another approach is now on offer. One Block Off the Grid's slogan
is "Solar power meets consumer power: Group discounts help you buy
home solar power." The purpose of 1BOG is to enable groups of a hundred residents to become a neighborhood solar community by helping
them purchase and install solar panels on their homes. It helps the community get the advantages of group purchasing (typically with discounts
of 15 percent off retail prices) and avoid the higher costs and the hassle
of trying to install power alone. The group educates and equips its members, vets solar installers, ensures quality, and helps secure financing.
The business works because 1BOG is paid from referral fees by the solar
installers for bringing customers to them. Initiated in San Francisco, the
idea has spread to New Jersey and Southern California.[129]

Putting It All Together

Investing in energy efficiency and renewable energy will generate jobs
and help build strong companies, communities, and countries. Researchers at the University of California–Berkeley concluded, "All states of the
union stand to gain in terms of net employment from the implementation of a portfolio of clean energy policies at the federal level."[130]
The new green energy economy will generate new manufacturing businesses, jobs retrofitting existing buildings, opportunities to build and
manage the new decentralized energy system, the ability to revitalize
farm income from biofuels, wind farms, etc. Traditional economists
who claim that acting to protect the climate is costly should be challenged to show why unleashing the new energy economy will not trigger,

as President Clinton asserts, the greatest economic boom since World War II.[131]

Some companies are not waiting for the government to lead. At the Frankfurt Motor Show in late 2009, Siemens unveiled a bold plan to construct a pan-European smart grid linking sites of distributed generation across Europe: it would connect the proposed Desertec project (a multi-billion-euro effort to link wind, solar thermal, and solar photovoltaic systems in the north of Africa with solar and biomass generation in southern Europe), massive offshore wind farms off the northern German and Danish coasts, and wave power off Scotland and Portugal. It would connect all of these big renewables systems with locally distributed generation on smart homes. In combination with a network of smart electric cars this would deliver a renewably powered Europe. Working with such partners as DONG Energy in Denmark, Better Place, and many others, Siemens sees its industrial future as built upon creating this energy system of tomorrow.[132]

In April 2010, Michael Weinhold, chief technical officer of Siemens's Energy Sector and an engineer, described to students at Berlin's Technical University how new ideas have shifted his focus from implementing small technical improvements to concerns of greater social responsibility. "We engineers need to make the energy system sustainable, so that the world can avert catastrophic climate change," he said. "Siemens already is showing politicians what's possible." He described some of the company's recent work: free-floating offshore wind turbines; the world's largest gas turbine in the combined-cycle process with a record-setting 60 percent efficiency; a new high-voltage direct-current (DC) power line in China that moves 5 gigawatts of CO_2-free hydropower across about 1,400 kilometers at about 95 percent efficiency. Then he described Desertec, which Siemens helped create, and the pan-European smart grid. "Only a few years ago, this project would have been labeled a passing craze," Weinhold told the students. "We can realize it, and we will realize it."

Weinhold described how a broad alternative-fuel mix—offshore wind power in the North Sea, solar photovoltaic from Italy and Spain, biomass and onshore wind in Germany, coupled with some conventional sources—would by 2020 enable 1 million electric cars to cruise German roads. The cars' batteries when connected to a smart grid could then serve as a giant power storage system. At night, people could plug in their electric cars to load their batteries with wind-generated power. Then, during daytime peak demands, the parked hybrid car plugged into the grid could feed excess power back for others to use.[133]

Siemens may be in the lead in implementing such technologies, but they are not alone. IBM is involved in more than 150 smart grid projects in various mature and emerging markets. In October 2010, the company announced that it had been chosen by Energy Australia to be the systems integration partner for the $100 million Smart Grid, Smart City initiative created by the EnergyAustralia Consortium, a partnership between IBM and GE Energy Australia, AGL, Sydney Water, Hunter Water, and local governments. The three-year project is beginning in 2011 across five sites in Sydney and the Hunter Valley region of Australia. It will allow residents to see real-time analysis of electricity usage for their households and even for individual appliances, to help them make better decisions about energy efficiency in their homes and cut their environmental impact. It was subsequently announced that Intel was joining the initiative with $100 million in Australian government funding to provide the smart meters for this project.[134]

There has never been a greater opportunity for entrepreneurs to combine the best energy efficiency technology with the wave of renewable technologies now sweeping the market. These companies will make a lot of money while helping communities enhance their energy security, improve quality of life, and enable all citizens to join the transition of the renewable-energy future.

4

Green Buildings, Green Neighborhoods:
Where Climate Capitalism Lives

Which sector of the economy is responsible for emitting the most green-house gases?

Manufacturing? No, the industrial sector releases about 18 percent of emissions. Then surely transportation? All those cars, trucks, trains, planes . . . ?

Good guess. As the next chapters describe, all the ways that humans use to move themselves around account for a whopping 34 percent of carbon emissions.[1] But the transportation sector isn't the worst offender, either.

The most powerful driver of global warming is the energy we use to construct and operate our homes, offices, and industrial facilities and keep ourselves comfortable inside them. The energy used in the build-ing sector is almost half (48 percent) of all energy consumption. Ac-cording to the U.S. Energy Information Administration, it is responsible for almost half of all the United States' annual greenhouse gas emis-sions. Globally the percentage is even greater, with 76 percent of all power plant–generated electricity used to operate buildings.[2] In communities with little vehicle traffic, buildings can drive 90 percent of emissions.[3] Buildings also use 13.6 percent of all potable water (15 trillion gallons per year) and 40 percent of raw materials and generate over a third of all waste.[4]

Done right, however, our buildings will cost less to build and maintain and will keep us comfortable year-round in all climates simply through good design that retains warmth in the winter and cool comfort in the summer and uses the sun's energy. This approach, called green building, is now a growth industry transforming the whole building sector. Oh, and it also largely solves the climate crisis.

David Johnston is an early green building pioneer. Winner of the European financial community's 2007 Sustainability Pioneer Award, Johnston created the first green building code in the United States, in Boulder, Colorado, and the first private-sector program, through Denver Homebuilders, in 1977. He was a consultant to the U.S. Department of Energy in the early 1970s, when he encouraged including energy efficiency and passive and active solar heating in DOE's buildings program. In the 1980s Johnston was head of the Passive Solar Industries Council, bringing the building trades into the field, until President Reagan destroyed America's government expertise in this. He was one of the early drafters of the LEED (Leadership in Energy and Environmental Design) standards.

One of green building's best implementers, Johnston is fond of saying, "Putting fancy solar systems on top of leaky buildings is like putting on a gold crown while wearing rags and shoes with holes in them." He points out that buildings are the perfect metaphor for what needs to be done not only to solve the climate crisis but also to implement profitable sustainability. The first and most profitable step is efficiency, and only then should supply options be considered. Think of a building as a balloon, he suggests. If a balloon is full of leaks it doesn't matter how much air you blow into it, it won't stay inflated. Similarly, a leaky building loses the energy you put into it.[5]

This chapter describes a wealth of ways we can invest in our communities and our economy by fixing up buildings and supplying them with climate-protecting energy. It profiles the growing group of Climate

Capitalists revolutionizing the construction trades by inventing ways of building that support more comfortable, affordable, and sustainable ways to live. It shows how they are transforming the construction industry into one of the biggest sources of climate protection and into a driver of economic renewal. Buildings can't be outsourced and they won't be put on a boat and sent to China. The workers needed to fix them are in our cities already. The materials and equipment are in local stores waiting for the investments that will rebuild our communities, one house, one storefront at a time.

Not the Color of the Paint

"Green building" refers to the practice of building homes, offices, and industries in ways that are environmentally responsible and resource-efficient throughout the life cycle of the structure. The best green buildings need no energy but the sun to keep those living and working within them comfortable year-round, whether in Bangkok or Alaska. Most green buildings feature the smart use of local, low-impact materials that do not have high embedded-energy content or require transportation over long distances, requiring commensurate amounts of fossil fuels. They use only low-toxicity interior finishes and are operated to exclude toxic cleaning supplies and other sources of pollution to maintain high air quality. Rooftop rainwater collection supplies water and the building provides on-site wastewater processing and irrigation. Landscaping includes drought-tolerant gardens and edible-plant cultivation. Thought is given to designing the structure for flexible use and future reconfigurations.

One early study estimated that, on average, building green reduces energy use by 30 percent, carbon emissions by 35 percent, and water use by 30 to 50 percent, and generates cost savings of 50 to 90 percent.[6] An early assessment of the benefits of green building found that green buildings' operating costs decrease 8 to 9 percent, their value increases over 7 percent, their return on investment improves more than 6 percent, their occupancy rates increase more than 4 percent, and their rent increases 3 percent.[7] The sale prices of energy-efficient buildings are as much as 10 percent higher per square foot than those of conventional buildings.[8] And many buildings do far better than this.

The Adam Lewis Center for Environmental Studies at Oberlin College is an elegant, comfortable, and functional living laboratory for students of the college and thousands of visitors. Stewarded from concept to completion by the great environmental educator Dr. David Orr, a member of the Oberlin faculty, the center produces more energy from its solar system than it uses, has its own wastewater treatment system, grows food in its landscaping, was designed with student participation, and continues to serve as a center for innovation. Dedicated in 1999, the building was the recipient of the 1999 American Architecture Award and was named by the American Institute of Architects one of America's Top Green Projects.[9]

At the dedication ceremony, Dr. Orr stated,

> We intended to create not just a place for classes but rather a building that would help to redefine the relationship between humankind and the environment—one that would expand our sense of ecological possibilities . . . A means to the larger end of improving how creatively we think. In the century ahead all of those who will be educated here must learn how to: Power society by sunlight and stabilize climate, disinvent the concept of waste and build prosperity within the limits of natural systems—in ways that can be sustained over the long term, preserve biological diversity and restore damaged ecosystems, and do these things while advancing the causes of justice and nonviolence.[10]

Dr. Orr credits the building with helping to inspire hundreds of Oberlin students to choose professions in ecodesign, green architecture, and related fields.

Green buildings cut the impact of the built environment on human health and the natural environment by efficiently using energy, water, and other resources. They improve employee productivity by creating healthy indoor environments with low toxicity. Green designs cut waste and pollution and are better stewards of the climate. They often use sustainable materials in construction—including reused, recycled content, and renewable materials—and feature landscaping that cuts water usage.[11]

A green building is far more resource-efficient than a conventional building, often incorporating a whole-systems approach that coordinates land-use planning and intelligent site selection and a layout that orients a building to benefit most from solar gain or shading, depending on its climate. Low-impact, waste-minimizing construction techniques are used and the impacts of the building on its surroundings and local community are considered. But climate protection is the core of what makes today's buildings green. Passive heating and cooling strategies, including cross ventilation, radiant barriers in the roof, daylighting and shading, and the use of energy-efficient appliances and lighting are key. Once the building is made as efficient as possible, renewable energy, such as solar electric cells, solar water heating, and integrated wind systems are used as appropriate.

Initially, builders thought that it would cost up to 2 percent to build more sustainable buildings. Experienced green builders now report that there is no hard evidence of any premium for building green, but even if this increase were required, as an investment, it results in average life-cycle savings of 20 percent of the total construction costs—more than ten times the initial investment.[12]

Where Do You Want to Live and Work?

Are you looking for more reasons to build green? Buildings are where we spend most of our time—the majority of us are inside upward of 90 percent of our time.[13] Shouldn't indoor spaces be magical places, comfortable, full of light and capable of inspiring the best in us? Sadly, few are. Environmental Protection Agency studies indicate indoor levels of pollutants may be up to ten times higher than outdoor levels.[14] The World Health Organization estimated that up to 30 percent of new or remodeled buildings around the world are the subject of complaints regarding poor indoor air quality. The EPA describes a condition called "sick building syndrome" that inflicts occupants with headaches; eye, nose, and throat irritation; dizziness and nausea; difficulty concentrating; and other ailments that disappear when they leave the affected building. Some building-related illnesses—including coughing, muscle aches, fever and chills—persist even after the afflicted leave the structure.[15]

The U.S. Green Building Council estimates that fully half of U.S. schools have sick building syndrome from molds, off-gassing from chemicals in building materials, carpets, and furniture, and toxic cleaning products introduced on a daily basis.[16] If I told you that I was going to imprison your children in a windowless space and systematically poison them with industrial chemicals, you'd fight. But that is precisely what we do in schools across the "civilized" world. For years schools have been designed without windows, with no natural ventilation, and with little regard to the toxicity of materials or cleaning products used to finish and maintain them. Yet studies have shown that over the course of a year students enjoying optimal daylighting in their classrooms progressed 20 percent faster on math tests and 26 percent faster on reading tests.[17]

All of us have shed clothes in the winter because the heating system is running overtime, and put sweaters on in the heat of the summer to deal with an overactive air-conditioning system. It doesn't have to be this way. This is a silly waste of money, and a shameful use of carbon energy. Occupants would be more comfortable in structures using good design and we would not be destroying our climate by artificially heating and cooling buildings in ways that make people miserable and sick.

It is possible, and, in fact, more cost-effective to build affordable structures that are delightful to be in and increase the productivity and health of the people inside them. An array of energy-efficiency measures implemented in buildings can increase worker productivity by 6 to 16 percent.[18] Even if energy savings are not sufficient to attract scarce management attention, deriving greater value from your employees should be. Employers typically pay 100 times more for people than for energy, and even a 1 percent increase in labor productivity will dwarf typical energy savings.[19] But it takes paying attention to energy efficiency to achieve that increased productivity. Better indoor air quality, a result of green design techniques, has been shown to improve worker productivity by 0.5 to 5 percent.[20] Improving indoor air quality could save U.S. businesses $20 billion to $200 billion in energy costs, as well as $58 billion in avoided sick time each year. The increased productivity would save another $200 billion a year.[21]

When asked whether merely locating workers in green buildings fosters innovation, almost 60 percent of corporate managers surveyed in a 2007 study answered in the affirmative.[22] The empirical evidence supports them. Experiments showed that energy-efficient lighting design resulted in a 27 percent reduction in the incidence of headaches, which accounts for 0.7 percent of overall employee health insurance costs at approximately $35 per employee annually.[23] A study at Herman-Miller showed a 7 percent increase in worker productivity following a move to a green, daylit facility. Paul Murray, director of environmental health, stated, "If you have a company that people want to work for because the company's doing the right thing as a corporate citizen, that will become a strategic advantage."[24] Customers, too, respond well to better design: in stores with skylights sales were up to 40 percent higher than in similar stores without skylights.[25]

A revolution is under way in lighting technology. The California Lighting Technology Center at the University of California–Davis and lighting engineers such as Clanton Associates can transform any room from dreary to a well-illuminated space that enables workers to see better, enjoy themselves more, and deliver superior work. The California Lighting Technology Center offers on its website a list of ten top measures you can implement in your home to save money and improve your quality of life.[26] Nancy Clanton, Clanton Associates' brilliant principal engineer and a green building pioneer, helped oversee the lighting for Oberlin's Adam Lewis building and is now leading the lighting retrofit of the Empire State Building. Many of the measures she is implementing can also deliver better living conditions in your business, from the use of full-spectrum lighting, which replicates full sunlight, to light shelves and sun tubes that deliver daylight even into interior spaces.

Many cities are finding great savings retrofitting their streetlights, stoplights, and other lighting with light emitting diode (LED) bulbs. Raleigh, North Carolina, became the first "LED City" in 2006. The city saved 40 percent compared with its existing high-pressure sodium fixtures by retrofitting one floor of a municipal parking deck. Garage users reported feeling three times safer after the LED lighting was installed.[27] Dan Howe, Raleigh assistant city manager, concludes, "We are moving forward with LED lighting whenever we can, including three solar-powered LED pole-lighting projects in places where line power is unavailable."[28]

Anchorage, Alaska, found that LED lights love cold weather, outlasting regular bulbs and saving significantly on maintenance. The city replaced about 140,000 cobra-head-style street lights throughout the city with LED fixtures, saving 50 percent over the replaced fixtures and keeping $360,000 a year in the city coffers.[29] Over a dozen universities have followed suit, as has Walmart. Participants report energy savings of 50 to 80 percent, depending on application and maintenance cost savings, reaching into six figures over the fixtures' lifetimes. According to the U.S. Department of Energy, such programs, if replicated across the country in the next twenty years, would cut electricity demand for lighting by a third, cut 258 million metric tons of carbon emissions, preempt the need to build forty new power plants, and achieve financial savings of over $200 billion.[30] LEDs do not contain the mercury and lead found in traditional lighting sources and compact fluorescent lights. Their durability and solid-state technology mean longer life and lead to less waste in the landfill.

Transforming an Industry

Green buildings are also the key to economic recovery. Sick buildings are part of a sick industry, the home-construction industry, which has infected the entire economy. The collapse of the mortgage bubble of the last decade nearly collapsed global finance. The Heritage Foundation acknowledged that the collapse of the subprime mortgage market created Depression-like conditions in the housing market and drove the economy into recession.[31] By April 2009, housing starts were at their lowest level since the Census Bureau began tracking housing starts in 1959.[32] This hit hard at an industry overwhelmingly made up of small businesses. Sixty percent of the National Association of Home Builders members build fewer than twenty-five homes per year and nearly 90 percent have less than $5 million in annual receipts.[33] But collectively the home-building industry represents over 13 percent of the $13.2 trillion U.S. GDP.[34]

Builders are not often considered the most innovative of tradespeople. Many in the construction trades, an industry described as a dynamically conservative one, work very hard to stay in the same place. This is not surprising of an industry whose basic unit of production is the pickup truck. Many people who have asked their builders to build "green" have found that unless the builder has done the type of task before, he is likely to say that it can't be done, that it will raise costs prohibitively, or that regulations won't allow it. It may be true, but often it is code for "I don't know how to do that . . ."

Yet despite this conservatism, an amazing transformation is taking place in many parts of the construction industry—they're going green. Builders are recognizing that their future lies in creating low-carbon buildings. McGraw Hill Construction's report "Trends Driving Change" states, "Green building has grown in spite of the market downturn. Green seems to be one area of construction insulated by the downturn, and we expect green building will continue to grow despite negative market conditions to be a $96 billion–$140 billion market by 2013."[35] The green market was 2 percent of nonresidential construction starts in 2005 and 10 to 12 percent in 2008, and will grow to 20 to 25 percent by 2013.[36]

The consulting giant Booz Allen Hamilton found that from 2000 to 2008, the U.S. green construction market generated $173 billion dollars in GDP, supported over 2.4 million jobs, and provided $123 billion dollars in labor earnings. Between 2009 and 2013 building green structures is predicted to create almost 8 million more U.S. jobs and pump $554 million into the American economy.[37]

In early 2010 *The Wall Street Journal* announced that half of all nonresidential buildings will be green by 2015. Since commercial buildings, a sector worth about $350 billion per year in the United States, accounts for 18 percent of U.S. total energy consumption and 11 percent of the total energy consumption in Europe, greening of this sector will make a significant contribution to greening the country.[38]

Tesco, a global powerhouse in the supermarket industry—with more than two thousand stores and 180,000 employees working in the UK, Europe, Asia, India, and North America, revenues of about £18 billion, and profits of £700 million—is committed to reducing their buildings' energy consumption and emissions. Since 2007 Tesco has focused on enhancing energy efficiency in their stores, building more efficient stores in seven countries, and recently opening a fourth UK prototype whose greenhouse gas emissions are just 40 percent of those in the company's standard stores.[39] The company's Cheetham Hill, Manchester, store achieved a 70 percent reduction in GHG emissions from operations and a 48 percent reduction in its energy costs.[40] Because of such efforts, at the end of 2008, Ceres, a nonprofit specializing in corporate responsibility, ranked Tesco as the company with the best climate change strategy in their sector.

Green Building Is Just Better Building

Many aspects of green building are ancient practices. In their 1980 book, *A Golden Thread: 2,500 Years of Solar Architecture and Technology*, Ken Butti and John Perlin describe how the Persians made ice in the desert using "wind catchers." These structures used air baffles to bend the wind, cooling it and the buildings through which it passed. As noted earlier, in the American Southwest the Anasazi people built passive solar structures whose ruins still deliver comfortable temperatures year-round, even with no windows. Socrates offered advice on the use of passive solar energy, Thomas Jefferson invented a passive cooling system, and vernacular architecture around the world uses good solar orientation, local forms of insulation, and other smart design techniques to maximize comfort.[41]

Before the advent of cheap fuel in the early twentieth century people were more canny about working with the earth and the elements when they created their homes. They husbanded their resources—planting woodlots for fuel and orchards. They planted shade trees to protect their houses from the heat of the sun in the summer and sited their houses to face south, to profit from the sun's warmth in the winter. Only when houses became commoditized and traded like baseball cards did we lose the connection between home and hearth and the earth.[42] The introduction of cheap fossil fuel energy allowed builders and occupants to become lazy and wasteful and the building sector to gain a fat carbon footprint. The good news is that there is no reason we cannot return to the best practices of earlier times. We can do better, and as this chapter and the next several show, we will.

Today, a green building has come to be defined as one built to the standards set forth by the U.S. Green Building Council's Leadership in Energy and Environmental Design rating system, called LEED. For example, the USGBC provides a working definition in its "Green Jobs Study":

> McGraw-Hill's "Green Construction Market" Definition: We define [a] green building as one built to LEED standards, an equivalent green building certification program, or one that incorporates numerous green building elements across five category areas: energy efficiency, water efficiency, resource efficiency, responsible site management and improved indoor air quality. Projects that only feature a few green building products (e.g., HVAC systems, waterless urinals) or that only address one aspect of a green building, such as energy efficiency, are not included in this calculation.[43]

LEED built upon the world's first green building rating system, the UK's Building Research Establishment Environmental Assessment Method (BREEAM), established in 1990. The Canadian Green Building Council (CaGBC), the Indian Green Building Council, the Green Building Council Italia, and others have all formally adopted LEED. In 2008 China launched its Green Building Council, meant to complement and expand on LEED.

Founded in 1993 by David Gottfried, Mike Italiano, and Rick Fedrizzi (who subsequently led the organization), the U.S. Green Building Council grew in part out of President Clinton's request to the American Institute of Architects to help "green" the White House; it became one of the fastest-growing nonprofits in history.[44] In 1998 volunteer teams of green designers, architects, sustainability thought leaders, energy-efficiency experts, and dozens of others created LEED version 1.0, covering energy and atmosphere, water efficiencies, building materials, and indoor air quality. To get LEED certification, a project must incorporate enough qualifying characteristics to gain a certain number of points. Buildings are submitted for LEED certification after completion, but increasingly the standards guide design and construction. Depending on the number of points the project receives, the building either is rejected or receives a "silver," "gold," or "platinum" LEED certification.

Organizers of the first USGBC conference, Greenbuild, in 1993, expected a few hundred construction tradespeople. Instead, the conference drew over four thousand architects, developers, builders, and product manufacturers. Since then Greenbuild has hit rock star status with the 2009 conference, which attracted 28,000 attendees and was headlined by Al Gore and Sheryl Crow. The USGBC and its partners around the world have swept the market, creating transparent, third-party-verified standards that enable any skilled professional to build structures that can authentically be called green. The LEED standard has become the leading certification program for the design, construction, and operation of green buildings. At a sustainability conference in 2007, President Clinton stated that henceforth all buildings should be LEED-rated, and Harvard University has announced that they can build to a LEED Gold certification for not a penny more than conventional building practices would cost.

In response to enormous and growing demand, the USGBC fine-tuned its program, introducing certification programs for, among others, new construction (LEED-NC), existing buildings (LEED-EB), and neighborhood developments (LEED-ND). A study by the New Buildings Institute (NBI) found that new buildings certified under the USGBC's LEED certification system use on average 25 to 30 percent less energy than non-LEED-certified buildings. The study found a correlation between increasing levels of LEED certification and increased energy savings. LEED Gold- and Platinum-certified buildings have average energy savings over conventional buildings approaching 50 percent.

USGBC membership comprises a thousand companies and organizations (including Natural Capitalism Solutions), seventy-eight U.S. chapters and affiliates, and more than 140,000 LEED Accredited Professionals. More than 43,000 commercial projects participate in the LEED green building certification system, representing over 9.7 billion square feet of construction space in all fifty states and in 106 countries.[45]

LEED-related construction spending added $830 million to the GNP, supported 15,000 jobs, and delivered $703 million in labor earnings between 2000 and 2008. Between 2009 and 2013, spending for LEED buildings is forecast to generate an additional $12.5 billion dollars in GDP, support 230,000 jobs, and increase labor earnings by $10.7 billion.[46]

Green buildings don't just save you money; they actually make it for you, too. A study by the Commercial Real Estate Information Company (CoStar) established that LEED buildings attract rent premiums of $11.24 per square foot over their non-LEED peers and have 3.8 percent higher occupancy.[47] In comparison to the average commercial building, green buildings have 13 percent lower maintenance costs and 27 percent higher occupant satisfaction.[48]

In Boise, Idaho, the spec builder Gary Christensen found that building the Banner Bank Building to LEED Platinum standards cost no more than a conventional building, but gave him a 32 percent return on investment while allowing him to attract 10 percent more tenants than planned with 15 to 20 percent less floor space than similar buildings. The building uses about half the water and three quarters the energy of a comparable conventional building, despite having four significant data centers not anticipated in the original design. Because the building's requirements forced its janitors to use green cleaning techniques to preserve air quality, the cleaning service extended these skills to its residential service as a Maid Brigade franchisee. The corporate office got wind of it, had the janitors present at a national conference, and within a year, Banner's standards were adopted nationally by this cleaning service, improving the working conditions of their twenty thousand maids and improving the health of thousands of customers.[49]

The Aldo Leopold Legacy Center near Baraboo, Wisconsin, a LEED Platinum building, is the first carbon-neutral building certified by LEED. The building's annual operations create no net increase in carbon dioxide emissions. The beautiful center is also a net-zero energy building, collecting all of the energy it needs from the sun.[50] Even in Wisconsin's cold winters and hot summers, the center uses 70 percent less energy than a building built merely to code. The roof-mounted solar array provides 110 percent of the building's energy needs on an annual basis.[51]

The EPA and the U.S. Department of Energy developed the Energy Star rating for energy-efficient appliances, but they added buildings to the rating system to further encourage energy efficiency as a way of reducing greenhouse gas emissions. The Energy Star program is a technical assistance and recognition program that provides owners and managers of buildings with free tools and resources to help them evaluate their energy performance and reduce energy use and greenhouse gas emissions. It helps organizations benchmark the performance of their buildings by means of the Portfolio Manager online energy-tracking tool. Buildings that perform in the top 25 percent of a cohort of their peers nationwide can be labeled Energy Star–certified as an indicator of superior energy performance.

These buildings consume on average about 35 percent less energy than non–Energy Star structures, and emit 35 percent less carbon.[52] Rental rates in Energy Star buildings command a premium of $2.38 per square foot over comparable non–Energy Star buildings and have a 3.6 percent higher occupancy rate. Energy Star buildings sell for an average of $61 per square foot more than their peers, and LEED buildings command $171 more per square foot.[53]

The Greenest Building: "Greening" Preexisting Structures Is Fixing Up the One That Is Already Built

Fixing up and "greening" existing buildings is another important facet of green building, and is generally far more energy- and resource-efficient than tearing a structure down and starting over. The Thomas Mott Homestead Bed and Breakfast, in Alburg, Vermont, originally built in 1838, has been remodeled over the years. In 2007, the inn's owner, Patrick Schallert, implemented some simple retrofits to make the inn more efficient. He started by installing insulation throughout the building. His next step was to install thirty-nine new high-performance energy-efficient windows, to minimize heat loss and make the building more comfortable. He also installed a new, continuous-flow hot water system, with a state-of-the-art boiler. Schallert's final touches included replacing all of the lighting with highly efficient compact fluorescents and planting trees on the grounds to provide shade in the summer. Because of Schallert's efforts, the inn saves about $10,000 annually, which over a period of six years covered the costs of the whole remodel. The investment will continue generating savings for years to come.[54]

The Wolcott Eco Office, at 28 Wolcott Street in Providence, Rhode Island, achieved similar performance from a green retrofit. Located in a former jewelry factory, it is now entirely heated, air-conditioned, and powered by the sun. The building is earth-sheltered, superinsulated, and passively heated and cooled. Its developer, John Jacobson, enabled the building to achieve net zero performance and even produce more energy than it needs. He did this without local tax breaks or incentives, and in the process put $1.1 million back into the local economy. He remarked, "Solar power is great for the environment but it is also great when businesses don't have to worry about rising energy costs."[55]

Deep Green

Passive solar design uses good architecture to minimize energy consumption and improve thermal comfort. The building is oriented to the sun to soak up its warmth, but is provided with shade to keep it cool on hot days. The building elements (architectural, structural, envelope, and passive mechanical) deliver the thermal performance that ensures comfort in whatever local microclimate the structure is built. A passive building in the American Southwest will look and be constructed very differently from one in Sweden, but the same concepts of passive design will eliminate requirements for mechanical systems that require fossil fuel–based energy, while keeping occupants comfortable at all times.[56]

In 1990 the physicist Dr. Wolfgang Feist created the *Passivhaus*, the "passive house," in Darmstadt, Germany.[57] Heated and cooled by good design, it requires no external air conditioning and uses only a small gas furnace for the coldest months to achieve dramatically higher comfort than conventional homes. Its energy use is 9 kilowatt-hours per square meter per year, as compared to the average German annual energy consumption for heating of some 170 kilowatt-hours per square meter per year. The Passivhaus achieved a 95 percent reduction in energy use, or twenty times greater efficiency.[58] Feist and others have since built more than six thousand passive houses, cutting their energy consumption to just 10 percent of the average for conventional buildings.[59] Feist founded the Passivhaus Institut (its American branch is Passive House Institute US), which now holds an annual global conference to promote the Passivhaus standard of energy efficiency.[60]

Passive design incorporates natural ventilation and daylighting, saving much of the electricity costs associated with lighting systems, the second-highest user of energy in a typical building. By creating open, airy spaces that are warm in the winter and cool in the summer, passive design cuts energy consumption from heating, ventilating, and air-conditioning systems, as well. [61]

The same passive design approach works in commercial buildings. The Sustainable Facilities Management Conference held in March 2010 in Melbourne highlighted green commercial buildings that leverage passive design to reduce energy demand. The conference showed how to achieve 68 percent reductions using passive ventilation and 42 percent energy cuts using passive daylighting. For example, Adobe Systems, the maker of Adobe Acrobat, spent $1.4 million to retrofit its California corporate headquarters with passive features, and they recouped their investment in fourteen months from 35 percent cuts in electricity and 41 percent reduction in natural gas consumption.[62]

In 2005 the global building firm Lend Lease created 30 The Bond, its Sydney headquarters—then Australia's greenest building. Holding numerous employee workshops to determine priorities when the company decided to retrofit an existing nineteenth-century building, the company set as its goals reduction in pollutants, increase in environment quality, water management (climate change has thrown Australia into permanent drought), waste management, and a green "break" area for employees. The result impressed Hunter Lovins as a stunningly beautiful space and one of the most functional and delightful office towers in the world.

An exposed four-story wall made of sandstone quarried by convicts early in Sydney's existence serves as the back wall of the atrium, providing insulation and natural cooling as well as a reminder of the site's history. The building was a brownfield industrial site, an old gasworks that was contaminated and had to be remediated before construction could commence. The first building in Australia to achieve a five-star rating under NABERS, the National Australian Built Environment Rating System, 30 The Bond was certified to have achieved a 20 percent carbon reduction over the already stringent targets set by its initial five-star design commitment.[63] To achieve this, the structure used a "chilled beam" cooling system (a first use in Australia of circulating cold water that convectively cools a structure), wintergarden rooms, a roof garden with native plants, decking made from sustainably harvested timber, and automatically controlled external shades that keep the heat from penetrating windows that provide external views for 60 percent of the occupants. The building features excellent indoor air quality by using only low-VOC (volatile organic compounds) carpets and paints.[64]

Lend Lease's honor at having Australia's greenest building was eclipsed in 2006 by the City of Melbourne's Council House2 building, which earned six stars, or LEED Platinum equivalent. The ten-story building features photovoltaic cells, chilled ceilings, blackwater wastewater recycling system (using recycled wastewater in toilets), all achieved within a conventional construction budget. Recycled timber louvers controlled by photovoltaic cells shade the building. By day the building is cooled by five shower towers, about 45 inches in diameter and twelve yards long, that draw air through water droplets that evaporate slightly, lowering air temperatures from around 94° Fahrenheit (35°C) to around 70° Fahrenheit (21°C) and water temperatures to about 54° Fahrenheit (12°C).

Wind-powered turbines help cool the building at night, storing that coolness passively in the structure's internal thermal mass of stone and concrete. Gas-fired cogeneration and recycling of the waste heat generated inside the building supplement the heating and cooling system.[65]

Then in June 2009, this building's energy efficiency was eclipsed by the opening of Melbourne's new convention center, also a six-star LEED Platinum building. Soaring facades, stunning angles, brilliant colors, and an array of textures all enhance what is now considered one of the greenest buildings in the world. It incorporates such innovative solutions as chilled floor slabs and displacement ventilation (low-velocity cool air that floods floor level and is lifted by hotter air, more efficiently cooling a space than high-velocity "mixed flow" ventilation) to reduce the need for air conditioning; a blackwater treatment plant that recycles wastewater for use in toilets; cooling towers and landscape irrigation; solar thermal panels that supply hot water for all public amenities; and the use of sustainably harvested timber veneer throughout the structure. Oh, and the new convention center generated a thousand construction jobs and will create another twenty-five hundred permanent jobs.[66]

As impressive as these structures are, projects that create "zero-energy" buildings—or, more accurately, buildings that need no external energy to keep them comfortable—are even better. In 2002, ZEDfactory, formerly Dunster Architects, completed the Beddington Zero Energy Development (BedZED) in a suburb of London, the largest mixed-use, carbon-neutral development in the UK and one of the first in the world. It incorporates ninety-nine homes and one hundred workspaces. Pushing the envelope of green building design, BedZED was responding to the fact that if everyone in the world lived as people conventionally live in the UK we'd need three more earths' worth of resources to support them. ZEDfactory set out to show that low-carbon, low-impact buildings can be a better way to live, accessible to all and more cost-effective. Not surprisingly, superinsulation and passive design were key principles followed by ZEDfactory.

Built from recycled, reclaimed, environmentally accredited, and local materials, the low-impact structures reduced the site's "embodied energy," the energy required to build it, by 20 to 30 percent. Efficiency came first: units are equipped with the latest energy-saving appliances, and have achieved water and energy savings of over 30 percent on water use from water-efficient appliances and fittings alone and approximately 90 percent on space heating. The structural steel is reclaimed from a building in Brighton. A combined heat and power plant is fueled by woodchips from waste timber that would otherwise be sent to a landfill. Photovoltaic panels meet the remaining energy demand at BedZED.

Bedzed was designed around a green transport plan, as the partners knew that sustainability couldn't be achieved by bricks and mortar alone and that greener lifestyle choices—lower-impact travel, food choices, and waste management—bring equally large dividends. BedZED is a socially inclusive community, with housing for tenants, key workers, and owner-occupiers. Residents feel a keen sense of community, holding regular farmers' markets, a music festival, and an organic Christmas dinner. The development offers car sharing, a sports facility, and an exhibition and visitor center. Its ninety-nine homes and one hundred workspaces are high-density, as dense as London's central-city neighborhood Soho, yet nearly everyone has a garden. It is a form of development suitable for inner-city areas, a model for minimizing urban sprawl, and a shining example of the future.[67]

ZEDfactory's target is "a zero carbon/zero waste society capable of running off the limited supplies of renewable energy available within our national boundaries." They've been rewarded with such prestigious awards as the 2003 EU Prize for Contemporary Architecture in 2003, the 2003 Stirling Prize Sustainability Award, and a President's Award from the Royal Institute of British Architects in 2008. ZEDfactory's recent project at the Nottingham University Ningbo Campus in China, which they named ZedSquared, seeks to create a replicable zero-carbon and zero-waste urban block in the country that perhaps currently leads in total carbon emissions.

ZEDfactory calls the project "the most important urban best practice demonstration in the world."[68] Indeed, China builds 7.5 billion square feet of commercial and residential space each year, more than the combined floor space of all the malls and strip malls in the United States.[69] Because little of this construction has thermal insulation, it requires

twice as much energy to heat and cool as do similar buildings in the
United States and Europe. The World Bank found that 95 percent of
new Chinese buildings do not meet the country's own codes for energy
efficiency.

Although green buildings are not new in Asia—Swire Properties and
Hongkong Land, one of Asia's leading property investment, management, and development groups, developed a local building certification
system in 1995—there are barriers. Fragmented ownership and incentives, short-term decision-making horizons, and isolated procurement
processes hinder change, even though many economically and technically feasible improvements are possible that confer enormous savings
in operating costs. But many builders in Asia do not know how to do
this. Worse, builders pay the up-front costs yet typically are not the ones
who ultimately benefit from putting in extra effort to make the building
perform more efficiently over its lifetime. To overcome this, Hong Kong
developers worked with the World Business Council for Sustainable
Development (WBCSD) regional partner, the Business Environment
Council, to develop BEAM, the Building Environmental Assessment
Method, a local version of LEED. In 2000, seeing the need for cross-
industry engagement, they established the BEAM Society.

BEAM benefits developers, landlords, and tenants by delivering cost
savings from more efficient use of energy and resources, in both construction and use of buildings. The scheme encourages innovative design and construction practices and has stimulated availability of local
supplies of environmentally friendly building materials previously unavailable in Hong Kong, including sustainable timber, low-toxicity paints,
and ozone-friendly insulation. It enables the creation of better buildings,
which provide healthy and productive accommodation, and cuts risk by
ensuring best-practice management. It facilitates more effective markets, as companies are able to give assurance of the green credentials of
their buildings, and tenants and buyers are able to communicate their
preferences.

BEAM recently released the fourth version of standards covering new
and existing buildings, offices, flats, and other developments. Almost
150 major developments in Hong Kong covering 6.8 million square

meters of space, including commercial and institutional buildings and some 36,000 residential units, are now certified to these green standards of building performance.

What was accomplished in Hong Kong promises to inform what will happen in mainland China. Kevin Edmunds, chief operating officer of the Business Environment Council, believes that public awareness and market demand for green buildings is growing. "BEAM is at a critical time and has the potential to scale up its impacts exponentially," he says. "We have been pushing and pushing and pushing. Now we are beginning to be pulled." Many council members have mainland interests, and the council has already established a subsidiary and projects across China. They intend to contribute BEAM's tools and experience to the development of greener buildings across the region. Its existence creates regulatory preparedness for both local and international standards. This is crucial, as buildings account for around 70 percent of total greenhouse gas emissions in Hong Kong, and more on the mainland. Two billion square meters of building space are added annually in China, the equivalent of nearly thirty new Hong Kongs going up every single year.[70]

Towns Going Green

Despite the savings to be gained from retrofitting existing structures, it is often easier to design to the highest standards when you're starting from scratch, particularly on the community level. When 95 percent of Greensburg, Kansas, was destroyed by a tornado in May 2007, the city council passed a resolution stating that all city buildings would be built to LEED Platinum standards, making Greensburg the first city in the United States to do this. The town turned to Greensburg GreenTown, a nonprofit organization created to help the residents learn about and implement the green building initiative. Daniel Wallach, a green-building pioneer, students and faculty from various business and design schools, and many others are helping to rebuild Greensburg as truly green.[71] The city's power will be supplied by ten 1.25 megawatt wind turbines; carbon offsets generated from the turbines are being managed by Native-

Energy, and have been purchased by charter supporters, including Ben
& Jerry's, Clif Bar, Green Mountain Coffee Roasters, and Stonyfield
Farm.[72]

Another green community is the Del Sur subdivision outside San
Diego; it is a LEED Platinum subdivision. The National Association of
Home Builders named this thousand-acre master-planned community
of three thousand eco-friendly homes the "greenest development." Fred
Maas, CEO of Black Mountain Ranch LLC, developers of Del Sur, observed, "We firmly believe that smart, sustainable design and construction represent the future of housing development in America."[73]

Older towns are going green, too. Eight miles east of Pittsburgh is
the Rust Belt city of Braddock. Home to the first Carnegie steel mill and
the first Carnegie library, Braddock was at its height in the 1950s and
'60s when it was a town bustling with businesses and more than twenty
thousand inhabitants. In the brutal postindustrial decline of the 1980s,
Braddock lost 90 percent of everything—its buildings, its businesses, its
people—winding up a city of vacant lots and boarded-up shops with a
population of two thousand that included teen gangs.

In 2001, John Fetterman moved to Braddock to work for Ameri-
Corps, fell in love with the town, became its mayor, and set about revitalizing the city—by going green. Braddock is converting a 130-acre
brownfield (former industrial site) into a site for eco-friendly businesses
involved with biodiesel, wind energy, collecting rainwater, and creating
an urban farm to export organic vegetables to the high-end restaurants
in Pittsburgh. In 2007 the recycling company Fossil Free Fuel arrived
to retrofit diesel cars and trucks to run on a mix of diesel and carbon-
neutral vegetable oil that would otherwise be dumped. Fossil Free Fuel
collects used oil and sells its products for $1 less than you pay at the
pump.[74] Fossil Free Fuel's nine-thousand-square-foot facility, more like
a retail store than a garage, offers a relaxed customer area, earth-plastered
walls, and free-trade organic coffee for waiting customers. Plans are under way to partner with a local university to undertake biofuel research
and build an on-site lab.[75] Watch for profiles of Braddock in Levi's ads.

Cities Going Green

In her landmark book *Cities and the Wealth of Nations*, Jane Jacobs showed that cities, not nations, are the main drivers of economic wealth and innovation. She also believed that cities foster the intelligence, innovation, ingenuity, and even improvisation that enable human society to deal with economic problems. The challenge of climate change may prove her right. In 2007, the United Nations reported that for the first time in history more people live in cities than in rural areas. The number is predicted to reach 70 percent by 2050.[76] Commenting on this transition, Thoraya Ahmed Obaid, executive director of the UN Population Fund, noted: "This wave of urbanization is without precedent. The changes are too large and too fast to allow planners and policymakers simply to react: in Africa and Asia, the number of people living in cities increases by approximately 1 million, on average, each week. Leaders need to be proactive and take far-sighted action to fully exploit the opportunities that urbanization offers."[77] Cities consume two thirds of total primary energy and produce over 70 percent of global energy-related CO_2 emissions.[78] And cities are home to the overwhelming majority of energy-consuming and carbon-emitting buildings in the world.

Architecture 2030, a nonprofit initiative supported by the American Institute of Architects and other nonprofit organizations, is promoting such aggressive energy and carbon reductions in the building sector to cities nationally and globally. Cities that take up the challenge commit to new construction and major renovations that will reduce carbon emissions and fossil fuel energy consumption by 50 percent and, by 2030, attain carbon neutrality in their entire building portfolio. Seattle, Portland, Dallas, Albuquerque, Boulder, and Vancouver, Canada, have joined the challenge.

Why? Perhaps their mayors read Architecture 2030's "Nation Under Siege, Sea Level Rise at Our Doorstep," which takes a sober look at the impact of sea level rise on the United States and then provides a two-pronged solution that, if begun immediately, would avert dangerous climate change that would otherwise displace millions of people. Using map overlays of current coastal cities, they show the calamitous impact of expected sea level rise on thirty-one urban areas and millions of people. The study calls for a moratorium on building coal plants, pointing out: "With 76 percent of all the electricity produced at power plants going to operate buildings, reducing the operating energy demand of the Building Sector is essential." Architecture 2030 calls for an immediate 50 percent cut in fossil fuel energy consumption for all new and renovated buildings and for incrementally increasing the percentage reduction allowed for new buildings to carbon-neutral by 2030.[79]

Sixty percent of all of New York City's carbon emissions come from its buildings.[80] Michael Northrop, director of the Sustainable Development Program of the Rockefeller Brothers Fund, has written:

> Take New York City, for example, where we have almost one million buildings. If we decided to reduce carbon emissions 30 percent in those buildings and systematically pursued that goal for 20 years, we would save tens of billions of dollars a year and create tens of thousands of jobs. It would be a whole new economy for New York to build on as it reels from the losses on Wall Street. Mayor Mike Bloomberg is going to need a strategy like this to rescue New York. Every city in America could do the same thing. Enormous savings and a massive economic engine would result. Wholesale, retail, shipping, manufacturing and retrofitting businesses would all grow steadily to meet the need. Sales of insulation, caulking, windows, doors, furnaces, boilers, air conditioners and dozens of other products would skyrocket. And we'd need tens of thousands of plumbers, electricians, carpenters, and contractors to make it happen.[81]

The U.S. Congress allocated almost $10 billion in stimulus money in 2009 to help accelerate the growth of businesses providing products and services for building retrofits. A 2009 study by Pike Research projected that, boosted by the stimulus money, the total market potential for building retrofits was as much as $400 billion in the United States alone.[82] A year and a half later, however, very little of the money has been spent. Of the $3.2 billion targeted for block grants to states and cities to provide jobs and improve energy efficiency, only about 8.4 percent of the funds had been spent by August 2010.[83] An even bigger program to weatherize the homes of low-income people around the country was also initiated in 2009. A federal audit in the late summer of 2010 found that only $368.2 million of that $4.73 billion had been spent; New York City, which got the biggest award, $80.8 million, had spent only $1.5 million, or less than 2 percent. Chicago, with a $27.6 million allocation, had spent under $40,000, or 0.1 percent.[84] In October 2010, the Colorado state government began issuing requests for proposals to groups to apply for grants under the program, more than a year after the money was allocated.[85]

Meanwhile climate capitalists have already been implementing the programs these plans were intended to encourage. Envirolution, an enterprising group of young New Yorkers, has been training young unemployed people to be building auditors and retrofitters. Energy audits are where the rubber hits the road in building efficiency. An auditor is a consultant hired to go through a facility and identify the most attractive energy efficiency and renewable energy upgrade opportunities to invest in there. The program is helping New York City's small-business community afford energy efficiency, while at the same time putting people to work as community energy consultants.[86]

Most commercial audits are conducted by highly skilled energy engineers and are thus expensive. KwhOURS, Inc., a commercial energy-auditing software company, has developed a mobile software program and hardware device to allow auditors to conduct better, faster, and cheaper audits. The software platform also serves as a training tool to bring less-skilled individuals into the industry by doing much of the work that previously required a lot of training, thus driving down the cost of identifying opportunities. Although its initial market is commercial energy auditors, KwhOURS is helping trainees from stimulus-funded home weatherization programs to enter the field. KwhOURS' software bridge allows these individuals to work in more complex commercial facilities, increasing the percentage of buildings that are audited while simultaneously creating green jobs.

The company is solving another problem as well. At present, only 15 percent of energy audits result in implemented cost- and energy-saving retrofits. KwhOURS helps facility owners who have had an audit performed but are unsure of how to follow through on these recommendations find the appropriate products, services, and financing options, thus speeding the adoption of energy-efficient technologies and driving billions of dollars of green commerce.[87]

In Boulder, Colorado, a city program called Two Techs and a Truck has equipped auditors to go door-to-door performing energy audits and at the same time implementing the straightforward retrofits, saving the homeowner money immediately and demonstrating the advantages of energy efficiency while helping the city meet its carbon-reduction goals.[88]

Rapidly developing countries like China are planning to build whole new cities that are not yet on our maps. China's Urban China 2020 program proposes to create four hundred new cities throughout the country to accommodate 600 million new city dwellers expected to move away from rural China by 2050.[89] China intends to do so while meeting the challenges and opportunities of a carbon- and energy-constrained future. Dongtan, on Chongming Island, near Shanghai, is the most widely publicized effort to create the world's first eco-city from scratch. In partnership with Arup, a global engineering cooperative, the island city was to be built before 2020, eventually becoming home to five hundred thousand residents.[90] The project has been fraught with delays and subject to criticisms that the Chinese authorities never intend to build green, but are just floating the Dongtan idea to cover the very ungreen building mania in which they are caught up.[91] Building an entire eco-city from scratch, however, is inherently bold, ambitious, and admirable. Arup's genius behind the concept, Peter Head, has noted, "It often takes decades to deliver new urban developments, in China and elsewhere in the world, and the development downturn in Shanghai affected the project." He does not believe that the project is dead, but notes that regardless, the very effort to develop Dongtan has yielded rewards and spurred others to think of similarly ambitious projects.[92]

In an even more unlikely place, oil-rich Abu Dhabi, it is claimed that Masdar City will be the world's first carbon-neutral, zero-waste city. Masdar City seeks to "become the Silicon Valley for clean, green and alternative energy, a global center where over fifteen hundred companies will converge to meet one of humanity's greatest challenges, climate change—a city where current and future technologies will be funded, researched, developed, tested, and implemented."[93] Masdar City, backed by Abu Dhabi's development entity, Mubadala, is already under construction. The 2.3-square-mile development is being designed with the goal of being the first zero-carbon, zero-waste, clean-technology cluster powered by renewable energy. Masdar plans to be a Mecca for the latest thinking in building design, renewable energy, and energy efficiency.

The Future of Green Building

The U.S. Green Building Council and its counterparts around the world are leading a revolution in the built environment. Buildings offer a lens through which to integrate all the aspects of Climate Capitalism: energy, transportation, water, food, communication, finance, and issues of health are all wrapped up with building systems.

That work is under way. In the case of a child challenging her parents, the Cascadia Green Building Council, a regional chapter of the USGBC based in Seattle, launched its own certification tool, the Living Building Challenge, in 2006; it goes far beyond even LEED Platinum by setting more stringent criteria for a "living building." Jason McLennan, the CEO of the Cascadia Green Building Council, says the Challenge is the most advanced green building standard in the world. "A living building must generate its own energy, use only water falling on site, be free of toxic materials, be on non-virgin land and maximize access to fresh air and daylight." The USGBC took the challenge in good heart, recognizing the Living Building Challenge and granting LEED Platinum status to any building achieving the Living Building status.[94]

Bob Berkebile, the founder of BNM Architects and the founding chair of the American Institute of Architects' Committee on the Environment, is a thirty-year veteran of sustainable design. At an event celebrating the U.S. Green Building Council's fifteenth anniversary, Berkebile stated,

I think it is safe to say that the U.S. Green Building Council has been the most transformative force in the design and construction industry by a factor of ten in my lifetime. However, given that, if you put this in terms of climbing a mountain we have done a good job of getting to the first base camp. That puts us in a position to do the real work. The fact is we have to move beyond thinking about doing less harm to doing something regenerative, restorative, and that is a leap we have to make. What is the real impact of our designs on the people we intend to serve? Are we improving their quality of life, their well-being, the vitality of their neighborhood, the city, the planet, or not?[95]

The green building pioneer David Johnston sees the built environment as a way to begin to knit these issues together. He views green building as a challenge to create ever-widening new systems, saying,

It is a hologram of how you define a whole system. We design houses as systems in the green building world. This offers the chance to begin relocalizing the economy, as we aggregate houses into neighborhoods as systems, into communities and into cities, all as systems. Each of those nested systems has to work in a harmonious network of flows, inputs, outputs, and thruputs to reach optimal efficiency of the larger world system. We have to start by getting it all right at the scale of the individual building to have any hope of getting the larger system right.[96]

5

Moving On

The twentieth century was three years old when Henry Ford founded Ford Motor Company and Orville Wright flew a plane for twelve seconds. By the end of the century mass production of cars was the norm and airplanes circled the globe. Advances in transportation now enable people to see the world, connect with friends and relatives, and expand their business activities globally. Nearly 30 million flights take off every day,[1] and only four nations emit more carbon than the United States' vehicle fleet. Give it another century and it will all change at least as much again.

In its white paper subtitled "Is Mobility as We Know It Sustainable?" the Global Insight Automotive Group warns that if present trends continue the number of cars and trucks on the road will nearly quadruple to 3 billion by 2035. This would require nearly four times the physical space, raw materials, and fuel consumed by the current in-use fleet and would generate up to four times more toxic and climate-changing emissions.[2] China, where only 6 percent of the population drives cars—the same as the United States in the 1920s—is predicted to have as many cars on the road by 2050 as there are total cars on the road today.[3] India's vehicle fleet is expected to increase fiftyfold.[4] This is not sustainable. And it won't happen using the cars of today.

The transportation sector is not the largest emitter of carbon dioxide. That, remember, is buildings. But vehicles are the fastest-growing emitters of greenhouse gases. In the United States, transportation is also the largest single source of air pollution. In 2006, it alone was responsible for over half of the country's carbon monoxide emissions, over a third of its nitrogen oxides, and almost a quarter of its hydrocarbons.[5] Already, 13 to 20 percent of global greenhouse gases come from various modes of transport: 2 percent from airlines, 3 percent from shipping, and most of the rest from cars and trucks.[6] That isn't the only high price we pay for our love affair with the car. In America car accidents claim more than three thousand lives a day.[7] The average cost of driving a car is 54 cents per mile, the cost of car ownership $8,000 a year; if you own an SUV, that's 68.4 cents per mile or $10,259 per year.[8] Owning and running an automobile soaks up 15 to 25 percent of an average American's disposable income, representing the second-largest household expenditure after the house itself (19 percent) and before food (13.7 percent).[9]

The litany of problems caused by automobiles doesn't stop there. The productivity costs of time spent commuting are substantial. In 1995, the most recent data available, the average American spent 443 hours annually behind the wheel of a car—that's fifty-five eight-hour workdays. In the Texas Transportation Institute 1999 study of sixty-eight cities, it was estimated that the total congestion "bill" for the country came to $78 billion, which was the value of 4.5 billion hours of delay and 6.8 billion gallons of excess fuel consumed.[10]

The United States uses 25 percent of the world's oil, but represents only 5 percent of the global population. Quite apart from the unfairness of this situation, how do Americans pay for it? They don't. In 2008, Charles McMillion, president and chief economist of MBG Information Services in Washington, stated, "It is remarkable that the United States still cannot competitively produce and sell enough to pay for imports and must continue borrowing almost $2 billion per day in today's global financial markets."[11] The money is borrowed from China and the sover-

eign wealth funds of the Middle East to buy imported oil, in competition with the Chinese, from the sovereign wealth funds of the Middle
East.

The companies that produce the carbon-rich petroleum that fuels
American cars are also heavily subsidized. The most recent estimates of
federal subsidies to the oil industry top a total of $60 billion for the
years 2002 to 2008.[12] An additional $16.8 billion went to produce corn-
based ethanol for cars. If that money had been spent on improving and
creating public transit infrastructure, more than twice as many jobs
would have been created than by putting the money into more fuel for
cars.[13] This is not Climate Capitalism, it is socialism for drivers, oil
companies, and fossil shareholders.

But travel by car or plane is an amenity most people do not wish to
lose. Mobility is precious to us all, but at what cost? Seventy-five percent
of Americans surveyed in 2007 by the National Association of Realtors
felt that being smarter about development and improving public transportation are better long-term solutions for reducing traffic congestion
than building new roads.[14] What we want are technological advances,
policy innovations, and entrepreneurial solutions that can deliver the
mobility we wish *and* a higher quality of life, which includes benefits to
communities and climate.

This chapter assesses the challenges the transportation sector faces,
explores new modes of moving people and stuff, and describes new ways
to profit from providing this different future. Focusing on desired outcomes rather than safeguarding the previous century's technologies offers opportunities for innovation that can simultaneously reduce our
dependence on fossil fuels and enhance global prosperity.

Cooler Wheels

The future of mobility could go in one of several widely divergent directions. Let's assume for now that the way we move people and things will
remain largely the same (it won't, and we'll get to that in the next chapter): people will continue to mostly commute alone—more than a quar-

ter of all driving now is to and from work and 75 percent of that is in a single-occupancy vehicle—and we'll still be driving cars that today's drivers would recognize. Even in such a future there remains a lot we can do to cut emissions profitably.[15]

If ever there was a time to reinvent the automobile industry, it is now. The weak economy, changes in taxes, and the existence of federal incentives for fuel-efficient vehicles are all driving demand for less carbon-intensive cars. And the auto industry is in turmoil. In 2009, General Motors, an iconic American business, entered bankruptcy and had to be bailed out by the American taxpayer. Unlike European and Asian carmakers, who correctly identified small fuel-efficient cars as the coming market, nearly every American automaker went down with their production lines still churning out trucks and SUVs.[16] This shift to smaller, more fuel-efficient vehicles was not sudden; the trends had been in the works for a while. Even China set higher fuel efficiency standards than the United States—which is why no car made in the United States can legally be sold in China.[17] Toyota swept to number one having set the aspirational goal of building an American car that could go coast to coast on one tank of gas. In 2006, Toyota's profits were almost precisely Ford's losses. In 2007 Toyota became the world's largest automobile manufacturer.

It is ironic that just as it was achieving world domination Toyota faltered and its shares slid to the lowest point since the depth of the recession. Its philosophy of innovation and quality fell victim to its relentless pursuit of growth. To beat Detroit, Toyota focused on building the big pickup trucks that conventional wisdom, and the ad agencies, said Americans wanted. Sacrificing quality in its flagship Prius hybrid and the smaller models that had built the brand, the company was then forced to recall millions of vehicles to correct safety defects. "Quite frankly," Toyota president Akio Toyoda acknowledged, "I fear the pace at which we have grown may have been too quick. We pursued growth over the speed at which we were able to develop our people and our organization, and we should sincerely be mindful of that. I regret that this has resulted in the safety issues described in the recalls we face today."[18]

If you are seeking examples of automakers taking advantage of the new and emerging markets for fuel-efficient cars, you pretty much need to look to imports. Ford is the only American carmaker on the list of the makers of the top twenty-one most fuel-efficient cars. The rest are Asian or European.[19] As a result, U.S. car buyers are limited in their choice of efficient cars. Of cars that a normal person can afford, only the Honda Civic hybrid and the Toyota Prius hybrid deliver fuel mileage of more than 40 miles per gallon. In contrast, Europeans can choose from more than 113 vehicle models getting at least 40 miles per gallon.[20] Ironically, two thirds of these more efficient vehicles are made by American car-makers or companies like Toyota and Volkswagen that have strong ties to American car companies—in fact, U.S. car companies make dozens of such fuel-efficient vehicles, but not in the United States.

Honda now has the most fuel-efficient fleet of vehicles in the United States. Has its drive toward more fuel-efficient, lower carbon-emitting vehicles reduced the company's competitiveness? Not hardly. Honda's shares have jumped and analysts believe that Honda, with its fuel- and carbon-efficient fleet, is poised to gain more market share.[21]

The same is true of three other foreign carmakers focusing on small, fuel-efficient cars. As the Chrysler brand lost 47 percent of sales in 2009, and GM's sales dropped 30 percent (the U.S. market as a whole slid 21 percent from the prior year), in 2009 Hyundai and Kia posted sales increases of 8 percent and 9 percent, respectively, over 2008; Subaru, although it sells only half the volume of cars as Hyundai, increased total sales 13 percent over 2008. One analyst, looking at the shift in car buying, observed, "Kia, as well as Hyundai, can attribute their growth to smart efforts to improve their product—across the board—plus [to] better marketing . . . [whereas] GM, Chrysler and Ford have, realistically, been dumping small cars into the market for years to offset EPA fuel-mileage penalties for their truck lineups. When market forces unearthed the weaknesses in this strategy, all three domestic makers got smacked in the face. We all know what has happened since."[22] Interestingly, GM's exit from bankruptcy in November 2010 was accompanied by the success of its hybrid pickup truck and the announcement of the Volt, a hybrid challenger to the Nissan Leaf.[23]

The title of world's most efficient car belongs to Volkswagen, and its entry isn't a hybrid. At 285 miles per gallon the 1L (for "one liter per 100 kilometers," which translates to 285 miles per gallon) is an ultra-lightweight, ultra-aerodynamic concept vehicle. The bullet-shaped carbon-fiber car has proved that the fuss about whether carmakers can possibly meet the slightly increased fuel efficiency standards in the United States is little more than whining.[24] In 2009, Volkswagen announced that by 2013 it will release a 170-miles-per-gallon diesel-hybrid version of the 1L.

Volkswagen is committed to engine efficiency. It partnered with John Deere, the U.S. Army, and Colorado State University's Engines and Energy Conversion Laboratory to commercialize a technology developed by the inventor Ed Van Dyne. While working at the Woodward Governor Company as its director of research, Van Dyne developed a device that combines the low-speed performance of a supercharger with waste heat recovery achieved by adding a transmission to a turbocharger—which increased vehicle efficiency by 36 percent over existing gasoline engines. In 2009, Woodward spun off Van Dyne's company, now named VanDyne SuperTurbo, Inc., to build products for the automobile industry. Volkswagen partnered with it and Colorado State to create transmissions and various other devices to dramatically increase vehicle efficiency.[25]

Transforming an Industry

Perhaps the biggest challenge that the auto industry must overcome is its dynamic conservatism: like the building trades, the car industry works very hard to resist change. The industry that fought basic safety standards and fuel efficiency standards now faces limits on carbon emissions; it must decide whether to respond by digging in and becoming even more uncompetitive or to use this development as a springboard for innovation.

The direction the tide is flowing is clear. On January 12, 2010, California's Air Resources Board approved legislation setting carbon limits on the auto industry. California's Low Carbon Fuel Standard requires that transportation fuel producers and importers in California reduce the average carbon intensity of their fuels incrementally every year from 2010 until 2020, at which point the fuels must reflect 10 percent less carbon intensity than the 2010 baseline. This will have the net effect of cutting 16 million tons of greenhouse gas emissions in the state.[26] Seeking to force the industry's hand, fourteen states have instituted California's policy.

In March 2010 the EPA announced the first national standards to address climate change. Starting with the 2012 model year vehicles, the rules require automakers to improve fleetwide fuel economy and reduce fleetwide greenhouse gas emissions by approximately 5 percent every year. The standards require that cars reach an estimated output of 34.1 miles per gallon for the combined industrywide fleet by model year 2016. The measures will reduce carbon dioxide emissions by about 960 million metric tons over the lifetime of the vehicles regulated, equivalent to taking 50 million cars and light trucks off the road in 2030. The enhanced fuel efficiency is predicted to save drivers $3,000 over the life of a new vehicle.[27]

The car industry's legal teams and public relations firms are very powerful, however, have shown a propensity for lawsuits, and have won their fair share while opposing any regulation of their industry. In February 2008, the Association of International Automobile Manufacturers sued to prevent California from setting stricter standards than the EPA's.[28] The Renewable Fuels Association sued California on behalf of the ethanol industry to block the state from setting low carbon fuel standards.[29] In December 2009 the National Petrochemical and Refiners Association followed suit. On February 2, 2010, the American Trucking Association fell into line, claiming, "The fuel prohibited from use in California will simply be used elsewhere, which will result in increasing overall GHG emissions as a result of less-stringent environmental standards in places where those fuels would ultimately be consumed."[30] The March 2010 EPA ruling will likely make this suit moot; but the opposition gives a sense of the lengths that the industry will go to prevent change.

However, as figures cited earlier show, the car industry will lose if it thinks it can avoid change. It will lose in the court of public opinion and, more important, in the companies' bottom lines. The time has come for U.S carmakers to spend more money on innovation and less on litigation. As consumers demand cleaner, more efficient vehicles, and governments, including the U.S., join Europe and others in setting a price on carbon, the U.S. auto industry has the choice of driving innovation or relegating itself to the off-ramp as low-emission, hybrid, electric, and highly efficient internal-combustion vehicles pass them by.

The remarkable success of Toyota's Prius suggests a pattern: the first out of the gate in the race to innovate to meet the sustainability imperative gets the spoils. The germ of the Prius idea dates from 1993, when Eiji Toyoda, Toyota's chairman, looked into the future of his industry and grew concerned. Higher gas prices and a swelling global middle class meant a changing demand. Shortly thereafter, Yoshiro Kimbara, then executive vice president in charge of R & D, set about developing a new car targeting 47.5 miles per gallon, a 50 percent improvement over Toyota's popular small car, the Corolla. The first Prius was unveiled in 1997; the estimated cost of development: $1 billion. A few hiccups and innovative responses later, by 2004, Jim Press, president of Toyota Motor Sales, the company's U.S. division, declared the Prius "the hottest car we've ever had."[31]

Happily, U.S. automakers appear to be realizing that the rest of the world is moving toward carbon regulation. After years of resisting fuel efficiency, U.S. carmakers are focusing on low-carbon and more fuel-efficient cars. The opening ceremony of the 2009 Frankfurt Auto Show featured slides on climate change and sustainability. The electric Porsche, the Tesla, and Mercedes' electric Smart car vied with biofueled cars from all the major automakers. The 2010 North American International Auto Show in Detroit similarly featured electric, hybrid, and fuel-efficient models.[32]

The recent history of the Ford Motor Company shows what U.S. companies can achieve. Ford had been the U.S. leader in green practices, with Bill Ford seeking to reposition the company before it was too late. Despite enormous criticism, his efforts paid off. An early entrant to the U.S. market with a hybrid, Ford was able to stave off bankruptcy.

Since 2007 Ford had cut labor costs by almost 22 percent. When it needed money, it borrowed it the old-fashioned way—from a bank, getting $23.5 billion in loans without government help. In early 2010, Ford Motor Company, the world's number two automaker, gained 25 percent in sales. As a result of its foresight, Ford made a $2.7 billion profit in 2009, and drove its stock price 700 percent over its fifty-two-week low. Ford succeeded because it recast itself as a leading player in the green car market.[33]

Business as Usual Gets a Little Less: Enter Electricity

The year 2011 will see the widespread entry into the vehicle market of electric cars, as well as robust sales of hybrids (cars that combine an internal combustion motor and an electric engine). Proponents of these new vehicles predict that 20 percent of all cars sold could be electric in five years or less. Power for these car owners will cost less than one dollar a gallon equivalent at average U.S. electricity prices, or free if you can power your car's battery from solar panels. To the extent that the power to charge the vehicle does not come from a fossil fuel–burning plant, the car is carbon-neutral. But even if fueled from coal-generated electricity in the United States, an electric car is cleaner than a gasoline-fired vehicle.[34]

Many people are already familiar with an electric vehicle (EV), but cars are far more than golf carts and are very impressive. Costs are starting to come down, too. Porsche will sell you a very sweet electric 918 Spyder or Boxter for $200,000, but fortunately the market is providing options at normal car costs as well. Nissan's battery powered Leaf, at $32,750 (or $25,280 with the tax rebate), has a hundred-mile range, enabling you to drive that far before recharging the battery. Mitsubishi i-MiEV plug-ins, with an anticipated range of forty-five to seventy-five miles, are expected to be on the market by the fall of 2011 at a cost below $30,000. Due in 2012 are Mercedes Benz's exceedingly cute Smart Electric and Chrysler Fiat's 500 Electric, both projected to have a hundred-mile range.[35] One of the most attractive electrics is the Citroën

Ev'ie. A four-seater, which like all the electric models has all of the conventional safety and comfort features of a "normal" car, the Ev'ie has some advantages over the car you now drive. Like most modern electrics this car features acceleration and handling any driver would envy. Like many hybrids it has "regenerative" braking, meaning that energy used to slow down the car—wasted in normal cars—is reclaimed by the battery for use by the motor. In London, which has climate protection policies in place to disincentivize automobile use, the Ev'ie is able to charge for free at "juice-up" spots, use high-occupancy vehicle lanes, and park for free—which makes the vehicle well worth owning, as those who drive in that city will instantly recognize.[36]

The Americans are determined to remain in this competitive set and deliver affordable contenders to wean drivers from petroleum. As mentioned above, the Chevy Volt, a hybrid with a flex-fuel engine, headlined GM's emergence from bankruptcy.

Ford is driving to retain its green leadership. The 2011 Ford Focus will offer a hundred-mile target range. Electrics are clearly part of its strategy to succeed. In 2010 Ford introduced an electric version of its small-business-friendly Transit Connect Delivery Van. Its 60- to 100-mile range options suit fleet sales, and its size makes it city-friendly. AT & T bought a fleet of these vans in the fourth quarter of 2010. Ford will release production runs of an electric car in 2011, its next-generation hybrid in 2012, and a plug-in hybrid in 2012.[37] Hybrids like the Prius use gasoline to drive electric motors that save fuel over conventional gasoline engines. A plug-in hybrid allows the user to charge bigger batteries from home, so that for most trips the car acts like a pure electric, but for longer distances the gasoline engine can extend the range. Ford's flex-fuel electric hybrid is capable of running off 85 percent ethanol fuel, called E-85, making the car even less dependent on imported, carbon-intensive petroleum. In 2014 Ford plans to bring out a hybrid averaging eighty highway miles per gallon. It will emit 60 percent less carbon dioxide than a conventional gasoline-powered vehicle, with carbon dioxide reduction as high as 90 percent if E-85 is used.[38] Ford has also partnered with Microsoft, whose Hohm smart-home software allows users to charge their cars when electricity prices are lowest.[39]

Start Your, er . . . Motors . . .

Opportunity breeds innovation and competition. Times are clearly tur-
bulent for the auto industry when start-up car companies are prospering
despite enormous barriers to entry, billion-dollar capital requirements,
massive supply chains, and the need for global distribution channels.
Historically, such ventures have been laughable. However, as the majors
pressed the snooze button a few too many times, entrepreneurs evolved
new efficient and alternative technologies to step into the breach.

Aptera Motors is currently taking orders for its futuristic-looking
electric hybrid vehicle, which goes 120 miles on a single charge and
achieves three hundred miles per gallon. The three-wheeled Aptera, legally a motorcycle, looks like a wingless Cessna plane, but it is not a toy,
cruising at eighty-five miles an hour. The fully enclosed two-seater is
eligible to use high-occupancy lanes. The company's cofounders, Steve
Fambro and Chris Anthony, an entrepreneur and boat builder, con-
ceived the idea for a glorified hybrid motorcycle and with the help of
the Pasadena, California, business incubator IdeaLab, brought the company to reality, selling early versions for $26,000 each.

The most hyped entrant in the electric vehicle market is California-
based Tesla (named for Nikola Tesla, a Serb inventor whose discoveries
formed the basis of modern alternating, or AC, current). Founded by
Martin Eberhard and Marc Tarpennin in 2003, the company is producing fifteen cars a week under its current CEO, Elon Musk, the founder
of PayPal. Tesla has also received significant funding from the Google
founders and Silicon Valley venture capital firms such as Draper Fisher
Jurvetson. Tesla officially launched its first product, the crazy-fast, all-
electric Tesla Roadster, as a prototype in 2006 (the first production model
was delivered to Elon Musk in February 2008). Proving that electric
vehicles can feature impressive torque, the Roadster accelerates from zero
to sixty miles per hour in 3.9 seconds. Even though Tesla is unlikely to
sell as many units as the Toyota Prius, by launching a lightning-fast, utterly quiet electric sports car, Tesla crushed the image of EVs as slow,
range-limited golf carts. Even with its amazing acceleration, the Tesla

goes 240 miles without a recharge. Recognizing, however, that its initial $100,000+ price point presents a barrier for both customers and the company's aspiration to compete with the big boys, Tesla is scheduled to introduce a slightly more affordable sports sedan, the Model S, in 2012.

Bankrolled for $60 million by the government of Qatar, Fisker Automotive took a different route, delivering a plug-in hybrid, the Fisker Karma, with a photovoltaic roof. Capable of going fifty miles on a charged battery, the Karma achieves one hundred miles per gallon using the motor. For sale now at $80,000, a $40,000 model should hit the market in 2011. The Fisker Karma should reach dealerships before Chevrolet's Volt.[40]

Mission Motors is bringing electric drive to another mode of transport, introducing race-winning electric motorcycles. Inducing sticker shock at $67,000, the bike won't be sweeping the neighborhood soon, but the company is showing off the battery pack, motor, controller, and the technology to link them, all of which can easily be transferred to any electric vehicle. "It's always much easier to take a technology down and make it cheaper," says CEO Jit Bhattacharya. "Our strategy from the start was to push the limits of what was possible and then to find the right partners for that technology."[41]

The challenge of charging electric vehicles will plague early adopters of plug-ins, but help is on the way. In California, a network of charging stations along Highway 101 opened in the fall of 2009. The corridor, a project of SolarCity, Tesla Motors, and the U.S. branch of Rabobank America, offers four solar-powered Clipper Creek 240-volt EV charger stations at Rabobank branches in Salinas, Atascadero, Santa Maria, and Goleta, and a fifth station at a public parking garage in San Luis Obispo. Spaced seventy to one hundred miles apart along Highway 101, the stations enable a Tesla Roadster to make the drive between San Francisco and Los Angeles with just one stop. Electric vehicle owners can recharge for free.[42] Free charging is also available at the solar array on the parking lots at Google's headquarters in Mountain View, California, and at the local general store in Hygiene, Colorado.

Such stations have been used mostly by owners of one of the oldest electric vehicles on the road. Chrysler was actually one of the early entrants into the EV market, selling Global Electric Motorcars (Gems) electric town cars for over twelve years. Essentially enclosed golf carts, the Gems make great sense for neighborhood driving. Like golf carts, they run on batteries that can be charged up at home. In 1998 the National Highway Traffic Safety Administration designated low-speed vehicles as a new class of motor vehicle: the Neighborhood Electric Vehicle (NEV). The low-speed vehicle classification allowed Gem cars to be driven on public roads if they met certain safety criteria, such as having safety belts, headlamps, windshield wipers, and safety glass. A two-seater starts at a bit over $7,000, and a four-seater goes for a bit over $10,000.

Fleets of the Things

Selling more fuel-efficient cars to individuals is only one of the emerging opportunities for climate capitalists. How about selling lots of them? Both United Parcel Service (UPS) and FedEx are investing in programs to cut their use of fossil fuels and increase the efficiency in how they move stuff. UPS's green fleet of propane, electric, electric hybrid, CNG, liquefied natural gas, hydraulic hybrid, and zero-emissions vehicles has logged more than 165 million miles since 2000.[43] In 2001, UPS began running hybrid trucks on a route in Huntsville, Alabama. In 2008, UPS placed new orders for two hundred hybrid electric vehicles and three hundred vans that run on liquefied natural gas. The purchase expanded the company's green fleet by 30 percent to a total of more than 2,200 low-carbon vehicles.[44] A Department of Energy study of UPS's hybrid fleet found them to be almost a third more fuel-efficient than UPS's conventional delivery fleet. The hybrid vans increase fuel efficiency by 60 to 70 percent in urban use and lower greenhouse gas emissions by 40 percent as compared to UPS's conventional diesel delivery trucks. What's more, the hybrids hold up under use.

Not to be outdone, FedEx is committed to improving its overall vehicle fuel efficiency by 20 percent by 2020.[45] In 2003 FedEx announced that they were testing hybrid vans and might convert their entire fleet to hybrids.[46] By 2008 they had 172 hybrids in operation, saving the company 83,000 gallons of fuel and cutting 950 tons of greenhouse gas emissions annually. The company announced that it was adding seventy-five more hybrids and testing the hydraulic hybrids, which, instead of using heavy, potentially polluting batteries, use lightweight components and clean fluid to power the vehicle while it's at slow speeds.[47] In 2010, FedEx rolled out four new all-electric vans to join its fleet of 1,800 hybrid and biodiesel vehicles. Based on electric trucks already on the road in Europe, including five in Paris, FedEx's vans are designed to give drivers a full eight hours' service before recharging. This made the FedEx fleet the largest hybrid fleet in the transportation industry and one of the largest alternative-energy vehicle fleets, period.

In Canada, Novex Couriers became the first courier company to grapple with the problem of the emissions from its hundred-plus fleet of cars, vans, and trucks. In 2003, Novex began gradually replacing its fleet with hybrid cars and biodiesel trucks. They also reduced emissions throughout their operations, cutting office energy use, paper use, and waste. Setting themselves the goal of a 100 percent clean fleet, Novex is unique in using a tool to track and monitor the company's performance in a transparent way. Want to see how they're doing? Go to www.novex.ca. Other courier companies have already achieved carbon neutrality, first by reducing emissions from their fleets and operations and then by supporting carbon offset projects to balance out the remainder of their emissions. That is how Elite Worldwide became the first carbon-neutral courier company in the UK, as did Urgent Couriers, in New Zealand.

Long-haul trucks, too, are becoming more efficient. In 2007, Walmart announced that it had increased the fuel efficiency of its fleet 15 percent by using a fuel additive mix, more fuel-efficient tires, and Auxiliary Power Units (devices on a vehicle that provide energy for functions other than propulsion) to power the various interior systems in a truck. The biggest piece of Walmart's solution will come from future hybrid diesel-electric engines, though. At a company quarterly meeting, Walmart, which operates America's second-largest private trucking fleet, announced that it was teaming with GM, Cummins Diesel, Peterbilt, and others to design hybrid long-haul trucks.[48] At an average price of $2.50 per gallon of diesel fuel, those measures would save $9,000 to $10,000 a truck per year.[49]

Combined with other measures Walmart was taking, this saved 28 or 30 percent from the 2005 baseline by the time the entire fleet was updated in 2010. In 2009 Walmart announced that it had already surpassed efficiency goals in its private fleet, achieving a 25 percent drop in fuel use from 2005 to 2008. The company set a new goal to double fleet fuel efficiency by 2015, and announced the testing of four new kinds of fuel-efficient commercial trucks. These include fifteen trucks to operate in Buckeye, Arizona, that will run on reclaimed cooking grease from Walmart stores; five Peterbilt Model 386 heavy-duty hybrids operating in Dallas, Houston, Atlanta, Washington, Baltimore, and Apple Valley, California; four Peterbilt Model 386 trucks that run on liquefied natural gas; and one full-propulsion (hybrid) Arivin Meritor electric-diesel hybrid operating in Detroit.[50] Full propulsion dual mode hybrid drivetrains give vehicles extended operation in battery-only zero-emission mode, and eliminate idling. They supply the "hotel load" that keeps the driver comfortable at rest stops, and enable the vehicle to run on electric power at speeds below 48 miles per hour, transitioning to diesel power only at highway speeds.

Each of the nine 386s will reduce carbon dioxide emissions by almost forty-five tons per year, compared to a diesel equivalent. The system cuts fuel use and lowers emissions by powering the heating, air-conditioning, and vehicle electrical systems with an auxiliary power unit while the engine is off.[51]

Existing fleets can be also made more efficient. ATDynamics (Advanced Transit Dynamics) designs and delivers the best-in-class fuel-efficiency technology for the freight transportation industry. Working with trucking fleets throughout North America, ATDynamics helps truckers save fuel and reduce vehicle emissions by installing drag-reduction technologies to improve the aerodynamics of tractor-trailers. The company's patented TrailerTail is the first and still the only rear fairing to be certified for fuel efficiency.[52] The company also installs trailer skirts to reduce side drag. In 2010 ATDynamics partnered with Navistar to develop next-generation trailer aerodynamics as part of the

U.S. Department of Energy–funded SuperTruck project, a five-year program aimed at improving the efficiency of the big rigs.

Andrew Smith, the entrepreneurial founder and CEO of ATDynamics, took the company from a winning business school competition idea to reality. "The trucking industry has the potential to realize $3 billion in annual fuel savings with existing aerodynamic options," says Smith. "While the add-on devices we provide today deliver up to 12 percent fuel savings at highway speeds, the SuperTruck project will allow us to exceed those aerodynamic efficiency gains by contributing to a ground-up redesign of truck-trailer combinations." Smith grinned. "This is the proverbial tip of the iceberg."[53]

Long-haul trucks can be made more efficient even when standing still. When drivers take their mandatory rest periods, they leave the diesel engine running, often for their entire ten-hour rest period to power the truck's "hotel load": the heating, air conditioning, sound system, television or whatever appliances the trucker has in the rig. Half a million long-haul trucks typically ply American roads, each one idling as much as 500 to 3,500 hours a year. Trucks going nowhere consume up to a billion gallons of diesel fuel a year, annually emitting 11 million tons of carbon dioxide, 200,000 tons of oxides of nitrogen, and 5,000 tons of particulate matter into the air.[54] When fuel was cheap, trucking companies looked the other way. Now, Walmart and other companies are installing idle-reduction Auxiliary Power Units in their trucks, saving, in Walmart's case, $25 million a year in fuel costs and cutting their trucks' carbon output by 100,000 cubic feet per year.[55] As of 2007, sixty truck stops in eleven states (out of a total of five thousand truck stops) permitted trucks to plug into local power supplies to power APUs or provided air conditioning for truck cabs.[56]

One of the best systems for running a truck's amenities is called IdleAire, created by a Knoxville, Tennessee, start-up. IdleAire saved more than 3 million hours of idling time over the ten-year life of the company, conserved about three million gallons of fuel, and cut more than 32,000 metric tons of diesel emissions. IdleAire provided a system of control consoles attached to tubes suspended from an overhead rack. Drivers would pull into a truck stop and attach one of the facility's

IdleAire units to a ten-dollar adapter that fit in their passenger window. They would open a control console, whereupon climate-controlled air, electricity, broadband Internet access, satellite TV, and long-distance phone service would become available. It was an expensive business, though, requiring a full-time IdleAire staff of about twelve to oversee an average of fifty parking spaces at each location. One parking spot cost $15,000 to build and had to be backed up by a customer-support team that was available 24/7 for technology-challenged truckers. "Building the technology from scratch, rolling it out, and supporting it isn't cheap," admitted Tom Badgett, one of IdleAire's founders.[57]

Unable to maintain financing, IdleAire filed for chapter 11 in 2008. It had operated in 131 locations in thirty-four states, serving 150,000 truckers and more than a thousand fleets.[58] As of March 4, 2010, however, IdleAire's website stated that a new group was working to restart IdleAire service. That would be good news for drivers who used to search for IdleAire facilities. "I go out of my way to find these IdleAire truck stops because they make for a better night's sleep and I know they're better for the environment," said one driver.[59]

Flying Fuelishly

Flying is a significant cause of the climate crisis, responsible for a growing percentage of human-caused climate change impact; it represents 12 percent of transport's share of carbon emissions.[60] Since 1990, CO_2 emissions from international aviation have increased 83 percent and are still rising. The Airports Council International estimates that the number of airline tickets sold per year will double to more than 9 billion by 2025. Much of the growth will come in rapidly developing Asia, where passenger numbers are increasing 10 to 15 percent annually.[61] Under current projections, emissions from flying are expected to triple by mid-century.[62]

Fortunately, innovation in transportation has not been limited to cars and trucks. Airplane engines are becoming dramatically more efficient, too. The Boeing 787 Dreamliner jet promises to be faster and 20 percent more fuel-efficient than current models, by making many of the plane's components out of composite materials and using better engines. General Electric was chosen by Boeing to develop the new jet engines in part because its Ecomagination unit had an established commitment to delivering much more efficient engines. Redesign of the plane to eliminate parts will also help to lighten the weight. The first prototype was airborne early in 2009, and Dreamliner deliveries are scheduled in 2011 for the fifty-six customers who preordered the new airplane.[63]

The airlines are desperate to increase efficiency, using ground holds in lieu of having planes circling in the air, investing in winglets to reduce drag, shutting engines down whenever possible when planes are on the ground, and optimizing flight planning for minimum-fuel-burn routes and altitude.[64] Airlines are also experimenting with eliminating paint on the planes, using lighter color schemes to reduce the need for air conditioning, even lighter-weight meals, and offering to ship luggage to your final destination. The Federal Aviation Administration believes that the greatest fuel efficiency gains will come from upgrading the air traffic control routes and technology, which are decades old, but boasts that aviation is already improving energy efficiency, moving 12 percent more people and 22 percent more freight than it did in 2000 while burning 4 percent less fuel and producing 8.4 million fewer tons of carbon dioxide. Nice, but much more is needed.[65]

Europeans are generally more energy-conscious than Americans, so it is not surprising that Europeans are leading in the airborne efficiency competition. In 2008 Lufthansa began informing passengers on its flights about all that it was doing to cut emissions. This is in part because in 2012 the European Union will begin regulating airline emissions. American airlines are still doggedly fighting the transition to a low-carbon world, resisting proposed charges by the EU on foreign airlines flying to major European cities, but they are losing. EU airlines say it is only fair that American airlines be required to meet the same standards, since they are operating in the same markets. If they are required to meet carbon emissions standards, it is projected that by 2020 they will be spending $50 billion annually to purchase offsets. The Europeans are right: American airlines should conform; more important, those airlines should want to do so. The UK-based Climate Trust has estimated that EU airlines that excel at fuel efficiency and carbon reduction will actually boost their profits by 20 to 40 percent over those that don't. Conversely, the laggards could see their profits decline by as much as 40 percent.[66]

Low-Carbon Transport Alternatives

If you are concerned with your personal carbon footprint, when you fly, you will want to do it on airlines that have made a commitment to cut their emissions. As with all such personal consumption choices, do business with the more responsible companies and buy offsets for travel you cannot avoid to eliminate your contribution to carbon emissions where you can.[67] That said, choosing not to fly and taking alternative modes of transport when you have that option may be one of the most important decisions you make personally to help the climate.

There are far more cost-effective ways to move people and goods than cars and trucks and planes.

Rail

Trains are not a new technology, but in response to emerging energy and climate constraints, new approaches to rail are sweeping the globe, especially high-speed rail. It requires fifteen lanes of highway to move as many people as one lane of track, a fact that has been noted and acted on in Europe and in Asia.[68]

Tokyo, Japan, has one of the most impressive rail infrastructures in the world, moving some 20 million people by rail per day, primarily on lines that are privately operated. At Shinjuku Station, a hub in Tokyo that connects rail and metro lines, more than 3 million passengers per day pass through the doors, making it the busiest station in the world.[69] Japan realized early the downsides of trying to move a lot of people by cars in a small, densely populated country. In 1964 Japan pioneered the bullet train, which travels at 131 miles (210 kilometers) per hour.[70] These trains now travel the world's biggest high-speed network, carrying 308 million passengers between March 2008 and March 2009.

Many Asian and European cities also excel in public transportation. The French have been running high-speed trains since 1989 and have hundreds that reach speeds of 186 miles (300 kilometers) per hour— meaning they cover a mile in 18 seconds. The Italians and Spaniards have likewise invested in high-speed-rail technology, and the Germans, British, and Russians soon will. North America, once again, lags behind. The first Japanese bullet train was faster than any train now operating in the United States. The only train that comes close, the U.S. National Railroad Passenger Corp's (Amtrak) Acela Express, carried 3.4 million passengers in 2008 at a top speed of 150 miles an hour between Washington and Boston.[71] Mostly, though, it goes considerably slower.

The dominant car culture and urban sprawl of the United States has fostered an acceptance of conventional wisdom that it is impractical to efficiently move large numbers of people by public transit, and so far general public indifference has undercut any incentive to contest this. A handful of cities, however—including New York, Boston, San Francisco, and Washington, D.C.—have invested in excellent and widely used public transportation systems. Portland, Oregon, may now be home to the greenest and most impressive public transit system. Combining bus, light rail, commuter rail, and a downtown streetcar line, Portland provides a wide variety of options for its five hundred thousand citizens. The city also invested in a cleaner transit system, virtually eliminating sulfur emissions and shifting to biodiesel for its buses. The city's Metropolitan Area Express train line uses regenerative braking, much like hybrid cars, to realize a 20 percent reduction in energy consumption. The streetcar, free within the downtown core, runs on electricity sourced from hydropower.[72]

The rest of America may finally be following in these cities' and the world's footsteps. The 2009 U.S. transportation initiative, called by Transportation Secretary Ray LaHood "an absolute game changer for American transportation," has allocated $8 billion for thirteen high-speed corridors across the United States. Train manufacturers from Japan, Germany, France, and Canada are eyeing the market, even as General Electric, maker of Ecomagination's more efficient locomotive engines, is determined to protect its home turf. GE has inked cooperation agreements with the Chinese and the State of California to help fund and build high-speed rail lines in California. But go figure, the first high-speed route is likely to connect Tampa and Orlando, Florida. Guess we're really in a hurry to get to Disney World faster. In the wake of the 2010 midterm elections, the fate of even that high-speed rail may be in question.

China is unquestionably the country most serious about fast trains, with 30,000 miles of route under construction and plans to provide high-speed links to all capital cities and cities with a population of over half a million.[73] The Chinese opened 1,200 miles of high-speed rail routes in 2010 alone. A route from Beijing to Shanghai—about the same distance as New York to Atlanta or Chicago—will open by the end of 2011 or early 2012, cutting that trip from ten hours to four. To cover the same-length route by train in the United States would take almost twenty hours, as Amtrak shares its tracks with freight and commuter trains.[74]

Plying the Waters

Perhaps the most promising contribution to low-carbon transport comes from the oceans. Shipping is one of the dirtier uses of fossil fuels, and a growing one. Shipping is expected to expand by at least 50 percent by 2050.[75] A ship's average annual fuel costs can be reduced by 10 to 35 percent by using skysails. This system uses a huge sail to let the wind pull cargo ships, superyachts, fishing boats, and other vessels through the water. The skysail, like a kite, is flown higher than a standard sail to take advantage of air currents high over the water's surface. Skysails can be used on boats with an effective load of 8 to 16 tons. Skysails with twice the capacity of those currently available will be offered in 2012, and a skysail capable of pulling 130-ton loads is planned. When the wind is right, fuel use can be cut by up to 50 percent. Any existing cargo vessel can be retro- or outfitted with a skysails system. Such ships can now receive a higher efficiency rating on the Carbon War Room's new ShippingEfficiency.org labeling system.

Two shipping companies are experimenting with another clever way to cut carbon emissions from heavy ships. Nippon Yusen Kaisha (the NYK Line) and Mitsubishi Heavy Industries, Ltd., are using an air-lubrication system to reduce CO_2 emissions at sea. Reducing frictional resistance between the hull of the boat and the seawater by bubbling air across the vessel's bottom, they can cut fuel use and thus CO_2 emissions by approximately 10 percent.[76]

Car Sharing

Let's be honest, cars are still the real transportation issue, and it's often handy to have a car. That doesn't mean you have to own one, though.

Enter car sharing. First offered by some European nonprofits, car sharing is an alternative to car ownership that has now spread to the United States. Car-share users pay a monthly fee to gain access as needed to a vehicle, typically located near them. The concept is similar to car rental, but allows members to use and pay for a car for an hour or two instead of in twenty-four-hour blocks, and at a much lower fee. In most of the six hundred car-share programs now operating around the world, a member books a car online, wields a smart card to open the car's doors, and enjoys the benefits of car ownership without having to pay the ongoing carrying costs.[77]

The largest car-share company in the world, Zipcar, was founded in 2000 in Cambridge, Massachusetts. It has grown rapidly, now counting more than six thousand vehicles in its fleet and nearly 300,000 drivers in North America and England. The poor economy since 2008 has helped Zipcar's growth, as it has other car-sharing programs. According to one report, "Since the recession started . . . Zipcar has had a 70 percent increase in membership to almost 300,000. Sixty percent of the new members said they had sold their cars or abandoned plans to buy them and decided instead to use Zipcar, which charges a small annual fee."[78] I-GO car sharing, a similar program in Chicago, reckons that "almost half of our members who own cars when they join I-GO sell them after six months of participation in the program. A similar number of participants either postpone buying a car or sell one before they join. Getting rid of all those fixed costs—monthly payments, gas, insurance, maintenance, parking—generates substantial savings: as much as $5,000 a year in reduced transportation costs for individuals, families, and businesses."[79]

A variant of car sharing is ride sharing. Made popular on Craigslist, the concept of using the Internet to match up people who have a car with spare seats and people who need a ride is gaining popularity. An array of programs now help people who are going to similar locations to carpool.[80] The founder of Zipcar, Robin Chase, created GoLoco, a Boston network that emphasizes social networking and attracts users through Facebook. NuRide, a similar entity, operates in the East and Midwest, enrolling employees of participating companies and then awarding ride-share points redeemable for discounts from local merchants. Claiming 25,000 subscribers and 1.25 million rides, NuRide charges a small fee for arranging each ride. Zimride works primarily through Facebook and claims about three thousand subscribers. ReadySetGoose initially started with 150 Microsoft HQ employees. The idea attracted government funding and is now available to all commuters in Washington State, through a partnership between Goose Networks, the Washington State Department of Transportation, and King County. It uses SMS messaging to connect users.

Jim Morris, a San Francisco Bay Area ride-share advocate, has proposed a scheme he calls SafeRide to increase the occupancy rate of vehicles.[81] Combining ideas from 511.org, San Francisco's transit website, Google Transit, Mapquest maps, Zipcar, SmartBike, Facebook, Myspace, eBay, and eHarmony, SafeRide would use GPS and cell phones as well as the Web to integrate the entire surface transportation system for the San Francisco Bay Area, linking drivers and riders in an attempt to match the convenience of personal vehicles. It would communicate to public transit services, vehicle-based radios, personal computers, and cell phones. Morris collects information on ride-sharing programs and helps those who wish to create them.

Ride sharing has traction in other countries, as well. Avego is a well-funded start-up in Dublin, Ireland. PickupPal.com is a Canadian program that allows people to post the rides they need and drivers to post prices they would charge riders. Pitching itself as "Drivers and passengers connecting online," it has local groups in Canada, the United States, and Australia. Participating drivers are expected to pay PickupPal 7 percent of what they collect. Members also transport cargo.[82]

Some cities are encouraging residents to use such programs to lose
that extra car, to cut down on infrastructure costs associated with sprawl
and provide a better quality of life. Seattle launched Way to Go Seattle,
which pays families to leave their second car at home. To get the program off the ground and generate some data, early participating households pledged to keep their extra car parked for six weeks, and keep a
journal of the alternative ways they traveled—by bus, foot, bicycle, or
taxi. In return they received a weekly check for eighty-five dollars. The
logs helped the city craft an educational campaign to show that people can use other means of travel and save money if they lose that second car.[83]

Employers can likewise encourage the use of non-car modes of
transport. Providing employee parking is a large expense to many employers, who must increase site costs to provide the spaces that many
employees would just as soon not use. Some employers "cash out" the
parking: an employer that has been providing free parking begins to
charge for it, but rebates that amount in cash to each employee. Those
who choose not to drive start earning more money. When undertaken
where alternative modes of transportation are available, such programs
consistently produce a 10 to 12 percent reduction in parking demand
and a commensurate drop in carbon emissions.[84]

Conclusion

Schemes like these may seem unrealistic to you today, especially if
you've just driven your car home from the store where you purchased
this book. Those of you who downloaded it to your iPad may feel a bit
more at home in the future that is fast breaking upon us. But as the next
chapter discusses, the chances that your life tomorrow, or even next
year, will look much the same as your life today and that your transportation choices will be what they were a decade ago are slim.

Hang on, we're going for a ride.

6

World Without Oil

Cars run on oil. So do airplanes, trucks, trains, ships, and most all other transportation modes. These industries are thus dependent on the oil industry, and the price it sets for a barrel of oil, the lifeblood of vehicles. Globally, 70 percent of oil use is for transport, with the remaining quarter going for feedstocks, petrochemicals, or specialty materials.[1] Even if one assumes that there's plenty of oil (not a good bet), the transportation industry, not to mention all of us who drive cars, needs to have stability in prices.

They don't. Oil prices fluctuated from $31 a barrel in 2001 to almost $150 a barrel in 2008, driving the largest transfer of wealth in human history as the thirteen oil-exporting countries raked in more than a trillion-dollar windfall in less than a year.[2] At the price peak, American drivers were aghast at paying as much as $5 a gallon, no doubt amusing their European counterparts who have long paid as much as $8 a gallon. It also sent shock waves through the American automobile industry as Americans began dumping big trucks and SUVs and bidding up prices for Priuses.

Oil prices then plummeted, as oil exporters damped the political backlash and the global recession slowed demand. Then they started to rise again. In 2009 gasoline prices rose more than 50 percent, costing American drivers $20.2 billion more than during the same period a year earlier. In the same time period, oil prices more than doubled, as investors used oil as a commodity hedge, imposing on drivers an additional cost of $100 billion in 2010. By late 2010, the price per barrel had crept back up to around $90, even though global demand remained slack (demand peaked at nearly 9.8 million barrels a day in August 2007).[3]

After 2007, demand for oil sank to a low of 8.5 million barrels a day in February 2010—a drop of 13 percent. But that response was driven largely by the collapsing economy. As astute analysts asked whether it makes any sense to manage our oil demand by periodic recessions, an analysis of the situation by the Energy Policy Information Center observed, "Alternative fuels, electrification, a focus on mass transit—those appear to be the very few tools available today to deal with the transportation sector's insatiable demand for oil. And until we seriously avail ourselves of those tools, we are left with the chilling close: The 'global economy is staring down the barrel of a series of boom-bust cycles that will be directly caused by the availability of oil.' Not a pretty picture."[4]

The analysis was referencing Michael Rothman, a former chief energy strategist for Merrill Lynch, who pointed out in the pages of the *Financial Times*, "The prosperity of the world hinges on oil . . . Demand for oil has become the most significant influence on the health of the global economy . . . The world economy may have become alarmingly dependent on the price of oil."[5]

Oil price oscillations are profit-and-loss issues for major industries. But they are life-and-death issues for billions of people around the world.

But what if we are running out of oil?

It's Just an Oscillation

Hold that thought for a moment. Imagine, instead, that rather than running out of oil we're only looking at vicious swings in the price of a barrel of oil. The winners in the transportation sector, as chapter 5 showed, will be those who focus on efficiency, more miles and freight moved at lowest cost, with the lowest impact on the environment. The smart money, and the lion's share of opportunity, awaits those who creatively respond to the market incentive of price instability. Americans love their trucks, but unless the industry can smooth out the wild oscillations in oil prices, drivers will join Europeans in transferring their loyalty to car companies that make more fuel-efficient vehicles. And sales figures from 2009 bear this out: although the best-selling pickup trucks—the Ford F-series, the Chevy Silverado, and the Dodge Ram— remain among the top ten bestsellers, the other seven are cars or small crossovers, which are really cars with larger cabins.[6]

More than 92 percent of Americans "expect gasoline prices to go back up in the near future"—including over half (52 percent) who "definitely" expect higher prices at the pump. Only a quarter of Americans say that they are *not* taking "expected future gasoline price increases into consideration in thinking about buying a new vehicle."[7] In 2007 the Civil Society Institute found that 85 percent of Americans—91 percent of Democrats, 77 percent of Republicans, and 85 percent of independents— agree with the statement: "We need higher federal fuel-efficiency standards for vehicles now in order to conserve more energy, making us less dependent on Middle Eastern oil, and to reduce the ill effects of global warming." That's what the market wants.

Will the American automobile industry position itself to respond? Although Chevy's hybrid truck is attracting a lot of attention, the current state of play is not very aggressive (see previous chapter). Cynics such as Stephanie Brinley, an automotive analyst with AutoPacific, Inc., an automotive market research company, believe that the future will look very like the past: "By 2015, we forecast the Compact Car group to see its share of an overall 15.4 million–unit market to be 21.4 percent. As a percent of American buyers, there isn't much change." She believes that those who buy into the conventional wisdom—that innovative vehicles are about to replace big SUVs—will likely find that, yet again, the conventional wisdom is wrong.[8]

But in the very near future the auto industry may not have any choice. What if we ARE running out of oil?

A Very Different Future

In his 2008 CNN documentary "We Were Warned: Out of Gas," the analyst Frank Sesno posits that a hurricane in the Gulf of Mexico takes out much of the Houston, Texas, refining capacity, the source of a quarter of U.S. gasoline. At the same time Middle Eastern terrorists pick this time of dislocation in the oil business to launch an attack on the oil-loading arms on the Saudi piers—they've tried various times unsuccessfully. This time they succeed. Once down, these facilities take three years to rebuild.[9]

In this plausible scenario, the United States finds itself "out of gas." Sesno profiles how, over the ensuing few months, the economy collapses, as oil tops $200 a barrel. He depicts the ugly consequences on the lives of average Americans, as deliveries of groceries dry up, shipments of pink fuzzy slippers never reach Walmart, and riots break out around the world as a lack of oil impacts developing countries far more seriously even than the United States. The global economy grinds to a halt.[10]

This could happen. Tomorrow.

Peak Oil Is upon Us

The dislocations portrayed in the documentary are realistic. In 2008, a heavy snowfall left grocery stores in midwestern states running out of food in just three days. The 2007–2008 spike in oil prices to almost $150 a barrel triggered the ensuing global recession, the worst since the Great Depression.[11] High gasoline prices forced various nations to ration gasoline supplies or attempt to end existing subsidies for oil. This caused riots in China (where ninety thousand protests raged in 2007), Myanmar, and Iran. In Nigeria, striking workers forced the government to rescind a decision to end fuel subsidies.[12] Most nations subsidize fossil-based energy in some form, but many oil producers, including Venezuela, Turkmenistan, Syria, Algeria, Angola, and Malaysia, use high fuel subsidies directly to stave off domestic unrest. When world oil prices rise, this becomes very expensive.

Sesno interviewed Matthew Simmons, the Houston banker who specialized in the oil trade. His sobering 2005 book, *Twilight in the Desert*, described an imminent peak in world oil production. Simmons pointed out that the extraction history of the supergiant oil fields looks essentially like a production curve drawn in 1956 by the Shell Oil geologist M. King Hubbert: oil extraction goes steeply up, and then, when the finite resource is half extracted, falls off as steeply as it went up. The shape of the curve, called Hubbert's needle or Hubbert's peak, gave its name to the theory of "peak oil."

Hubbert postulated that world oil production would peak early in the twenty-first century. He accurately predicted the peaking of U.S. fields in the 1970s. In 2001, Kenneth Deffeyes, a geologist at Princeton, predicted that world oil production would peak in 2005; recently, the U.S. Energy Information Administration concurred.[13] Simmons believed that the tipping point would occur when the oil fields in Saudi Arabia can no longer meet demand, which he believed would be very soon. He claimed that the Saudis are already injecting seawater to increase pressure and enable greater extraction, thereby shortening the life of their fields. If true, this is very serious news for the world transportation system. Hell, it's pretty damn serious news for the world as a whole.

Under this theory, the world is not truly out of oil, but it will soon lose the ability to extract enough of it cheaply enough to satisfy exponential growth rates. Over half of the oil ever used by humans has been extracted since 1988, 90 percent of it since 1958. If Hubbert, Deffeyes, the U.S. Energy Information Agency, and Simmons are right, peak oil has occurred. That fact will soon change everything about how the earth does business, and utterly transform how we get about.

It is clear that many major fields are peaking. The Cantarell field in Mexico peaked in 2003 at 2.2 million barrels a day. Today the Mexican oil company Pemex struggles to extract a quarter of that amount from Cantarell, and officially admits that the field is declining at 12 percent per year; others believe that the decline is faster than that. The Mexicans could be excused for being a bit coy about the real figures: Pemex's revenue—a large part of which comes from the sale of Cantarell's oil—makes up 40 percent of the Mexican government's income. Mexico, one of the United States' biggest sources of oil, is now exporting only about 1 million barrels a day, much less than before, and a number that the Mexicans project will go to zero over the next ten years.[14] Mexican political stability, already a bit shaky, could collapse if the recognition that peak oil will impoverish the country becomes widespread.

In 2005, Bloomberg reported that Kuwait's Burgan field, previously the world's second largest, had peaked, dropping to 1.7 million barrels a day from its peak of 3 million.[15] British North Sea oil peaked in 1999. Iran, a major oil extractor, began importing refined product in 2007. China entered the world oil market at about this time, as did India.

Skeptics Coming Around

This information is not new, but for many years official energy experts have dismissed the concept of peak oil. The International Energy Agency (IEA) was one such denier. With a website that boasts, "Governments and industry from all across the globe have come to rely on the IEA's World Energy Outlook to provide a consistent basis on which they can formulate policies and design business plans," the IEA's decades of statements rejecting the prospect of oil shortages comforted the many who want to believe that the future will mirror the past.[16]

In 2007 the IEA reversed its assertions that the world is awash in oil, suddenly warning that the world could face an oil supply shortage within five years that would raise oil prices to record heights. These prices, the agency warned, would be driven by increased demand for oil in the fast-growing Asian and Middle Eastern economies, political instability in some oil-rich countries, and the inability of the oil majors to expand their extraction to meet expanded demand.[17] The report was not widely publicized and remained largely ignored.

In late 2009, however, an article in *The Guardian* reported that a "senior official" at the IEA had accused the agency of deliberately understating how close the world may be to running out of oil, saying the agency did not want to trigger panic buying. This unnamed source alleged that the administration of George W. Bush had influenced the supposed watchdog agency to underplay the rate of decline from existing oil fields while overplaying the chances of finding new reserves. The article reported that "a second senior IEA source, who has now left but was also unwilling to give his name, said a key rule at the organisation was that it was 'imperative not to anger the Americans' but the fact was that there was not as much oil in the world as had been admitted. 'We have [already] entered the "peak oil" zone. I think that the situation is really bad,' he added."[18]

In December 2009, Dr. Fatih Birol, the chief economist of the IEA, acknowledged that unless trends changed,

In terms of non-Opec [countries outside the big oil producers' cartel], we are expecting that in three, four years' time the production of conventional oil will come to a plateau, and start to decline. In terms of the global picture, assuming that Opec will invest in a timely manner, global conventional oil can still continue, but we still expect that it will come around 2020 to a plateau as well, which is, of course, not good news from a global-oil-supply point of view.[19]

An article in *The Economist* observed,

By contrast, oil optimists like Cambridge Energy Research Associates (CERA) argue that high prices will lead to improved technology that will enable oil firms to find new oilfields; make it economically feasible to extract oil under more challenging geological conditions or manufacture it from coal or natural gas; and increase the amount of oil that can be recovered from existing fields. This, they argue, will allow demand to be met for at least a couple of decades. After that, CERA reckons, 'supply may well struggle to meet demand, but an undulating plateau rather than a dramatic peak will likely unfold.' Until now, official estimates from the IEA were far closer in spirit to those from the likes of CERA than the pessimists. Mr. Birol's statement suggests that the IEA has extended a tentative foot into the other camp.[20]

Dr. Birol conceded, after analyzing extraction trends from eight hundred different oil fields, that the annual decline in the older fields could average 8.6 percent by 2030. "Even if oil demand were to remain flat," he admitted, "the world would need to find more than 40 million barrels per day of gross new capacity—equal to four new Saudi Arabias— just to offset this decline." Unfortunately, the average size of new discoveries has been declining since the mid-1960s. Between 1960 and 1989 the world discovered more than twice the oil it produced. But between 1990 and 2006 cumulative oil discoveries have been about half of extraction.[21]

In March 2010, officials of the UK government met to discuss the possibility that there might not be as much oil available to the world as "previously thought."[22] The meeting, called to quell industry fears stemming from the news reports about the IEA, may have done the opposite. It released a report by the Industry Taskforce on Peak Oil and Energy Security, commissioned after the announcement that the IEA may have cooked its books. The report, with a foreword written by the previous chairman of Shell Oil, warned,

Plentiful and growing supplies of oil have become essential to almost every sector of today's economies. It is easy to see why, when we consider that the energy locked into one barrel of oil is equivalent to that expended by five labourers working 12 hour days non stop for a year. The agricultural sector perhaps makes the case most starkly: modern food production is oil dependent across the entire value chain from the field to the delivered package. Within modern cities, for example, life in the suburbs will become extremely challenging without plentiful supplies of affordable oil. Yet in recent years, a growing number of people in and around the energy industry have been warning that global oil supply will soon fail to meet demand, even if the global demand drops, because the world is on or close to its peak of oil production. Peak oil production is the point at which the depletion of existing reserves can no longer be replaced by additions of new flow capacity. Conventional wisdom holds that the peak is many years in the future, allowing a timely transition to alternatives that can replace falling oil supply. However, the International Energy Agency has warned of an oil crunch by 2013. Other authoritative voices warn of severe problems earlier than this.

We hope our work to date will act as a wake-up call for fellow companies, for government, and for consumers. For one is surely needed.[23]

The report recommended immediate acceleration of the "green transport revolution," the ongoing introduction of lower-carbon technology and trials of sustainable biofuels for private vehicles but also extending to the general transport network. It urged the government not to cut investment in public transport and to combine a focus on new clean technologies with "wide scale behavioural change promoted through incentives and education to produce a modal shift to greener modes of transport."[24]

Climate activists have long argued that it will be necessary to limit oil extraction and use to protect the climate. The IEA chief economist argues, conversely, that climate protection may be the only thing that can stave off peak oil:

Mr. Birol reckons that coordinated action to restrict the increase in global temperatures to 2°C will restrict global demand for oil to 89 million barrels per day in 2030, compared with 105 million that would result if no action is taken. That could push back the peak of production, as it would take longer to produce the lower-cost oil that remains to be developed. Action on climate change, Birol argues, may yet save the world from an early supply crunch.[25]

It's a Scary World Out There

The latest entrants into the peak oil debate are the world's militaries. In late 2010 a leaked internal draft of a study prepared for the Future Analysis department of the Bundeswehr Transformation Center, a think tank tasked with fixing a direction for the German military, drove home the geopolitical implications of peak oil.[26] It warned that there is "some probability that peak oil will occur around the year 2010 and that the impact on security is expected to be felt 15 to 30 years later." An article discussing the report summarized some of its main warnings:

> Oil will determine power: . . . Oil will become one decisive factor in determining the new landscape of international relations: "The relative importance of the oil-producing nations in the international system is growing. These nations are using the advantages resulting from this to expand the scope of their domestic and foreign policies and establish themselves as new or resurgent regional, or in some cases even global leading powers."
>
> Increasing importance of oil exporters: For importers of oil more competition for resources will mean an increase in the number of nations competing for favor with oil-producing nations. For the latter this opens up a window of opportunity that can be used to implement political, economic or ideological aims . . . "This could result in a more aggressive assertion of national interests on the part of the oil-producing nations."
>
> Politics in place of the market: A supply crisis would roll back the liberalization of the energy market. "Bilateral, conditioned supply agreements and privileged partnerships, such as those seen prior to the oil crises of the 1970s, will once again come to the fore."
>
> Market failures: "Shortages in the supply of vital goods could arise" as a result, for example in food supplies. Oil is used directly or indirectly in the production of 95 percent of all industrial goods. Price shocks could therefore be seen in almost any industry and throughout all stages of the industrial supply chain. "In the medium term the global economic system and every market-oriented national economy would collapse."
>
> Relapse into planned economy: Since virtually all economic sectors rely heavily on oil, peak oil could lead to a "partial or complete failure of markets . . . A conceivable alternative would be government rationing and the allocation of important goods or the setting of production

schedules and other short-term coercive measures to replace market-based mechanisms in times of crisis."

Global chain reaction: "A restructuring of oil supplies will not be equally possible in all regions before the onset of peak oil . . . If there were economic crashes in some regions of the world, Germany could be affected. Germany would not escape the crises of other countries, because it's so tightly integrated into the global economy."

Crisis of political legitimacy: The Bundeswehr study raises fears for the survival of democracy itself. Parts of the population could perceive the upheaval triggered by peak oil "as a general systemic crisis." This would create "room for ideological and extremist alternatives to existing forms of government." Fragmentation of the affected population is likely and could "in extreme cases lead to open conflict."[27]

Or, put differently, even if you're not concerned about climate change you should be terrified of running out of oil. Saving the world and saving it from an early supply crunch turn out to be one and the same thing.

But we'd better get about it.

In a report on peak oil commissioned by the U.S. Department of Energy, the oil analyst Robert L. Hirsch wrote, "Without timely mitigation, the economic, social and political costs" of world oil supplies peaking "will be unprecedented." Even a worldwide emergency response "10 years before world oil peaking" would leave "a liquid-fuels shortfall roughly a decade after the time that oil would have peaked."[28]

Many people believe that it is foolish to wait. The Post Carbon Institute, long called a peak oil alarmist, has teamed with a British-born movement called Transition Towns to help communities cope with both the sort of emergency scenario Frank Sesno portrayed and the more durable global catastrophe of peak oil. Believing that national governments will act too late and implement too little, this international grassroots movement is helping communities build resilience to survive peak oil, climate change, and the economic crisis. The Transition Towns movement empowers citizens to seek local solutions and strengthen local ability to provide food, energy, and the necessities of life. The model is based on four assumptions:

1. That life with dramatically lower energy consumption is
   inevitable, and that it's better to plan for it than to be taken by
   surprise.
2. That our communities currently lack resilience to deal either
   with short-term crises or the more slowly unfolding disaster of
   peak oil.
3. That we have to act collectively, and we have to act now.
4. That by unleashing the collective genius of our communities it is
   possible to design new ways of living that are more nourishing,
   fulfilling, and ecologically sustainable.[29]

Resources for communities interested in implementing low-carbon
futures include the Post Carbon Cities Manual, the Transition Handbook, and Local Action for Sustainable Economic Renewal (LASER),
Natural Capitalism Solutions' *Climate Protection Manual for Cities*.[30]
These detail actions that municipalities and citizens' groups are taking
to meet local needs with local, renewable resources. The Transition Network lists the hundreds of communities around the world that are already implementing these measures.

Fueling the Future

The best way to become independent of oil is to produce dramatically
more efficient cars. Every additional mile per gallon that the U.S. vehicle
fleet achieves saves 350,000 barrels a day of oil.[31] There is no strategy for
getting off oil that makes sense without making the vehicle fleet dramatically more efficient.

This can actually happen quite quickly, if the political will is there.
Lester Brown points out, in *Plan B 4.0*, that on January 6, 1942, one month
after the bombing of Pearl Harbor, President Roosevelt turned to the
American auto industry, then the world's greatest concentration of industrial might, and ordered the production of 45,000 tanks, 60,000 planes,
20,000 anti-aircraft guns, and 6 million tons of merchant shipping. From
April 1942 through the end of 1944, essentially no personal cars were

produced in the United States. Road and highway construction halted and pleasure driving was banned. All consumer goods that could help the war effort were rationed, including tires, gasoline, fuel oil, and sugar. Cutting back on consumption freed up capacity and resources that drove the war effort. Between 1942 and 1944, the United States produced 229,600 aircraft and more than 5,000 ships, far exceeding the initial goals. In three and a half years, U.S. industrial might turned the tide and won the war.[32]

Transforming how we build cars seems a far less daunting task than that.

The necessary other half of any sensible strategy to deal with peak oil or climate chaos is to fuel our vehicles in renewable ways that do not destroy the climate. The end of oil doesn't have to mean the end of fuel.

Petroleum is not the only or even the best way to run a vehicle. Rudolf Diesel, the inventor of the diesel engine, used peanut oil to run his motor. Henry Ford and Charles Kettering, the head of research at General Motors in the early days, both believed that ethanol would power their inventions. In 1925 Ford famously remarked, "The fuel of the future is going to come from fruit like that sumac out by the road, or from apples, weeds, sawdust—almost anything. There is fuel in every bit of vegetable matter that can be fermented. There's enough alcohol in one year's yield of an acre of potatoes to drive the machinery necessary to cultivate the fields for a hundred years."[33]

In the past decade biofuel production has exploded. World production surpassed 100 billion liters of annual production in 2009. On a net energy basis, it is displacing 1.15 million barrels of crude oil each day, and cutting approximately 215 million tons of greenhouse gas emissions annually. This included 74 billion liters of ethanol, which cut greenhouse gas emissions by over 87 million tons (an amount equaling Austria's total 2007 emissions) and 16 billion liters of biodiesel, which cut emissions by 36 million tons (more than Croatia's 2007 carbon footprint). Together, the carbon reduction equaled the national greenhouse gas emissions of Monaco, Liechtenstein, Iceland, Latvia, Luxembourg, Slovenia, Estonia, Lithuania, and Croatia.[34] Global production of biofuels is projected to double between 2009 and 2015, with the United States expected to see a

30 percent increase in its production, the largest.[35] But Brazil, the world's poster child for biofuel success, will remain the world's top exporter of ethanol.[36] Brazil is in this position because it took oil shortages seriously the first time around.

Sweet Fuel

The 1973 oil embargo, which sent world oil prices soaring for the first of now four times, hit Brazil hard. Brazil is dependent on imports for over 80 percent of its oil, and Brazil's economy was nearly destroyed. Unlike most of the rest of the world, Brazil decided to act. In 1975 Brazil implemented the National Alcohol Program. Petrobras, Brazil's state oil company, was required to purchase a set amount of alcohol and blend at least 22 percent ethanol into its fuel. Almost $5 million in low-interest loans encouraged the industry to comply.[37]

Today Brazil is the world's second-largest ethanol producer, behind the United States, and gets 48 percent of its transportation fuel from ethanol made from sugarcane at a cost cheaper than gasoline.[38] Between domestic petroleum extraction and domestic production of alcohol, Brazil has entirely weaned itself from global oil addiction. The energy yield from sugarcane ethanol is seven times greater than that from corn ethanol (corn is the preferred feedstock for the American ethanol industry). The introduction of flex-fuel cars into Brazil in 2003 enabled three quarters of its vehicle fleet to run on ethanol, making the country energy-independent. In contrast, in the United States only 12 percent of the vehicles produced by General Motors are flex-fuel, and only 1 percent of American gas stations sell E-85, a blend of 85 percent ethanol with petroleum gasoline.[39]

Biofuel critics have rightly warned that unsustainable production of monocultures, clearing of forest land, and the use of unsustainable agricultural practices make first-generation biofuel production efforts a threat to biodiversity and to the integrity of ecosystems essential to climate protection.[40] For sugarcane to be considered a sustainable solution it is also essential that Brazil correct the horrific working conditions of laborers in the cane fields, and deal with the negative impacts of growing a sugar monoculture that requires inputs of chemical fertilizers, pesticides, and fuel to harvest the cane. It must also ensure that it is not cutting rainforest to grow sugarcane, otherwise the enterprise will do more damage to the climate, hardly a solution.[41]

Fair enough, but Brazil's program set out to make the country energy-independent, not carbon-neutral or socially responsible. Given peak oil, the rest of the world may very well face the same imperative. Still, unsustainable practices are just problem switching, not problem solving, and in 2010 Brazil's president, Luiz Inacio "Lula" da Silva, signed a law requiring that Brazil cut greenhouse gas emissions by 39 percent by 2020, meeting a commitment made at the Copenhagen climate talks. He also pledged that the government of Brazil would slow deforestation of the Amazon rainforest by more than 70 percent between 2008 and 2018—a move that will also reduce greenhouse gas emissions significantly.[42]

Corn ethanol production faces many of the same issues. Critics rightly point out that it requires vast tracts of land that could be producing food, cannot be maintained without intensive artificial inputs, requires more energy to make than it produces, and depends on enormous federal subsidies. Lester Brown pointed out that the corn that would be required to make enough ethanol to fill an SUV with fuel once would feed a hungry person for a year.[43]

Second-Generation Biofuels

These are all legitimate criticisms and the industry surely must do better. Lester Brown has said, "To understand the environmental and health consequences of biofuels we must look well beyond the tailpipe to how and where biofuels are produced. Clearly, upstream emissions matter."[44]

Enter second-generation biofuels. Researchers at the University of Minnesota's Institute on the Environment are arguing for a shift to producing ethanol from switchgrass, prairie biomass, and *Miscanthus*, a genus of perennial grasses, to reduce the environmental and health impacts of expanded biofuels production. The researchers evaluated the full life-cycle costs of various fuel types produced from the three sources, as well as the impacts of fertilizer and pesticide runoff into rivers and lakes. Increased use of nitrogen fertilizers for corn production has been linked to the creation of a dead zone of low oxygen in the Gulf of Mexico. The researchers found that "total environmental and health costs of gasoline are about 71 cents per gallon, while an equivalent amount of corn-ethanol fuel costs from 72 cents to about $1.45, depending on the technology used to produce it. An equivalent amount of cellulosic ethanol, however, costs from 19 cents to 32 cents, depending on the technology and type of cellulosic materials used."[45]

The use of food-quality grains to produce fuel for our cars may have been an easy putt for agribusiness and distillation industries keen to keep doing what they've always done while securing federal subsidies and higher profits, but it is far from the only way to produce liquid energy to move ourselves around. Cellulosic ethanol, described in the Minnesota study, can be made from any woody material: wood waste, sweet sorghum, walnut hulls, and a huge variety of waste products.

A Canadian company called Iogen claims that it can replace half of the gasoline in the United States with cellulosic ethanol. Using "enzymatic hydrolysis," Iogen strips the lignan (the woody structural component) from the sugars in cellulose. The sugars can then be fermented, and if all goes well the remaining lignan can be burned to power the rest of the process. The company's product fueled flexible-fuel Chevrolet Impalas for the United Nations Climate Change Conference (COP 11) in Montreal in 2005, ferrying delegates between the convention center, their hotels, and the airport.[46]

In the spring of 2010, Iogen converted straw and waste from a dairy herd at Mrs. Mclaren's Double Diamond Farms in Ontario, Canada, to ethanol to fuel the Ferrari race team to second- and third-place finishes in the Bahrain Grand Prix. Mrs. Mclaren hauls at least five truckloads of straw each week to Iogen's Ottawa facility. In neighboring Saskatchewan, six hundred farmers have contracted to supply straw to a new Iogen facility now under construction.[47] Iogen's ethanol will then power the Ferrari team for the entire Formula One season.

This only begins to suggest the opportunities for companies and entrepreneurs looking to get rich off the demand for fuel in a world of declining oil. Any fatty material can be turned into biodiesel, and some of the sources of that fat are piquant. A Formula 3 racecar in the UK is running on waste chocolate from a Cadbury's plant. Indeed, its steering wheel is also biological, sourced partly from carrots, while the mirrors and aerodynamic front wing are formed from potato starch and flax fiber. The Canadian company AMEC is turning diapers into diesel, keeping 180 million disposable diapers a year, a quarter of Quebec's output, out of landfills and producing 11 million liters of diesel. Considering that diapers can take a hundred years to decompose, turning them into domestic fuel seems a good alternative.[48]

Changing World Technologies of Carthage, Missouri, uses "thermodepolymerization" to turn turkey guts, feathers, waste, "anything but the gobble," into an oil that can then be made into diesel, gasoline, or jet fuel. Its plant, running since 2008, is making three thousand barrels of "turkey crude" each week. An adjacent ConAgra slaughterhouse supplies the raw material. A federal grant of $17 million helped create the $40 million factory. The process is competitive against $80-a-barrel petroleum, a level breached in spring 2010.[49]

Tyson Foods formed a renewable-fuel division to take the same approach. Tyson produces 2.3 billion pounds of chicken, hog, and animal fat from its operations each year that could be converted into about 300 million gallons of fuel. It is the "equivalent of 20,000 barrels a day of feedstock that can be turned into renewables," Jeff Webster, senior vice president of strategy and business development for Tyson, told an investor conference in 2006. It's "the equivalent of bringing renewable content to one-third of the [diesel used] . . . within the U.S."[50]

Creating fuel from waste fat is now such a conventional technology that McDonald's is using the grease from its fryers to make biodiesel for its UK trucking fleet. But a Beverly Hills liposuction surgeon has taken the technology to a whole new level. He uses fat suctioned from his patients to make biodiesel (quite illegally). The good doctor derives a gallon of biodiesel from each gallon of fat, running his Ford SUV and his girlfriend's Lincoln on the results of over seven thousand liposuctions. "They lose their love handles and help the Earth at the same time," he said.[51]

The oily residue from brewing coffee is 10 to 15 percent usable oil that can also be refined into a biofuel. The world's annual coffee grounds production, about 15 billion pounds, could offset as much as 340 million gallons a year of imported oil.[52] Polystyrene cups, waste from cattle production, or special crops like jatropha can all be converted to fuel. Interestingly, many of these technologies lend themselves better to small-scale production in developing countries than as a basis for megacorporations to change their business to another industry, but still control fuel production. Jatropha, for example, has proved difficult for commercial operations to grow in plantations. The leading producer of jatropha oil for fuel conversion, D-1 Oils PLC was an investors' darling, until BP (formerly British Petroleum) declined to invest further in the company, citing difficulties in commercializing jatropha production.[53] Jatropha can grow on marginal land, and with very little water, but its harvestability and oil yield then become unattractive to commercial growers. By mid-2010, D1 Oils PLC was undergoing a major reorganization.

Meanwhile, in Mali, where 99 percent of the rural population lives without electricity, a project called Garalo has partnered with Access, a private power company that provides a guaranteed market for the farmers to buy small-production runs of jatropha oil for electricity production. Funded by a grant from Amader (a government company in charge of rural electrification) and the FACT Foundation, an international NGO, each system generates 300 kilowatts, feeding a distribution grid of approximately eight miles that supplies 247 households. Homes pay for connection to the system and for any energy used and also make a contribution toward street lighting. Payment defaults are under 10 percent.

By staying small, Garalo ensures that villages' natural resources (land and jatropha) are processed and used to provide local energy security while keeping the money in the communities and supplying low-cost electricity to off-grid rural communities. Garalo encourages farmers to interplant jatropha with food crops, which limits the negative impact of large plantation biofuel production on food security. [54]

Parts of the world rich in forests are turning to their main resource, woody materials, to produce fuels. A wide array of companies is coming to market with wood gasification facilities. Modern variants of the gasifiers that provided fuel for a million German vehicles in World War II can turn any woody waste into a suite of biofuels and other feedstocks. ALL Power Labs, a Berkeley-based start-up, combined "junkyard fabricators and university-trained Ph.D.s to develop a do-it-yourself kit to turn garbage into vehicle fuel." They have shipped 150 such kits to users on five continents. So long as the wood is sustainably harvested such systems make great sense.

Pond Scum to the Rescue

Of all of the second-generation biofuels, algae may be the most exciting. Critics deride the approach as trying to make fuel from pond scum, citing the fact that in at least ten years of trying it hasn't become commercially viable and it isn't apt to become so anytime soon. The Department of Energy disagreed, granting $78 million in funding in 2010 to various efforts to make fuel from algae. The National Alliance for Advanced Biofuels and Bioproducts received $44 million to develop "a systems approach for sustainable commercialization" of algae-based gasoline, diesel, and jet fuel. Algae-based biofuel doesn't compete with food or livestock feed, can use marginal land and degraded water, and can make use of CO_2 emissions. The National Advanced Biofuels Consortium, led by the National Renewable Energy Laboratory and Pacific Northwest National Laboratory, got an additional $33.8 million to develop algae-based hydrocarbon fuels that will feed into existing refining and distribution facilities.[55]

They are all following in the steps of Exxon and Craig Venter, who in 2009 invested $600 million over five years to find the most suitable strain of algae, figure out the best way to grow it, and develop ways to mass-produce algae economically with existing energy infrastructure.[56]

Critics point out that biofuels have a way to go before they move from an asterisk as a fuel source into a sustainable industry. In 2006, only 150 million gallons of biodiesel were produced while Americans consumed 62 billion gallons of regular diesel.[57] Of course, if vehicle efficiency cuts the number of gallons of diesel, gas, and oil needed, biofuels could play a larger role.

But as usual, entrepreneurs are seeking to prove such conclusions wrong. Clean Power, a company in Berlin, New Hampshire, is building a wood-fueled combined heat and power plant to sell electricity and steam to a nearby paper mill. From an adjacent sewage treatment plant they will reclaim wastewater to supply their facility. The nutrients in the sewage and CO_2 piped in from their smokestack will be used to raise algae to make biodiesel. The waste heat and electricity will run growlights for the algae.[58]

High Flying: Virgin Airlines

Richard Branson offers an inspiring counterpoint to the slow pace of government research. In 2008, Branson committed all of the profits from Virgin's various carbon-generating businesses to funding the search for carbon-neutral fuels. When queried why, he replied, "Look, I run an airline, I'm going to need fuel. We live in a carbon-constrained world."[59] Branson's airline indeed does use a lot of jet fuel: 700 million gallons of it each year. As oil prices rose into 2008, Virgin's costs rose by more than a billion dollars over three years. Declaring that the climate crisis was "an emergency far worse than World War One and World War Two put together," Branson began experimenting with alternative fuels, investing $3 billion in corn and cellulose ethanol. He is now putting his research money into second-generation biofuels.[60]

Branson's Virgin Airlines is so committed to fighting climate change that it has created a thirty-point manifesto that includes such ambitious goals as improving fuel efficiency by 30 percent by 2020 and generating 100 percent of the electricity that runs its UK operations from renewables.[61] On Sunday, February 24, 2008, Virgin Atlantic became the first commercial airline to take off with biofuel, in this case a mix of coconut oil, babassu oil, and jet fuel. The Virgin Boeing 747 flew from London to Amsterdam. Branson described it as an historic event on the way toward a low-carbon future for the airline industry. The feat was replicated soon after when an Air New Zealand 747 flew on a 50 percent mix of biofuels.

Some environmentalists were less than enthusiastic. The chief scientist at Greenpeace, Doug Parr, called Virgin's biofuel experiment "high altitude green wash." Parr argued, "The scientific evidence is now clear—using the finite amount of land we have to grow biofuels is bad for the world's poor, bad for biodiversity and bad for the climate. Instead of looking for a magic green bullet, Virgin should focus on the real solution to this problem and call for a halt to relentless airport expansion."[62] Steve Howard, CEO of the Climate Group, disagreed, and called Branson's extraordinary commitments to tackling climate change "groundbreaking."[63] It is precisely because Parr has a point that Howard, too, is correct.

Solix Biofuels, Inc., a spin-off company of Colorado State University's Engines and Energy Conversion Laboratory, has commercialized growing lipid algae to produce fuel biocrude, green diesel, biojet, biodiesel, methane, chemical intermediates, feed, and other important products.[64] A study by Dr. Bryan Willson, a CSU professor, showed that turning algae into a biofuel is more environmentally friendly than producing either petroleum diesel or soy biodiesel. The study evaluated the complete process for each fuel, including such factors as the amount of energy required to grow algae, the diesel burned by trucks used to move the algae biodiesel from processing facilities to the pump, and the energy used to make fertilizer.[65]

Do-it-yourselfers can get into the act as well. Numerous books and videos show how to make alcohol at home, and how to make biodiesel in your garage.[66] If the Cassandras warning of peak oil are correct, this is the new growth industry.

Building a Better Place

Liquid fuels are not the only way to power a vehicle. In October 2007, Project Better Place was launched with $200 million in financing from

Morgan Stanley, Israel Corp, and VantagePoint Venture Partners. Better Place's founder and CEO, Shai Agassi, on track to become CEO at SAP, left the world of enterprise software to launch a start-up transportation business in response to a question posed at the 2005 World Economic Forum: "How do you make the world a better place by 2020?"

Creating a sustainable, environmental solution transforming transportation from fossil fuels to renewably produced electricity, Better Place proposes to build the infrastructure to enable electric vehicles to go mainstream. "To ensure that we can confidently drive an EV anytime, anywhere, Better Place is developing and deploying EV driver services, systems and infrastructure. Subscribers and guests will have access to a network of charge spots, switch stations and systems which optimize the driving experience and minimize environmental impact and cost."[67]

And they are doing it. Better Place teamed with the government of Israel, keen to get off of imported oil for obvious reasons, and the Danish Oil and Natural Gas company (DONG) to implement the first electric car refueling systems. Using the business model of mobile phones, Better Place proposes to sell battery electric cars (it has already contracted with Renault to buy 100,000 Fluence EV family-sized, all-electric sedans, with another 100,000 on order). They propose to sell the cars for $12,000, then, for $300 a month (or less if you drive less) sell the service of swapping out and recharging the batteries at specially designed and operated renewable charging stations. The Better Place proposition is to deliver mobility for the same time commitment and price point that people now spend to refuel gasoline cars—except that it will be renewably powered, all-electric transportation that emits no CO_2 or other pollutants. And helps the world break its addiction to oil.

Aiming to be the dominant infrastructure provider in the rapidly growing EV market is no modest or inexpensive task. Better Place secured significant financing from private and institutional investors, with a January 2010 $350 million investment round led by HSBC that took Better Place to a valuation of over $1 billion.[68] In addition to its projects in Israel and Denmark, Better Place has undertaken EV infrastructure projects in Australia, Canada, Japan, and the United States, where it has sought agreements to roll out the model in Northern California and in

Hawaii. In late 2010, Better Place announced a program to run switchable battery taxis in San Francisco and San Jose, modeled on the successful taxi service it has been running in Tokyo for several years.[69]

Better Place's success has led others into the market. France made a major commitment to electric vehicles, which is one reason why Renault says it will launch four electric car models in the next several years. Agassi and DONG are cooperating with Siemens to roll out the pan-European smart grid described in chapter 3.

Virtual Transportation Solutions

The best way to avoid the cost and carbon impacts from transportation is to avoid travel altogether. Over the past several years, significant advancements in communications technologies have vastly increased the options for individuals and professionals to keep in touch regardless of time zone, geographic distance, or other barriers, all without the need to get on a plane or in a car.

Skype, a now-ubiquitous tool for keeping up with loved ones, is increasingly used for business communications. In the third quarter of 2009, Skype users made 27.7 billion minutes of Skype-to-Skype calls, one third of them video calls. And, of course, Skype-to-Skype calls are free. With over 20 million people online at peak times, and growth close to 60 percent per year, "Skype is now the largest provider of cross-border communications in the world, by far."[70] Interesting achievement for an entrepreneurial start-up that launched without a visible business model other than to get bought by eBay.

Many corporations now routinely hold multistate or transnational meetings with no one leaving his or her office, or building. Participants enter their company's videoconference room, are visually patched together by a technician, and conduct their business as if they were sitting in the same room. Hewlett Packard's Halo Telepresence solution is one such offering, helping corporate clients save money on travel costs and dramatically cut their carbon footprints. "Halo is a virtual meeting tool that gives users a 'tele-immersive' experience," boasts the company. "It creates a lifelike encounter so natural that many users report forgetting whether they met a colleague in person or over Halo."[71] Not yet impressed? How about the fact that the Human Resources Department at HP saves $300,000 per year and reduces its travel budget 43 percent using Halo to conduct preliminary job interviews.[72] Every flight not taken saves money, reduces lost work hours, and cuts emissions. HP estimates that with Halo an average multinational can easily avoid 200 flights per year, saving 600,000 tons of emissions. As companies around the world face climate legislation, that savings equals about $10 million per year (at 2010 prices) in carbon offset purchases they will not have to make.

The same climate benefits of video conferencing apply to virtual shopping. In 2008, Climate Cooler, a California-based carbon-tracking company, was hired by eBay to determine the greenhouse gas emissions impacts of buying used products online as compared to traditional bricks-and-mortar commerce. Using emissions data from buildings, transportation, and data centers, Climate Cooler found that "eBay's business model reduces the global warming impact of retail by extending the useful life of a wide array of products and encouraging product reuse and recycling," and that "eBay's business model avoids the typical greenhouse gas emissions of retail stores and warehouses."[73] Buying a used HP Pavilion laptop on eBay, the Climate Cooler study found, saves over 50 percent of the emissions of buying a new one.

Scale this up. In 2007, the sale of used laptops on eBay saved over 69,000 tons of greenhouse gas emissions compared with purchasing new machines. Even more impressive results were found when buying used golf clubs and Coach handbags. The primary savings came from displacing the need for 138 million square feet of retail space, the equivalent of 735 big-box retail stores, the attendant retail warehousing space, and the associated emissions from their operations.[74]

A Very Different Future

For all of the reasons listed in this chapter, how we move people and stuff around is likely to change dramatically, and much else will change in consequence. Transport choices have driven the design of cities and suburbs; helped determine where we live, work, and shop; even how we interact with our neighbors and neighborhoods. Much of our life is structured around how to move and store cars. Relatively little attention is given to how to create delightful communal spaces in which we live and interact. In many of the world's cities, gridlock, smog, and sprawl erode quality of life. Where the car culture predominates, anyone too young, old, or infirm to drive is relegated to second-class citizenship.

In *Suburban Nation: The Rise of Sprawl and the Decline of the American Dream*, the "new urbanists" Andres Duany, Elizabeth Plater-Zyberk, and Jeff Speck ask us to imagine what life could be like if the money that now subsidizes car culture and consequent suburban sprawl were spent to create human-scale, walkable cities with public transport and all of the services that have been squeezed out by subsidized automobility.[75] American taxpayers spend the equivalent of $3.50 in taxes for each gallon of fuel used to underwrite the construction of highways and parking. Add in costs for mitigating air pollution and emergency medical care for vehicle wrecks and the cost rises to $9 a gallon.[76] What else might we do with all that money?

That question is being answered in some of the great cities around the world, as livable-city advocates implement policies to encourage the creation of urban space that is not dominated by cars.

One of the earliest innovations came from Curitiba, Brazil. In 1974, Curitiba introduced, among many improvements, a concept called bus rapid transit (BRT). A hybrid of light rail and buses, BRT designates lanes for buses and encloses and elevates bus stops. The system works like rapid transit, with fares paid on entry into loading enclosures. As the bus arrives, big doors open, everyone gets on or off, and the bus is gone. At rush hour there is one minute between buses. The system has been so successful that it accounts for more than half of all trips in Curitiba and has inspired similar programs in Quito, Bogota, Panama, Mexico City, and even Los Angeles.[77] Interestingly, Bogota helped to finance the development of its BRT system by introducing it as a carbon-reduction project, making the system eligible for carbon credits. Named the first transportation project approved as a UN Clean Development

Mechanism–certified project, BRT is expected to reduce CO_2 by 14.6 million tons over thirty years of operations.[78] Bogota has used its BRT program to expand pedestrian and cycling lanes and to implement a *"pico y placa"* program that allows passenger vehicle owners to use their car every other day. At a cost of $2 million per kilometer instead of $20 million per kilometer for light rail, bus rapid transit is a very cost-effective way to cut carbon, supply transportation, and guide land-use planning.[79]

Congestion pricing—charging cars to enter a city center when it is crowded—and spending the resulting revenues to strengthen public transit is a livable-city approach that has been used in London and Singapore. Some cities have banned cars from entering downtown.[80] This represents a sea change in how millions live and offers opportunities for the forward-thinking. In 2000 the British government began a comprehensive effort to discourage car use by requiring that all new development be accessible by public transit, stating, "Developments comprising jobs, shopping, leisure and services should not be designed and located on the assumption that the car will represent the only realistic means of access for the vast majority of people."[81]

Walkable Cities

Cities that are designed to speed ever greater numbers of cars through them may make it easier to get somewhere else, but are lousy places to live and raise children. As hard as this might be to imagine, no city had cars before the twentieth century, and as oil and carbon constraints worsen, many may find themselves carless in the twenty-first. Such islands as Sark (Channel Islands), Mackinac (Michigan), Hydra (Greece), and, most famously, Venice remain car-free. Many old sections of towns have streets too narrow for cars, and the people who live there have chosen to keep it that way. A growing number of cities are creating more delightful neighborhoods by implementing traffic-calming measures to enhance the ability of people to walk, to bike, and to be safe from cars. At least one suburb has chosen to become essentially entirely car-free.

Vauban, Germany, an upscale suburb of Freiburg, in southwestern

Germany, has all but banned cars. Residents are allowed to own them, but must garage them in a separate facility at the edge of the town, and pay $40,000 for the privilege. The garage also houses car sharing, so that the 70 percent of residents who live there without a car can have access to one when they need it.[82] Built around a tram that runs through the center, Vauban features mixed-use neighborhoods with groceries and services sprinkled around energy-efficient town houses and gardens. Built in 2006, the homes are passive solar structures, needing no heating infrastructure even in cold and cloudy Germany. Many of the 5,500 residents chose to move to Vauban to raise children away from cars, and 57 percent of them sold their car when they moved in.[83] A global organization, World Carfree Network, works to promote Vauban's approach and has sponsored nine Towards Carfree Cities conferences.

Even in the United States, the global center of car dependence, car-free communities are emerging. Quarry Village is a planned community in the East Bay area near San Francisco that would be built to be car-free. Homes would be affordable, net-zero-energy town houses. The almost 1,000-person subdivision would be connected to the Bay Area Rapid Transit system.[84]

Many new developments are connecting to transit without going all the way to banning cars. An annual survey conducted by PricewaterhouseCoopers and the Urban Land Institute found that consumers prefer mixed-use, transit-oriented developments (TODs) centered with access to commuter rail, light rail, heavy rail, streetcar, or electric trolley bus systems.[85]

This should not be surprising. One study found that working families in twenty-eight U.S. metropolitan areas spend about 57 percent of their incomes on the combined costs of housing and transportation. Roughly 28 percent of income is spent for housing and 29 percent for transportation. Although the share of income devoted to housing or transportation varies from area to area, the combined costs of the two expenses are surprisingly constant.[86] This is in part because many people are forced into what Scott Bernstein of the Center for Neighborhood Technologies calls the "drive till you qualify market," meaning accepting the forced trade-off between affordable housing and a long commute.

But if a family moves from an area requiring three cars per household and 35,000 vehicle-miles of travel per year to one where a household needs just one car and has transit access, housing costs may increase by $5,000, but transportation costs will be cut by $12,000, for a net reduction in the cost of living of 18.3 percent. Even moving from a location requiring two cars and 25,000 miles per year to one where the household needs just one reduces costs by 9.4 percent.[87]

Scott Bernstein has run the numbers, showing not only that communities offering mass transit increase their real estate tax base, but also that homes within them hold their value better than does the market at large, even during recession. "Economic success requires the availability of urban amenities such as mass transportation," Bernstein notes.[88]

Christopher Leinberger, a University of Michigan real-estate scholar and the author of *The Option of Urbanism*, confirms that such developments are more desirable to live in. "You've got huge pent-up demand and that pushes up prices." Leinberger reports that walkable urban properties cost on a square-foot basis between 40 and 200 percent more than suburban homes.[89] Conversely, there appears now to be an established link between greater car dependency and mortgage failure. A study reported in *The Journal of Sustainable Real Estate* suggests that mortgage default rates are higher in sprawling, auto-dependent areas. The authors of a report titled "Location Efficiency and Mortgage Default" looked at more than 40,000 mortgages in the Chicago, Jacksonville, and San Francisco metro regions, all of which have struggled with higher-than-average foreclosure rates. Researchers found that areas with high rates of vehicle ownership tended to have higher default rates, after adjusting for income disparities.[90]

Interest in transit-oriented development that maximizes access to mass transit and nonmotorized transportation with centrally located rail or bus stations, surrounded by relatively high-density commercial and residential development, is growing in the United States and around the world.[91] Transit-oriented development will only become more popular, as changes driven by energy costs and climate change sweep communities. This increase in interest is behind the abrupt shift in policy announced by the U.S. transportation secretary, Ray LaHood, when he announced that his department would no longer favor "motorized transportation at the expense of nonmotorized." A few days after speaking at the National Bike Summit in the summer of 2010, LaHood announced the Transportation Department's support for the development of fully integrated transportation networks. It called on states and cities to provide convenient and safe amenities for bikers and walkers. "Walking and biking should not be an afterthought in roadway design."

Bike riders were thrilled. Members of the National Association of Manufacturers were not, and retorted, "Treating bicycles and other non-motorized transportation as equal to motorized transportation would cause an economic catastrophe."[92] But it's not clear that this is true. It would surely come as an enormous surprise to such cities as Amsterdam and Copenhagen, where tens of thousands of people commute each day by bicycle using specially constructed traffic lanes. A 30 percent increase in such nonmotorized travel in the United States would lead to an estimated savings of $163.8 billion per month (nearly $2 trillion dollars a year) that could be used for discretionary purchases. Meanwhile, gridlock costs the average peak period traveler almost forty hours a year in travel delay and costs the United States more than $78 billion each year, according to the Texas Transportation Institute.[93]

In urban areas bike lanes can accommodate seven to twelve times as many people per yard of lane per hour as car lanes—just one reason merchants like bicyclists. Not only do bike lanes allow for more shoppers, but studies have shown that people who bike and walk to an area spend more money than those who drive to the same location.[94]

Which means the bicycle industry is poised to grow. The League of American Bicyclists' 2009 policy research report, "The Economic Benefits of Bicycle Infrastructure Investments," demonstrated that the bicycling industry adds $133 billion a year to the U.S. economy, supports 1.1 million jobs, and generates $17.7 billion in federal, state, and local taxes. A diverse range of companies are positioning themselves to benefit, from manufacturers of electric bikes to Google Maps, which in 2010 added bike directions to its maps.

When it comes to bike travel, once again China is at the forefront. Although its rapidly growing middle class is increasingly interested in acquiring passenger cars, China has a long and storied tradition of commuter cycling, more recently with electric bikes. In 2006, 5 million electric bikes were sold in China. By 2006, electric bike sales topped 15 million.[95] One of China's electric bike leaders is a company named Luyuan—"green power" in Chinese—with 1,800 employees, that sells more than 500,000 electric bikes each year in China and abroad.

Electric bikes are just gaining traction in the West. More than a dozen manufacturers deliver an array of products. There's the $14,000 Optibike carbon fiber model featuring GPS and a performance-monitoring system, and the $1,000 IZIP Twist & Go tricruiser electric tricycle with cargo capacity. Sports enthusiasts can choose the sporty E+ electric mountain bike. Most models retail for under $2,000 and are considered bicycles until their motors exceed 750 watts and their top speed exceeds 20 miles per hour, at which point they are considered cars and must be registered. Do-it-your-selfers can even buy kits to convert their existing bicycles into electrics.[96]

Perhaps the boldest embrace of the potential in commuter cycling is Bicycle Transportation Systems of Colorado, which has developed the Transglide 2000, an enclosed cycling system that, the maker claims, leads to a 90 percent increase in efficiency by removing the cyclist from the elements and providing a constant directional tailwind.

Conclusion

Moving people and stuff is a major source of carbon emissions. The way we have chosen to do it—with cars, trucks, and planes—also forces cities to develop in unappealing ways. It is time to imagine a different future. Cities like Vauban offer a vision of a superior way of living and getting around. Entrepreneurs are showing that we can still drive and fly, but in ways that solve the climate crisis. It is clear that applying more imagination to the problems facing us is an important part of Climate Capitalism.

But a cautionary tale of the future of transportation comes from Douglas Adams's novel *The Restaurant at the End of the Universe*:

The trouble with most forms of transport, he thought, is basically one of them not being worth all the bother. On Earth—when there had been an Earth, before it was demolished to make way for a new hyperspace bypass—the problem had been with cars. The disadvantages involved in pulling lots of black sticky slime from out of the ground where it had been safely hidden out of harm's way, turning it into tar to cover the land with, smoke to fill the air with and pouring the rest into the sea, all seemed to outweigh the advantages of being able to get more quickly from one place to another—particularly when the place you arrived at had probably become, as a result of this, very similar to the place you had left, i.e., covered with tar, full of smoke and short of fish.

And what of matter transference beams? Any form of transport which involved tearing you apart atom by atom, flinging those atoms through the sub-ether, and then jamming them back together again just when they were getting their first taste of freedom for years had to be bad news.[97]

7

Growing a Better World

Thomas Jefferson wrote in a letter to George Washington that "agriculture is our wisest pursuit, because it will in the end, contribute the most to real wealth . . . and happiness."[1] Were he alive today, Jefferson would be sorely disappointed with the state of American, and global, agriculture. According to the National Institutes of Health, four of the six leading causes of death in the United States are linked to unhealthy diets. The way food is grown is unsustainable, what we eat today is less nutritious than the same foods used to be, and our meals are often toxic. Exposure to pesticides, antibiotics, hormones, and other chemicals laced throughout our food supply is increasingly linked to such conditions as ADD, ADHD, antibiotic resistance, and early onset of puberty, as well as diseases such as cancer and diabetes.[2] Oh, yes, and all of this is contributing to climate change.

The connections between agriculture and climate change are numerous: fossil fuel–dependent agricultural practices; poor land-use choices; toxic chemicals; the energy used in manufacturing, refrigeration, food processing, transportation, packaging, and retailing; and the lost ability to feed ourselves with locally produced food all contribute. A report by the Union of Concerned Scientists concluded, "The currently dominant system of industrial agriculture—which voters and taxpayers have unknowingly promoted and subsidized through ill-considered government food and farm policy choices—uses huge amounts of water, energy, and chemicals, often with little regard to long-term adverse effects." The report cited inefficient irrigation systems, farming practices that leach chemical fertilizers and insecticides into ground and surface waters and spread oxygen-depleting microorganisms that disrupt ecosystems and kill fish, and the unmanageable mountains of waste that are the hallmarks of industrial-style CAFOs (confined animal-feeding operations).[3] Such problems are not confined to the West. Huge algae blooms threaten the health of China's lakes, and according to a 2010 report released by the Chinese government, half of the pollutants that are poisoning the country's waterways come from agriculture.[4]

Modern industrial agriculture is part of a broken, negative feedback loop in which agricultural practices contribute significantly to global warming, and then agricultural yields are put at risk by those changes in the climate. The mere process of converting wildlands around the planet to agricultural uses releases 5,900 million tons of CO_2-equivalent gases into the atmosphere each year, more than the total annual emissions of the United States.[5] Clearing land for agriculture and ranching, responsible for 97 percent of deforestation in Latin America, 94 percent in Southeast Asia, and 90 percent in Africa, not only breaks up the soil, but releases the carbon that the trees in the forest had sequestered, thereby keeping it out of the atmosphere.[6]

Michael Pollan, a leading writer and advocate for sustainable food systems, stated in a letter entitled "Farmer in Chief" that he sent to President Obama shortly before his election:

Whenever farmers clear land for crops and till the soil, large quantities of carbon are released into the air. But the 20th-century industrialization of agriculture has increased the amount of greenhouse gases emitted by the food system by an order of magnitude; chemical fertilizers (made from natural gas), pesticides (made from petroleum), farm ma-

chinery, modern food processing and packaging and transportation
have together transformed a system that in 1940 produced 2.3 calories
of food energy for every calorie of fossil-fuel energy it used into one
that now takes 10 calories of fossil-fuel energy to produce a single calorie of modern supermarket food.[7]

Remember the tales told by the first settlers who plowed the American Great Plains of their awe as they turned over dense black soil ten
feet deep? After 20 years of intense conventional tillage, most agricultural soils lose 50 percent of their soil carbon.[8] And after 150 years of
unsustainable agricultural practices, that carbon-rich soil has been reduced to mere inches. The tripling of world grain production over the
past fifty years has come at a high cost.

At the same time that modern agriculture is worsening climate
change, many organizations are concerned that, unchecked, climate
change will destroy humankind's tenuous ability to feed itself. For every
1°C rise in temperature above the norm, yields of wheat, rice, and corn
drop 10 percent. This is scary, given that more than a billion people in
the world already suffer from malnutrition.[9] In 2010, the hottest year yet
on record, record floods on three continents and unprecedented heat
and drought in Russia led to soaring wheat prices. In July 2010, grain
prices rose by 66 percent, Russia banned wheat exports, and the World
Bank called for action to prevent disastrous global food shortages.[10]

These types of events had long been predicted. In 2007 James Spellman, consultant with the United Nations Foundation, warned the
World Agricultural Forum,

> Climate change has an impact on prosperity. If climate change is not
> mitigated or understood early enough, the ability of a country to gener-
> ate a livelihood may be impacted by increased disease, new pest pat-
> terns, diseases that plants weren't accustomed to in northern regions.
> It's a profound re-engineering of the entire agricultural system.[11]

Sir Gordon Conway, former head of the Rockefeller Foundation and
chief scientist of the UK's Department for International Development,

issued an even bleaker warning for Africa in 2009. Observing that the continent is already warming faster than global averages, Professor Conway stated that Africa will be hit especially hard with droughts, floods, storm surges, crop failures, and hunger. "Projected reductions in crop yields could be as much as 50 percent by 2020 and 90 percent by 2100," he stated.[12]

U.S. Secretary of Agriculture Tom Vilsack optimistically stated that "Agriculture is the foundation on which recovery from the global recession and financial and food price crisis will be built, especially for developing countries which derive much of their income from agricultural production."[13] Perhaps. But only if agriculture changes dramatically. As with the sectors described in previous chapters, much about the way we now conduct agriculture—even if it did not threaten the climate— is not contributing to greater human happiness and is not even good business.

The good news is that fundamental economic factors are already driving many of the necessary changes. Implemented intelligently, measures to transform farming can enhance profits and make the sector a major contributor to the climate solution. This will be Climate Capitalism at its best.

What's Wrong with Conventional Agriculture?

The bad news is that this prospect is far from being realized just yet. Michael Pollan, the author of the bestselling *Omnivore's Dilemma*, observed that the U.S. food system now uses 16 to 19 percent of the fossil fuels consumed in the country and accounts for slightly more greenhouse gas emissions. He went on to describe the industrial-food system as one in which "we are eating oil and spewing greenhouse gases."[14]

The U.S. Department of Agriculture disagrees with his accounting of fossil fuel consumption in the food system, counting only direct fuel to arrive at an agricultural energy use of a little over 1 percent of the fossil fuels used in the United States.[15] The Earth Policy Institute points out, however, "The U.S. food system uses over 10 quadrillion Btu (10,551 quadrillion Joules) of energy each year, as much as France's total annual energy consumption. Food is an energy intensive business, but growing it only accounts for one fifth of this."[16] Much of the rest is used in fertilizer manufacturing and in the diesel and gasoline used by farm vehicles to plant, till, and harvest crops. These account for 28 and 34 percent, respectively, of the energy used in agriculture.[17]

Fertilizer use is often the largest part of a product's carbon footprint. When PepsiCo analyzed the carbon burden of the value chain of its Tropicana brand orange juice, it was stunned to find that the single largest source of carbon emissions derived not from processing, packaging, and transporting the juice, but from the use of nitrogen fertilizer to grow the oranges. The energy it took to produce the fertilizer made this the single largest source of carbon in the life cycle of juice. [18] Shifting to organic production, and thus eliminating the use of artificial fertilizer, would cut the carbon footprint of its product. Instead, PepsiCo chose the high-tech route of using ground sensors to control water and fertilizer pumps to cut its costs and its carbon footprint.[19]

But fertilizer accounts for only 21 percent of overall food-system energy use. Here, the word "system" is key; the food system encompasses all that we as a society do to supply ourselves with a meal or a snack. The Earth Policy Institute found that roughly 32 percent of the food system's energy requirement is gobbled by home refrigeration and food preparation. Processing food—drying it, canning it, freezing it—uses 16 percent, while almost 14 percent of total energy use in the food system goes to food transport—equal to two thirds of the energy used to grow the food. The energy used in packaging and in running retail stores, restaurants, and caterers accounts for the remaining roughly 18 percent.[20]

In 2004, the United Nations' Intergovernmental Panel on Climate Change estimated that global agriculture contributes 13.5 percent of global greenhouse gases, and a recent Greenpeace announcement placed agriculture's greenhouse gas contribution as high as 32 percent (this included both direct and indirect emissions from farming, land-use impacts, transportation, packaging, and processing).[21] Vegetarians provocatively claim that producing red meat, dairy products, chickens, fish, and eggs accounts for 58 percent of these food-related emissions.[22] A 2006 UN report concluded that livestock raising was responsible for 18 percent of global greenhouse gases.[23]

In 2010, however, UN scientists acknowledged that claims of the impact of meat production were flawed. Analysts had included impacts common to all industrial activities but had not counted those when analyzing the footprint of any other sector.[24] The numbers also counted as a contributor to climate change the clearing of forestland in the Amazon for cattle ranching. The UN promised a revised report, but none has yet emerged.

Whatever the exact figures, industrial meat production drives the emission of significant amounts of climate-destroying gases. Many critics of the meat industry point to the harm done by methane, a particularly potent greenhouse gas that is produced by enteric formation (burping and flatulence) from cattle (1,792 million tons of CO_2-equivalent gases each year).[25] This argument fails to take into account that cows aren't really adding more methane to the planet so much as cycling what's already above ground. Methane emissions from enteric fermentation represent the transformation of carbon already in circulation between the earth and the atmosphere. The number of ungulates roaming the planet today is not significantly larger than the herds of prehistoric bison and other ungulates. Sorry, the real issue is the burning of fossil carbon, causing a net increase in atmospheric carbon concentrations.[26]

Agriculture's real impact, whether from meat or vegetable or grain production, depends totally on the production methods used. There are dramatically more sustainable ways of growing our food—producing vegetables, grains, meat, and fiber.

Jonathan White, a proprietor of Bobolink Dairy & Bakehouse, producers of 100 percent grass-fed cheeses and wood-fired breads, describes the difference between feeding cattle grass, their natural diet, and grain, as in feedlots. He points out,

> Grain-fed cattle produce much higher-energy waste than grass-fed cows, who ferment out most of the fermentable carbs, leaving mostly just lig-

nan behind. Grain- or silage-fed cattle's waste is pretty rich stuff, with a lot of protein as well as carb bypassing. Drive down past a 2,000-cow feedlot in Los Banos in the Central Valley [of California] some fine day, and you'll smell what I mean. But there is also the issue of the carbon released by the growing of the grain, specifically the massive amount of coal or oil needed to make the electric power to fix synthetic nitrogen. Grasses' leguminous fellow travelers [such as clovers that live among grasses] fix nitrogen for free, from sunlight.[27]

He's right about grain feeding versus pasture feeding. Unfortunately, the 95 million conventionally raised cattle in the United States are taken off the pastures where they were healthy, and "finished" in concentrated animal-feeding operations, or CAFOs. There they ingest grain and oil crops such as soy—food that grazing animals with their multiple stomachs were never designed to eat—to fatten them for slaughter. Half of all the agricultural land in the world is used to grow oil and grain crops to feed cattle.[28] In 2008, 70 to 80 percent of grains grown and acreage farmed was used to produce America's 11 billion meat, milk, and egg-laying animals, 95 percent of which were raised in confinement. This includes nearly 69 million pigs, 300 million commercial laying hens in battery cages, 10 billion meat chickens, and half a billion turkeys that live in abusively close quarters. In addition, about 33 million beef cows and 9.7 million dairy cows are confined in crowded feedlots or dairy barns that foster diseases. A 2008 study by *Consumer Reports* found that 83 percent of the 525 meat chickens tested had salmonella or campylobacter. Deadly diseases were found in 63 percent of chickens tested.[29]

Michael Pollan describes such operations as "vast cities of animals in confinement." The preconditions making such operations possible, he says, are, first, the agricultural subsidies that enable operators to buy grain for less than it costs to grow it and, second, FDA approval for the profligate use of prophylactic antibiotics and hormones, "without which the animals in these places could not survive their crowded, filthy and miserable existence. There is nothing inherently efficient or economical" about these operations, he concludes. "The F.D.A. should ban the routine use of antibiotics in livestock feed on public-health grounds, now that we have evidence that the practice is leading to the evolution of drug-resistant bacterial diseases and to outbreaks of *E. coli* and salmonella poisoning. CAFOs should also be regulated like the factories they are, required to clean up their waste like any other industry or municipality."[30]

Raising beef this way also reduces its nutritional value. Cattle are intended by nature to eat grass; fattening them on soybeans and corn so that they bulk up faster reduces levels of beta-carotene, vitamin E, omega-3s, conjugated linoleic acid (CLA), calcium, magnesium, and potassium in the meat.[31] The University of California Cooperative Extension and California State University–Chico, under a grant from the W. K. Kellogg Foundation, studied the health benefits of raising cattle exclusively on grass. A literature review of fifty-five articles, letters, websites, and commentaries by scientists representing a wide variety of institutions found that ranchers who produce grass-fed cattle may rightfully claim that their product is more healthful than conventionally produced meat.[32]

Plant-based agriculture is a climate change driver as well. Soil that has been decarbonized requires intensive amounts of artificial fertilizer to enable it to grow "industrial" crops. Producing and using all of the petrochemicals in fertilizer releases even more carbon and other greenhouse gases, especially nitrous oxide, a gas three hundred times more potent per ton than carbon dioxide in causing global warming.[33] Plowing and poor nutrient management then releases the nitrogen from soils in substantial quantities.

To understand why all this is a problem, let's do a little soil and health science. Nitrogen is necessary for life, and is a key component of DNA and the other building blocks of life. But people and other animals cannot obtain the nitrogen that they need just by breathing it in. They have to eat it. In its molecular form (N_2), it is an inert element. To be biologically available it must be converted to nitrate (NO_3), ammonium (NH_4), or organic nitrogen ($[NH_2]_2CO$), otherwise known as plant protein. Biologically available nitrogen enters the soil naturally when lightning oxidizes atmospheric nitrogen and rain brings it to the ground. Leguminous plants such as clover also "fix" atmospheric nitrogen in the soil, using rhizobium soil microbes that live in a symbiotic relationship with the roots of these plants. The microbes break down the N_2 into forms usable by plants. Animals get the nitrogen that they require by eating plants.[34]

In healthy soil, other microbes convert any excess organic nitrogen, or the nitrogen that enters the soil when living things decay, back into N_2, completing the nitrogen cycle.[35] When the nitrogen cycle is in balance, this is a normal function. But artificial fertilization upsets this balance, and excessive use of artificial nitrogen drives the cycle ever faster, resulting in excess nitrogen in the soil.[36]

Excess nitrogen in the soil fuels the microbes that convert organic nitrogen back into N_2 gas and release it into the atmosphere. Nitrous oxide (N_2O), a by-product of synthetic fertilizer and manure from CAFOs and other industrial processes, is a very potent greenhouse gas, and is also now the number one threat to the ozone layer. N_2O is not regulated by the Montreal Protocol on Substances That Deplete the Ozone Layer, meaning there is no global effort to reduce its emissions.[37]

The reactive forms of nitrogen in fertilizer are also frequently washed from the soil, winding up in drinking water, where they poison farm animals and humans.

The best hope for control of these substances and their effects on climate change is a conversion to sustainable agriculture, which is a good idea anyway. Again, agriculture as currently practiced is putting the climate at risk, which, left unchecked, will destroy much of industrial agriculture as it is currently being practiced. Changing temperatures and precipitation levels will affect yields.[38] As the summer of 2010 showed, droughts, desertification, and floods will all worsen the ability of the planet's people to feed themselves.[39]

Dr. Stephen Chu, U.S. secretary of energy, in a 2009 interview on climate risks, stated, "You're looking at a scenario where there's no more agriculture in California. When you lose 70 percent of your water in the mountains, I don't see how agriculture can continue. California produces 20 percent of the agriculture in the United States. I don't actually see how they can keep their cities going."[40]

Chu's warning was corroborated by a 2009 study released by the National Academy of Sciences. Researchers predicted that climate change would lead to a 20 percent reduction in runoff from the snowmelt that feeds the Colorado River basin by 2050; and Colorado River water is already overallocated.[41] In that case nearly nine of every ten scheduled deliveries of water from the Colorado River basin would be missed, a particular problem because the Colorado basin allotments were set forth during the twentieth century at a time when the region was wetter than studies suggest was actually normal. If climate change forces drier conditions, delivery shortfalls will be even greater than predicted.[42]

Climate deniers have opined that increasing the CO_2 on the planet would be good for plant growth. Unfortunately, research warns that increased carbon dioxide levels may actually inhibit crop growth, instead of accelerating it as was previously believed.[43] Except weeds. Weeds like increased CO_2.

There are, however, ways to use agricultural land that are much less carbon-intensive than conventional agriculture, and are more profitable, too.[44]

It's Possible

There are ways to conduct agriculture that return carbon from the air to the soil, making sustainable agriculture a significant part of the solution. A new, sustainable relationship between agriculture and the climate can be created, and as with Climate Capitalism generally, it will be more profitable. If humans are to sustain and expand food production and security, agriculture must be transformed to mitigate climate change, not worsen it. An unlikely example shows how a profound transformation in agricultural practice is indeed possible.

In 1990, an island nation that was more than 57 percent reliant on foreign oil, pesticides, and food imports for its population's caloric intake found itself suddenly bereft of its external support. Out of necessity, the government launched an organic revolution that had to double food production without access to fossil fuel, while cutting imports by more than half, even while producing sufficient export crop to keep the country's foreign exchange afloat.[45]

The nation turned to its scientific infrastructure for needed technology and for human resources, and substituted native technology for the energy-intensive inputs that were no longer available to it. Farmers combined biopesticides and biofertilizers (locally made microbial pesticides and fertilizers that are nontoxic to humans) with earthworm culture, waste recycling, biological pest control, composting, and other sustainable practices. This enabled them to avert a catastrophic shortfall of food and sustain the population. Localized organic food production, the basis of what the government called the "Alternative Model" of farming, promoted "ecologically sustainable production" by replacing the dependence on heavy farm machinery and chemical inputs with traditional practices of animal traction, crop and pasture rotation, soil conservation, organic soil inputs, and biological pest control. Rural populations were reincorporated into agriculture, not just as labor but as experts. Their knowledge of traditional farming techniques helped generate new, more effective technologies. The model not only helped stem the flood of rural migrants to cities, but provided the nation with food security.

The transformation was undertaken for survival, not ideological reasons, and it worked. You haven't heard about it because the nation is Cuba. Cuba's way of life had been subsidized by the Soviet Union, which paid premium prices for sugar and supplied Cuba with cheap oil. With the fall of the Soviet Union in 1989–90, Cuba's way of life ended. As its agricultural system, previously sustained by cheap Soviet oil and food, collapsed and the U.S. tightened its embargo, Cuba faced catastrophe.[46]

By 1993 all state farms, previously covering 80 percent of the nation's farmland, had been privatized into employee-owned shareholder enterprises. Farmers' markets and free-market pricing, experimented with and abandoned for ideological reasons in the 1980s, were reinstated, to rave reviews from shoppers. Organic, locally based farming became the norm in a country that had previously prided itself on having the most industrialized, chemical-intensive agricultural sector in Latin America.[47]

What Cuba accomplished the globe must now achieve. The end of cheap oil and impending carbon and resource constraints will make the transition to sustainable agriculture an imperative for all of the world's people.

Organic farms tend to be more energy-efficient than conventional operations. An extensive study begun in 1978 by the Swiss government found organic farms to be 20 to 56 percent more energy-efficient than conventional agriculture.[48] Flex Your Power, a California partnership promoting energy efficiency, found that organic farms are 50 percent more energy efficient than conventional farms.[49] A UK government study found that "organic systems had a lower energy input largely because of an absence of indirect energy inputs in the form of nitrogen fertilizer." Compared to conventional agriculture, the study estimated, scientific field comparisons showed that large organic arable production used 35 percent less energy per unit of production, and organic dairy operations used 74 percent less. An organic apple orchard plot produced superior apples, greater profitability, and greater energy productivity than a conventional adjacent plot.[50]

Fortunately, many studies have shown that it is possible to feed even a growing population by means of organic, low-carbon-production techniques.[51]

Agricultural scientists at the University of California–Davis reviewed 154 growing seasons' worth of data on various crops grown on rain-fed and irrigated land in the United States. They found that organic corn and organic soybean yields were 94 percent of conventional yields, and organic wheat yields were 97 percent. Organic tomatoes showed no yield difference.[52] A study by researchers at the University of Michigan also found that in developed countries, yields were almost equal on organic and conventional farms. In developing countries, interestingly, food production could double or triple when organic methods were used. This is because farmers in developing countries cannot afford carbon-intensive fertilizer, machines, and other artificial inputs anyway, and a shift to organic production would result in higher yields than less-sophisticated attempts at conventional mechanized agriculture.[53]

In 2007 the Food and Agriculture Organization (FAO) of the United Nations recognized this, stating explicitly that organic agriculture can meet local and global food security challenges. Noting that conventional agriculture, together with deforestation and rangeland burning, are responsible for 30 percent of the CO_2 and 90 percent of nitrous oxide emissions worldwide, the report concluded that a worldwide shift to organic agriculture can fight world hunger and at the same time tackle climate change. Evidence presented to the FAO by the Danish Research Centre for Food and Farming confirmed the potential of organic farming to provide more than enough food to feed the world, while cutting environmental impacts. Studies by the Food Policy Research Institute showed that a 50 percent conversion to organic farming in sub-Saharan Africa would enhance food security, help feed the hungry, and reduce the need to import subsidized food. At the same time, it would produce a diverse range of certified organic surpluses that could be exported at premium profit.[54]

Along with requiring less energy and providing greater security, such methods are also more profitable.[55] Economic analyses by the University of Maryland showed comparable returns in organic systems even without calculating the price premium for organic foods (which command higher prices on the free market). In recent years, price premiums for organic grains have varied from 35 to 240 percent, offering great opportunity to wean farmers from price support subsidies.[56]

In *The Omnivore's Dilemma*, Michael Pollan profiled the financial and personal successes of the Salatin family of Polyface Farm. As described at the Polyface website, in 1961 the Salatins set out to farm on what had been described as the Shenandoah Valley's most worn-out, eroded, abused property, in Staunton, Virginia. Disregarding conventional wisdom, the Salatins embraced low-carbon sustainable agricultural practices on their land. They planted trees, built huge compost piles, dug ponds, and rotated cows to different fields using portable electric fencing, raising all their animals using perennial prairie polycultures of grasses.[57] Producing sought-after meat, eggs, and forest products, Polyface Farm is today a financial and agricultural success, validating the family's mission to develop emotionally, economically, and environmentally balanced agricultural practices.

They are not alone in this endeavor. TK Ranch, in Alberta, Canada, raises cattle fed on certified organic pastureland. Use of pesticides, herbicides, and feeding animals with animal by-products, growth hormones, and doses of antibiotics are all banned. The ranch uses "low-stress" techniques throughout the animal's life cycle, including roundups, weaning, and finally the meat slaughtering process. The flavor of its premium meat—sold directly to organic and natural-food markets and high-end restaurants such as the Banff Springs Resort—is intensified by dry aging for twenty-one days, rather than the usual twenty-four to thirty-six hours that regular commercial beef gets. The bottom line: even with the closing of the American border to Canadian cattle ranchers from a mad cow disease scare, the TK Ranch is thriving.[58]

Allan Savory, the creator of Holistic Management, the approach used by TK Ranch, teaches his methods at the Savory Institute, located in Albuquerque, New Mexico. His institute works to restore the vast grasslands of the world through the teaching and practice of Holistic Management and Holistic Decision Making. The institute's worldwide consulting and training activities enable practitioners to turn deserts into thriving grasslands, restore biodiversity, bring streams, rivers, and water sources back to life, and combat poverty and hunger, all while working to brake global climate change. Holistically managing grazing animals is, it turns out, one of the best ways to reclaim depleted land. It is also one of the more important ways to recarbonize the soil and sequester greenhouse gases.

Savory points out that even achieving zero emissions from fossil fuels will not avert major catastrophe from climate change, because grassland and savanna burning will continue and desertification will accelerate as soils become increasingly unable to store carbon or water.[59] To avert disaster, Savory argues, a global strategy is required that cuts carbon emissions by substituting benign energy sources for fossil fuels and implementing effective livestock management practices. Only the latter can deal with biodiversity loss and biomass burning and reverse desertification that is not caused by atmospheric carbon buildup.[60]

In 2010 the Buckminster Fuller Challenge Award recognized Savory's decades of work. His Operation Hope, a combined effort of the Africa Centre for Holistic Management in Zimbabwe and the Savory Institute, is transforming degraded Zimbabwe grasslands and savannas into lush pastures with ponds and flowing streams, and demonstrating how this approach to climate protection also enhances African agricultural livelihoods. The Buckminster Fuller Challenge Award, which recognizes initiatives that take a "comprehensive, anticipatory, design approach to radically advance human well being and the health of our planet's ecosystems," selected Savory's work to accelerate the development and deployment of whole-systems solutions to climate change and sustainable development. Operation Hope's demonstrated success in land management contradicts accepted practice and theories of letting land rest after animal grazing. Instead, Savory's Holistic Management process reestablishes the symbiotic balance between plant growth and herd animals. On over 30 million acres around the globe this practice is helping land managers bioremediate barren land back into thriving grasslands, and increase crop yields to ensure food security for people.

A growing number of cattle operations are moving to more sustainable practices, from the grazing techniques just described to implementing systems to use manure in more climate-friendly ways.[61] The Mason Dixon Farm in Gettysburg, Pennsylvania, is a pioneer in this practice, capturing the methane produced by its 2,300 Holstein milk cows and 1,700 replacement heifers. Operating with the motto "Change is inevitable, success is optional," they have found that climate protection activities are also more profitable than conventional farming. The farm is a sophisticated dairy business that includes two thousand acres of crops that supply the forage needs of its cows, which produce more than 30 million pounds of milk a year.

A family business, Mason Dixon is headed by Richard Waybright, whose grandchildren are the ninth generation to live and work on the farm. Waybright and his team have realized a number of impressive achievements. For decades visitors have marveled at how the farm responded to the energy crisis of the late 1970s by using "cow power" to make the farm energy-self-sufficient. Since 1977, the farm staff has designed and built all new buildings to house the herd, including a barn passively heated by sunlight in which five hundred cows are free to move about. In 1979, Mason Dixon Farms began operating the first plug-flow anaerobic digester at a commercial farm. This device captures methane emissions from cattle manure and uses it to produce energy.

In recent years such practices became eligible for carbon offsets, but Mason Dixon made the practice profitable long before the availability of carbon credits.[62]

Since the late 1970s, the farm has produced enough electricity for its own operations, dramatically cutting operating costs, and sold excess energy to the grid, increasing farm revenues. Today, three digesters turn manure to biogas that fuels five generator sets that reliably produce power. Recovered heat from the engines is circulated as heated water through the digester to increase biogas production, estimated at 120,000 cubic feet of gas per day, and to warm drinking water for the cows, increasing milk production. Excess heat keeps the buildings on the farm comfortable. The composted manure provides superior bedding for the cows, and eliminates the need to buy commercial bedding, while the digester solids are sold as soil amendment, increasing revenues. The nutrient-rich slurry is spread on the silage fields in which silage crops are grown, decreasing the need for commercial fertilizers and lime, increasing crop yields, and cutting irrigation needs in dry periods. Richard Waybright sums up the integrated system, saying, "Our farm has been 'cow powered' since 1979. Our cows not only provide the public with a healthy and wholesome product, they provide our farm with our electricity needs."[63]

Such whole-systems farming uses the complementary interactions among land, cattle, pigs, and chickens to almost completely eliminate external inputs, and produce healthier animals, milk, and meat in the process. Cutting dependence on external inputs shields farmers from increasingly volatile fuel prices, too. Vermont farmers, always an independent bunch, have long seen the wisdom of this. As their numbers decline (from 2,500 dairy farms in 1993 to 1,400 in 2010) they have adopted more sustainable strategies for survival. Some are switching to organic production. Ordinary milk sells for $12 a hundredweight, while organic produce brings at least $30 a hundredweight. The Blue Spruce dairy in Bridport, Vermont, is using the Mason Dixon system with its thousand Holstein cattle. Installing the anaerobic digestion electricity system cost Blue Spruce $1.3 million, but now it enables them to sell $120,000 worth of electricity a year, for a seven-year payback. The electricity produced on the farm would power four hundred homes, but it is being bought by nearby Green Mountain College, which is eager to cut its own carbon footprint.[64]

Organic Agriculture Sequesters Carbon

More sustainable agriculture can also increase the amount of carbon that is held in the soil. Studies conducted over many years by the University of California–Davis, the Rodale Institute (an organic farm institute in Kutztown, Pennsylvania), and others have shown that such practices increase (not just maintain) the quantity of soil-held carbon through a variety of mechanisms.[65] Farming operations that use more natural agricultural practices that do not rely on such chemical inputs as artificial fertilizers, pesticides, and herbicides have higher levels of beneficial soil fungi. Mycorrhizal fungi help the soil build organic (carbon) matter. Because these operations do not use chemical pesticides and support more diverse habitats, farms using crop rotations and animal manure also enjoy higher biodiversity than fields farmed with industrial agricultural practices and monocultures. Organic fields also have reduced nitrogen runoff and release of nitrous oxide.[66] Numerous studies show that systems that integrate livestock with vegetable production, use perennial pastureland, and use organic production techniques (including long crop rotations, planting leguminous crops and cover crops, use of manure produced by livestock as fertilizer) improve soil carbon retention, reduce pollution, and deliver higher profitability.[67]

Combining no-till agriculture (farming without plowing) with organic agriculture sequesters carbon in the soil even better. This conclusion was supported by the twenty-seven-year-long (and still running) Farming Systems Trial, the most extensive side-by-side comparison of organic and conventional corn and soybean production systems in the United States. A joint project of the Rodale Institute, land grant universities, federal researchers, and academics, the study has developed a scientific database and generated numerous academic papers.[68]

Working in conjunction with Cornell University (a land grant university), the Rodale Institute has shown that diversified organic agriculture using cover crops can reduce fossil fuel energy use by 33 to 50 percent compared with conventional agriculture systems and by 75 percent compared with conventional tillage farming.[69] The test plot that was organically managed showed an increase of over 30 percent in soil organic matter and 15 percent in soil nitrogen over the twenty-seven years of testing so far. The Rodale Institute has gone further, combining the advantages of organic production with an innovative organic no-till system.[70] Such systems increase the soil's ability to hold moisture and cut soil erosion, so that in dry years organic corn and soybean yields exceeded those raised through conventional practices by 28 to 75 percent.[71] Why? Because each kilogram of organic soil can absorb twenty times its weight in water. The presence of increased organic soil matter opens the structure of the soil surface, increasing water percolation by 25 to 50 percent over soil that lacks comparable tilth.[72]

The organic and no-till approach enables soil to sequester two to three times the amounts of atmospheric carbon, over 1,000 kilograms per hectare per year, compared with conventional no-till agriculture, which sequesters 370 kilograms per hectare per year.[73] This process of capturing atmospheric carbon as organic matter in the soil contributes to improved soil quality and productivity. The Rodale Institute's modern compost technology can increase soil carbon sequestration by more than 2,000 to 3,000 kilos per hectare per year (roughly 7,000 pounds of CO_2 per acre per year). If the sequestration rates recorded in the Rodale test sites were achieved on all 434 million acres of cropland in the United States, nearly 1.6 billion tons of carbon dioxide would be sequestered each year, or close to a quarter of the total 2006 U.S. fossil fuel emissions. Put differently, every two acres put under organic management is the equivalent of taking one car off the road.[74]

These conclusions have since been strengthened by European research showing that applying organic fertilizers such as compost to agricultural land could increase the amount of carbon stored in these soils and contribute significantly to the reduction of greenhouse gas emissions.

By one estimate, using only 20 percent of the surface of agricultural land in the EU as a sink for carbon would sequester about 8.6 percent of the total EU emissions-reduction objective.[75]

The market for organic produce continues to grow. In 2002 the U.S. organic market was worth $9 billion a year. Between 2000 and 2007 the industry had a compound annual growth rate of 18 percent, and by 2008 it had risen to an annual value of $24.6 billion.[76] Although rates slowed in 2008 with the economic collapse, organics still experienced well over twice the overall growth rate of the whole food and beverage industry.[77] Organics are now a $60 billion-a-year global market, and this figure is projected to rise to $96.5 billion by 2014.[78]

In 2008, 5 million hectares (2 million acres) of agricultural land were certified organic, up from 3 million hectares (1.2 million acres) in 2007. Growth was strongest in Latin America and Europe. Globally, there are almost 1.4 million organic producers.[79] By 2010, 35 million hectares (14 million acres) of land were managed organically around the world, by almost 1.4 million producers, with more than a third of organic producers in Africa. On a global level, the organic agricultural land area increased in all regions, in total by almost 3 million hectares (1.2 million acres), or 9 percent, compared to 2007.[80]

Conventional Agriculture Cuts Carbon Loss and Enhances Profitability, Too

Conventional agriculture practitioners are also finding ways to cut carbon and reduce their negative impacts, even though their gains are not as impressive as those achievable with the organic approach. Conventional no-till farming, or "direct seeding," cuts the loss of soil carbon caused by plowing. It also cuts costs. With direct seeding the soil is broken only in narrow strips as "openers" place fertilizer and seed into the soil. Farmers who have practiced direct seeding report requiring 30 percent less nitrogen fertilizer to grow the same amount of crop as a conventional grower. No-till farming, a practice common with dry land, results in as much as 25 percent more water retention in the soil. Irrigated no-till farmers need to apply less water and gain increased "water transmissibility."[81]

The Pacific Northwest Direct Seed Association (PNDSA), an agricultural group in the Palouse region of eastern Washington and western Idaho, has been aggregating commitments by its farmers to practice direct seeding and then selling credits for the carbon retained from this approach through the Chicago Climate Exchange.[82] Founded in 2000 by farmers and university researchers in Oregon, Washington, and Idaho, PNDSA in 2002 became the first farm group in North America to compile and register a listing of direct-seed acres available for purchases of carbon offsets. Members committed to direct-seed these acres for ten years. The resulting "stored carbon" was then marketed as a lease to Entergy, an electricity-generating company willing to pay the growers to offset Entergy's CO_2 emissions. Grower contracts were completed and money transferred to the producers in November 2002. To secure the value of the carbon sequestered in the soil, Entergy contracted to lease an annual trade of 3,000 tons of CO_2 sequestered for ten years. PNDSA was paid $75,000 to aggregate its growers for the duration of the sequestration project. PNDSA contracted with seventy-seven members farming 6,470 production acres to meet this obligation. PNDSA then paid growers to direct-seed their designated acreage over the ten years, sequestering over half a ton of CO_2 per acre per year. PNDSA now represents grower-members farming over 600,000 acres in the Pacific Northwest and Montana.

This is essentially free money for the farmers. With direct seeding the residues from the prior crops are left in the field, increasing soil fertility and providing higher yields. The practice cuts such input costs as water, labor, equipment, and fuel. This means saving 3.5 gallons an acre, or 1,750 gallons on a 500-acre farm, and keeping between 0.5 and 0.66 tons per acre of CO_2 per year out of the atmosphere, equal to not burning about a twenty-gallon tank of gasoline per acre per year. It reduces soil erosion by up to 90 percent and surface runoff by up to 69 percent, cutting sedimentation 93 percent. This is important, as agricultural runoff, usually carrying fossil fuel–based fertilizer, has already created over 60 dead zones in the world's oceans, places where the high nitrogen levels have spawned algae blooms that strip that region of the ocean of sufficient oxygen to support life. Preventing runoff also reduces the need to dredge streambeds and clean irrigation ditches, which in turn enhances water quality and wildlife habitat. Because of the reduced amount of work, farmers can practice direct seeding on more acreage and because the unbroken soil holds more water they can use less irrigation. But what has garnered attention and money is the ability of direct seeding to increase the soil's organic content and thus increase the carbon content of the soil by one ton per hectare per year or more.

The project is externally monitored and verified by local National Resource Conservation Service Districts. It complies with the Kyoto Protocols, providing additionality, duration, permanence, and no leakage. Additionality means that the carbon sequestered is in addition to any that would have been sequestered under a "business as usual" scenario. Permanence means that the carbon sequestered will be maintained in a carbon sink, such as agricultural soil, for a sufficiently long time to matter. Duration refers to the length of the contract. Leakage refers to impacts that would occur if the practice caused participants to take actions that would increase greenhouse gas emissions elsewhere.

The PNDSA example is particularly interesting because it was made possible by a partnership between the state land grant universities, the environmental group Environmental Defense Fund, the farmers, and Chicago Climate Exchange. The Environmental Defense Fund created a one-page offer that it circulated among a consortium of energy companies that had committed to cut their emissions. PNDSA chose to lease the carbon credits rather than sell them, giving the energy companies only temporary management of the land involved. This way the farmers keep ownership of the carbon credits at the end of the contract, and the energy companies are forced to reduce their emissions, create an internal sequestration system, or renegotiate their leases with the contracting farmers.

PNDSA's goal is to stimulate research to develop a whole-farm accounting of carbon and carbon-equivalent changes occurring as a result of direct-seed cropping practices. Their vision is to have a yield of carbon equivalents for the farms of each of their members on the basis of all of the environmental and management decisions that a farmer might choose to make. Many farm organizations are now promoting and benefiting from no-till practices. In 2005 the Iowa Farm Bureau began working with the Chicago Climate Exchange to aggregate the carbon sequestration of its farmers' conversion to no-till and organic farming, getting payments for them from the carbon market.

Biochar

As important as it is to sequester carbon—lock it up—in the land by the management of agricultural lands, if climate chaos is to be prevented, society must find ways to sequester more carbon by drawing it from the air. Once again, farming and forestry have an important role to play, and a substance called biochar is a crucial part of the solution. Biochar is similar to charcoal, but, as described below, it differs because it is produced not primarily for fuel but as a soil amendment, as a way to enrich agricultural lands while locking up carbon.

Biochar production is rapidly emerging as a viable agricultural enhancement strategy that is also a climate change mitigation solution. A two-thousand-year-old practice now improved by modern technology, the manufacture of biochar is one of the few ways that carbon can be extracted from the atmosphere and sequestered that is relatively inexpensive, widely applicable, and quickly scalable. How does biochar work to sequester carbon dioxide? As plants grow, they soak up CO_2. This has led to the reasonable call by climate protection advocates for mass tree planting. But when biological material burns or rots, it releases its carbon back to the atmosphere. If, instead of being allowed to rot, trees and plants are converted to biochar and the biochar is put back into the soil, the carbon can be sequestered for very long periods of time, even up to thousands of years.[83] In effect, you are pulling carbon out of the air and breaking the carbon cycle.

Biochar is essentially charcoal, but made in a much more benign process than typical charcoal production. Charcoal production is an important energy source globally—nearly 3 billion people worldwide rely on burning wood (usually from local forests) for cooking.[84] But as conventionally practiced, charcoal production in developing countries drives deforestation and is exceedingly wasteful of the wood and the carbon. Inefficient use of charcoal also contributes to indoor air pollution and greenhouse gas emissions by the people who use it.

Biochar production is quite different. Biochar is created through pyrolysis, a process by which woody material is heated at low temperatures with little oxygen until it is carbonized. The process can produce energy (heat and power), but unlike burning fossil fuels it is a carbon-neutral process; it neither adds nor subtracts carbon from the atmosphere. Done intelligently, the production process delivers usable energy in the form of charcoal, a very valuable product in developing countries where it is the primary cooking fuel, and the biochar to be used as a soil amendment. Other by-products may be a bio-oil and syngas. These can be used to make substitutes for petroleum-based oil or natural gas to fuel transportation or as another substitute for charcoal.

Sustainable biochar production results in only part of the woody material's being turned into a fuel. The other 50 percent or more of the biomass's carbon becomes the biochar, which, when placed in soil, stays there, representing a near-permanent carbon sink that has actually removed carbon from the active carbon cycle, reducing overall atmospheric CO_2.[85]

Biochar in soil increases water retention and crop yields, reducing the need for fertilizer. It thus goes one step further. By enhancing plant growth, it encourages the removal of even more CO_2 from the atmosphere. Because biochar can be made in simple, homemade devices and on a small scale, biochar production also represents a start-up opportunity that can create rural jobs.[86]

The International Biochar Initiative and its U.S. affiliate, the U.S. Biochar Initiative, are among the leading voices in the promotion of biochar use around the world. They point out,

> The carbon in biochar resists degradation and can hold carbon in soils for hundreds to thousands of years. Biochar and bioenergy co-production

can help combat global climate change by displacing fossil fuel use and by sequestering carbon in stable soil carbon pools. It may also reduce emissions of nitrous oxide. We can use this simple, yet powerful, technology to store 2.2 gigatons of carbon annually by 2050. It's one of the few technologies that is relatively inexpensive, widely applicable, and quickly scalable. We really can't afford not to pursue it.[87]

Dr. Tim Flannery, one of Australia's most eminent scientists and the author of *The Weathermakers*, states, "Biochar may represent the single most important initiative for humanity's environmental future. The biochar approach provides a uniquely powerful solution, for it allows us to address food security, the fuel crisis, and the climate problem, and all in an immensely practical manner."[88] In an interview Flannery explained, "Now if you used these agri-char based technologies and you have your aggressive reforestation projects for the world's tropics, you could conceivably be drawing down in the order of 10 to 15 gigatonnes of carbon per annum by about 2030. At that rate we could bring ourselves down below the dangerous threshold as early as the middle of this century." This is an extremely exciting prospect, but, Flannery warned, "Whether the world can actually get its act together and do that is another matter."[89]

Biochar has its critics. In a 2009 article, George Monbiot, a leading advocate of climate change mitigation, slammed biochar and the numerous well-respected climate change scientists who promote it as a "cure-all" for climate change.[90] His concern is that large areas of land will be deforested or converted in order to mass-produce biochar, diverting that land (and those forests) in a manner similar to the ethanol craze of the past decade. He specifically points out that one company, Carbonscape, planned to plant 930 hectares (376 million acres) of trees specifically for the creation of biochar.

Clearly, unsustainable plantations created for any purpose are a bad idea. The International Biochar Initiative is committed to the *sustainable* implementation of its technology. An array of companies are undertaking biochar production on a smaller scale. Dynamotive Energy Systems, based in Vancouver, Canada, converts agricultural and forestry waste into bio-oils for fuel and creates biochar as a by-product. In a series of studies on farms in Quebec that are using Dynamotive's biochar, the company found that the biochar increased crop yield by 6 to 17 percent and reduced the depletion rate of nutrients from the soil by 44 percent.[91]

Highly efficient cookstoves can enable the rural poor to create biochar as a by-product of fuel production. Biochar stoves are capable of burning virtually any type of readily available biomass, so they do not require users to chop down native trees. Re:char, founded by a social entrepreneur named Jason Aramburu, is developing such small-scale, mobile pyrolyzers for on-site use at farms, vineyards, and food-processing plants in Africa. The units will produce biochar and bio-oil from wood and agricultural waste. Bio-oil can be upgraded for use in stationary diesel engines for carbon-negative power generation.[92]

In another part of the world, a young entrepreneur is using biochar as the basis for development in Haiti. Nathaniel Mulcahy, the founder of WorldStove LLC, spent two months on the earthquake-devastated island in 2010. Working with the support of the United Nations and several other international organizations, he showed how LuciaStoves, efficient biochar-producing cookers and stoves, can lift people from poverty. In the shambles left by the earthquake, Mulcahy was forced to innovate. His team brought together and trained a community of artisans on how to build Emergency LuciaStoves and institutional stoves for schools, orphanages, hospitals, and camps. Not having tools, they took apart old cars, built a forge, and made the tools they needed. They built several prototype biochar stoves from scratch, and developed prototype odor-free, aerobic, biochar-based composting latrines. They also created an integrated system whereby local residents in Haiti can make cookstoves, sell biochar, and ultimately use biochar to reclaim Haiti's soil fertility.[93]

Its few critics notwithstanding, biochar is about to hit the big time. Entrepreneurs who have made their mark in other industries are bringing to biochar production the sorts of talents, investment capital, and management skills that have taken other technologies mainstream. EcoTechnologies Group LLC, a company created to assist technology inventors to find projects in the green economy, is focusing on the simultaneous production of biochar, electricity, and heat from next-generation conversion technologies to develop a truly closed-loop (zero-waste) and fully sustainable business model in Hawaii, the most import-dependent state in the Americas. EcoTechnologies' Hawaiian Mahogany Project will grow three thousand acres of a fast-growing nitrogen-fixing tree called albzia; beneath the trees they will grow a cattle feed called Guinea grass. Even though it will be an albzia plantation, in a state where the competitive vegetation is miles of sugarcane plantations this approach is considerably more sustainable than conventional farming. The high-protein treetops and Guinea grass will become cattle and fish feed, the wastes from which will be impregnated into the biochar and returned to the land to fertilize future crops or sold as soil amendment to the sugar plantations.

"If Hawaii can demonstrate such efficiencies and sustainability along with financial viability, then no state on the mainland with similar resources would have an excuse to use fossil fuels. In the future, we will not be afforded the luxury of waste," says EcoTechnologies' cofounder Jeff Wallin. "The business case is sustainable and profitable without depending on tax subsidies or CO_2 credits, but they will help in finding interested financial partners." The environmental future is upon us and, as Wallin observed, "Nature does not negotiate."[94]

We Are What We Eat

If the health of the planet doesn't move you to action on its behalf, perhaps your own health will. Many observers are now linking unsustainable industrial agriculture with childhood diseases and obesity and the growing number of maladies afflicting modern eaters.

Robyn O'Brian was a Wall Street money manager with an MBA who began to investigate the chemicals now plentiful in our food after her child was born with food allergies. She now leads a mothers' crusade to transform agriculture. Her groundbreaking book, *The Unhealthy Truth: How Our Food Is Making Us Sick and What We Can Do About It* (2009), describes how research conducted primarily in Europe confirms the toxicity of America's food supply. O'Brian traces how industrial agriculture has pressured politicians to the point that the United States is one of the few countries in the world that allows its food supply to contain toxins that can be blamed for the increases in allergies, ADHD, cancer, and asthma in children. These include artificial hormones injected in cows to increase milk production, genetically modified corn and soybeans (now virtually all of the corn and soybeans produced in the United States are genetically modified), and pesticides that disrupt the hormones of our endocrine system. These "endocrine disrupters" are molecules that mimic the actions of human and animal hormones and disturb important hormone-dependent activities such as reproduction.[95]

Factory farmers continue to use enormous quantities of the most toxic poisons. In 2004, California strawberry farmers used 184 pesticides, applying an average of more than 335 pounds of pesticides per acre. In 2006, four of the six most-used farm pesticides in California were among the most dangerous chemicals in the world, yet only two states, California and New York, collect information on pesticide use on farms.[96]

From 1997 to 2002 there was a doubling of individuals afflicted with peanut allergy in the United States. According to one report, one out of seventeen American children under the age of three now has a food allergy. According to the Centers for Disease Control, there has been a 265 percent increase in the rate of hospitalizations related to food allergies. O'Brian cites studies showing that migrants to the United States from, say, Japan, increase their likelihood of developing cancer fourfold. In 2009, the World Health Organization reported:

> The global cancer burden doubled in the last thirty years of the twentieth century, and it is estimated that this will double again between 2000 and 2020 and nearly triple by 2030. Until recently, cancer was considered a disease of westernised, industrialised countries. Today the situation has changed dramatically, with the majority of the global cancer burden now found in low- and medium-resource countries.[97]

Michael Pollan, in his "Farmer in Chief" letter to President Obama, noted that without reforming how we produce food, we will not be able to control health-care costs. "Four of the top 10 killers in America today," Pollan noted,

> are chronic diseases linked to diet: heart disease, stroke, Type 2 diabetes and cancer. It is no coincidence that in the years national spending on health care went from 5 percent to 16 percent of national income, spending on food has fallen by a comparable amount—from 18 percent of household income to less than 10 percent. While the surfeit of cheap calories that the U.S. food system has produced since the late 1970s may have taken food prices off the political agenda, this has come at a steep cost to public health. You cannot expect to reform the health care system, much less expand coverage, without confronting the public-health catastrophe that is the modern American diet.[98]

Strong words, but the Centers for Disease Control estimates that one in three American children born in 2000 will develop Type 2 diabetes. What is the link between the public-health catastrophe of the modern American diet and Climate Capitalism? Pollan is only one of many agricultural experts who argue that all of the aspects of unsustainable agriculture are interrelated, from its carbon burden to its cost on our health. He urges the government to require a bar code on all food products that will provide information on the carbon footprint of the product and the oil required to make and deliver it, and with pictures that tell the whole story "of how that product was produced: in the case of crops, images of the farm and lists of agrochemicals used in its production; in the case of meat and dairy, descriptions of the animals' diet and drug regimen, as well as live video feeds of the CAFO where they live and, yes, the slaughterhouse where they die." To be sure, shortening the chain between producer and consumer is the best way to improve the quality of the food we eat, yet Pollan—acknowledging that most consumers know little about the modern food chain—sees provision of information through technology as another way to break a "culture of ignorance and indifference among eaters."[99]

Indeed, one of the challenges to reforming unsustainable agriculture is that few people know where their food comes from. Most children believe milk comes from a carton and that soda is one of the basic food groups. A number of efforts are under way to remedy this, beginning in schools, where children are being taught to grow their own food in school gardens and to cook so that they better understand proper nutrition. Much of this has been made possible by the vision and dedication (and funding) of Alice Waters, the legendary chef, founder of Chez Panisse in Berkeley, California, and for more than thirty years one of the sparkplugs behind the organic and healthy food movements.

Waters's Chez Panisse Foundation recruited Ann Cooper, a graduate of the Culinary Institute of America and previously the executive chef at the renowned Putney Inn, in Putney, Vermont, to bring nutrition and edible schoolyards to the Berkeley school system. In her book *Lunch Lessons: Changing the Way We Feed Our Children*, Cooper describes her work transforming a lunch program in which 95 percent of the food was processed, to one in which 90 percent is fresh and cooked from scratch, with ingredients that include organic chicken or turkey, sunflower seeds, fresh avocado, strawberries, and other in-season items, many raised locally. Food not made on the premises, like fresh tamales and muffins and vegetable calzones, is supplied by small local businesses.[100] Satisfied with her work in Berkeley, in 2009 Chef Ann moved to the Boulder, Colorado, school system to repeat her magic there.[101]

Others are undertaking similar projects. In Kissimmee, Florida, Dr. Arthur Agatston, the founder of the South Beach Diet, initiated a program using four of the Osceola County district schools as a clinical laboratory to deal with the fact that the obesity rate in adolescents has tripled since 1980 and is still rising. After the first two years of patients' following the recommended nutritional regimen, the program seemed to be working, and obesity rates were down.[102] In rural Arkansas a program makes nutrition a part of the math, science, and reading curriculums. This emerging movement to educate children about healthy nutrition includes one Harlem school in which all cafeteria meals are cooked from scratch and Santa Monica, California, schools, in which salad bars feature produce from the local farmers' market.[103] By linking what children eat, where it is grown, and the sustainable practices necessary to transform agriculture, these programs are practicing Climate Capitalism.

Some of the companies that are making the biggest investments in climate protection are also investing in healthier food. The Indian-born CEO of PepsiCo, Indra Nooyi, is leading the $39 billion food-products company in a massive rebranding of itself away from its flagship product, fizzy sugar water. Nooyi has promised that by 2010, half of Pepsi-Co's U.S. revenues will come from the sale of healthy products and that the company will invest in renewable energy.[104] And even as she campaigns against obesity and shifts the company from being one that shows up on the EPA's list for purchasing renewable energy credits to one showing up on the list for direct investment in renewable energy, Nooyi has driven up company earnings and shareholder value.[105] Nooyi's mantra, "Performance with purpose," seeks to give Wall Street what it wants and what the planet needs. "It doesn't mean subtracting from the bottom line, but rather that we bring together what is good for business with what is good for the world," she says.[106]

This is a prescient move. In 2007 studies from around the world began to collect compelling evidence that sustainably grown food is healthier. Of three European studies reporting the benefits of organic crops, the largest was a four-year EU-funded study of organic and conventional crops. In side-by-side plots covering a total of 725 acres near Britain's Newcastle University, organically grown wheat, tomatoes, potatoes, cabbage, and lettuce were found to contain 20 to 40 percent higher levels of antioxidants than conventionally grown veggies. A ten-year study by a University of California–Davis team analyzed dried tomato samples from side-by-side organic and conventionally farmed plots just west of the university. The organic tomatoes contained 79 percent more of one antioxidant and 97 percent more of another. A second UC Davis study confirmed the results of higher levels of polyphenols, vitamins, and minerals in organic produce from blueberries and strawberries to kiwi and corn.[107] Dr. Alyson Mitchell, a professor in the Department of Food Science and Technology at UC Davis, remarked, "Whether it's corn, tomatoes or peaches, modern commercial crops have been bred for high yield, resistance to disease, long shelf life, uniform size and an attractive appearance—anything but taste, or nutrition." She stated that her recent tomato study showed that organic farming methods using manure and compost instead of synthetic nitrogen fertilizers not only built healthier soil but pushed plants to produce more of their defense mechanisms, which are often antioxidants.[108]

Urban Agriculture

As consumers rethink the sort of food that they wish to eat, cities are beginning to rethink where they get their food. This is in part because the modern food delivery system is vulnerable: the average molecule of food travels up to 2,500 miles before someone eats it.[109] As Michael Pollan, among others, has observed, the logic for this—New York City's getting its produce from California rather than the "Garden State" next door—rests on cheap, fossil fuel–based energy. As fuel costs rise, and as regulations force corporations to account for the costs associated with their carbon footprints, the economic sense of sending salmon caught in Alaska to be filleted in China and then shipped back to California evaporates.[110]

Forward-thinking regions, like King County, surrounding Seattle, and Boulder County in Colorado, are taking these "food miles" very seriously. They are buying agricultural land, in part to preserve the natural beauty of their viewsheds but also to enable local production of food as a strategy for reducing their carbon footprints. And in the event that peak oil or another serious dislocation drives up the costs of food, they are protecting their ability to grow enough food to support their populations.[111] High-end subdivisions are even incorporating organic farms as amenities to increase sales of all their lots, often garnering as much as a 61 percent premium over conventional tract developments. The Urban Land Institute is tracking two hundred such projects now under development.[112]

Perhaps in reaction to all of this, Americans are flocking to community gardens and urban "green markets," long a feature of many European cities.[113] In China, urban farming in back gardens, on little plots,

and on rooftops provides more than 85 percent of urban vegetables—
even more in Beijing and Shanghai—plus significant amounts of meat
and tree crops.[114] More recently a rebirth of victory gardens, a practice
encouraged by governments during World War II, has led First Lady
Michelle Obama to plow up some of the White House lawn to plant an organic garden. Tiny container gardens are giving even the most asphalt-
and concrete-surrounded urban dwellers a way to grow some vegetables.

Another way to shorten the supply chain for food is community-
supported agriculture (CSA), also called subscription farming. Arriving
in the United States in 1986 after becoming established in Switzerland
and Japan in the sixties, CSA has spread widely, allowing nongardeners
to get a fresh weekly delivery of garden produce and enabling local farmers to get necessary cash to finance their operations. For over a quarter
century Japanese housewives have avoided the risks, health and otherwise, of industrial agriculture through subscription relationships (called
teikei partnerships) with local farmers.[115] Like the Japanese housewives,
CSA members generally pay for all or part of the season's produce in
advance, thereby providing farmers with a guaranteed income and an
important source of, sometimes literally, seed capital.[116] By 2004 there
were over 1,700 of these operations in every region of America, providing support for hundreds of small farms and clean local food for thousands of families. CSAs also strengthen an urban-rural matrix, building
networks of families who are cultivating new and healthy aspects of
community life and helping to shape a new vision of agriculture.[117]

High-end restaurants are also joining this "locavore" movement.
They aim mostly to provide the higher quality that comes from locally
grown organic produce, but also to demonstrate their climate consciousness. In an exclusive Fugu bar in Kyoto, the owner, on being comple-
mented on his sake, picked up the phone and called the owner of the
sake brewery to enable the woefully unprepared American guest to
complement the producer directly.[118]

In Boise, Idaho, the Red Feather restaurant pampers its patrons with
exquisite cuisine, all sourced within the Boise Valley. Like the Fugu proprietor in Kyoto, the Red Feather's owner, Dave Krick, can reel off the
names of every farmer who supplies his establishment, reciting how the

potatoes are grown with no poisons, and why his own hand-made oyster crackers taste better than those trucked in by restaurant suppliers.
All compost goes to an industrial worm farm in the historic building's
basement, where the worms produce castings rich in nitrogen, phos-
phorus, potassium, magnesium, and calcium. This could be sold as an
added revenue source, but it is given back to the local farmers whose
partnership makes the Red Feather such a desirable and profitable restaurant (see http://justeatlocal.com).

Grocers are getting into the act, too. The People's Grocery in West
Oakland, California, has teamed up with local farmers to bring an end
to the "food desert" phenomenon common in many low-income neighborhoods whereby there are plenty of liquor stores but no groceries. At
the same time they are supporting local agriculture and local jobs. Recently, the USDA has undertaken to support such efforts by enabling
users of food stamps to spend them at grocery stores specializing in local produce and at farmers' markets. At the opposite end of the spectrum, Walmart, pledging to be the world's largest retailer of organic
produce, is also seeking to feature local produce and thus to cut the
food miles of its products.[119]

Detroit may seem an odd place for an urban farm, but the entrepreneur John Hantz believes that urban farming may be the only way to
revitalize what has been described as "a desolate, postindustrial city-
scape." Once home to 2 million residents, Detroit is down to less than
half that, with forty thousand acres of unused land, and one of the nation's highest unemployment rates.[120] But where dilapidated houses, no
longer even serviced by the city's water or sewage departments, and
blocks of burned-out structures and rubbish currently stand, Hantz
imagines orchards and urban agriculture taking root and revitalizing
neighborhoods. He believes this enough to put $30 million of his own
money into the project, called Hantz Farms LLC, starting with fifty
acres on Detroit's east side. The for-profit venture will hire five hundred
people over the next decade to make it happen.

Hantz's proposal has its critics. City officials may have a hard time
keeping their city functioning, but they are adept at generating red tape.
More troubling, local community gardeners fear that Hantz's scheme is

"just a business," and want him to buy the land and give it to them. It is a business, and time will tell whether Hantz's vision proves a success, but the American Institute of Architects supports his most basic conclusion: "Detroit is particularly well suited to become a pioneer in urban agriculture at a commercial scale."[121]

Elsewhere urban agriculture is already under way. At the peak of its popularity, Cleveland's Galleria Mall had approximately two hundred shops. The economic collapse of 2008, however, left it an abandoned structure. A regional bank took over a quarter of the space, the Cleveland Metropolitan Bar Association took a bit more, but the operation was not economically viable until urban entrepreneurs turned the remaining space into a vertical farming operation. The mall's low humidity turns out to be perfect for growing lettuce. Its promoters hope to turn the Galleria into an urban ecovillage, attracting solar panel companies, health-food stores, garden supply companies, vegetarian restaurants, and more into the former retail center.[122] The Galleria at Erie View Mall has rebranded itself Cleveland's Center for Green Technology.

Much of the emerging urban agricultural landscape sounds and looks cutting edge, but it draws on the well-established, pioneering work of Dr. John and Nancy Jack Todd, founders of the New Alchemy Institute in Falmouth, Massachusetts, and creators of the bioshelter concept. Beginning in the 1970s they showed that it is possible, and economically desirable, to create buildings that house people comfortably year-round with no external inputs of energy. Because the structures are essentially solar greenhouses, they also enable occupants to raise a rich bounty of fresh vegetables and fish, while treating the wastes generated by living in such structures. Their 1980 book, *Village as Solar Ecology*, remains a classic in the literature of ecovillages, local food production, and sustainable living.[123]

Successful Failure: Agriculture for the Rest of the World

In many ways modern agriculture is the epitome of the success of the industrial age. Where premodern farmers had to rely on nature's rhythms of the sun and the weather, the modern "miracles" of massive irrigation systems and genetically modified crops have given the illusion of setting human cleverness above the wisdom of natural processes.

This triumph was achieved, however, only because of the temporary luxury of cheap fossil fuels and government subsidies. As Michael Pollan has argued, it is decidedly not the result of the free market. "Rather, it is the product of a specific set of government policies that sponsored a shift from solar (and human) energy on the farm to fossil-fuel energy" and enabled monoculture farming, and with it a vast increase in productivity.[124] The U.S. National Research Council reports that such practices enabled American farmers to achieve efficiency gains of 158 percent per unit of energy used since 1948. Output grew 1.58 percent on an annual basis while inputs only grew at 0.06 percent.[125] Sounds great . . .

Pollan, however, sees a darker reason for the "success" of industrial agriculture:

> This did not occur by happenstance. After World War II, the government encouraged the conversion of the munitions industry to fertilizer—ammonium nitrate being the main ingredient of both bombs and chemical fertilizer—and the conversion of nerve-gas research to pesticides. The government also began subsidizing commodity crops, paying farmers by the bushel for all the corn, soybeans, wheat and rice they could produce. One secretary of agriculture after another implored them to plant "fence row to fence row" and to "get big or get out." As Wendell Berry has tartly observed, to take animals off farms and put them on feedlots is to take an elegant solution—animals replenishing the fertility that crops deplete—and neatly divide it into two problems: a fertility problem on the farm and a pollution problem on the feedlot. The former problem is remedied with fossil-fuel fertilizer; the latter is remedied not at all.[126]

The agricultural analyst Will Allen writes,

> In 1945, only five percent of the nitrogen used on U.S. farms was synthetic. Now, more than ninety-five percent is. Before the synthetic take-

over, farmers grew fertilizer crops and applied small amounts of composted manure for fertility and tilth, to increase organic matter, and to feed the microorganisms that delivered healthy soil. These techniques and more modern ones are used by both organic and non-organic farmers today and enable them to produce high yields of quality produce, meat, fiber, oilseeds, and grains. Farmers all over the world are getting higher yields of calories per acre on diversified organic farms than on monocultural chemical or GMO farms.[127]

Some of the greatest opportunities in the transformation of agriculture will be in the developing world. The International Fund for Agricultural Development found in 2005 that farmers in developing countries who switch to organic agriculture achieve higher earnings and a better standard of living. Studies conducted in China, India, and six Latin American countries showed that farmers made more money as organic farming also reduced the health and financial risks posed to them by chemical pesticides and fertilizers. Organic practices also benefit the environment with improved soil management.[128] The study concluded, "Marginal and small farmers in China, India, Latin America and most probably in other developing countries, have a comparative advantage in shifting to organic agriculture, as the technologies they [already] use are often very close to organic practices."[129] Markua Arbenz, executive director of the International Federation of Organic Agriculture Movements, the global governing body that certifies organic production, agreed, stating in 2009, "We have learned in recent years that conversion to organic agriculture supports food security, climate change adaptation, and biodiversity conservation."[130]

This is a welcome revolt against the so-called Green Revolution. A product of the 1960s and 1970s, the Green Revolution initially took the world by storm. In an all-out push to modernize farming throughout Asia, and especially in India, synthetic inputs and intensive irrigation replaced traditional agriculture methods to increase yields.[131] In some ways it proved an enormous success. Grain production doubled in less than twenty years. Previously famine-stricken regions of rural India became breadbaskets, producing enough wheat and rice to export a surplus. Farmers who had previously grown as many as thirty different crops adopted techniques of monoculture and double-cropping, or harvesting twice a year by generating a second "rainy season" through irrigation. Yields increased enormously as biodiversity plummeted.

However, increasingly farmers found this industrialized approach did not provide a sustainable foundation. Soil fertility declined, water pollution became rampant, workers suffered health problems, including soaring cancer rates from using industrial chemicals often banned in Western countries, and fields did not sustain their peak yields. In addition, because synthetic inputs are heavily reliant on fossil fuel energy, the Green Revolution forced communities to become dependent on foreign inputs of oil, accompanied by significant exports of cash. In a telltale spiral of impossibility, falling water tables demanded the use of pumps, which required more imported fuel, all of which depleted water tables ever faster. India's once booming agriculture center is now heading for collapse.[132]

No longer able to sustain the yields of a few years ago, Indian farmers are increasingly concerned that they will not be able to meet the demands of tomorrow. In 2009, in a reflection of the global recession and consequences of climate change, Indian farmers came up short. In Punjab, failing monsoons led to dried-up aquifers, forcing farmers to dig wells deeper, driving them into a spiral of debt. The widespread application of insecticides gave rise to insect strains that are immune to the chemicals and now destroy more and more crops. To sustain comparable yields farmers now buy up to three times as much fertilizer as they did thirty years ago. The Punjab State Council for Science and Technology proclaimed that the state's agriculture program "has become unsustainable and unprofitable." Food prices began to rise over 10 percent annually. In August 2009, India announced that it was being forced to import food, especially lentils and edible oils. "The situation is grim, not just for crop sowing and crop health but also for sustaining animal health, providing drinking water, livelihood and food, particularly for the small and marginal farmers and landless labourers," stated India's farm minister, Sharad Pawar.[133] The chairman of the Punjab State Farmers Commission summed up the situation: "Farmers are committing ecological and economic suicide." Some are also literally committing suicide. In 2009 the shift in the monsoon rains caused crop losses on a massive scale, leading over 1,500 farmers in India to commit suicide that summer.[134]

In contrast, shifting away from the so-called modern practices to refocus on traditional, sustainable agricultural methods has been shown to reinvigorate communities. In 2007 the UN Food and Agriculture Organization determined that organic agriculture would positively contribute to food security, climate mitigation, water security and quality, agrobiodiversity, nutritional adequacy, and rural development.[135] Sustainable agriculture methods involve treating farms as holistic systems, where the relationship between all inputs is considered. In best cases, farmers use only what is produced on-site, such as using manure from livestock as a fertilizer for crops instead of synthetic fertilizer, which is derived from imported natural gas. Such sustainable practices restore soil structure, build healthy topsoil, nurture soil microbes, and promote biological activity, all of which contribute to long-term productivity and nutritious crops. Water use is optimized and the best practices in irrigation are applied. Farmworker safety and investment in local dollars sustain farming communities. Additionally, higher soil fertility also sequesters atmospheric carbon dioxide.

As the demand for foods produced by sustainable agriculture methods explodes throughout the world, this growing industry promises not only to be profitable but also to reconnect communities with traditional respect for soil, water, and air. Because more people are needed to do the work recently done by chemicals, organic farming increases labor demands and employment opportunities. This is one reason the citizen-based Development Research Communication and Services Center in West Bengal is working with surrounding states in northeastern India to transition to sustainable agriculture. The center sees organic farming as a means to ensure food and livelihood security for India's rural poor. Its work has been so successful that some organic farmers are actually producing more than their communities need. This is hardly a new concept for Indian farmers. "In the past, integrated rice-fish-duck-tree farming was a common practice in wetlands. This does not only meet peoples' food, fodder and fuel wood needs, but it provides superior energy-protein output to that obtained from today's monoculture practice of growing high-yielding varieties."[136]

There are many ways to reform agriculture in developing countries. One of the best examples of how this can be done profitably is being practiced on some of the most desolate ground in Egypt. SEKEM, the only corporation to win the Right Livelihood Award (the "Alternative Nobel Prize"), is using sustainable practices to grow third-party-verified organic products (vegetables, fruit, spices, cotton, plant-based pharmaceuticals, and cosmetics) in the Egyptian desert (the name means "vitality from the sun"). The operation employs two thousand people and provides housing, health care, schools, and now a four-year university. To ensure the value added to their products is fully understood, SEKEM partners with a European labeling service to educate its customers. A ten-point rating on a bar code label enables customers to key into a computer-based system that explains how each product was made and the fact that it is being sold in a fair-trade transaction.

Reinventing Agriculture

A growing number of critics of current agricultural practices are calling for a beyond-modern approach that would combine the best of traditional agriculture with the best of science and community organization to deliver abundant, sustainable food and high-quality ways of life to all the world's people while helping to solve the climate crisis. From the Rodale Institute, one of the original centers of scientific research into organic agriculture, to the Soil Association of the UK, to the Massachusetts-based E. F. Schumacher Society, to the Agroecology Lab at UC Davis, to authors such as Michael Pollan and Will Allen, these visionaries describe an agriculture that will build diverse and more profitable agro-ecosystems. These will replace the vast monocultures characteristic of modern agriculture and will be more resilient in the face of climate change than monocultures. Practitioners of sustainable agriculture will take a longer view of production, seeking not "to maximize yield in any optimum year, but to maximize yield over many years by decreasing the change of crop failure in a bad year."[137]

An even bolder vision of sustainable agriculture is emerging at the Land Institute in Salina, Kansas, promoted by Dr. Wes Jackson, a McArthur Genius Award winner. Jackson's approach, called Natural Systems Agriculture, is to shift agriculture away from monocultures of annual plants intensively managed to a polyculture of perennial strains carefully selected to deliver abundant yields of nutrients and quantity. Perennials develop large, efficient root systems that are not disturbed each planting season. This program is based on working with the plants that nature has endowed Kansas with naturally.

Jackson explains:

> Essentially all of the high-yield crops that feed humanity—including rice, wheat, corn, soybeans, and peanuts—are annuals. With cropping of annuals, alive just part of the year and weakly rooted even then, comes more loss of precious soil, nutrients, and water . . . Across the farmlands of the U.S. and the world, climate change overshadows an ecological and cultural crisis of unequaled scale: soil erosion, loss of wild biodiversity, poisoned land and water, salinization, expanding dead zones, and the demise of rural communities. The Millennium Ecosystem Assessment (MEA) concludes that agriculture is the "largest threat to biodiversity and ecosystem function of any single human activity."[138]

The Land Institute's goal is to develop an agricultural system with the ecological stability of the prairie and a grain yield comparable to that from annual crops. Prudence, they say, requires one to first look to nature, the ultimate source of our food and production, no matter how independent we may think that we have become. Essentially all of the natural land ecosystems within the ecosphere, from alpine meadows to rainforests, boast mixtures of perennial plants. By contrast, Jackson observes, annuals are opportunists that sprout, reproduce, throw seeds, and die. Perennials hold on for the long haul, protect the soil, and consequently better manage nutrients and water to a fine degree. In this regard perennials are superior to annuals, whether in polyculture or monoculture. The Land Institute's long-standing mission is to perennialize such major crops as wheat, sorghum, and sunflower, as well as to domesticate a few wild perennial species to see if they can produce food like their annual counterparts. The goal is to grow them in various mixtures depending on what each landscape requires. Using pre-agricultural ecosystems as a standard, the institute is attempting to bring the ecological integrity of the wild to the farm, below as well as above the ground's surface.

The Institute aims to end the situation in which "agricultural scientists from industrialized societies deliver agronomic methods and technologies from their fossil fuel–intensive infrastructures into developing countries, thereby saddling them with brittle economies . . . New perennial crops, like their wild relatives, seem certain to be more resilient to climate change," Dr. Jackson writes. "Without a doubt, they will increase sequestration of carbon. They will reduce the land runoff that is creating coastal dead zones and affecting fisheries and maintain the quality of scarce surface and ground water." In short, Dr. Jackson hopes to save the planet while producing greater economic stability at the same time. [139]

Nature Needs Us

In his book *Gardeners of Eden: Rediscovering Our Importance to Nature*, Dan Daggett profiles a dozen small agricultural operations across the American West that are, like Dr. Jackson's, reclaiming the land by working with the ecology that is there, not against it.[140] Daggett shows that although humans have come in recent years to behave like an alien species, rapaciously taking from the land what they desire, for most of human history we lived on land as natives, working with the place in which we lived in ways that enhanced it, and us. "Nature creates conditions conducive to life," says Janine Benyus, of the Biomimicry Institute. Bees feed themselves and their hives by pollinating flowers. Beavers, nature's engineers, cut trees and build dams in ways that slow erosive rivers and create meadows. Daggett argues that we all need to become native to the places that support us, and by so doing, learn the role that nature needs us to play in its spectrum.

Sustainable agriculture makes sense. It makes financial sense. It makes ecological sense. And it is humanity's best insurance policy against the onslaught of climate chaos. The farmer-poet Wendell Berry put it best when he observed that in such systems sunlight nourishes the grasses and grains, the plants nourish the animals, and the animals then nourish the soil, which in turn nourishes the next season's grasses and grains, and us. Animals on pasture harvest their own feed and dispose of their own waste—all without our help or the use of fossil fuel. In such a whole system humans can find their place and make a good life. This, Berry says, includes the use of technologies conducive to the creation of healthy community, time for conversation, good food, frugality, fidelity, and the miracle of life. Most of all, it offers connection to a place one can call home and to the interconnectedness of all life.[141]

8

Carbon Markets: Indulgences, Hot Air, or the New Currency?

Using energy efficiently and leveraging new technologies in all sectors is the cornerstone of Climate Capitalism. However, another profitable market is emerging as thousands of companies buy carbon offsets to help them meet their emissions targets. Carbon offsets are purchases of someone else's saved carbon or newly generated renewable energy. Those who reduce their carbon emissions can sell these offsets to those who have not lowered their emissions. Some buyers are required to offset their emissions by treaties that their national governments have signed under the Kyoto Protocol that mandate carbon-reduction requirements. Companies operating in the European Union are subject to such mandates.

But carbon trading isn't restricted to regulated markets. Many individuals and businesses choose to buy offsets to compensate for the carbon they emit from personal travel or business operations even though no regulation obliges them to do so. Interface, STMicroelectronics, HSBC, Whole Foods, and Nike are companies that use offsets to fulfill their voluntary corporate social responsibility pledges.[1] Organizations from

Natural Capitalism Solutions to the World Bank offset any emissions that their energy efficiency or renewable energy projects have not yet eliminated.

Critics scoff that offsets are just a way to assuage guilt and that it is cheaper to pay for offsets than to do "the right thing" by investing in energy efficiency and renewables.[2] Kevin Smith of Carbon Trade Watch mocks offsets as operating under the principle of "polluter profits rather than polluter pays." Others complain that even binding agreements will not be enforced.

The critics are wrong. Intelligent offsetting is a responsible thing to do in a time of climate crisis. If an offset drives the real reduction of existing direct carbon emissions, it is a legitimate way of cutting total carbon emissions. Guilt and shame may be involved, but combined with self-interest they are useful motivators. If the opinions of shareholders, investors, and the media matter to your company, offsets make good business sense.

Thousands of books, websites, and media reports cover every arcane aspect of offsets, carbon trading, and the relative merits of "cap and trade" as opposed to taxes.[3] This chapter cannot possibly present all of that information, but given that carbon trading represents a massive business opportunity that you disregard at your peril, no conversation about Climate Capitalism would be complete without at least a brief primer on how the carbon markets work, what the controversy is about, and how the regulatory environment and the voluntary standards are evolving to meet the growing demand for carbon offsets. Along the way, the chapter will explore some of the business opportunities emerging in the identification and development of carbon offset projects and the resulting opportunities for wholesale and retail carbon offsets. It presents vignettes of innovative companies, governments, and nonprofits that are finding carbon trading a route to profitability.

Let the Battle Begin

Two facts should be obvious: first, all offsets are not created equal. Measures that both remove as much carbon from the atmosphere as the offset activity emits, and remove carbon that would not otherwise have been removed, are valid. This concept, called "additionality," although much argued over, is simple: if the carbon reduction was going to be achieved anyway, why should someone be paid extra to do it? There is actually a good reason why they might, but offset providers are seeking to appear squeaky clean and to avoid any hint of impropriety.

Second, some carbon offsets are controversial. Scams, some of which make the climate crisis worse, have been perpetrated. For example, critics charged that the UN Clean Development Mechanism (CDM) was tricked by Chinese entrepreneurs into paying them $6 billion in carbon credits to destroy HFC 23, a potent greenhouse gas and marketable by-product created in the manufacturing of refrigerants. A mere $100 million, the critics charge, would have been enough to allow the Chinese to buy the equipment necessary to destroy the gas their current operations were creating. Worse, they claim that because the carbon credits netted the factories twice what they would have gotten from simply selling the gas, the Chinese built more factories to manufacture more gas so that they could be paid to destroy it. UN officials have recently put a hold on all HFC reduction projects. Nonetheless, the damage to the credibility of carbon markets was done.[4]

None of this should deter you from offsetting the carbon you cannot eliminate, however. The solution is simple: learn to offset responsibly. There are four steps to carbon responsibility:

1. Conduct an inventory of your current emissions to set a baseline.
2. Establish meaningful targets for reductions.
3. Reduce, reduce, reduce.
4. Offset what you can't eliminate with high-quality, certified carbon offsets.

As entities seek to address their carbon emissions, their first step is to get a baseline of their existing carbon emissions and then develop a strategy for reducing them by setting targets for reduction. Most companies, small and large, don't have the necessary expertise to conduct this analysis, let alone formulate cost-effective strategies for mitigating their impacts on climate change, however.

Enter Point Carbon, a world-leading provider of independent analysis and consulting services for global power, gas, and carbon markets.[5] Point Carbon has more than thirty thousand corporate, government, and professional subscribers from 150 countries. Its CEO, Per-Otto Wold, stated prior to the global climate summit in Copenhagen in 2009 that while he did not expect a firm deal to replace Kyoto from COP 15, he did expect one shortly after: "I expect that there will be a price on carbon long into the future."[6]

The world needed him to be right. As climate chaos worsened, however, the world policy apparatus found itself largely out of bullets. Unfortunately, Copenhagen failed to deliver a global agreement to replace the Kyoto Protocol. Expectations for the 2010 global summit in Cancun were downplayed, as it was clear that the world's nations were not ready to commit to a replacement to Kyoto. Much to many people's surprise, Cancun reached a last-minute consensus to move forward on policies for reducing carbon emissions from deforestation and degradation (the approach described below called REDD+). International forest protection was a leading element in a balanced broader package. The nations also created a fund to help the developing world implement climate protection. But they deferred for another year the tough work of agreeing to the deeper reductions in carbon emissions essential to keep the world's climate from warming into catastrophic levels. The Cancun Accord urged industrial countries to move faster on emissions cuts, noting that scientists believe that industrial countries must cut greenhouse gas emissions by 25 to 40 percent from 1990 levels within the next ten years. Current pledges amount to only about 16 percent.

As limited as the accords were, they represented the first time in three years that the 193-nation UNFCCC meeting adopted any climate action whatsoever. This at least had the value of restoring faith in the unwieldy UN process after the Copenhagen breakdown.

But the continuing failure to set a global carbon reduction mechanism has left the world of carbon markets in a fragile state. Players in the carbon market realize that they are going to have to hang on until 2012 before finding out whether there will be a global agreement. It also likely means that a lot of bilateral and regional country agreements will be reached in 2011.

Carbon markets remain the best tool for driving reductions in emissions, and so it is worth understanding how they work.

The field of greenhouse gas emission reporting and offsetting gained coherence when the World Resources Institute and the World Business Council for Sustainable Development partnered to develop the Greenhouse Gas Protocol, the most widely used international accounting tool for government and business leaders to quantify and manage greenhouse gas emissions. The protocol is the foundation for nearly every greenhouse gas standard and program in the world, from the International Organization for Standardization to the Climate Registry. Companies required by the various mandatory schemes to report their emissions typically hire experts to do the calculations, or buy custom software. For example, the 2009 start-up Hara Software enables big companies to monitor energy use and water and to cut their impact through efficiency. Hara Environmental and Energy Management's content database shares information on efficiency programs and products to help companies reduce energy use and carbon impact. It is now in use by dozens of organizations, including corporations such as Coca-Cola and Intuit. The cities of Palo Alto and San Jose expect to save more than $2 million and cut their greenhouse gases by 15 percent over the next three years using Hara.

These systems allow companies to calculate how much carbon their operations are emitting, and often guide users to energy efficiency measures that will make good sense. But the emissions that remain should be offset, either by buying someone else's reductions or by buying someone else's addition of renewable energy.

PepsiCo, as part of its three-year commitment made to the Environmental Protection Agency, became the first Fortune 500 Company to go from zero to 100 percent renewable power in one quarter. How? Pepsi had been installing solar energy systems in many of its facilities for years. Then, in 2007, PepsiCo bought over 1.1 million megawatt-hours of renewable energy credits, representing 100 percent of its total electricity use.[7] Pepsi stated that its green-power efforts, especially purchasing renewable energy credits (RECs), were just one part of the company's "responsibility to continually improve all aspects of the world in which we operate."[8] Then in early 2010, PepsiCo decided to invest not only the $1.2 billion each year that it had been spending on RECs, but a total of $30 billion in on-site renewables. It will still buy some RECs, but decided it would rather invest in its own facilities.[9] Companies selling to PepsiCo would do well to take notice. Like Walmart, the corporation has stressed that its green-power initiative was only one part of a larger commitment to sustainability, and it would be encouraging its entire supply chain to increase its energy efficiency and renewable energy.

Despite initial challenges, the market for carbon credits, offsets, and RECs is growing. The climate crisis is real, and responsible people who cannot (or choose not to) curtail their carbon-emitting activities will seek ever more ways to offset.

The first step in establishing a carbon market is setting a price on carbon. While there is substantial disagreement within the scientific, public policy, and business communities over the best mechanisms to reduce carbon emissions, essentially everyone agrees that putting a price on carbon is necessary. Emissions trading does that by limiting (capping) the amount of carbon that can be emitted, then letting market forces determine the value of one ton of carbon emissions (and the carbon equivalent of other greenhouse gases).

The Carbon Market

The global carbon market came into existence with the 1997 Kyoto Protocol, which established a "cap-and-trade" mechanism to meet the greenhouse gas limits set by the world at the Rio Earth Summit. The heart of a cap-and-trade system is a governmental regulation setting an upper limit, a cap, on allowable emissions for target industries within a geographic region covered by the Protocol. Companies within that region that reduce their emissions more than required can then trade their "unused" emissions to companies that exceed their allowable limits. Cap-and-trade systems establish clear limits that allow a market-established price on carbon emissions to create incentives to reduce emissions.

The Kyoto Protocol introduced "flexible mechanisms" to allow variability in approaches to carbon reduction including emissions trading, the Clean Development Mechanism (CDM), and Joint Implementation.

The Clean Development Mechanism is a tool to reduce global emissions by creating carbon offset projects in developing countries and then selling those offsets in the form of credits in regulated markets such as the European Union Trading System. CDM was introduced to help developing countries gain access to low-carbon technologies and to create cheaper offsets than would likely occur by implementing offset projects in more developed countries with higher land and labor costs. Given that climate change is a global phenomenon, and emissions released into the atmosphere anywhere worsen climate chaos for the whole earth, the physical location of offset projects need not be near the source of the emissions being offset.

Since the launch of the Clean Development Mechanism, more than 2,400 projects have been officially registered, which is predicted to lead to the reduction of more than 2 billion tons of CO_2 by the end of the first phase of the Kyoto Protocol, which ends in 2012.

Joint Implementation (JI) is another flexible mechanism; it allows a country seeking to meet its obligations under the Kyoto Protocol to claim offset credits generated outside its borders. The difference between JI and CDM projects is that JI projects occur within developed countries whereas CDM projects occur within underdeveloped countries. To date only thirty-eight projects have been approved through the JI mechanism, most likely because the costs of energy efficiency and renewable energy projects in developed countries are frequently much higher than in developing countries.

Many climate experts—including Dr. James Hansen, a climate change expert who heads the NASA Goddard Institute for Space Studies—would prefer to set the price by government fiat through taxing carbon-based fuels at the point at which they come out of the ground or into a country. The benefit, they claim, is that everyone would know precisely what that price is, and the system thus cannot be "gamed." Market mechanisms, such opponents argue, fluctuate and are inherently messy. A tax, they claim, would be predictable and unavoidable.[10]

A tax is also, at least in the United States, politically dead on arrival. Worse, the earth does not care what the price of carbon is, it cares how much carbon emissions are being reduced, something a tax without a cap will not control.

More important, carbon markets work—if the supporting governmental policy is in place. When companies have an incentive to cut carbon because they get paid to do it, doing so becomes a part of their business and they take it seriously. Certainly the carbon markets have seen volatility, with prices ranging from nearly $50 a ton to pennies a ton as investors gain and lose confidence. In the wake of the world's failure to agree on a new trading regime in Copenhagen, and the U.S. Senate's failure to pass binding legislation, the price of carbon fell dramatically. In the United States it fell almost to nothing. In Europe, the price of carbon fell from a high of €25 to €8 a ton. But by October 2010, prices had started to rebound, hitting €12.[11] Subsequent measures have only strengthened the price per ton.

Despite the volatility, there is no doubt that the European Union market is continuing to cut carbon emissions. By early 2009, EU emissions had fallen 3 percent in one year. Some of the reduction was assigned to the slower economy, but analysts agreed that 70 percent of the reduction is due to emissions trading and to a growing renewable-energy sector. In fact, even in the face of a tough economy in which many companies sold off carbon credits to raise cash, prices did not fall to zero, leading analysts to conclude that the European market was working as designed. In the tougher climate regime anticipated after 2012, prices are expected to rise again.[12]

Such markets have worked before. The whole concept of carbon markets is drawn from the regulated sulfur-reduction system in the United States that successfully cut acid rain. Once companies applied themselves to reducing sulfur emissions it turned out to be far faster and cheaper just to eliminate them. All of the horror predictions that the requirement would bankrupt companies turned out to be wrong.

The sulfur cap-and-trade program resulted in 100 percent compliance and achieved a net reduction of 22 percent (7 million tons) of sulfur below mandated levels.[13] The markets created under the Kyoto Protocol carbon market are also working.

The European Union: The First Regulated Carbon Market

The heart of the Kyoto Protocol is the regulated market for the developed countries. The European Union Emissions Trading System (EU ETS) is the cap-and-trade system created to meet Europe's commitment to carry out the Kyoto Protocol. Each member state of the EU sets a limit (cap) on the amount of allowable emissions for all carbon-emitting businesses in the country that fall under the EU ETS. Each facility is then allocated allowances equal to that established cap. If a business is able to cut its carbon lower than its allowance, this creates a carbon credit that the business can trade. If the business emits more than its allowance it needs to buy credits to meet its obligation.

In January 2005, the Emissions Trading System (ETS) came into force with companies within the United Kingdom reporting their emissions and purchasing offsets through the UK ETS. Under this mandatory system, major greenhouse gas emitters in Europe, who collectively account for more than 40 percent of the world's total greenhouse gases, were obliged to cut their emissions or purchase carbon credits. In 2008, despite the economic downturn, trading volume exceeded $95 billion. The European Union has committed to reducing its emissions by at least 20 percent by 2020 over 1990 levels. This predictable reduction and the increased industry obligations that fall under it will significantly drive the carbon emissions market.

The EU rolled out its platform and beginning operations quickly, fully cognizant that bugs would emerge that would require changes to the system. One major blunder quickly emerged: the system encouraged participation by eastern European nations by granting them credits for their extensive forests. In the process the system had authorized more credits than there was carbon being emitted, and the price of carbon crashed. However the system adjusted rapidly, and the price rose. Amazing. The market worked.

Analysts now believe that the revised ETS directive, which sets the EU-wide cap for the next twelve years, will provide regulatory stability and predictability, ensuring an investment-friendly environment. With an overall cap that cuts emission allowances from 2013 onward, the price of carbon credits should rise, eliciting investment in efficiency and renewable energy.[14] As this happens, investments in developing countries will become more attractive. For example, the Spanish utility Endesa, regulated by the mandatory carbon market in force in the European Union, buys UN-monitored CDM carbon credits to fund the construction of renewable energy in developing countries, or plants trees there because these are cheaper offsets than the carbon credits issued by the EU carbon market.[15]

A U.S. Market Emerges

Following the successful conclusion of the Kyoto Protocol, American climate activists returned to the United States eager and expectant. The U.S. Senate, however, refused to ratify the international accord. As activists searched for an alternative, the economist Dr. Richard Sandor, now considered the "father of carbon markets," observed, "Governments don't make markets, traders do. I'm a trader, let's make a market." In 2003, Sandor's team created Chicago Climate Exchange, the first entrant into the U.S. carbon market.

A verified, rules-based trading regime, CCX was the world's first and North America's only integrated trading system to reduce emissions of all six major greenhouse gases. The choice to join CCX was voluntary, but that choice became contractually binding once a member opted in. Members, including such major companies as DuPont, STMicroelectronics, Ford Motor Company, Motorola, Sony Electronics, and others joined because they believed that a regulated regime was coming, because they wanted to learn how to reduce their emissions, because they believed it would be good marketing, and for a variety of other serious business reasons. Other members, including Natural Capitalism Solutions and World Resources Institute, joined as buyers, offsetting all of their carbon emissions this way. Colleges (the University of Oklahoma and Presidio Graduate School), cities (Chicago), and counties (King County, Washington) were also members. CCX became the world's biggest market for stationary (from buildings and power plants) carbon-emissions reductions, with offset projects globally. In 2008, CCX's trading volume tripled from 2007 levels, rising to nearly 70 million tons of CO_2 equivalents, and the value of these trades reached $300 million, up from just $72 million the year before.[16] CCX members contracted to cut their emissions by 6 percent by 2010.

CCX rules required that the big industrial members cut their emissions 4 percent through 2006, but members actually reduced much more, hitting 8 percent cuts in aggregate. This may be the most potent rejoinder to those who claim that such markets are just opaque ways to generate unearned wealth. The savings were indeed making the companies richer, but they were also responsible for real reductions in the greenhouse gases emitted by CCX members, and eliminated 185 million metric tons of CO_2. CMX governed 17 percent of U.S. stationary emissions, 20 percent of the U.S. power industry, and 20 percent of the Dow Jones Industrials. CCX also became the trading floor used by the Regional Greenhouse Gas Initiative, the first mandatory carbon market in the United States. CCX traded futures contracts for federal allowances in anticipation of whatever mandatory national system might be introduced.

CCX operated internationally as well, opening the Tianjin Climate Exchange in Tianjin, China, partnering with the China National Petroleum Corp (Petro China), as well as the city of Tianjin. CCX's India Climate Exchange gathered twenty members to establish targets for a private cap and trade in India. CCX also partnered with the European Climate Exchange, which now trades 85 percent of the European Trading System futures market.

In addition to demonstrating that the concept of a carbon market will attract and be profitable to companies, CCX showed that it is good for developing nations, working with local development groups in Kerala state in India to use carbon credits to jump-start biogas production. A Kerala NGO named Anthyodaya pioneered the use of carbon credits for farmers. Anthyodaya aggregates carbon emission offset credits for CCX and pools the credits generated from the operation of biogas plants for sale in the exchange. "When farmers use biogas in their kitchen," explains Peter Thettayil, the executive director of Anthyodaya, "they prevent the emission of methane and carbon dioxide (from kerosene), two of the major greenhouse gases." But using biogas cost the farmers more than government-subsidized kerosene. The carbon credits, earned by around 16,000 farmers for their contribution toward controlling emission of greenhouse gases, were traded at CCX, providing the farmers with sufficient annual income to tip the scales in favor of using biogas. CCX heard about Anthyodaya's work, contacted the group, conducted a site visit in 2006, and shortly thereafter issued checks to the farmers averaging around a thousand rupees.[17] "When I joined the programme I never thought I'd get the amount so easily," said K. V. Chacko, a farmer participating in the program. "I am now aware of global warming and related issues," he added. "Biogas plant is part of our farming infrastructure. The cowdung slurry from the plant is an excellent manure. Now, we know we are doing something good by using biogas and got a reward for that."[18]

Such programs not only deliver genuine development, they also help educate businesspeople across the world about the importance of using markets to solve environmental challenges. CCX proved such a successful model that in April 2010 it was acquired by Intercontinental Exchange for $622 million. By August, however, the fallout from the failure in Copenhagen and cowardice by Democrats in the U.S. Senate and by the Obama administration on climate change was beginning to bite. Intercontinental Exchange was forced to lay off half its staff. In November ICE closed Chicago Climate Exchange.[19] The institution that had proven that carbon markets work was destroyed by political incompetence and self-interest. Pathetic.

Regional Markets

Dereliction of duty by federal and international climate negotiators led state governments to craft a series of regional agreements, particularly in North America. The New England states went first, creating the Regional Greenhouse Gas Initiative (RGGI), comprising ten Mid-Atlantic and northeastern states. RGGI is the first mandatory, regulated carbon market in the United States. As the United States considers federally regulated emissions standards and eventually joins Europe and other developed countries in a global accord, the regional initiatives will merge into the federal and international agreements. But for now they are picking up the slack as the national and international agreements lag behind the more responsible action of local and regional governments.

The RGGI system is working. It sells more than 90 percent of its permits at auction, using 55 percent of the money to invest in energy efficiency, 15 percent to fund renewable energy in the region, and, in several states, 12 percent to help relieve budgetary deficits.[20]

In 2007, seven western states—Arizona, California, Montana, New Mexico, Oregon, Utah, and Washington—joined forces with four Canadian provinces—British Columbia, Manitoba, Ontario, and Quebec—to launch the Western Climate Initiative "to identify, evaluate, and implement collective and cooperative ways to reduce greenhouse gases in the region, focusing on a market-based cap-and-trade system." As part of the initiative, the nonprofit group Climate Action Registry links state and regional initiatives across most of the United States, Canada, and northern Mexico. The registry is a key part of the mechanisms that need to be in place to enable a formal market in saved carbon to emerge.

Such efforts at creating markets remain under attack. In February 2010, Arizona pulled out of creating a cap-and-trade system for fear of negative economic impacts, even though all studies of climate protection efforts show that they create jobs and drive prosperity. Alaska considered similar cowardice but chose to remain a member of the initiative.[21] In mid-2010, Valero and Tesoro Corporation (two oil companies), Koch Enterprises, and an Ohio coal company spent over $10 million to fund an initiative, titled Prop 23, to overturn the California Climate Protection Act AB 32, the now implemented California law mandating a cap on carbon emissions and establishing the basis for a market in saved carbon.[22] They clearly feared the success of market mechanisms in driving a transition from dirty forms of fossil energy to a clean-energy future. Happily, activists and ordinary citizens rallied in support of California's stance on carbon and overwhelmingly crushed the proposed destruction of California's climate protection regime. California also elected a governor sworn to strengthen the state's leadership in the green economy.

Other carbon markets have emerged in national cap-and-trade schemes. Since 2008 new national schemes have been proposed in China, Japan, Australia, New Zealand, Mexico, Chile, and Colombia, among others. Concerns over the slow pace of post-2012 negotiations within the UN and lack of consensus regarding an approach to carbon regulation has driven these national efforts. Some of these national proposals have also included bilateral agreements such as Japan's August 2010 announcement of plans to link their emerging national markets, bypassing the stalled negotiations for a post-2012 UN-sanctioned global agreement.[23]

Voluntary Approaches

As the number of international, national, and regional agreements seeking to enforce or at least encourage carbon reductions has grown, so too have the number of voluntary standards. More than ten voluntary carbon-offset standards have been propounded to provide a measure of credibility for the dizzying array of participants and carbon project developers in the voluntary carbon market around the globe. Companies can report their emissions to the Voluntary Carbon Standard and buy certified reductions from the Gold Standard. Other sustainable carbon standards include the Climate, Community & Biodiversity Alliance and Social Carbon. Companies can track carbon and report emissions using the International Organization for Standardization's ISO 14064 standards, which "provide tools for assessing and supporting greenhouse gas reduction and emissions trading," and the Department of Energy's 1605(b) program. Walmart chose the Carbon Disclosure Project (CDP) as its registry for the carbon footprint reports from its suppliers (described in chapter 1).[24]

Because the majority of small and medium-sized entities that wish to trade carbon do not have a core competency or the networks to build relationships with offset purchasers, they turn to wholesalers and retailers to sell their offsets for a commission or at a discount. These retailers sell carbon offsets to companies and governments in the regulated market and to anyone, from consumers to companies, on the voluntary market. As the market matures, there has been an ongoing shakeout, with retailers who are not providing the highest-quality certified offsets losing out to those who can satisfy consumers who want to know that their offset purchases are actually causing real reductions in carbon emissions and helping people and communities achieve a higher standard of living.

How do you choose amid the plethora of options?

Just as all offsets are not created equal, offset providers, too, vary in quality. Carbon Fund, based in Maryland, received the Readers' Choice Award from TreeHugger.com because "The organization is a top-notch, reliable and trustworthy provider of carbon offsets and you can trust that your funds are going directly towards projects that reduce carbon emissions."[25] The nonprofit enables you to calculate your personal carbon footprint, then choose from a variety of offsets, including renewable energy development and methane reduction, tree planting, and rainforest protection.

The Australian organization Carbon Offset Watch surveyed twenty carbon offset retailers in order to assist carbon offset buyers in making their selection. Retailers that earn outstanding ratings

performed well in all or most assessment categories and during the assessment period . . . sold a high proportion of offsets accredited by high-scoring standards—Gold Standard, CDM, VCS and Greenhouse Friendly. They also had a high proportion of offsets from projects that change or prevent the underlying activities that create greenhouse gases, such as energy efficiency, renewable energy and diversion of waste from landfill. There is a very high likelihood that an offset purchased from these retailers will deliver real, additional greenhouse gas emission reductions.[26]

Freddy Sharpe, CEO of Climate Friendly, one of three offset retailers that received an outstanding rating, commented that the quality of offsets in the voluntary sector, where a wide variety of offset certifications exists, will increase in importance:

> Voluntary markets are too important to leave to "caveat emptor." We provide complete assurance across all of our processes, from measuring carbon footprints, through procuring the highest quality available offsets and to registration, tracking, and retirement of offsets. We do this through adhering to international standards and protocols, ensuring independent third party verification and auditing of our processes and services, and providing full transparency to our clients. Greenwash not only damages corporate reputations but, much more important, risks damaging consumer trust in buying green products and services. This would limit one of society's most effective mechanisms for responding to climate change.[27]

As stated above, additionality is the assurance to a buyer of a carbon credit that his money is really eliciting a reduction in carbon and not merely further enriching someone who would have made the reduction anyway. Standards that require at least as much evidence of additionality as the UN's Clean Development Mechanism are considered high quality.

Many offset buyers particularly value the co-benefits associated with carbon offset projects. Co-benefit projects not only generate quality carbon offsets but also provide such additional sustainability benefits to local communities as economic growth, improved environmental conditions, and enhanced health for local residents. Although the UN's CDM program requires some co-benefits, three current standards—the Gold Standard; Climate, Community and Biodiversity Standards (CCBS); and Plan Viro—exceed the CDM's co-benefits requirements.

The Gold Standard is an international nonprofit organization that created the leading verification protocol of the same name. Endorsed by sixty major climate-protection, environmental, and development organizations, the standard meets the quality demanded by the CDM and requires developers seeking its certification to demonstrate proof of local sustainable benefits. The World Wildlife Fund calls the Gold Standard "an independently audited, globally applicable best practice methodology for project development that delivers high-quality carbon credits of premium value along with sustainable development co-benefits associated with the projects."[28]

Carbon offset projects can be certified as Gold Standard Voluntary Emissions Reductions (GS VER) or as Gold Standard Certified Emissions Reductions (GS CER). The latter are used to complement CDM-JI projects by enabling these offsets to meet the regulatory requirements of CDM while also demonstrating the projects' extra sustainability benefits.

Although relatively few Gold Standard projects have been developed and verified, hundreds of proposals are currently registered. It is a good bet that Gold Standard Verified Emissions Reductions and complements to CDM processes will become increasingly popular as a way to meet the stringent criteria of the CDM processes of the Kyoto Protocol while providing a rigorous, credible certification of a project's additional benefits.

Reducing Carbon Emissions: How Low Do You Go?

Different organizations set different targets for their carbon reductions. The FIFA World Cup and companies like Pepsi have chosen to offset all of the carbon that their various activities emit.[29] Others are less ambitious, choosing to offset the emissions from participants traveling to a conference, or a particular event like a hotel stay or a car rental.[30] The National Football League offset the emissions from the 2007 Super Bowl by planting three thousand trees and buying renewable energy credits.[31] Given that we all emit dramatically more carbon than the earth can sustain, any meaningful reduction is a good start. As reducing and offsetting emissions comes to be the norm, however, we can all tighten our focus on carbon neutrality, and indeed seek negative carbon emissions as the goal.

There are several ways to achieve carbon neutrality. The best approach to climate protection is to implement energy efficiency throughout an organization's operations (see chapter 2). It is worth it to invest as much as you can in achieving energy efficiency to protect against rising energy prices, let alone what carbon emissions will cost companies in the future. Typically a business will not be able to cut all of its emissions through efficiency, but it should always seek to eliminate as many as it can cost-effectively, because this will be the cheapest way to reduce its impact, as well as the fastest, cheapest, and best way to drive its profits. By 2007 DuPont had cut its emissions almost four-fifths below what they were in 1990, the year that the Kyoto Protocol set as its baseline year (described in chapter 1). EcoSecurities and ClimateBiz surveyed sixty-five multinational corporations and found that three-fifths of them had implemented a carbon management strategy, and another third were in the process of developing one. Nearly all of the companies surveyed said energy-efficiency measures such as upgrading insulation and using low-energy lighting were the easiest carbon reductions to implement.[32]

Once it has cut emissions as far as it can through efficiency, a company or community that wants to be able to call itself carbon-neutral should install renewable energy sources to meet its remaining needs for power. This will save money in the long run, guarantee energy security indefinitely into the future, and underpin local economic vitality and the creation of jobs. Ferreira Construction combined energy efficiency and solar power to make its 41,000-square-foot Branchburg, New Jersey, headquarters a net-zero building, one that produces more energy than it uses. Featuring 1,276 rooftop solar panels, a highly efficient boiler system, and a radiant-slab heating system, the building is a model throughout the state for cost-effectiveness.[33] By installing solar panels, Ferreira is supporting the economic viability of another Branchburg company, Voltaix (see chapter 3), which makes the gas feedstocks that are part of the production process of the solar panels used on the Ferreira HQ's roof. Installed by local contractors, the panels also keep money in the local economy that would previously have left Branch-burg to buy electricity generated at distant power plants.

On the other coast, Applied Materials installed a 2.1-megawatt solar array on its Sunnyvale, California, headquarters, relegating Google's 1-megawatt array, previously the largest in the state, to second place. Like Google, Applied Materials erected many of the panels so they act as shading structures in their parking lots, supplying renewable power for electric and plug-in hybrid cars. Applied Materials' system will pay back its investment in less than ten years, eliminate more than 2,700 tons of carbon dioxide emissions, or roughly the annual output of 450 cars, provide work for local contractors, and also support Applied Materials' business, which, among other things, is to make the machines that make the solar panels.[34]

The next-best option is for a company to buy renewable energy cred-its to offset its emissions. In 2008, Intel made the largest single voluntary purchase of renewable energy credits ever, 1.3 million megawatt-hours of electricity, or enough electricity to power more than 130,000 average American homes annually. The net effect was the equivalent of taking 185,000 passenger vehicles off the road for a year. In 2010 Intel upped its renewable energy credit purchases by 10 percent, raising the company's renewable commitment to cover 51 percent of its power use. This com-plements the company's own renewable installations, ranked as one of the ten biggest in the southwest, including a 1 megawatt ground-mounted photovoltaic installation at Intel's Folsom, California, facility.[35]

Forest Offsets

In 2007, the Vatican became the first carbon-neutral state by accepting a donation from a start-up Hungarian carbon-trading company, which promised to plant enough trees to offset the Vatican's emissions that year.[36] Planting trees to soak up the carbon emitted by an entity's use of fossil fuels is a commonly used offset, but has been controversial. Scien-tists debate whether taking land in temperate climates, which had not previously been tree-covered, and darkening it by covering it with trees might not warm the earth more than the carbon those trees remove from the air might cool it.

The importance of keeping standing forests in tropical regions standing is noncontroversial. Every hour, deforestation releases as much carbon into the atmosphere as 8 million people flying from London to New York. Stopping this deforestation is probably the fastest and cheapest way to prevent climate chaos.[37] Forests are felled for lumber, to clear land for corporate agriculture, to grow palm oil plantations for biofuels, and to provide wood for cookstoves and brick making.

The Global Canopy Programme, an alliance of leading rainforest scientists based in Oxford, UK, estimates that the loss of tropical forests accounts for up to 25 percent of global emissions of greenhouse gases. Because of this, Indonesia became the third largest GHG emitter, followed closely by Brazil. Only two industrial giants, the United States and China, each emit more. "Burning tropical forests drives global warming faster than the world's entire transport sector; there will be no solution to climate change without stopping deforestation," states Andrew Mitchell, head of the Global Canopy Programme.[38] He points out,

> Consumers "eat" rainforests each day—in the form of beef-burgers, bacon and beauty products—but without knowing it. The delivery mechanism is a global supply chain with its feet in the forests and its hands in the till. Because of growing demand for beef, soy and palm oil, which are in much of what we consume, as well as timber and biofuels, rainforests are worth more cut down than standing up.

Fixing this situation requires no new technology, just political will and a system of enforcement and incentives to make the trees worth more to governments and individuals when they are left standing rather than felled. This is where the carbon markets and offsetting can come in. "The focus on technological fixes for the emissions of rich nations while giving no incentive to poorer nations to stop burning the standing forest means we are putting the cart before the horse," says Mitchell. A Global Canopy Programme report, "Global Forest Footprints 2009," concludes, "If we lose forests, we lose the fight against climate change."[39]

The government of Norway and Prince Charles, the Prince of Wales, are determined to act. Norway is investing $2.7 billion from its oil revenues to keep massive tracts of endangered rainforest from being cut. Other countries are helping as well. In an effort to achieve carbon neutrality by 2020, Costa Rica planted more than 5 million trees (more than one tree per person) in 2007, the highest per capita planting in the world. Industries, including the banana sector, supported Costa Rica's initiative, which includes increasing the percentage of renewable energy generation to well over 90 percent and implementing energy efficiency and energy-saving appliances. In 2008 the UN Environment Programme leveraged Costa Rica's work by creating the Climate Neutral Network, whose goal is to federate the small but growing group of nations, local authorities, and companies who are pledging to significantly reduce emissions en route to becoming zero-emission economies, communities, and businesses. Early members besides Costa Rica included Iceland, New Zealand, and Norway. Recently, Ethiopia, the Maldives, Monaco, Pakistan, and Portugal; the cities of Brisbane, Cape Town, Copenhagen, Curitiba (Brazil), Rizhao (China), Sydney, and Vancouver; and corporate entities, including Bayer, Dell, Deutsche Bank, Interface, Japan Airlines, and Microsoft.[40]

Such initiatives appear to be having an effect. By early 2010, the rate of deforestation began to slow. The UN Food and Agriculture organization (FAO) stated that although the loss of forests remains alarming, the deforestation rate in the last decade had declined from 16 million hectares (6.5 million acres) annually in the 1990s to a rate of 13 million hectares (5.26 million acres) in 2010. The FAO's report "Global Forest Resources Assessment 2010" found that more than 7 million hectares (2.8 million acres) per year of new forests, especially in China, were being planted, for a net rate of loss since the year 2000 of 5.2 million hectares (2.1 million acres) per year, compared to 8.3 million (3.4 million acres) in the 1990s. The biggest losses of forest occurred in Brazil, Indonesia, and Australia, but Brazil, supported by President Lula da Silva, has set the political goal to reduce deforestation by 80 percent by 2020 (see chapter 6).

One of the few successes of the Conference of the Parties in Cancun in 2010 (COP 16) was the work to strengthen the REDD (Reducing

Emissions from Deforestation and Forest Degradation in Developing Countries) program. The insipid Copenhagen Accord at least recognized the crucial role of reducing emissions from deforestation and forest degradation and agreed on the need to provide funds for forest protection to such actions through the immediate establishment of a mechanism including REDD-plus, so that developed countries can fund forest preservation efforts. REDD+ is a UN-sanctioned program focused on helping developing countries avoid deforestation.[41]

After Copenhagen, an organization called Pure Planet, headquartered in San Francisco, was formed by a group of social entrepreneurs to use carbon markets to drive reforestation projects, coupled with fair-trade economic development, and simultaneously to work for a zero-carbon world. It offers carbon credits for small- to medium-scale projects in the developing world that confer a local sustainable development impact, enabling individuals seeking to offset their emissions to pay others to keep standing forests intact and conduct reforestation campaigns while supporting local farming communities in developing countries. Since 2008, Pure Planet has planted 3 million trees and conserved 300,000 hectares of primary forest. Its goal is to plant a minimum of 12 million trees by the end of 2012. Founded by social entrepreneurs, including Ryan Fix and Tristan Lecomte, the founder of Alter Eco, a leading fair-trade brand, the program works with fifty fair-trade cooperatives in thirty countries around the world, helping farmers plant a mix of native trees on deforested farmland both to provide additional revenue to farmers and to increase productivity of the farms while effectively reducing CO_2 levels in the atmosphere. The funding comes from the sale of carbon credits on the voluntary market, simultaneously creating additional revenue for local communities and fighting climate change. Pure Planet uses the highest verification standards for carbon-offset projects whenever possible, maintaining successful and long-lasting reforestation projects. To ensure maximum transparency, its planted parcels are tracked and recorded by GPS and are viewable by the public using Google Earth. Its projects currently have or are in the process of achieving Clean Development Mechanism validation for registration with the United Nations Framework Con-

vention on Climate Change, Voluntary Carbon Standard (VCS) validation, or SGS certification. This covers projects of planted trees, smaller
projects, and reforested areas that are not eligible for CDM and VCS
validation because of their size or other technical limitations (SGS S.A.,
formerly Société Générale de Surveillance, is a Swiss company offering
inspection, verification, testing, and certification services).

Profitable Business Opportunities in the Carbon-Trading Sector

The competition to become carbon-neutral will intensify in coming
years. The first countries and companies to act did so to capture both
the first-mover advantage and marketing advantages. Prior to the global
climate summit in Copenhagen in December 2009, participants were
getting into the carbon markets to make money. After the failure of
COP 15 to do anything, this rate of market entry slowed. But in spite of
that setback, the inexorable march of climate chaos and customer demand for companies to behave in more responsible ways will force
companies and countries to get much more serious about cutting their
carbon emissions.

If North America, China, and other major emitters enter the regulated market, the demand for offsets would become substantially higher
than the credits available for purchase, creating significant opportunities for new and existing companies to get into the business of developing offset projects to sell the resulting carbon offsets to wholesalers or,
in direct sales, to trading systems such as the EU ETS. EcoSecurities
will be one of those players. It is already one of the largest developers
and traders of CDM carbon offsets in the world, with 378 projects in
thirty countries in its portfolio, amounting to more than 100 million
carbon offsets projected through 2012.[42] Its COO, Adrian Fernando,
ticked off such first-in-industry achievements:

- The first carbon-offset certification system in the world was licensed
  by EcoSecurities to Société Générale de Surveillance (SGS), the

largest commodity certification company worldwide, in January 1997.

- The first CDM project registered under the Kyoto Protocol was EcoSecurities' NovaGerar Landfill Gas to Energy Project in Brazil in 2004.
- In 2005 EcoSecurities structured the CDM component of the first project in the world to receive certified emission reductions (CERs): the La Esperanza Hydro Project in Honduras.
- In December 2009 EcoSecurities successfully registered its 195th CDM project.

Interested? So was JP Morgan. In July 2009 the bank acquired Eco-Securities for $204 million.[43]

EcoSecurities' activities to promote projects in the least-developed countries included the introduction of Programmes of Activities (POAs), allowing multiple small-scale projects such as home solar systems and cookstove projects to be bundled together under one project design document (PDD) for approval by the UN's CDM executive board. Such POAs support co-benefits projects that are highly sustainable, but whose small size made them economically unviable under the previous approval process. Reflecting on key concerns for the private sector given the continued lack of a global binding political accord, Fernando noted,

Countries involved in the Copenhagen conference pledged $100 billion in finance, and the EU has previously stated that at least half of this would need to come from the private sector. With over 378 projects currently in our portfolio we have shown that we can mobilize the necessary resources needed to help the transition of developing countries down a low-carbon pathway. However, much more clarity is needed in terms of the post-2012 landscape before private-sector organisations can make further investments. The climate-change problem is immediate and action is required now. What remains to be seen now is whether or not the international community can come together to agree to binding commitments to significantly reduce greenhouse gases and provide clear rules of engagement for the private sector post-2012. It will be important for the United States and New Zealand to join a binding international agreement.[44]

One of the cleverer uses of market mechanisms to protect the climate is emerging at a company called EOS Climate. Developed as a 2008 thesis project by three of Hunter Lovins's forward-thinking MBA candidates, EOS Climate is creating a profitable business that would guarantee permanent greenhouse gas reductions by expediting destruction and decommissioning of chlorofluorocarbons and other ozone-depleting substances (ODS). In addition to damaging the ozone layer, these chemicals are also highly potent greenhouse gases, up to 11,000 times more threatening to the climate than carbon dioxide. The Montreal Protocol successfully phased out production of ODS, which was the reason these gases were not included in the Kyoto Protocol, but the Montreal Protocol stopped short of regulating use or disposal of ODS already in existence, and their recycling and reuse has been encouraged. Consequently, large quantities of ODS manufactured prior to their production phaseout deadlines remain in widespread legal use worldwide. The founders of EOS Climate realized that unless this regulatory gap was filled, and incentives provided for collection and destruction of ODS (rather than mandated, which would be impossible to enforce and too expensive for government budgets), these chemicals would be released to the atmosphere from older equipment, appliances, and building infrastructure, representing the equivalent of billions of tons of CO_2.[45]

EOS Climate's founders set out to use carbon finance to leverage aggressive, near-term climate action. Securing funding in 2009 from Firelake Capital, EOS Climate is transforming management of these dangerous chemicals, still pervasive across the economy. Against a backdrop of international climate negotiations and anticipated U.S. climate legislation, EOS acted to create a new market:

- Educated industry and policy makers about the environmental imperative for policy and market-based incentives for management of global ODS banks.

- Created a quantification/monitoring methodology in conformance with ISO standards, incorporated under the Voluntary Carbon Standard and Climate Action Reserve.
- Developed an integrated value chain with partners in the United States and abroad to address every aspect of ODS recovery, transport, analysis, destruction, and project financing, where all parties participate in the upside as carbon markets evolve and costs are reduced.
- Developed demonstration projects in North and South America, Africa, Europe, and Asia.
- Created verified carbon credits that generate a new source of revenue for leading-edge equipment manufacturers, building owners, appliance recyclers, and other businesses.
- Delivered high-quality, transparent emissions reductions that provided early-stage liquidity for emerging, precompliance greenhouse gas markets.
- Developed new technologies to demanufacture equipment, separate CFCs (chlorofluorocarbons) from insulation foam, and convert ODS to benign, marketable products.

EOS estimates that their programs, along with those of competitors who will inevitably enter the market, will cost-effectively eliminate emissions of hundreds of millions of tons of greenhouse gases by 2020, accelerate the transition to more advanced technologies, create thousands of jobs, and buy time to build the bridge to a clean-energy economy.

CO2IMPACT Social Carbon, cofounded by Boyd Cohen, one of this book's authors, is a carbon project development company currently creating the first Gold Standard project in Colombia. CO2IMPACT was one of the first twenty organizations in the world to become a Gold Standard Majority Pledger, committing to develop more than 50 percent of its carbon offsets to achieve the Gold Standard certification.

Cohen founded CO2IMPACT in November 2009 with his wife, Elizabeth Obediente, a former petroleum engineer in Venezuela, who had previously directed Latin American operations for a carbon consultancy in Vancouver. Cohen and Obediente recognized that unmet demand for charismatic carbon offsets (projects that have a particularly appealing story to tell) represented a gap in the project development market and created CO2IMPACT to fill it. In its first year of operation, CO2IMPACT raised angel investment from First Light Ventures and others.

Starting in Huila, Colombia, a region with about 1 million people and at least five artisan brick-making communities, CO2IMPACT is using the carbon market to cut pollution that is harming residents and the climate. All the members of the community—men, women, and children—work virtually nonstop in hundreds of highly polluting artisan kilns, producing bricks for the construction sector, suffering rampant respiratory illness and even death. The region is stuck in poverty, unable to diversify its economy or create value-added products. Lacking marketing skills or leverage, the hard-working artisans are pressured into selling their bricks at the prices set by distant purchasers, who arrive in their community with trucks and money in hand. Bricks that should sell for 300 pesos are frequently bought in Huila for less than 100 pesos.

CO2IMPACT is helping the community form local associations and secure competitive financing for the purchase of eco-efficient kilns. These will reduce harmful contaminants and emissions, while allowing the artisan communities to diversify their economies, using the new kilns to make tiles, roofing, and other more value-added, differentiated products. The increased efficiencies will also free children to go to school more regularly and allow others in the community to participate in the economy beyond working in the kilns.

CO2IMPACT works with local NGOs to bring capacity to the communities with which it works. In Huila an NGO called Corciencias is helping the community understand how to diversify and market its new products. By enabling increased revenues and efficiencies, these projects can help the artisan communities and their families escape the vicious cycle of poverty. With increased efficiencies and a shift toward a more professional approach, child labor will be less necessary than with their previous inefficient and unprofitable operations. Furthermore, CO2IMPACT shares a significant percentage of the revenues it gets from its offset projects with the local community and its NGO partners, allowing them to tap into additional financial benefits from their emissions reductions.

There is rising demand for such social/charismatic carbon offsets. CO2IMPACT has received three offers to purchase offsets from its Huila project and from other projects in its pipeline from some of the largest carbon-offset brokers in the world. Social carbon offsets sell at a premium because they combine ways to reduce carbon with effective development programs. The model is working and has led to projects worth more than $20 million in CO2IMPACT's portfolio.

Although this model of using carbon offsets to support economic development is relatively new, CO2IMPACT is not the only player in the carbon markets to use it. Ecosystem Restoration Associates (ERA), based in Vancouver, is also leveraging carbon markets to generate positive local impacts much closer to home. They were recently awarded the highest certification level from the Climate, Community and Biodiversity Standard Ecosystem for their community-based reforestation program in British Columbia. ERA was rewarded with a contract announced in September 2010 to sell 1.8 million tons of forestry-based offsets over a three-year period from their Canadian activities to Forest Carbon Group, a carbon-offset broker based in Germany.[46]

Nexus, an alliance of social ventures and NGOs, is conducting a similar initiative in Asia. Nexus is committed to leveraging carbon finance "to reduce poverty, reduce emissions of greenhouse gases, and where possible achieve other benefits such as improved human health and conservation of biodiversity, in a sustainable manner." Nexus is also a Gold Standard Majority Pledger. Though a young organization, Nexus is becoming an important voice and support system for the social carbon markets in the coming years.[47]

Conclusion

Capitalism, business, and indeed naked greed are some of the most powerful motivations for solving the problem of climate change—so let's unleash them through Climate Capitalism and visionary business models.

Governments have failed to solve the climate crisis. As this recognition grows, businesses, communities, states, and the growing civil society sector must step up to the plate to innovate in creating carbon markets, implementing self-regulation, and creating offsets that not only cut carbon but empower people in poor communities to begin solving their own problems. This entrepreneurialism may be messy, but it represents our best hope in facing an uncertain future.

9

Adapting to Climate Chaos

Much of the global conversation about climate change, and much of Climate Capitalism, is focused on mitigation, or the actions we can take that curb climate change, most of them profitable. Thousands of individuals, companies, NGOs, cities, and governments realize that moving to a low-carbon economy, and fast, is the key to profitability and survival. Mitigation—blunting the forces that lead to climate change—is only part of the story, however. Adaptation, figuring out ways to deal with the consequences of climate chaos, is no less profitable, and will be essential to preserving any quality of life in a world beset by climate chaos.

Activists, scientists, and policy experts committed to reducing greenhouse gas emissions have feared that any shift in the public's attention from mitigation to adaptation would be perceived as a sign of defeat. Embracing adaptation, they worry, is an admission that runaway climate change is inevitable and investments in lowering carbon emissions are too little, too late, and should be abandoned.

Their fear is understandable. And it is right, in part: adaptation advocates believe it is already too late to avoid dangerous climate change, and we would be utter fools to delay implementing sensible adaptation measures. But in larger part, it is wrong. As this book argues, the best mitigation actions to prevent climate chaos are profitable and should be (and increasingly are being) undertaken anyway for good business reasons. They are also the best way to avoid the worst, and still preventable, impacts of climate chaos. Furthermore, the most compelling rebuttal of those who fear that adaptation will divert action from mitigation is that the same logic applies to adaptation as applies to mitigation: it's good business. Many adaptive measures are profitable and should be implemented regardless of whether you care about climate change or not. And the best adaptive measures also help mitigate climate change.

It is not a matter of either-or. As Dr. John Holdren, President Obama's science adviser and an eminent climate scientist, makes clear, "We basically have three choices: mitigation, adaptation, and suffering. We're going to do some of each. The question is what the mix is going to be. The more mitigation we do, the less adaptation will be required, and the less suffering there will be."

In "Learning to Love Climate Change" in *Newsweek*, Sharon Begley wrote:

> It's such a polite, unthreatening word: "adapt." The kind of thing you do as you roll with the punches or keep a stiff upper lip, modifying your behavior to a new situation. But as it will be used in 2008, adaptation is a euphemism for widespread, expensive changes that will be needed to cope with climate change. Although some adaptations will be modest and low tech, such as cities' establishing cooling centers to shelter residents during heat waves, others will require such Herculean efforts and be so costly that we'll look back on the era beginning in 1988, when credible warnings of climate change reached critical mass, and wonder why we were so stupid as to blow the chance to keep global warming to nothing more extreme than a few more mild days in March.[1]

As the summer of 2010 showed, climate change impacts are already being felt all around the world. More severe droughts and floods, the increased strength of hurricanes, rapid glacier loss, and rising sea levels—already threatening the existence of Tuvalu and the Maldives—all make clear that although every possible resource should be devoted to mitigation so that the problem does not get worse, adaptation is already necessary.

The longer the world puts off achieving a globally binding, fair, and ambitious mitigation accord to replace the Kyoto Protocol, the more quickly it will have to gear up adaptation strategies and the costlier they will be. Heather McGray, of the World Resources Institute, recently noted: "If we don't have some very substantial mitigation soon, we're going to have a lot, a lot, a lot of adapting to do. If we do have some mitigation moving soon, we will still have a fair amount of adapting to do."[2]

The state of California, long a leader in responding to climate change, issued the "2009 California Climate Adaptation Strategy Discussion Draft," the state's guide to adaptation.[3] Covering the need to protect biodiversity and habitat, infrastructure (roads, levees, buildings, and so forth), oceans and coastal resources, public health, water and working landscapes (forestry and agriculture), the report summarized the best-established science on the impact of climate change in these seven specific sectors and provided recommendations on how to manage them to protect against those impacts. The report was prepared in response to Governor Arnold Schwarzenegger's November 2008 Executive Order specifically asking the Natural Resources Agency to identify how state agencies would respond to rising temperatures, changing precipitation patterns, sea-level rise, and extreme natural events. It is sobering reading.

Adaptation is already being undertaken the world over: the Alaskan Inuit village of Shishmareff is moving to higher ground and building a wall to protect against storm surges destroying its coastal houses.[4] Efforts are being made to shore up the Trans-Alaska Pipeline, endangered by melting permafrost. The Dutch are building floating subdivisions that will rise and fall with changing sea levels. None of this is much use, however, to the millions of Bangladeshis who live in the low-lying areas that are now regularly flooded by ever more common and more intense cyclones. More than 500,000 Bangladeshis from Bhola Island became climate change refugees overnight as half of their island was lost to rising sea levels and heavier Himalayan glacier melt.[5]

Adaptation has now become a market segment. A representative of the U.S. Climate Change Adaptation Industry states, "The . . . industry is just emerging, slowed by state and federal deficits, by the lack of projections firm and specific enough to plan by, and by denial about just how serious the impacts will be."[6] But emerging it is. And small pockets of entrepreneurs and business leaders around the globe have awoken to the possibility of minimizing current and future suffering from the effects of climate change while generating profits. These leaders have recognized that the impacts of climate change on communities and companies around the globe will be monumental, and adaptation, like mitigation, will create Climate Capitalism opportunities for companies, organizations, and governments that can develop cost-effective and profitable solutions to climate chaos.

This chapter looks at two sets of Climate Capitalism challenges and opportunities: existing industries and emerging sectors. Existing industries, most prominently insurance, energy, construction, and tourism, face both threats and opportunities. Insurers face ever greater exposure because of the increase in natural disasters. Energy companies are coping with spiking demand for cooling. The construction sector is responding to infrastructure damaged by ever larger storms and demands for innovative housing. Finally, as beaches erode, hurricanes threaten vacation seasons, ski resorts warm, and destination sites vanish beneath rising water levels, tourism stands to lose significant revenue to climate change. All four industries must adapt, and all four have cost-effective or even potentially profitable solutions available to help them.

Emerging sectors in the adaptation marketplace also offer significant potential for profits, running the gamut from finding innovative solutions to delivering potable water to inventing controversial geoengineering approaches. Opportunities exist, too, to help communities and companies adapt to the changing climate. It is hard to identify a single industry that will remain untouched by escalating climate change. Reviewing how the most exposed established industries—insurance, energy, construction, and tourism—and the most creative new markets are responding to adaptation suggests strategies and models others can and likely will be forced to adopt.

Existing Industries in the Line of Fire . . . and Floods . . . and . . .

Insurance

The insurance industry is in climate chaos' gunsights (see chapter 1). In 2010, the monsoon-induced floods in northwest China and Pakistan dwarfed the 2010 storms that savaged New England, Nashville, Arkansas, and Oklahoma.[7] In Pakistan alone, the 2010 floods inundated a fifth of the country, killing over 1,600 people, injuring another 2,500, damaging 30 percent of farm land, and putting 20 million people at risk of disease and food shortages.[8] UN Secretary General Ban Ki-moon described the disaster as a "slow motion tsunami."[9] Climate change is clearly agnostic, as flooding in India subsequently left another 2 million homeless.[10]

In 2005 Hurricane Katrina cost the United States well over $200 billion, or the equivalent of what it spent over a four-year span in wars in Iraq and Afghanistan, forcing the insurance industry to pay out an estimated $60 billion in claims.[11] It also killed over two thousand people. Scientists agree that the warmer Gulf waters caused by climate change increased the intensity of Katrina and led to more extensive damage than average earlier hurricanes.[12] Even without a Katrina-sized hurricane, 2008 imposed on the insurance industry $200 billion in catastrophic losses globally, the third-highest amount in history—certainly an unappealing trend.[13]

Insurance companies have responded by undertaking efforts to mitigate and adapt to the crises posed by climate change. In March 2009, the National Association of Insurance Commissioners (NAIC) adopted a mandatory requirement that insurance companies disclose to regulators the financial risks they face from climate change, as well as actions the companies are taking to respond to those risks.[14] While some states are resisting this order, others, such as Florida, are urging their insurance companies to comply.

As a graph from a recent Ceres report shows, the insurance industry is increasing its activities across a range of mitigation and adaptation solutions.[15]

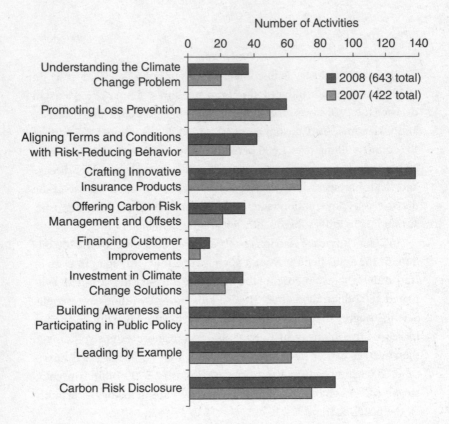

Capitalizing on the trend in corporate governance that compels companies to protect themselves from the effects or risks associated with climate change, the insurance industry now offers to indemnify boards of directors and companies from liability due to climate change litigation. This strikes us as a lousy business proposition, but the insurers obviously feel that companies with carbon exposure or those that are significant emitters of greenhouse gases represent a new opportunity, which is why Zurich and Liberty Mutual both launched such insurance services in 2008.[16]

Insurers have also introduced micro-insurance policies aimed at low-income populations at high risk of climate-related catastrophes. A majority of the more than 7 million policyholders reside in developing countries where food and water shortages already present grave risks.[17]

In August 2010, a group of academics and researchers at the United Nations University published a report entitled "Solutions for Vulnerable Countries and People." In it they suggest that it is essential that the poor in developing countries be insured against the largest impacts of climate change. "Many risk management activities, such as risk identification and mapping, risk pricing, and vulnerability assessment, are useful for a variety of adaptation measures. In this way, investing in risk reduction promises multiple dividends: lower losses, safeguarding development goals, lessened volatility for government planning and budgets, and benefits for other adaptation measures."[18] A 2010 micro-insurance pilot project in Mexico led to 50,000 microinsurance policies being sold with a goal of an additional 200,000 policies sold by the end of the year.[19]

MicroEnsure, founded in 2005, is one of the world's first insurance intermediaries focused on insurance products for the world's poor. Operating in ten countries in Africa and Asia, MicroEnsure offers a range of insurance services to the poor in the same way that microcredit organizations provide many poor communities with access to small amounts of capital. MicroEnsure provides insurance against drought and extreme weather events, all of which will be worsened by climate change.

Depending on how it adapts to the realities of climate change, the insurance industry is poised either to lose its shirt or to gain significant market share. Providing climate change–related insurance products to the Fortune 500 or the global poor at the base of the economic pyramid may enable insurance companies such as Zurich, Liberty Mutual, and MicroEnsure to survive and even thrive in an age of the now-inescapable consequences of climate chaos. But the insurance products also underscore why adaptation cannot replace mitigation. Adaptation alone will simply add the cost of paying for the increasing insurance burden to the economy. Only mitigation offers a chance to curtail the additional expense of defending against predictable disasters and cleaning up after them.

Energy

Ironically, climate change will negatively impact the very energy companies that are its leading cause. Hotter weather is driving the demand for more cooling, much of which is now powered by electricity, most of which is produced by the coal-fired generators driving climate change. A report produced by the Natural Resources Defense Council, "The Cost of Climate Change," estimates that the rise in demand for air-conditioning and refrigeration in the United States alone will add "more than $200 billion for extra electricity and new air conditioners, compared with almost $60 billion in reduced heating costs. The net result is that energy sector costs would be $141 billion higher in 2100 due to global warming."[20] This may sound like more business for the utilities, but, as discussed in chapter 2, utilities that help their customers use energy more efficiently are those that will prosper.

The less-sustainable utilities will face greater challenges. The heat waves of 2003, 2006, and 2007 forced the closure of several nuclear reactors because they could not be cooled. In August 2007, the Tennessee Valley Authority shut down Browns Ferry Unit 2 and reduced the power output from other reactors to 75 percent because the Tennessee River water was too hot to adequately cool them. The TVA had to buy power from elsewhere to meet demand, which was at an all-time high because of the heat wave. European reactors have faced similar closures, or been required to waive safety rules and rules designed to limit damage to aquatic life from the discharge of overly hot water.[21] In 2009, France was forced to import 1,000 megawatts of power a day, as high temperatures forced the closure of a third of its nuclear stations to keep the casings of reactors from exceeding design tolerances.[22]

What about hydropower? From the Sierra Mountains in California to the Three Gorges Dam in China, hydropower will be limited by changes in rainfall and snow pack. Venezuela, which derives most of its energy from hydropower, offers an interesting example. Venezuela has gone from a net exporter of hydroelectric energy to coping with severe energy shortages caused by prolonged drought.[23] Venezuelans now face both water and energy shortages as a result of a nine-meter drop in water levels at the country's Guri Dam.[24] Left with few options, in January 2010 the government announced rolling blackouts throughout the country, an extremely costly adaptation strategy that reduced economic efficiency and sowed social discord. A far better strategy would have been aggressive implementation of energy efficiency, timely diversification of the country's renewable energy portfolio, and proper maintenance of its energy infrastructure.

Energy companies that move toward the renewable and distributed energy solutions discussed in chapter 3 will be the best prepared for adapting to climate change. As the energy sector both contributes to the problem and has to react to it, renewable-energy solutions are important to both mitigating the impacts of climate change and adapting to them.

Ethanol production in particular will be severely impacted by climate change. Corn-based ethanol is susceptible to droughts as well as the consequent increased political and economic pressure to use still-productive land for food production instead of energy crops, as climate change cuts the productivity of farmland. Companies producing alternative energy will need to adapt by diversifying their product portfolio into crops like algae that do not require crop acreage. Renewables, such as wind and solar, that can coexist with farmland will help energy growers reduce their exposure to climate change impacts and offer growth opportunities. Princeton professor Van Jones points out that integrating wind turbines and sustainable agriculture into midwestern agricultural land can give farmers a diversified cash flow: lease payments for the turbines, biofuel production, and carbon payments for sequestering carbon by converting to organic agriculture.[25]

As more severe storms damage our energy infrastructure, the energy sector will find that mitigation and adaptation measures go hand in hand. Moving away from coal-fired power plants is the obvious way to mitigate climate change. However, as the Venezuela example illustrates, reliance on large centralized sources of power, even renewable ones like hydropower, can still leave a region susceptible to the impacts of climate change. A proper adaptation solution requires much greater efficiency, use of more inherently resilient distributed forms of energy that are less dependent on grid-delivered energy, and a mix of renewable energy solutions.[26]

The Construction Industry: Building Resilience

The NRDC's report "The Cost of Climate Change" estimated that if climate change is left unchecked, residential real estate losses in the United States by 2100 would be $360 billion dollars per year.[27] Wherever substantial communities are exposed to damage or destruction from storms or rising water levels, there is risk to property and infrastructure. Hurricane Katrina alone damaged 360,000 homes valued at over $48 billion.[28] The rebuilding of New Orleans, however, points to a possible solution.

The actor Brad Pitt responded to the devastation of Katrina by launching the Make It Right Foundation to help rebuild. In partnership with Morphosis Architects, the foundation is building floating homes able to rise with storm surges in the badly hit Ninth Ward neighborhood. Morphosis describes the floating homes as

> a new kind of house: a house that can sustain its own water and power needs; a house that can survive the floodwaters generated by a storm the size of Hurricane Katrina; and perhaps most importantly, a house that can be manufactured cheaply enough to function as low-income housing. To protect from flooding, the FLOAT House can rise vertically on guide posts, securely floating up to twelve feet as water levels rise. In the event of a flood, the house's chassis acts as a raft, guided by steel masts, which are anchored to the ground by two concrete pile caps each with six 45-foot deep piles.[29]

Other architectural firms are meeting the challenge of climate change. Dura Vermeer is an innovative Dutch firm that has developed similar adaptation solutions for coastal communities. The Dura Vermeer homes, capable of withstanding a thirteen-foot rise in sea level, are selling at €260,000 and are quite popular with locals in the Netherlands and foreigners alike.[30] Dura Vermeer recently secured a contract to build similar eco-friendly floating homes on the Thames River in London.[31]

Tourism

Tourism is a crucial component of economies around the globe, accounting for about $2,008 billion in travel and hospitality spending in 2008, or 3.4 percent of total global GDP. World Tourism and Travel Council calculations that include economic sectors driven by tourism count $5,890 billion a year, or 9.9 percent of global GDP.[32] Many local and regional economies depend almost entirely on tourism for their economic survival. Small island states that have the largest percentage of GDP associated with tourism, especially those in the Caribbean, face some of the biggest threats from climate change. Tourism is disrupted through the loss of beaches from more intense storms, coastal inundation from sea level rise, degradation of coastal ecosystems, saline intrusion into ground water, storm damage to critical infrastructures, and the bleaching of coral reefs from warmer, more acidic oceans. As sea levels rise, island states also face significant threats of flooding, losing resort properties to storm surges—indeed, of disappearing right off the map.

The president of the Maldives, Mohammed Nasheed, has been a highly vocal advocate of acting fast to mitigate and adapt to climate change. He has a compelling reason: the 1,100-plus islands that make up the Maldives face ever more dire threats of disappearing into the rising Indian Ocean. Speaking at the Times World Forum on Enterprise and the Environment in Oxford, UK, in 2009, President Nasheed warned, "We feel that climate change is not an environmental issue, it's a security issue, it's a human rights issue." Referring to his plan to become the first country in the world to achieve a zero-carbon economy by 2019 through a $110 million investment, he stated, "We know that the Maldives becoming carbon neutral is not going to de-carbonize the world and stop us from annihilation. We know that. But at least we could die knowing we've done the right thing."[33]

Such acts of mitigation will not be enough. Even as the Maldives builds embankments and sea walls, it has initiated an even more dramatic adaptation strategy. In 2008, the country began diverting a por-

tion of its billion-dollar-a-year tourist revenue into an insurance policy
to buy a new home for the whole population. "We do not want to leave
the Maldives," Nasheed said, "but we also do not want to be climate
refugees living in tents for decades."[34]

Nasheed is not alone in fearing the worst consequences of climate
change for his country. The Honorable Isaac V. Figir, vice speaker of the
Federated States of Micronesia, warned, "The fear of submergence is
not mere science fiction though that is all too easy for skeptics to dis-
miss. I have no doubt that at current levels of emissions of greenhouse
gases (or even at levels where there is only a nominal decrease in the
level of emissions of greenhouse gases) submergence is a possibility." He
went on to point out that Micronesia is at grave risk long before it risks
submergence. "A long, long time before that point is reached, our reefs
could be dead, our fishes fleeing, our groundwater completely salinated,
our food crops depleted and our islands made inhabitable. Needless to
say, our economies destroyed."[35]

One of the most obvious adaptation measures for small island states,
building sea walls to protect their coastlines from rising sea levels, is
exceedingly costly. Jamaica would have to spend the equivalent of
19 percent of its GDP on it. Barriers to protect the Maldives' capital,
Male, which has a mean height of about eight feet above sea level, would
cost approximately $4,000 per meter of barrier.[36] However, the cost of
not doing it, in human lives and damaged and destroyed property, is
likely to be much more. The cost to rebuild New Orleans's levees damaged by Katrina to insurance-certified levels approaches $10 billion.[37]
Advocates who argued for strengthening the levees before the storm, at
what would have been a fraction of that cost, were clearly prescient.[38]
"Be prepared" is the cornerstone of all good adaptation policy.

Rising sea levels are far from the only threat to tourism. The recent
2010 Winter Olympics in Vancouver, dubbed the "Spring Olympics" by
some wags, saw mountain communities long reliant on snow for their
ski industries scrambling to adapt to barren slopes. The general lack of
snow cost Olympic organizers millions of dollars while they worked to
make snow, even resorting to helicopters to dump buckets of the white
stuff on crucial competition venues. If warming trends continue, only

Swiss ski resorts over 1,600 meters in elevation will have reliable snow. This leaves 66 percent of the current ski resort industry in need of a different source of revenue.[39] Many have adapted by turning to snow-making facilities, but these demand greater energy use and require abundant water supplies. The wiser choice, evidenced by such premier ski resorts like Whistler in Canada, is to retool a resort's offerings to attract summer vacationers. Whistler now attracts more warm-weather tourists than skiers.

Golf courses, another water-intensive enterprise, also face significant challenges as a result of climate change. As many regions around the world experience longer and more intense droughts, this favorite pastime may contract to the driving range in many parts of the world. Using water and energy to make snow to save ski resorts is not a wise idea for the planet, and neither is spraying potable water on golf courses when local populations lack drinking water. Companies such as Aquaspy, with offices in the United States and Australia, sell a stop-gap solution that minimizes water consumption on golf courses. Their smart water controller ensures that water is not dispersed unless it is needed. Ultimately, however, even reducing water consumption on golf courses in drought-prone regions is unlikely to offer sufficient savings.

Another industry at risk is beach resorts. In 2003, Natural Capitalism Solutions worked with the Dolphin Head Trust in Jamaica to create a business plan for the development of ecotourism to replace the all-inclusive "sun and sand" resort-based tourism that does little to benefit Jamaicans, and is now threatened by climate change.[40] The project is focusing instead on local bamboo production and on the creation of an eco-resort in the Dolphin Head Mountains, to offer Jamaicans a better route to prosperity as well as an alternative form of tourism that can endure even in a hotter world.[41]

Ecotourism, defined as "responsible travel to natural areas that conserves the environment and improves the well-being of local people," represents an opportunity for destinations with natural beauty such as mountains, rivers, coral reefs, and rainforests to both mitigate and adapt to climate change.[42] Globally, ecotourism since the 1990s has been growing at more than 20 percent per year, three times faster than the overall tourism industry, as 85 percent of tourists would prefer to patronize operators that protect the environment.[43] Featuring renewable energy and other sustainable technologies, it offers lower-carbon-footprint tourism than mainstream tourism, as operators reduce the footprint of their tours and their accommodations offerings. Because ecotourist operations can help deliver electricity to local villages and serve as an example of more sustainable living, enabling locals to see how renewable power and resource efficiency can enhance their lives, it also serves as a mitigation measure. It is also a better business for local communities than conventional tourism, as ecotourists spend more, sometimes twice as much, as traditional tourists. Ecotourism operators frequently educate clients on the sensitivities of local ecosystems, and this understanding has the potential to influence tourists to reduce their carbon footprints when they return home.

New Adaptation Opportunities

While existing industries are being forced to exercise innovative adaptation strategies in response to climate chaos, arguably the greater Climate Capitalism opportunities exist in the emerging sectors of the adaptation marketplace. Given the nature of the unfolding disaster, no needs are more pressing than ensuring the fresh water supply, preventing floods, and preparing for disasters.

Water

Climate change is already disrupting water supplies around the world, with the rural poor in developing countries hit particularly hard. An issue far more severe than preventing hurricanes and floods is that over a billion people, one in eight around the world, lack access to clean drinking water, a situation that will only get worse.[44] Droughts in China threatening agriculture and melting glaciers in Bolivia limiting water for rural villages and major cities alike, as well as water rationing in California, all led analysts at Goldman Sachs to conclude that water will be "the petroleum for the next century." They warn that a "catastrophic water shortage could prove an even bigger threat to mankind this century than soaring food prices and the relentless exhaustion of energy reserves."[45] Sir Nicholas Stern, author of the UK government's *Stern Review on the Economics of Climate Change*, likewise cautioned that underground aquifers could run dry at the same time that melting glaciers play havoc with fresh supplies of usable water that feed the world's rivers.[46]

Reduced access to potable water is not just an issue for developing countries. A 2010 report found that "more than 1,100 U.S. counties—a full one-third of all counties in the lower 48 states—now face higher risks of water shortages by mid-century as the result of global warming, and more than 400 of these counties will be at extremely high risk for water shortages."[47] By 2100, costs to the U.S. economy from water shortages resulting from climate change are estimated to equal nearly $1 trillion annually.[48]

Delivering potable water to replace the diminishing supplies is an entrepreneurial opportunity. A recent study on climate change adaptation published by Oxfam singled out water as a source of significant Climate Capitalism opportunities: "Climate change–driven growth in the water management sector will generate jobs for engineers; planners; and those who specialize in manufacturing and constructing water supply, storage, and purification infrastructure."[49]

An innovative Swedish company, Solvatten, has developed a personal solar-powered water filter for distribution to rural residents in developing countries. Using a patented UV-radiation technology, Solvatten filters hold up to ten liters and can purify dirty water up to three times each day. Solvatten has partnered with Tricorona, one of the largest carbon brokers in the world, to distribute the filters in target regions of Africa and beyond.[50] Tricorona, recently acquired by Barclays for $150 million, and Solvatten will distribute more than five thousand of their filters in western Kenya as part of a carbon-offset project. Because the filters enable users to avoid cutting down trees for fuel to boil dirty water, water filters count as carbon mitigation. Tricorona is helping Solvatten market their filters for carbon-reduction projects with the goal of leveraging carbon finance so that the costs to the end user can be eliminated. The carbon finance provider obtains the bulk of the carbon-offset revenues, enabling a return on investment, while helping the poorest and most exposed populations adapt to climate change.

Innovative Water Technologies, based in Colorado, takes solar-powered water purification to another level. Their Sunspring Water Purification System uses the sun to purify enough water to fill the needs of up to five thousand people per day. The purifier recently gained fame when more than one hundred of them were used in the Haiti disaster relief effort. Innovative Water Technologies not only generates profits from the sale of their water purification system but also enables the people where they are installed to generate income and employment. A cofounder of Innovative Water Technologies, Jack Barker, noted:

> One Sunspring costs $25,000, but it lasts for 10 years. If you sell the water at just 4 cents a gallon—20 percent of what water is going for right now in Haiti—the payback period would be four months. You can create a local microfinance model; NGOs can help support hospitals, community centers, or schools. This can be sustainable within itself.[51]

It is critically important, however, that solutions actually work. Play-Pumps International seemed like a brilliant solution: use children's merry-go-rounds so that play generates the spinning action that powers a water pump. The idea attracted $10 million in U.S. funding and Laura Bush's patronage.[52] Alleged to be able to deliver 1,400 liters of water per hour to a surface storage tank standing seven meters above the ground, the actual experience was considerably less exciting. One analysis in *The Guardian* calculated that children would have to "play" for twenty-seven hours every day to meet PlayPumps' stated target of providing 2,500 people per pump with their daily water needs. The systems were also costly, averaging $14,000, considerably more than an ordinary hand pump. They required specialized maintenance, as well, and although the water storage tanks were supposed to generate further income when the sides were leased as billboards, with the revenue paying for pump maintenance, most are now standing unused.[53]

FogQuest, a Canadian nonprofit run entirely by volunteers, has devised a solution to capture water from fog near rural villages, deploying large mesh canvases that can capture up to 200 liters per day. The Fog-Quest solution requires no energy, since wind pushes the fog past the mesh canvas. Once collected, the water moves by gravity from the hillside to the nearby village. The value of this technology can be seen in Yemen, a country experts predict will be the first in the world to run out of water. The capital, Sanaa, a city of 2 million that is growing rapidly as rural residents flee insurgencies and the increasingly severe water shortages in the countryside, has about ten years at current rates of usage before its wells run dry. FogQuest collectors in Yemen demonstrated the ability to produce about 180 liters per day, enough clean water to support a family of nine people.[54] The project also made clear the necessity of follow-through. Yemen suffers from violent winds and the collectors, made from inadequate cloth imported from Saudi Arabia, tore apart. FogQuest is a small nonprofit, lacking resources to return to Yemen and conduct repairs. They had turned the project over to a local nonprofit and the families benefiting from the water collection. The collectors have since fallen into disuse, with residents content to have water sold to them from trucks that ply the country. They may feel differently when the wells, now rapidly being depleted, are exhausted.

Disaster Preparedness and Response

In 2009, Istanbul experienced significant flooding, now blamed in part on climate change. The CEO of the World Wildlife Fund in Turkey noted in September 2009 that "ecological flood management is the safest and most cost-effective solution . . . If future damage is to be prevented, the climate change adaptation process has to start immediately."[55] It's sound advice. Companies providing products and services that rapidly and effectively assist citizens, communities, and governments will be in demand. The majority of emerging adaptation market entrepreneurs focus on flood prevention, providing temporary shelters and emergency communications services, and fire protection and prevention.

Governments invest millions of dollars in flood prevention to protect vulnerable communities. Seeking to capitalize on this, Solid Applied Technologies, headquartered in India, developed sensors for flood warning systems. One of their technologies, Aquascan, allows remote monitoring of reservoir and river levels. To date they have sold more than eighty units to be deployed in the region of Maharashtra, India, which contains rivers and reservoirs vital to sustaining life in the region. In the dry season, water is allocated to individual users and the agricultural sector, depending on water levels. In monsoon season, when floods threatening property and livelihood are common, Aquascan enables government agencies to have nearly real-time readings of remote water sources, not only informing decisions regarding water allocation but also providing an early warning system against floods. Residents can also access this information by sending an SMS text into the Solid Applied Technologies communication service.

As climate-related extreme weather events around the world increase, there will be a significant increase in the number of environmental refugees. Janet Sawin of the World Watch Institute noted that "human migrations are expected to increase as average global temperatures continue to rise and we experience rising sea levels, more severe weather disasters, and other impacts as a result."[56] The Intergovernmental Panel on Climate Change has estimated that by 2050 there could be as many as 150 million environmental refugees around the globe.[57] Being able to provide temporary shelter will be an important part of meeting their challenges.

In response, Worldwide Shelters has developed temporary shelters for people displaced from disasters. They placed more than three thousand such shelters in Haiti following the devastating earthquake in early 2010. Working with NGOs, governments, and humanitarian aid groups, Worldwide Shelters sells and distributes their temporary shelters to displaced individuals around the world.

Rafael Smith, a fellow of the Boulder-based Unreasonable Institute, designed an even cleverer solution. His Uber Shelter is a temporary two-story structure, complete with a stove, light, even a porch. Unlike tents, the shelter is solid enough to be built onto, providing modular solutions appropriate at the different stages of a disaster. Foldable and stackable on a shipping pallet, the Uber Shelter provides immediate simple shelter during initial response to provide stability in a crisis. Because the basic model can be the core of a permanent structure, it brings security as the situation stabilizes. It can then be made into durable housing as the area manages the transition to reconstruction, at all stages offering local construction jobs as the structure is upgraded.

Many parts of the world are at increased risk for fires as a direct result of climate change. Regions prone to long periods of drought and record temperatures will experience significant exposure to wildfires, leading to the loss of life and property and further deforestation. One study in Australia found that the forest fire index in that country alone had increased between 10 and 40 percent since the mid-1980s.[58]

According to the Russian Meteorological Center, the summer of 2010 brought the deadliest heat wave in Russia's recent history, the most intense in the last thousand years. The ensuing fires and intense heat took the lives of up to 15,000 people and cost the Russian economy approximately $15 billion.[59] Michael Tobis, a climate scientist at the University of Texas, is "hazarding a guess . . . that the Russian heat wave of 2010 is the first disaster unequivocally attributable to anthropogenic climate change."[60] Many have argued that northern countries such as Canada and Russia might actually benefit, at least in the short term, from climate change, as growing seasons would be longer and there would be fewer deaths from extreme cold. The Russian heat wave has showed that even northern countries will suffer short-term chaos, damage, and loss of life from climate change. "There ought to be, coming out of this [Russian heat wave], a greater awareness that many hazards come with climate change," observed Kevin Trenberth of the National Center for Atmospheric Research.[61]

The most effective means for Climate Capitalism to minimize the risk, intensity, and impacts of forest fires is by properly valuing ecosystem services in the economy. The World Wildlife Fund (WWF) has long advocated incentivizing diverse and sustainable uses of forestry land to create natural buffers and forestry practices that minimize fire risk. Multiple use of the land, the WWF argues, creates landscape discontinuity and fire breaks. An economy based solely on extraction of timber does not value the services that intact forest ecosystems give to all of us.

For example, healthy forests are less susceptible to catastrophic fires, provide better watersheds, support biodiversity, and sequester carbon.[62] Fully valuing this is a more honest form of accounting but is rarely done.

To support healthy forests, the Forest Stewardship Council has developed a land and forest management certification program that encourages more sustainable forestry practices to help ward off forest fires. By mid-2010, more than 135 million hectares of forests around the globe had achieved FSC certification. FSC-certified wood products now sell at a premium and are commonly specified in the construction of green buildings, a powerful incentive for forestry companies to manage their forests to FSC standards. In 2008, the Rainforest Alliance published a report analyzing the impacts of FSC practices in the Maya Biosphere Reserve in Guatemala. They found that the incidence of forest fires declined from 6.5 percent of the land area in 1998, when FSC was first introduced to the reserve, to only 0.1 percent in 2007, after nearly ten years of sustainable forestry management using FSC practices.[63] Jose Roman Carrera of the Rainforest Alliance noted, "These numbers show that certification is a real tool for the market and for conservation. In these communities, FSC certification helped strengthen business structures, enhanced fire prevention measures and delivered low-impact harvesting practices."[64]

A high-tech solution to provide early detection of forest fires has been proposed by the Center for Biomedical Engineering at the Massachusetts Institute of Technology. In partnership with Voltree Power, a Boston-based company specializing in bioenergy, they have developed a wireless network of sensors that use Voltree's patented bioenergy-harvesting technology to draw their minimal power needs from the trees themselves. The first trial of this innovative solution was introduced in 2009. The result, Voltree states, is "a new, efficient, and green means for fire prediction and detection. Developed under the oversight and guidance of the United States Forest Service as well as the Bureau of Land Management, the system employs sensors for air temperature, relative humidity, [and] voltage and is capable of generating alerts in the event of a fire." Information travels from sensor to sensor until reaching a central monitoring station, which, through a satellite microwave uplink connection, can send the data to numerous agencies and, indeed, users worldwide.

Where there is a climate change problem there are climate capitalists looking for solutions. Some of them are looking to geoengineering, defined by the National Academy of Sciences as "options that would involve large-scale engineering of our environment in order to combat or counteract the effects of changes in atmospheric chemistry."[65] The benefits achievable through geoengineering could be far greater than the types of solutions discussed so far, but geoengineering also carries wider risks. Although geoengineering solutions have fascinated the scientific, government, and business communities seeking to assist the earth and its inhabitants in adapting to climate change, they have drawn their share of detractors.

Some geoengineering solutions, such as ocean iron fertilization, which aims to inject iron into the top layers of oceans to enhance marine ecosystems, are attempts at carbon sequestration, which might qualify them as climate change mitigation solutions. Many adaptive geoengineering solutions involve solar radiation management, which aims to reduce the amount of solar radiation the earth is exposed to through a range of innovative and largely untested man-made technologies.

In 2009, the World Bank conducted a competition entitled "100 Ideas to Save the Planet." Eduardo Gold, a Peruvian inventor, was among the twenty-six winners, for his solar radiation management proposal to literally paint formerly glacier-covered Peruvian mountains white. By creating this reflective surface on the mountain peaks, Mr. Gold hopes he can "re-grow" glaciers by cooling the surfaces enough to enable ice to reappear.[66] Mr. Gold's proposal also showcased why the many critics of geoengineering in the climate change scientific community oppose such measures. Such solutions are untested, may be exorbitantly costly, and have many unintended consequences, say such critics as a doctoral candidate at Carnegie Mellon, Katherine Ricke. She and her colleagues recently published research suggesting that solar radiation management techniques could have negative consequences such as reduced rainfall and that in some microclimates, geoengineering could be too successful and result in the overcooling of small geographic regions while having no impact whatsoever on neighboring communities.[67] One fact is inescapable: so long as politicians fail to implement regional accords to curb climate change, the climate continues to change. The less effective we are at using mitigation to address the problem, the more important adaptation—including geoengineering solutions—will become.

Conclusion

The majority of *Climate Capitalism* has properly been focused on mitigation responses to climate change. If the world is to avert the worst of the climate crisis, our collective focus must be on reducing global contributions to climate change by cutting greenhouse gas emissions by at least 80 percent. This is also where the immediately profitable opportunities lie. A rapid switch to focusing on adaptation solutions would divert resources from our paramount need to shift to a low-carbon economy.

In some ways, however, separating adaptation from mitigation is artificial. Many mitigation solutions, for example, solar-powered water purification, are an excellent form of adaptation. Renewable and distributed energy are not only necessary climate change mitigation solutions, but are some of the best adaptation strategies, enabling communities to have the resilience to survive when traditional grid energy sources are wiped out by storms. Energy-efficient ecohomes built to withstand floods make sense, regardless of how quickly or how high sea levels rise. An adaptation solution that helps monitor and speed responses to catastrophic forest fires also serves a mitigation function because forest fires are responsible for the release of significant amounts of greenhouse gases, accounting for 4 to 6 percent of the total greenhouse gases released in the United States in 2007.[68] Similarly, localized food systems, such as vertical farms and rooftop gardens, reduce a community's dependence on international food supply chains while cutting emissions from fertilizers and transportation.

Climate capitalists seek economic opportunities in the context of averting runaway climate chaos that will also enable communities to adapt to a world transformed by climate change. It is a certainty that carbon markets and industry will blend both mitigation and adaptation solutions. Yet mitigation should be considered the primary challenge. As a shrewd commenter on a popular blog by the University of Texas climate scientist Michael Tobis put it: "To mix metaphors; putting the cart (adaptation) before the horse (mitigation) is like digging yourself into a hole and adapting to the hole instead of stopping digging."[69]

10

A Future That Works

The 2008 financial collapse that evaporated $50 trillion in assets world-wide caught almost everyone by surprise, but not Nessim Taleb. The author of the bestselling *The Black Swan: The Impact of the Highly Improbable*, Taleb accurately predicted the timing and causes of the economic melt-down. He did so not because his crystal ball is better than everyone else's, but because he pays attention to low-probability, high-consequence events ("black swans")—events that, he believes, are on the increase.

And they are changing everything.

Future winners, Taleb suggests, will be those who are prepared to accept that such events can and indeed will happen, and then expose themselves to the information that will allow them aggressively to exploit them. He's talking about climate capitalists.

Conventional wisdom says that acting to protect the climate will be very costly. It holds that the world can't possibly afford it, particularly in a down economy. This book has shown that the contrary is true: those who embrace Climate Capitalism are on the most dependable route to prosperity, now and in the coming decades.

Business as Usual Isn't Safe Anymore

Business as usual will not endure, and it would be a recipe for disaster if it did.[1] Conventional best practices are no longer sufficient to deal with the challenges facing the world.[2] The fact that many of the world's major eco-systems are tipping into collapse; the advent of peak oil chronicled in chapter 6; the looming food shortages outlined in chapter 7; the water crises described in chapter 9—these drivers of change mean that business as usual is no longer a safe place to be.[3] The Sustainability Imperative—the recognition that doing business in ways that are better for people and the planet is more profitable—is the climate capitalists' prime directive. It will also mean that success will go to the nimble.

Consider just a few of the surprises that occurred during six months in 2010:

- The BP oil spill devastated the Gulf of Mexico's environment and economy and now threatens the company's survival. Then a second Gulf oil rig blew.
- A "flash crash," caused the Dow Jones Industrial Average to lose 999 points in a single half hour.
- The Greek economic collapse threatened the economies of Portugal, Ireland, Italy, and Spain, and underscored the weaknesses of the Eurozone. All are dwarfed by the de facto bankruptcy of California, the eighth largest economy in the world.
- 2010 became the hottest year on record with nineteen countries posting all-time temperature records; Pakistan recorded temperatures of 129 degrees, setting the record for Asia, shortly before suffering the worst flooding in its history. Both firsts threatened the economic stability of the country.
- In May Pakistan test-fired two nuclear-capable missiles, as did India six months later.
- Russia suffered a heat wave that precipitated massive fires and so reduced its wheat crop that the country, Europe's breadbasket, banned exports, hiking food prices globally.

None of these events should have surprised anyone, but they all did.

Perhaps the biggest surprise is that despite overwhelming evidence, climate change became taboo, banished by economic fears and wedge politics, as political panderers labeled it a hoax. The discredited environment-versus-jobs arguments suddenly found a second life as Republican talking points, and Democrats, too cowed to respond, gave up the fight. Unless human-caused emissions of greenhouse gases, now higher than at any time in human existence, are immediately reduced, however, we'll lose a lot more than savings and jobs. A 2009 report by the International Institute for Environment and Development found that adapting to climate change will cost the world $1.5 trillion every year—two to three times prior estimates ($1,240 trillion in 2010 dollars). And that is if the world can hold CO_2 concentrations to no higher than 450 parts per million.[4] Business as usual will deliver concentrations approaching 850 parts per million or more.

Dr. Rajendra Pachauri, chairman of the UN's Intergovernmental Panel on Climate Change (IPCC), told an international gathering of representatives of 114 governments, "Climate change is for real. We have just a small window of opportunity and it is closing rather rapidly. There is not a moment to lose. We are risking the ability of the human race to survive."[5] The former U.N. secretary general Kofi Annan put it a bit more simply: "The very basis for life on earth is declining at an alarming rate."[6]

Climate chaos is not a future threat. It is real and already causing misery around the globe. Left unchecked, it will get far worse. The evidence is everywhere around us. Devastating fires sweep across not only Russia, but Australia, Greece, Spain, and the western United States. Droughts cripple agriculture in Russia, India, China, Africa, and California. The drastic melt-off of glaciers in Greenland and the polar regions threatens to raise sea levels at the same time that the loss of glaciers in the Himalayas will restrict water access to 40 percent of people on earth, from China to India.[7] Disappearing sources of water could affect 1.8 billion more people by 2080.[8] Heat waves across the globe devastate grain crops and worsen outbreaks of diseases. At the same time, major storms have increased, causing floods from Pakistan to China to Europe

to the southeastern and midwestern United States. Hurricanes sweep
the Caribbean and Latin America, as cyclones batter the Philippines
and Burma. Even the genocide raging in Darfur has been recognized by
the UN to be the result of the forty-year drought caused by the warming
climate.[9] The United Nations Development Programme warns that
agricultural systems will begin to fail owing to increasingly variable
weather patterns, leaving large numbers of people facing malnutrition.[10]
The Global Humanitarian Forum reports, "Already today, hundreds of
thousands of lives are lost every year due to climate change. This will rise
to roughly half a million in 20 years . . . Climate change is already responsible for forcing some fifty million additional people to go hungry
and driving over ten million additional people into extreme poverty."[11]

Left unchecked, climate change will overwhelm most nations' abili-
ties to cope. The worst effects are already being felt by people who had
the least to do with causing the problem—underscoring the moral urgency for action by the industrialized nations whose economic activities have caused the crisis.[12]

Climate Chaos Is Now Scientifically Undeniable

In March 2009 the International Alliance of Research Universities' scientific congress in Copenhagen reviewed and updated the state of global
climate science that underpinned previous Intergovernmental Panel on
Climate Change reports. Many of the 2,500 researchers in attendance
had contributed to the IPCC reports. Participants from nearly eighty
different countries gave more than 1,400 scientific presentations.[13] In its
"Synthesis Report" the congress concluded, "The scientific evidence has
now become overwhelming that human activities, especially the combustion of fossil fuels, are influencing the climate in ways that threaten
the well-being and continued development of human society." The solutions called for were "rapid, sustained, and effective mitigation based on
coordinated global and regional action."[14]

In light of this and similar science from around the world, the NASA
scientist Dr. James Hansen advises, "Don't ask what's possible; ask what's

necessary."[15] What's necessary, he has been warning for several years, is reducing the concentration of CO_2 in the atmosphere to at most 350 parts per million. That is the upper "safe" limit. Sustained concentrations of CO_2 over that, he argues, are not "compatible with the planet on which civilization developed and to which life on earth is adapted."[16]

But CO_2 concentrations in the atmosphere were at 392 ppm in September 2010,[17] well beyond the 350 level that leading scientists believe is "safe." And by "safe" they mean that humanity has a fifty-fifty chance of avoiding climate catastrophe. If a friend told you, "Come drive with me, there's a fifty-fifty chance we'll get into a fatal car wreck," you'd get into another car. Even at 350 ppm, the world would still be well above the historic level of CO_2 concentration, 280 parts per million, under which the earth's ecosystems evolved.[18] And even if the world stopped burning fossil fuels today, concentrations and warming would go up for a while because of time lags in the system.[19] Perhaps worse, an internal briefing paper produced by the UN Framework Convention on Climate Change at the Copenhagen climate negotiations in December 2009 showed that even the most ambitious emissions reduction targets currently offered by developed and developing countries, including the European Union nations and the United States, would set the world on course for warming of around 5.4° Fahrenheit (3° Celsius).[20]

Despite efforts by climate deniers to confuse the public, the overwhelming scientific consensus is that if the nations of the world fail to act decisively in the next few years, it may become impossible to prevent runaway climate change that will end life as we know it on earth.[21] Dr. Pachauri stated, "If there's no action before 2012, that's too late. What we do in the next two to three years will determine our future. This is the defining moment."[22]

What We're Up Against

In his 2001 book, *Eco-Economy: Building an Economy for the Earth*, Lester Brown quoted Øystein Dahle, former Exxon vice president for Norway and the North Sea, who said, "Socialism collapsed because it did not allow the market to tell the economic truth. Capitalism may collapse because it does not allow the market to tell the ecological truth."[23]

The Nobel Prize–winning economist Joseph Stiglitz pointed out that financial allocations are driven by market signals. But these signals are distorted because the nations of the world "price" many of the world's priceless resources (a stable climate, or the pollution that endangers it) at zero. "Not surprisingly, this has led to inefficient outcomes, with emissions levels too high and too little effort devoted to energy conservation and research," he says. He echoes essentially all other economic observers when he writes, "Providing a strong, stable carbon price is the single policy action that is likely to have the biggest effect in improving economic efficiency and tackling the climate crisis."[24]

The business-as-usual crowd would prefer that we continue the practice of what Randy Hayes, director of the World Future Council's U.S. Liaison Office, calls "cheater capitalism." The chief apologist for this approach to business was the economist Milton Friedman. Friedman extolled the belief that the job of a corporate executive was simply to look after the profitability of his enterprise. Issues of the larger world belonged to the realm of policy, he argued, ignoring the fact that corporations influence that, too, with fleets of lobbyists. The former CEO of General Electric Jack Welch echoed that the only social responsibility of business is to create jobs and shareholder value.[25] These icons of twentieth-century business wrote in cavalier disregard of the fact that this way of doing business has brought the global economy and the world to the edge of a crumbling cliff. The ground that companies and communities, very much including you and me, stand on, which the world has long taken for granted, is collapsing. The global climate crisis, high and rising energy prices, the loss of ecosystems worldwide, water shortages, food crises, debt-ridden economies, and the growing demand for commodities by China and India are only a few of the forces that will inevitably change everything about the way we do business.

Many deny the need for change and seek to shore up the precipice even as it erodes. One way they do this is by pouring billions of your and my tax dollars into supporting the status quo, climate-destroying technologies.

While it has never been easy to get an accurate count of how much is spent to make energy look cheaper than it really is, and to keep the incumbent industries happy, it is a big number. As described in chapter 3, for the United States estimates range from a high of $87 billion a year to the more recent calculation by the Environmental Law Institute at over $72 billion in the study period between 2002 and 2008.[26] The National Research Council estimated in 2009 that indirect subsidies for fossil fuel energy in the United States were $120 billion in 2005. Whatever the number, worldwide subsidies supporting fossil fuels dwarf those for renewables. Subsidies to solar, wind, biofuels, and the other young and developing renewables industries are roughly 1 percent of the subsidies given to the fossil fuel industries.[27] Further, in the United States, most of the largest subsidies to fossil fuels are written into the tax code as permanent provisions. By comparison, subsidies for renewables, by one estimate totaling $29 billion in the United States for the past several decades, are time-limited initiatives implemented through energy bills with expiration dates that limit their usefulness.[28] Bloomberg New Energy Finance reported that federal renewable subsidies are finally rising, reaching between $43 and $46 billion in 2009, but handouts to the existing fossil industries, which Bloomberg estimates at twelve times as much, dwarf any renewable support.[29]

Similarly, inefficient use of energy by governments helps perpetuate the status quo. The U.S. federal government spent more than $24.5 billion on electricity and fuel in 2008 and projects that if it achieved its commitment to reduce greenhouse gas emissions by 20 percent it would save between $8 and $11 billion in avoided energy costs by 2020.[30]

America is hardly the only culprit. In 2010 the International Energy Agency released a study of the global subsidies that prop up the climate-destroying forms of energy. The IEA concluded that in 2008, the last year for which numbers are available, the use of fossil energy worldwide was underwritten by well over $557 billion in government support in thirty-seven developing countries.[31] This does not count direct payments to fossil industries or subsidies for nuclear power or other polluting forms of energy. The IEA estimated that merely phasing out these perverse subsidies between 2011 and 2020 would alone cut primary global energy demand by 5.8 percent by 2020. That would be huge, equivalent to the current energy consumption of Japan, Korea, Australia, and New Zealand combined. It would reduce global oil demand by 6.5 million barrels of oil a day (predominantly in the transport sector) in 2020, or around one third of current U.S. oil demand. Dr. Fatih Birol, chief economist of the IEA, observed that removing subsidies was a policy that could change the energy game "quickly and substantially." He's right. Retaining current subsidies, on the other hand, would be responsible for emissions of 2.4 gigatons of CO_2, equivalent to the current combined emissions of France, Germany, Italy, Spain, and the UK.[32]

The subsidies are unlikely to be eliminated anytime soon, however. The fossil industry spends a lot of its own money to convince the public that they are just fine. In 2010, The Global Climate Coalition, an oil industry association—its members include Amoco, the American Petroleum Institute, Chevron, Chrysler, Cyprus AMAX Minerals, Exxon, Ford, General Motors, Shell Oil, and Texaco—spent at least $63 million on publicity campaigns to make you believe that any reduction in the use of fossil fuel will cripple the economy and ruin business.[33]

The United States Chamber of Commerce, also a member, funded teams to visit every local Chamber of Commerce across the country to claim that the science of climate change isn't settled, that there is no proof of climate chaos, and that even if the climate is changing, the real issue is American jobs. They claim that any legislation that raises the cost or reduces the amount of energy that the United States uses will strangle our way of life and be ruinous to business.[34]

True conservatives, climate capitalists, and others committed to unleashing American ingenuity and ensuring prosperity know that change is necessary, but it will not come without a fight.[35]

We Need a Miracle

Sydney Harris once penned a cartoon in which two scientists are scribbling equations on a chalkboard. In the middle one of them writes, "Then a miracle occurs." The other scientist objects, saying, "I think you need to be a little more explicit here in step two."

Any sober look at the climate chaos now ravaging the globe and the efforts by the incumbent industries to remain dependent on the technologies of the last century makes it clear that we need a miracle.

Perhaps not surprising to a capitalist, our best hope for the source of that miracle is the business community. Already the smarter American companies are renouncing the worst excesses of the old way of doing business. In the autumn of 2009, PG&E, Nike, Apple, GE, and the utilities Pacific Gas and Electric, Public Service of New Mexico, and Exelon resigned from the U.S. Chamber of Commerce, announcing that business needs representation from an organization that appreciates the need and potential benefits to industry of being part of the climate solution.[36] Ford Motor Company, no longer a Global Climate Coalition member, won a 2009 EPA award for improving energy efficiency in the United States by 5 percent, saving itself approximately $16 million in the process.[37]

A 1995 survey by the consulting firm Arthur D. Little showed that just 4 percent of the 187 responding companies took environmental issues seriously in their business decisions. By 1998, that number had grown to 90 percent of 287 businesses polled by *Industry Week* magazine. More than 80 percent of Fortune 500 companies have created environmental charters and most multinational firms, responding to stakeholder pressures, have designed environmental strategies.[38] Additionally, corporate codes of conduct, such as the Ceres Principles, are increasingly common and improve industrial responsibility toward the environment.[39]

By 2010, a corporate commitment to sustainability was common. At that year's World Economic Forum at Davos, Switzerland, *Corporate Knights* magazine announced that more than 70 percent of the top global companies are on a sustainable path.[40] Companies are formalizing their sustainability communications by reporting to third parties like the Carbon Disclosure Project (from 235 reports filed in 2003 to 2,204 in 2008, a nine-fold increase) and the Global Reporting Initiative (from 175 reports to 1,226 in 2008, a seven-fold jump).[41] The *Financial Times* analyst Alan Smith found that "corporate social responsibility (CSR) has become such an important concept that in some situations it is soon to be required by law that publicly listed companies disclose ethical, social and environmental risks in its [*sic*] annual report."[42]

When such magazines as *Time*, *Newsweek*, and *Bloomberg Businessweek* all feel compelled to provide annual lists of the hundred most sustainable companies, joining the ranks of the Dow Jones Sustainability Index and the Global 100, the trend is clear.

The explanation for this trend is not, as some snarky commentators have alleged, CEOs undertaking charity by playing at being green.[43] The reality is quite the contrary. Ernst & Young's recently released 2009 Business Risk Report concluded that "in order to maintain their corporate image and reduce environmental impact, companies must take proactive measures, including more complex decisions regarding capital spending, production procedures, and installed technologies" for climate protection. The report found that, despite uncertainties in the regulatory environment, companies must prepare for changes in regulation and carbon-trading schemes. But the report pointed to regulations as the second risk, specifically mentioning increased regulatory restrictions of energy-resources extraction. It listed the 2008 surge in oil prices and brand reputation as the primary reasons that companies must be prepared to manage the "risk of radical greening around them." It placed what it called "the need for social acceptance and corporate social responsibility" in the top ten risks facing business. "The risk will rise again in the future," the report concluded, stating that "successful companies will be those who put environmental policy at the top of their agenda and adapt their business to that goal. A consumer products commentator argued, 'As growth resumes and environmental degradation continues this will re-emerge as a very powerful force in shaping business.'"[44]

Even the *Harvard Business Review*, as described in chapter 1, has acknowledged what most everyone in the field recognizes: sustainability is now the key driver of innovation.[45] Michael Porter, a professor at Harvard Business School, asserts that "managers must start to recognize environmental improvement as an economic and competitive opportunity. It is time to build on the underlying economic logic that links the environment, resource productivity, innovation and competitiveness."[46]

Transforming the Economy

This tectonic shift in how global business views the issue of sustainability is a great start to crafting a new economy, but it remains insufficient. So long as Americans continue borrowing more than a billion dollars a day to buy fossil oil from distant and unstable parts of the globe, no durable recovery is possible.[47]

In 2009, Jonathan Porritt, an adviser to the Prince of Wales, warned, "People seem blind to the fact that the causes of the economic collapse are exactly the same as those behind today's ecological crisis—and behind accelerating climate change in particular." Porritt wrote in support of the UK government's chief scientific adviser, Sir John Beddington, who predicted, "A 'perfect storm' of food shortages, scarce water and high-cost energy will hit the global economy before 2030." Porritt warned, "There is a simple conclusion here: the self-same abuses of debt-driven 'casino capitalism' that have caused the global economy to collapse are what lie behind the impending collapse of the life-support systems on which we all ultimately depend." He believes that the storm will hit by 2020.[48]

A growing number of commentators recognize that the current economic crisis is different from prior market downturns. The *New York Times* columnist Thomas Friedman argues, "Let's today step out of the normal boundaries of analysis of our economic crisis and ask a radical question: What if the crisis of 2008 represents something much more fundamental than a deep recession? What if it's telling us that the whole growth model we created over the last 50 years is simply unsustainable economically and ecologically and that 2008 was when we hit the wall—when Mother Nature and the market both said: 'No more.'"[49]

Friedman's right. The economic system that has given so many of us such a high standard of living is based on Hayes's cheater economics. The future's prosperity will depend on our success in shifting to a whole new way of doing business: to Climate Capitalism. This is what the companies described in this book that are staying the course with energy efficiency, that are publishing sustainability codes of conduct, that are pledging to cut their carbon emissions, are sensing. They recognize that they are the leaders of this new way of doing business. They know that their shareholders will be better for it, and they are committed to leaving a legacy that future generations will revere.

Many astute analysts describe the needed transformation. They call for communities to relocalize and reclaim control over where their energy comes from. They welcome decisions and policy changes that will give citizens a resilient future in the face of peak oil and the ravages of climate change.[50] Many books such as *Climate Code Red: The Case for Emergency Action*, by David Spratt and Philip Sutton, and *Straight Up*, by Dr. Joseph Romm, set forth brilliant policy prescriptions. Others— Bill McKibben's *Earth: Making a Life on a Tough New Planet*, James Gustave Speth's *The Bridge at the Edge of the World: Capitalism, the Environment, and Crossing from Crisis to Sustainability*, Dr. David Orr's *Down to the Wire: Confronting Climate Change*, and Tim Flannery's *Now or Never: Why We Must Act to End Climate Change*—acknowledge that the situation is dire and that much is already irrevocably lost.

This is no doubt true. The world has left matters until very late. However, much remains to save, and there is no more important work ahead of us. The single overriding point of *this* book is that doing that work also happens to be the best route to profitability and competitive advantage.

Business remains the most potent force for good on the planet, and in this new century business leaders such as Walmart's Rob Walton and General Electric's Jeffrey Immelt are proving the views of predecessors like Milton Friedman and Jack Welch wrong. They are showing that investing in climate protection is not only smart corporate risk reduction, but simply better business.

Principles of Climate Capitalism

The CEOs of the companies implementing greater sustainability in their business practices may not recognize it, but they are following the principles set forth a decade ago in this book's predecessor, *Natural Capitalism*. These principles have proved to be some of the best guides a company can use as it embraces sustainability in its own operations. They also represent a roadmap to a sustainable economy.

The first principle, buying time by using all resources as efficiently as possible, is cost-effective today and is the best way to address many of the worst problems facing humankind while delivering premium returns on investments. There are many smart companies implementing this principle, from measuring and managing their carbon footprints with the Carbon Disclosure Project, to Mi Rancho Tortilla's saving $175,000 a year by implementing efficiency measures because it knows it has to do so to meet Walmart's Sustainability Scorecard. It and the other small businesses participating in Natural Capitalism Solutions' "Solutions at the Speed of Business" program are enjoying returns on investment ranging from 100 percent to more than 600 percent. Perhaps the best example of the success of efficiency is GE's use of the Ecomagination campaign to regain the company's status as an innovation leader.[51] This commitment, little more than greenwashing when CEO Jeffrey Immelt announced it (all that GE did was to rebrand as "green" some of the products it was already making), is now the engine driving the company's growth. Even in a down economy, Ecomagination revenues rose from $5 billion in 2005 to over $25 billion in 2010. It enabled GE to cut its emissions by 22 percent in 2009 compared to its initial goal of 1 percent in 2004. By 2015 GE reckons to cut the energy intensity of its operations by 50 percent.[52] In his annual letter to shareholders, Immelt confirmed that Climate Capitalism is good for the bottom line, reporting, "Ecomagination is one of our most successful cross-company business initiatives. If counted separately, 2009 Ecomagination revenues would equal that of a Fortune 130 company and Ecomagination revenue growth equals almost two times the company average."

Efficiency buys time, but unless that time is used to redesign how businesses are run and how products are made and delivered, no amount of efficiency will solve the climate crisis or enable us to create a truly sustainable economy.

Smart climate capitalists are also implementing the second principle of Natural Capitalism: redesign how we make and deliver all products and services using approaches such as cradle-to-cradle concepts, Biomimicry, the circular economy, Design for the Environment, and others.[53] Nature makes a wide array of products and services that run on sunlight, producing neither waste nor toxics. The design of macroeconomic systems and microeconomic enterprises should mimic healthy, native ecosystems in diversity, adaptability, resilience, and local self-reliance. As Biomimicry's founder, Janine Benyus, says, "After 3.8 billion years of research and development, failures are fossils, and what surrounds us is the secret to survival. The more our world looks and functions like this natural world, the more likely we are to be accepted on this home that is ours, but not ours alone."[54]

The Calera company is using seawater and 92 percent of the carbon dioxide waste from the Moss Landing, California, power plant to create cement in the same way that sea creatures create their calcium silicate shells. Every ton of cement the process makes sequesters half a ton of CO_2, in just the way that coral reefs are formed. Investors include Vinod Khosla and Peabody Coal.[55]

Recognizing that green plants do not see CO_2 as the biggest poison of our time but rather use it to create starches and glucose, the building blocks of life, Dr. Geoff Coates at Cornell and other scientists are mimicking this process, using CO_2 and catalysts to make polycarbonates, a biodegradable plastic that is almost 50 percent CO_2 by weight. "It's highly abundant and really cheap," says Dr. Coates. He is using similar catalysts to create Styrofoam from orange peels.[56] Existing companies have huge opportunities to "intrepreneur" sustainable solutions, as well.[57] GE worked with Walmart to commercialize more cost-effective LED lightbulbs and other efficiency technologies. Because of such success, GE committed $10 billion more to Ecomagination research and development to grow its portfolio of environmentally sensitive products, services, and technologies. The fact that the Chinese 11th Party Congress passed the Circular Economy Initiative, now a guiding factor in China's massive investment in renewable energy and energy efficiency, should give all Western economies pause.[58]

Achieving a truly sustainable economy will also mean managing institutions so they are not just efficient and innovative, but also restorative of human and natural capital, the third principle of Natural Capitalism.

Business as usual has degraded intact ecosystems and human communities around the world. To reverse this we will need to change how we define success. Ecosystem services such as a healthy climate, soil fertility, and the restorative capacity of an intact biosphere are not presently on any company or country's balance sheet. Yet they underpin the capacity of the planet to sustain life and thus the economy. So long as our economic and accounting system treats them as having a value of zero, it will be impossible to implement any sort of capitalism that can deliver enduring wealth and well-being.

Honest Accounting

The profession of accounting arose when managers realized that if they did not have honest information about the financial status of their company they could not manage intelligently. Today, an equally momentous transition is needed in how businesses and governments keep accounts. Business practices that do not tell the ecological truth, that "externalize" environmental and social costs, and that drive companies and all of us to exceed the carrying capacity of the ecosystems to support life (and, lest the obvious be missed, all economic activity) need to be recognized as bad and unethical business.[59] The explicit warning in the UN's Third Global Biodiversity Outlook is that if ecosystems don't survive, neither will businesses. As Ray Anderson, the business leader who chaired the President's Council on Sustainable Development, bluntly asks: "What's the business case for ending life on earth?"[60]

Respectable economists are beginning to ask similar questions. Efforts such as Natural Capitalism Solutions' work to create a comprehensive Integrated Bottom Line analysis have attracted the interest of the Institute of Chartered Accountants of England and Wales.[61] Economists and others are also asking whether humans exist only to serve economic goals, as Madison Avenue has assumed, or whether the economy should be so designed that it serves humanity. It is not an easy issue to grapple with. The American economy is now 70 percent dependent on consumer spending, which is why, after the 9/11 attacks, President Bush implored

Americans to "go shopping" to protect the American economy (the Nobel Prize–winning economist Paul Krugman wondered whether there might be a nobler way for Americans to show support for their country[62]). It is why, after the economy collapsed in 2008, reforms were aimed more at ensuring the health of banks and Wall Street than the preservation of intact ecosystems, human communities, and Main Street.[63]

But the questions are now being raised again.

Economic measures such as the gross national product are intended to indicate whether the economy is healthy. We are expected to be happy when GNP grows, and worried when it falls. But GNP is actually a very strange measure. It really only counts the flow of money and stuff as it changes hands in economic transactions. The more money gets spent, goes the conventional wisdom, the better off we are. But if you volunteer at a home for the elderly, you've done nothing to increase the GNP. A divorcing cancer patient who gets in a car wreck adds handsomely to the GNP as money changes hands for insurance, repairs, lawyers, and medical bills. Is she better off than she would be if she weren't ill and divorcing and hadn't had a car wreck? Clearly not.

The usefulness of the GNP measurement has been questioned since it was invented in the 1930s. Simon Kuznets, one of the architects of national income accounting, himself warned, "The welfare of a nation can scarcely be inferred from a measure of national income."[64]

On March 18, 1968, Robert Kennedy put the value of GNP in perspective elegantly:

> Too much and for too long, we seemed to have surrendered personal excellence and community values in the mere accumulation of material things . . . The gross national product counts air pollution and cigarette advertising, and ambulances to clear our highways of carnage. It counts special locks for our doors and the jails for the people who break them. It counts the destruction of the redwood and the loss of our natural wonder in chaotic sprawl . . . Yet the gross national product does not allow for the health of our children, the quality of their education or the joy of their play. It does not include the beauty of our poetry or the

strength of our marriages, the intelligence of our public debate or the integrity of our public officials. It measures neither our wit nor our courage, neither our wisdom nor our learning, neither our compassion nor our devotion to our country, it measures everything in short, except that which makes life worthwhile.[65]

In light of business practices that threaten not only life as we know it but quite possibly life itself, now might be an opportune time to ask, "What's the economy for?"

Is the point of the economy to enrich the 20 percent of the population that owns 80 percent of global wealth, at the cost of misery for the rest? Should good capitalists not seek to enhance and productively use all forms of capital, human and natural, as well as manufactured and financial, to durably create more wealth?

This concept seemed quaint to most economists until 2009, when the Nobel Prize laureates Dr. Joseph Stiglitz and Dr. Amartya Sen, and the French economist Jean-Paul Fitoussi, released the report of the two-year project they chaired nicknamed by some the Quality of Life Commission—officially it was the Commission on the Measurement of Economic Performance and Social Progress.[66] Convened by President Nicholas Sarkozy of France, the commission brought together Nobel Prize winners and keepers of national accounts from across the world. They concluded that assessing a population's quality of life will require metrics from at least seven categories: health, education, environment, employment, material well-being, interpersonal connectedness, and political engagement. They also decided that any nation serious about progress should start measuring its "equity"—that is, the distribution of material wealth and other social goods—as well as its economic and environmental sustainability.

In the wake of the report's release, the European Union's statistical office and the Organization for Economic Cooperation and Development began debating how to implement more representative indicators of genuine well-being and to move the focus away from gross domestic product (the European version of GNP). "We want policies that reflect our values, but nobody says what those values are," Stiglitz told a *New*

York Times reporter. "The opportunity to choose a new set of indicators is tantamount to saying that we should not only have a conversation about recasting G.D.P. We should also, in the aftermath of an extraordinary economic collapse, talk about what the goals of a society really are."[67]

The British statistician Nic Marks, in a TED talk on the Happy Planet Index, explored what makes life worthwhile, noting that when people are actually surveyed and asked this question they say that they most want happiness, then love, then health, and only belatedly list money. If these are the natural human aspirations, Marks asks, then "Why are statisticians not measuring that? Why are we not thinking of the progress of nations in these terms, instead of just how much stuff we have?" He cites the Happy Planet Index, created by the New Economics Foundation, which plots the "happy life years" of a country's citizens as against the ecological footprint of that country. For example, the United States and the Persian Gulf states in the Middle East both use a lot of resources to deliver quality of life to their citizens. Well, most of them. In contrast, Afghanistan and those in sub-Saharan Africa use relatively few resources, but condemn their people to an average life span of forty-five hard years. Marks cites an evidence-based study exploring what enables people to be happy. The answers: social relationships, being active, taking notice of one's surroundings, life-long learning and curiosity, and the quintessentially uneconomic activity of giving. All are activities that have no cost to the climate or the ecological integrity of the planet. "Happiness," concludes Marks, "does not cost the earth."[68]

Some countries have been shifting their approach to national accounts. The concept that the Stiglitz commission was debating has come to be called Gross National Happiness, or GNH, a notion first put forth by the king of the tiny Himalayan kingdom of Bhutan in 1972.[69] It codifies the practice of Buddhist economics profiled in E. F. Schumacher's landmark book *Small Is Beautiful*.[70] Faced with an economy that was stagnating as it sought to pursue Western ideas of enhancing productivity, the king of Bhutan decided to focus instead on providing sustainable economic development, preserving and promoting cultural values, conserving the environment, and practicing good governance.

Dasho Karma Ura, president of the Center for Bhutan Studies in the capital, Thimphu, notes, "Defining happiness is not what is important. What is important is providing the conditions through which people can achieve happiness as they understand it."[71] GNH guidelines are now being adopted in Brazil, India, Haiti, and France. The Canadian Index on Well-being, Measures of Australia's Progress, the State of the USA Index, and the Living Planet Index of the United States are all efforts to measure the well-being of their country's citizens.[72] The growing discipline of community indicators is a local version of the same approach (see www.sustainablemeasures.com).

Bhutan and others have recognized that the developing world cannot lift itself from poverty in the same inefficient way that the West has done. Bhutan's prime minister, Jigme Thinley, stated, "Happiness is very serious business. The dogma of limitless productivity and growth in a finite world is unsustainable and unfair for future generations."[73]

On the other hand, there are many desirable areas in which there can be limitless growth—community well-being, education, knowledge, music, culture, happiness, and so on. The one thing that cannot grow indefinitely is the use of finite, nonrenewable resources or the emission of greenhouse gases.

Yet as Dr. Tariq Banuri, director of the Division for Sustainable Development in the UN Department of Economic and Social Affairs, and other development experts point out, the only approach that has ever lifted the world's poor out of poverty has been economic growth of the traditional, resource-consuming sort. People in developing countries need more resources, not fewer.[74]

But enabling all of the world's people to achieve the standard of living enjoyed in the West, if done in the same inefficient way that Europe and America did it, would require at least three more earths' worth of resources. One metric of the health of the planet, "The Living Planet Report," warns, "The Earth's regenerative capacity can no longer keep up with demand—people are turning resources into waste faster than nature can turn waste back into resources."[75]

To put a sharper point on the debate, it has been pointed out by Buckminster Fuller and others that infinite growth in physical stuff in a finite world is the ideology of a cancer cell, and a violation of the operating rules of the planet on which we all live.[76] Observers as far back as Thomas Malthus pointed out that a constantly growing population that makes exponentially increasing use of finite resources cannot depend on those resources' remaining available. And yet nearly every modern economic theory states that companies, nations, and the economic system must "grow" if economic collapse is to be avoided. The Great Recession made clear the fragility of a world economy devoted to that approach. Climate change, along with the profound stresses on species and ecosystems, proves how unsustainable any such "economic development" predicated on endless growth is. It's no wonder an increasing number of "ecological economists" are asking whether this underlying ideology of growth makes sense anymore.[77]

The landmark 1972 book *Limits to Growth*, commissioned by the Club of Rome, raised the question of whether the traditional economic assumption that indefinite growth in the throughput of materials, products, and money (what GNP measures) is sustainable.[78] The authors concluded it was not. The book, which sold more than 9 million copies, was viciously attacked, and many of its predictions of collapse were proved wrong. Critics crowed, forgetting, perhaps, that it was precisely because enough readers took its argument seriously and implemented an array of efficiency technologies and policy changes that the world postponed the predicted collapse.

But the time thus purchased was not used to implement fundamental reforms in the way we keep score or the way we run the economy. In *Beyond the Limits*, the twenty-year follow-up to *Limits to Growth*, Donella H. Meadows and her coauthors reported that all of the system dynamics she had described decades ago were still operating.[79] They had been pushed out into the future by better coping mechanisms, but unless fundamental changes in the way we do business are implemented, the foretold collapse will still ensue. The Meadows team ran four scenarios of how the future might turn out. In three of them ecological resources and the economies dependent on them collapsed. In the fourth, we make it.

The executive summary of *Beyond the Limits* concluded:

If present growth trends in world population, industrialization, pollution, food production, and resource depletion continue unchanged, the limits to growth on this planet will be reached sometime within the next hundred years. The most probable result will be a sudden and uncontrollable decline in both population and industrial capacity.

It is possible to alter these growth trends and to establish a condition of ecological and economic stability that is sustainable far into the future. The state of global equilibrium could be designed so that the basic material needs of each person on earth are satisfied and each person has an equal opportunity to realize his or her individual human potential.

If the world's people decide to strive for this second outcome rather than the first, the sooner they begin working to attain it, the greater will be their chances of success.[80]

The follow-up volume was, like the original, dismissed, but in 2008 no less a bastion of business interests than *The Wall Street Journal*, observing rising commodity prices prior to the collapse, wondered whether these shortages of raw materials might mean that the old *Limits to Growth* thesis had been right after all.[81]

The debate continues today. Humankind seems determined to push beyond the environment's thresholds of hospitality to our species. In a study sponsored by the Stockholm Resilience Centre, "Planetary Boundaries: Exploring the Safe Operating Space for Humanity" (published in a special edition of the journal *Ecology and Society*), twenty-eight of the world's most respected scientists identified nine critical environmental boundaries, concluding that humans have already passed three: climate change, loss of biodiversity, and nitrogen loading of our waters. We are close to exceeding several of the remaining six, they warned.[82]

If the world is to fix the mistakes of the past and create a better future, it will have to do it in a very different way than the industrial practices to date. In 2009, Joseph Stiglitz and Sir Nicholas Stern agreed. They teamed up to advise President Obama, writing, "The investments necessary to convert our society to a low-carbon economy—investments that can change the way we live and work—would drive growth over the next two or three decades. They would ensure that growth, with accompanying improvements in standards of living, was sustainable. The path that we have been on is not." They describe a recent paper by the Peter G. Peterson Institute for International Economics, a nonpartisan research institute, that demonstrates that spending $10 billion to insulate U.S. homes and federal buildings would create and sustain up to 100,000 jobs between 2009 and 2011, while saving the economy up to $3 billion a year between 2012 and 2020. Stern and Stiglitz wrote, "This type of investment and those in green technology and infrastructure would not only provide a short-term stimulus but also improve the U.S. competitive position. As the world moves to a low-carbon economy, there will be a competitive advantage for those who embrace these technologies."[83]

Some hopeful examples of a new approach are emerging. Costa Rica uses one quarter the resources of the United States per capita but delivers to its people a longer life span, the highest literacy rate in the world, and, by the results of the recent Gallup poll, the happiest citizens in the world. The country is 99 percent powered by renewable resources; it abolished its military to invest instead in social programs, education, and health care; and it has committed to be carbon-neutral by 2021.[84]

On a different scale of magnitude, and perhaps therefore more important, China has begun to engage in this conversation. A good thing, because if China succeeds in its stated goal of making half of its citizens middle class by 2025, and does it in the same ecologically unsound way that Western nations did, it will render irrelevant the efforts of the rest of the world to protect the climate. "If China cannot meet its own energy-efficiency targets," warns the International Energy Agency's chief economist, Dr. Fatih Birol, "the chances of avoiding widespread environmental damage from rising temperatures are very close to zero." In its headlong rush to satisfy the demands of its consumers, China has become even less energy-efficient than it was earlier. With most of its energy from fossil fuels, China's CO_2 emissions continue to rise. In 2010 China showed the largest six-month increase in emissions tonnage ever by a single country.[85] And economists the world around are calling on China to step up its consumerism as the last great hope for enabling economies to grow in the traditional way. A recent *New York Times* story exhorted,

> For the rest of the world, the Chinese consumer is one of the best hopes for future economic growth. In the years ahead, when the United States, Europe and Japan will have no choice but to slow their spending and pay off their debts, China could pick up the slack. Millions of Americans—yes, millions—could end up with jobs that exist, at least in part, to design, make or sell goods and services to China. This possibility helps explain why Democrats, Republicans, economists, business consultants, corporate executives and labor leaders all devote so much time to urging China to consume more.[86]

The seriousness of the challenges facing China is not lost on its leaders. In 2005, President Hu Jintao proposed creating a "Green GDP," an environmental metric with which to evaluate the performance of every official in the country. This would have embraced full-cost accounting in which economic gains would be balanced against ecosystem losses. The Green GDP was to have recalculated gross domestic product to reflect the cost of pollution. The pioneering attempt was abandoned in 2007, however, when the results became politically unpopular after they showed that China's real growth rates, when ecological and social losses were counted, were close to zero. The project was redefined as an academic exercise and stripped of any official influence.[87] And China went on "growing."

Perhaps the academic exercise is being taken off the shelf and dusted off. In 2010, in tandem with its massive green-energy push (see chapter 3), China began closing inefficient factories. It has already closed over a thousand inefficient coal plants and is now the world's largest investor in wind and solar, and has been increasing vehicle efficiency standards. Will these measures make a dent? A third of China's economic recovery package, about 3 percent of its GDP, was spent on green-technology investment in the form of high-speed-rail trains and infrastructure, wind energy, solar energy, and energy-efficient lighting.[88] Despite its goal of cutting energy use by 20 percent and greenhouse gas emissions by 40 to

45 percent per unit of GNP in 2010 compared with 2005, Chinese emissions are projected to grow more than the rest of the world's combined increase by 2020. China is increasing its use of coal and is now the world's largest importer.[89] Unless something changes, China, with one fifth of the world's population, will emit more than a quarter of humanity's energy-caused greenhouse gas emissions.[90] In fairness and by way of comparison, on a per capita basis, China would still be a better performer than the United States is today, which with 5 percent of the world's population produces 25 percent of greenhouse gas emissions from burning fossil fuels. But again, the earth doesn't care about statistical profiles. It only cares how much carbon is being emitted.

Perhaps the nations of the world are, like China, beginning to realize that change is necessary. In 2009 the United Nations Environment Programme released "Global Green New Deal," which calls for transforming all of the globe's economies.[91] Pointing out that every 1 percent drop in growth in developing economies translates into 20 million more people forced into poverty, the report states,

> An expanded vision is critical to the lasting success of a world economic recovery. Reviving growth, ensuring financial stability and creating jobs should be essential objectives. But unless new policy initiatives also address other global challenges, such as reducing carbon dependency, protecting ecosystems and water resources and alleviating poverty, their impact on averting future crises will be short-lived. Without this expanded vision, restarting the world economy today will do little to address the imminent threats posed by climate change, energy insecurity, growing freshwater scarcity, deteriorating ecosystems, and above all, worsening global poverty. To the contrary, it is necessary to reduce carbon dependency and ecological scarcity not just because of environmental concerns but because this is the correct and only way to revitalize the economy on a more sustained basis.[92]

Efforts such as South Korea's Green Recovery, allocating 95 percent of its $36 billion recovery package, about 3 percent of its GDP, to green measures, and America's $80 billion in green stimulus investments are a start, but they fall short of Sir Nicholas Stern's benchmark that green measures should be 20 percent of global economic recovery spending, and the UN's target of 1 percent of GDP.

Jonathan Porritt, the founder of Forum for the Future, outlined how solutions must be based on sustainable approaches, stating, "As regards appropriate remedies, the link between today's recession and the perfect storm that awaits us in 2020/30 couldn't be clearer: sort out today's calamity by investing in infrastructure and technologies to help avoid tomorrow's infinitely worse calamity."[93]

In 2010, the United Nations scheduled a world summit to be held on the Green Economy in 2012, twenty years after the world summit that created the sustainable development agenda, Agenda 21. The UN's Achim Steiner, the brilliant under-secretary general and executive director of the UN Environment Programme, commented on the need for such a gathering:

> The financial, fuel and food crises of 2008 are in part a result of speculation and a failure of governments to intelligently manage and focus markets. But they are also part of a wider market failure triggering ever deeper and disturbing losses of natural capital and nature-based assets coupled with an over-reliance on finite, often subsidized fossil fuels. The flip side of the coin is the enormous economic, social and environmental benefits likely to arise from combating climate change and reinvesting in natural infrastructure—benefits ranging from new green jobs in clean tech and clean energy businesses up to ones in sustainable agriculture and conservation-based enterprises.[94]

What's to Be Done?

Randy Hayes says that the cure for cheater economics is "ecologizing capitalism":

> The rise of a new ecological economics paradigm including awareness in regional carrying capacities (scale), just distribution, and the "clean-

est is cheapest" true cost pricing system would be as historically significant as any since the advent of the industrial revolution. This economic
system would still employ the efficiencies of the market system to allocate energy and resources. Yet, this economic system could halt the
shredding of the web of life—a web that supports us all.[95]

Randy and others have set forth how practicing ecological capitalism would shift the world to a market in which doing the right things,
delivering clean energy, and solving the climate crisis would happen
naturally because it is better business. Practicing full-cost accounting
would enable everyone to see the price of sending armies to protect access to Middle Eastern oil fields as the digits rolled over at the gas pump
(whose hidden price was five dollars per gallon of gas even before the
Iraq war). Such a system would make transparent the fact that resources
in deepest Africa are being purchased by the Chinese, and that access to
lithium in Afghanistan is being "protected" by American troops. The
cost of burning coal would be accounted for in every electricity bill,
with the degradation of the atmosphere and your lungs, the costs of
treating your children's asthma, mercury from coal burning rendering
fish unsafe to consume, and the cost of dealing with climate damages
you yourself are causing broken out as line items. The billions of dollars
in myriad subsidies you now pay through your taxes would be abolished and the real cost of supplying energy to you would be manifest.
Such true-cost pricing would give us an economy in which individual
choices actually would aggregate to wise societal decisions. Such transparency, such truth in pricing, is an inherent requirement of a truly free
market, and is wholly absent now.

How, then, can we achieve such honest economics? A first step is to
see the world as the set of interlinked systems that it really is and to understand the feedback loops that drive present behavior. Donella Meadows's book *Thinking in Systems: A Primer* reveals how the world that
exists today is created and reinforced by a system of forces.[96] By understanding that network, we can all find the leverage points that enable us
to intervene effectively.[97]

As you begin to explore the systems that support you, it is worth questioning whether the systems that enable you, your family, and your community to meet your needs for energy, water, food, housing, and transportation are resilient. Can they withstand the sorts of shocks that, for example, peak oil will impose on us? At present, the answer is no. Organizations like the Post Carbon Institute and Transition Towns, described in chapter 6, are working with communities across Europe and the United States to enable citizens to increase the resilience of their essential systems. Publications like the LASER manual (Local Action for Sustainable Economic Renewal) and the *Climate Protection Manual for Cities* can help you implement more resilient systems in *your* community.[98] The new Economics Foundation and other similar organizations provide a wealth of publications on what is needed and what is already happening to transform our economy into one that meets the needs of people, while preserving the capacity of the planet to support life. As Joseph Stiglitz pointed out, "Spending money on needed investments— infrastructure, education, technology—will yield double dividends. It will increase incomes today while laying the foundations for future employment and economic growth. Investments in energy efficiency will pay triple dividends—yielding environmental benefits in addition to the short- and long-run economic benefits."[99]

As this book has shown, the legacy industries of agriculture, car manufacturing, energy production, water supply, and all of the other outmoded bits of our economy will need to be transformed. This process is already under way, but far more is needed.

Market mechanisms are incredibly powerful tools, and if used intelligently can solve most of the problems facing humankind. Tax shifting—ending subsidies to unsustainable use of resources, and raising taxes on depletion and pollution—is one way to implement true-cost accounting and pricing. The American cap-and-trade system was used in the case of sulfur dioxide and it largely ended the problem of acid rain. Yet an unholy coalition of industry and political "conservatives" has prevented the use of cap and trade in the United States to bring down carbon emissions and to solve the climate crisis. Carbon trading is functioning in Europe, and has driven a far more efficient use of energy, saved companies and citizens, and reversed the growth in carbon emissions. Why won't we use it here?

Leadership for a World That Works

It's frustrating. We have all the technologies needed to solve the crises facing the world. We know the policy measures that work and that will drive the changes needed. Unleashing a true and honest free market would largely implement the new energy economy. And yet the elections of late 2010, the collapse of the Chicago Climate Exchange, and the failures of the COP meetings in Copenhagen and Cancun show that the world is gridlocked.

It is perhaps necessary to remember that throughout history, no change has come without struggle. There remains a very important role for government and for political leadership. Tracing back at least to the administration of Ronald Reagan, an ongoing campaign in the United States has delegitimized the role of government. And we have stood placidly by, even though this plays to the strength of entrenched interests far more than to the interests of citizens. A system that rewards 11,140 lobbyists in Washington, D.C., twenty five for each and every member of Congress in office, has transformed what started as a representative democracy into a market democracy: How much representation can *you* afford to purchase?[100] Oil and gas companies don't have this problem. The *Climate Progress* blog reported in September 2010:

The oil, gas, and coal industries have spent over $2 billion lobbying Congress since 1999. These three industries combined spent a whopping $543 million on lobbying in 2009 and the first two quarters of 2010. Meanwhile, alternative energy companies spent less than $32 million on lobbying efforts in 2009 and have only spent $14.8 million this year. The 20 biggest-spending oil, mining, and electric utility companies shelled out $242 million on lobbying from January 2009 to June 2010. Trade associations that generally oppose clean energy policies spent another $290 million during this time. This is over $1,800 in lobby expenditures a day for every single senator and representative.[101]

Is this system working for you, for your family, for your community? If not, perhaps it is time to change the system.

Industry apologists suggest that all the economy needs is for government to get off the backs of business. Isn't that like a bad lightbulb joke? How many economists does it take to screw in a more efficient lightbulb? None, the free market will do it. Except it won't. Chapter 13 of this book's predecessor, *Natural Capitalism*, downloadable for free,[102] as well as the paper "Climate: Making Sense and Making Money," describes the myriad barriers that keep markets from functioning as they should, outlines how truly free markets ought to work, and shows how they can be used to protect the climate.[103]

Markets make very good servants, but they're not good masters, and they're a lousy religion. There's also an important role for communities of faith in reminding us that markets aren't God, and that there are important questions to answer about what it means to be human, and why we are on this planet. The goal isn't "He who dies with the most toys wins."

A good exercise in market humility is actually to go back and really read Adam Smith, whose *Wealth of Nations* is often cited by free marketeers. The "Father of Markets" was quite clear that markets allocate scarce resources *efficiently* in the short term, and that this is all that they were ever designed to do. Markets were never intended to take care of grandchildren. That's our job. That's the job of a free people coming together and asking, "What kind of a world do we want to live in? What kind of world do we want to leave behind?"

Interestingly, academics who have revisited Adam Smith's work have found that judging from what he was writing shortly before he died, Smith may have been the father not just of markets but of sustainability. Mishko Hansen, a former investment manager currently researching ethical issues in business and economics at Cambridge University, points out that Adam Smith, in *The Theory of Moral Sentiments*, the book he was working on when he died, carefully distinguished between economic activity that is beneficial to nations, enabling them to afford military forces to protect their boundaries, and economic activities that bring happiness to individuals. A moral philosopher, Smith rejected the notion that greed is good, stating in *The Theory of Moral Sentiments*, "Hence it is, that to feel much for others, and little for ourselves, that to restrain our selfish, and to indulge our benevolent affections constitutes the perfection of human nature; and can alone produce among mankind that harmony of sentiments and passions in which consists their whole grace and propriety." And, "The chief part of happiness arises from the consciousness of being beloved."[104] Smith recounts the story of the king who desires to become great so that he can enjoy his later repose surrounded by friends and family, and how it was a fool's pursuit, depriving him of a lifetime of enjoyment of family and friends that had been his all along:

> The pleasures from which we propose to derive our real happiness are almost always the same with those which, in our actual though humble station, we have at all times at hand and in our power. Except for the frivolous pleasures of vanity and superiority, we may find, in the most humble station, where there is only personal liberty, every other [pleasure] which the most exalted can afford.[105]

These passages and others prompt Hansen to ask, "Then why all this writing on the wealth of nations? Smith was writing not about how economic growth was going to lead to happiness or well-being, but rather how a country should become economically prosperous, and hence militarily powerful. He believed that people living in conditions of relative freedom and equality could be very happy with almost nothing in the way of material goods (his example was North American Indians), but that they needed to ensure that they would not be subjugated and made miserable by more militarily powerful forces."[106]

Remember the discussion in chapter 1 of the waves of innovation that have taken place since the First Industrial Revolution? America has that opportunity to drive economic prosperity. Investments in the technologies of the green economy are precisely the innovations that can lift our nation and all others out of the recession and out of poverty while solving the climate crisis. And yet we stare at them as if they are out of our reach, as if we are content with the way it was in the last century. We would do well to remember that the nation that innovates has led the world, politically, economically, and militarily. Thomas Friedman warns:

> America is about to learn a very hard lesson: You can borrow your way to prosperity over the short run but not to geopolitical power over the long run. That requires a real and growing economic engine. And, for us, the short run is now over. There was a time when thinking seriously about American foreign policy did not require thinking seriously about economic policy. That time is also over.[107]

It is time for capitalists to reread *The Wealth of Nations* and to free our energy markets from corporate socialism such as perverse subsidies that make energy look cheaper than it really is to us and to the earth. But it may be even more important for us to read, perhaps for the first time, the father of capitalism's greater work and answer the important question that cannot be answered by armies and economies: What is it that will make you happy? What will *your* legacy be? The entrepreneur Ray Anderson is fond of saying, "When you meet your Maker, what will your conversation be about? Last quarter's share price?"

I don't think so . . .

It is in this spirit that Lester Brown writes,

> This energy transition (to energy efficiency and renewables) is being driven by an intense excitement from the realization that people are now tapping energy sources that can last as long as the earth itself. Oil wells go dry and coal seams run out, but for the first time since the industrial revolution we are investing in energy sources that can last forever. This new energy economy can be our legacy to the next generation.[108]

In his book *Hot, Flat, and Crowded*, Thomas Friedman argues that America has lost its way, its ability, even willingness, to take on big challenges. Of a world that is in the grip of "petro-dictatorships, buffeted by surprises, rising populations, rising poverty, the extinction of plants and animals, and waning energy supplies," Friedman exhorts:

> How we address these interwoven global trends will determine a lot about the quality of life on earth in the twenty-first century. I am convinced that the best way for America to solve its big problem, the best way for America to get its "groove" back, is for us to take the lead in solving the world's big problem . . . The task of creating the tools, systems, energy sources, and ethics that will allow the planet to grow in cleaner, more sustainable ways is going to be the biggest challenge of our lifetime. But this challenge is actually an opportunity for America. If we take it on, it will revive America at home, reconnect America abroad, and retool America for tomorrow. America is always at its most powerful and most influential when it is combining innovation and inspiration, wealth-building and dignity-building, the quest for big profits and the tackling of big problems. When we do just one, we are less than the sum of our parts.[109]

Climate chaos is not an American problem only, and the United States alone cannot provide the solution. The truth is that solving the climate crisis will require something from all of us. It cannot be done without you, whether you are in high school or contemplating retirement. But perhaps it is time for the middle-aged pundits who helped to create the climate mess to step back and invite young people into leadership to craft future solutions, as Bill McKibben, the professor who founded 350.org, has been doing. In the final days of the United Nations climate negotiations in Copenhagen, officials restricted access to all but a very few nongovernment observers, including McKibben. Decidedly over thirty, he gave his pass to a young person in his group. Bill remained outside in the streets with the millions of mostly young people from around the world who were calling for change. As he says, "350.org, created by seven college kids and me, is now a global organization which CNN stated created the most widespread day of action in the planet's history—5,200 actions in 188 countries."[110]

But young or old, it is time to act. Martin Luther King once said:

We are now faced with the fact that tomorrow is today. We are confronted with the fierce urgency of now. In this unfolding conundrum of life and history there is such a thing as being too late. Procrastination is still the thief of time. Life often leaves us standing bare, naked and dejected with a lost opportunity . . . Over the bleached bones and jumbled residue of numerous civilizations are written the pathetic words: "Too late."[111]

What Kind of Future Do *You* Want?

The people of the world know that climate change is a vital issue. In mid-2010, the HSBC bank surveyed 15,000 consumers in fifteen countries whose populations make up over 50 percent of the global total.[112] The survey found that climate change is one of the top three concerns globally, on a par with economic stability and terrorism. Sixty-four percent of respondents in China claim to be making a significant effort to help reduce climate change, compared to 23 percent in the UK, 20 percent in the United States, and 11 percent in Japan.

The report, titled "Climate Confidence Monitor," also reveals that one in three people in Vietnam, India, and China believe climate change can be halted, compared to just one in twenty in France and the UK. Survey respondents in Hong Kong and Vietnam also rank climate change as their number one concern.[113]

David Brower, perhaps the greatest environmentalist of our time, was fond of asking, "What do we want the future to look like in fifty years? Let's do a little dreaming. Aim high," he said. "Navigators have aimed at the stars for centuries. They haven't hit one yet, but because they aimed high they found their way."

In the 1939 World's Fair in New York, the General Motors exhibit, called Futurama, portrayed the joys of suburban living and inspired generations of Americans to covet that unsustainable lifestyle. What if we could use advanced communications and visualization technologies to help the world's citizens envision a sustainable society? Bill Becker, executive director of the Presidential Climate Action Project, is creating just such a project, called "The Future We Want." Realistic computer-generated visuals will place you into the buildings, neighborhoods, energy systems, cities, and mobility options that a clean-energy economy would offer. The project's immersive media will show you what it would feel like to walk around in a future that has learned to mitigate and adapt to climate change. Its interactive tools will allow you to help design that future. Such images, widely disseminated and absorbed, could result in a public less afraid and far more excited about achieving a low-carbon future, less prone to denying climate change, and more likely to support the enlightened public policies needed to make the transition to a sustainable future.

This is not a liberal agenda, or a red or a blue wedge issue. Newt Gingrich envisions "a dynamic American economy producing its own energy, independent of dictators, using science and technology to create an exciting future, and continuing its role as the most prosperous and technologically advanced country in the world." John McCain's ads in his presidential campaign spoke of ending "a reliance on oil," "a threat to our climate," "a threat to our economy," and "a threat to national security." McCain said, "Much of the world's oil supply is controlled by states, regimes and a cartel for which America's well-being is not exactly a priority." As McCain spoke, a map of Iran was shown, followed by a picture of a smiling President Hugo Chavez of Venezuela and President Mahmoud Ahmadinejad of Iran.[114]

All of us want much the same things: prosperity, security, and lives filled with meaning. If we allow business to go on as usual, none of us will have them. Climate chaos will rob us all.

We have the ability to cut our energy use at least in half through the efficiency technologies described in chapter 2, to meet all of our remaining needs with the renewable energy profiled in chapter 3, to create buildings that keep their occupants comfortable year-round with no energy but the sun, and to design the livable communities portrayed in chapter 4. Chapters 5 and 6 showed how we can meet our needs for transport. Chapter 7 set forth the ways to provide abundant, healthy food. In chapter 8 we profiled the capacity of markets to solve the climate crisis; chapter 9 described opportunities offered by the need to mitigate and adapt to mild climate change (and pointed out that there *is* no way to adapt to unmitigated climate chaos). This final chapter sketches the outlines of how to transform our economy.

All at a profit.

We know what we need to solve the challenges facing us. Let's unleash this new-energy economy. We *can* entrepreneur our way out of the crisis and create a far higher quality of life.

The authors of *Beyond the Limits* wrote:

Is any change really possible? Can the world actually ease down below the limits and avoid collapse? Is there enough time? The truth is that no one knows. The world faces not a preordained future, but a choice. The choice is between models.

One model says that this finite world for all practical purposes has no limits. Choosing that model will take us even further beyond the limits and, we believe, to collapse.

Another model says that the limits are real and close, and that there is not enough time, and that people cannot be moderate or responsible or compassionate. That model is self-fulfilling. If the world chooses to believe it, the world will get to be right, and the result will also be collapse.

A third model says that the limits are real and close, and that there is just exactly enough time, with no time to waste. There is just exactly enough energy, enough materials, enough money, enough environmental resilience, and enough human virtue to bring about a revolution to a better world.[115]

In *The Lord of the Rings*, J.R.R. Tolkien's tale of great evil threatening the chances for all the people of his fictive Middle Earth to live lives of happiness, the wise wizard, Gandalf, declares to a narrow-minded bureaucrat who refuses to look beyond his borders at the disaster threatening to extinguish life, "The rule of no realm is mine, but all worthy things that are in peril as the world now stands, those are my care. And for my part, I shall not wholly fail of my task . . . if anything passes through this night that can still grow fair and bear fruit and flower again in the days to come. For I too am steward, did you not know?"[116]

Not a bad maxim of leadership.

But remember: in Tolkien's story it was the fun-loving, unassuming little Hobbits, who liked their second breakfasts and wanted nothing more than to return to their quiet lives in their quiet shire, who took on their shoulders the awesome task of meeting the challenges that threatened the world. They were scared and uncertain, but in the end all the kings and warriors and wizards could just stand by as these little people saved the world.

Real leadership is extraordinary courage by ordinary people.

This little blue marble, Earth, suspended in space, is the only place in all the known universe where there is life.

Will you protect it?

Appendix: How to Calculate and Offset Your Carbon Emissions

CarbonFund.org is a carbon offset provider that has a very easy-to-use calculator, so that you can calculate your emissions and purchase offsets at one website: www.carbonfund .org/site/pages/individuals/individual_business_carbon_offsets.

Here are some other popular calculators, in order of increasing stringency:

www.liveneutral.org/calculator
www.carbonfootprint.com/calculator.aspx (also an offset provider)
www.epa.gov/climatechange/emissions/ind_calculator.html
www.climatecrisis.net/takeaction/carboncalculator
www.safeclimate.net/calculator
www.bp.com/extendedsectiongenericarticle.do?Categoryid=9015627&contentid= 7029058
www.b-e-f.org (an offset provider with a calculator that lets you "look under the hood" and answers your questions)
www.nature.org/initiatives/climatechange/calculator (this will likely give you the highest carbon footprint)

If you are on Facebook, check out the Makemesustainable application: http:// makemesustainable.com/tour/my_calculator.html.

Notes

1: Entrepreneuring the Solutions

1. "Credit Crisis—The Essentials," *New York Times*, April 1, 2009.
2. As described in Donella Meadows, Dennis L. Meadows, and Jorgen Randers, *Beyond the Limits: Confronting Global Collapse, Envisioning a Sustainable Future* (White River Junction, Vt.: Chelsea Green, 1993), the converging crises now facing the globe are not caused by any one factor. They reflect a systemic breakdown that can only be understood and responded to in a whole systems way. See also Donella Meadows, *Thinking in Systems* (White River Junction, Vt.: Chelsea Green, 2008).
3. Tom Raum, "Can't Do Nation: Multiple Crises Fray US Optimism," Associated Press, June 4, 2010, http://abcnews.go.com/Business/wireStory?id=10828334.
4. Edward Mazria, "Nation Under Siege, Sea Level Rise at Our Doorstep," keynote speech delivered at the University of San Diego, October 29, 2007, p. 11, www.architecture2030.com/pdfs/nation_under_siege_lr.pdf.
5. This phrase was introduced by L. Hunter Lovins in speeches in 1999. It became the title of a *Harvard Business Review* article in 2010. See David A. Lubin and Dan S. Esty, "The Sustainability Imperative," *Harvard Business Review*, May 2010.
6. Goldman Sachs, "Introducing GS Sustain," report, June 22, 2007. This is just one of more than twenty similar studies all showing essentially the same thing: more-responsible companies are better-run businesses.

7. Lela Davidson, "Walmart Meeting Focused on Sustainability," Bizzia.com, June 7, 2009, www.bizzia.com/articles/Walmart-meeting-focused-on-sustainability.

8. Ron Scherer, "Number of Long-Term Unemployed Hits Highest Rate Since 1948," *Christian Science Monitor*, January 8, 2010.

9. Dr. Rosina Biernbaum, personal communication, Sundance Climate Conference, November 13, 2008.

10. Gary Pfeiffer, DuPont CFO, speech delivered at a Conference Board conference, 2005.

11. Andrew Winston (Eco-Strategies), personal communication and Colorado State University talk, March 8, 2010.

12. STMicroelectronics, "Sustainable Development Report," 2003, www.st.com/stonline/company/environm/sustdev/sustdev03.pdf.

13. Jeff Hohensee (senior consultant at Natural Capitalism Solutions), personal communication, Natural Capitalism Solutions headquarters, December 2008.

14. 2009 1E PC Energy Report: 1E Study: www.1e.com/energycampaign/index.aspx.

15. Ariel Schwartz, "Ford Saves One Million Dollars . . . by Shutting Off Computers," *Fast Company*, March 23, 2010; Julie Morrison, "Study Shows Turning Off Computer at Night Saves Energy, Big Bucks," *Flint Journal*, April 13, 2009.

16. Jeff Hohensee, personal communication, Natural Capitalism Solutions headquarters, December 2008.

17. According to Verlyn Klinkenborg, "Light Pollution," *National Geographic*, November 2008, 30 to 60 percent of energy consumed in lighting is unneeded or gratuitous; Lumina Technologies, "Survey of 156 California Commercial Buildings' Energy Use" (Santa Rosa, Calif.: August 1996); The Good Human (website), "Why in the World Do Businesses Leave Their Lights On at Night?"

18. "JohnsonDiversey Ups GHG Reduction Target to 25%," Environmental Leader, November 6, 2009.

19. Andrew Revkin, "Greens Debating Tactics Instead of Ideas," *New York Times*, August 5, 2010.

20. *Market Consultation on the FTSE4Good Climate Change Criteria*, FTSE4Good Index Series, August 2006, www.ftse.com/Indices/FTSE4Good_Index_Series/Downloads/FTSE4Good_Climate_Change_Consultation_Aug_06.pdf.

21. "Disasters Escalating Four-Fold as Climate Change Hits Poor Hardest, Says Oxfam," November 22, 2007, www.oxfam.org/en/node/231.

22. Society for Environmental Journalists, "Environmental Refugees: U.S. and World Examples," December 19, 2007.

23. Jeffrey Ball, "11 Insurers Turn Up *Kyoto* Heat," *Globe and Mail*, May 7, 2003, page B11.12; "Global Warming Is a Threat to Health of Corporations," *Wall Street Journal*, April 16, 2003.

24. Douwe Miedema, "Climate Change Means Big Business for Reinsurers," Reuters, November 14, 2006.

25. Evan Mills, Richard J. Roth, Jr., and Eugene Lecomte, "Availability and Affordability of Insurance Under Climate Change: A Growing Challenge for the U.S.," a Ceres report, December 2005.

26. John Morrison and Alex Sink, "The Climate Change Peril That Insurers See," *Washington Post*, September 27, 2007.

27. Eugene Linden, "Cloudy with a Chance of Chaos," *Fortune*, January 17, 2006.

28. For a comprehensive list of climate-related shareholder resolutions, see Investor Network on Climate Risk, http://www.incr.com/Page.aspx?pid=874.

29. John Broder, "Companies Must Disclose Climate Risk," *New York Times*, January 27, 2010.

30. Francis X. Lyons, "Sarbanes-Oxley and the Changing Face of Environmental Liability Disclosure Obligations," *Trends* 35, no. 2 (November–December 2003).

31. In Germany, only "heavy" industry is currently required to report greenhouse gas emissions.

32. Dr. Russell Read (chief investment officer, California Public Employees Retirement System), "Written Testimony Prepared for the U.S. Senate Banking Subcommittee on Securities, Insurance, and Investment," October 31, 2007, www.incr.com/netcommunity/Document.Doc?id=204.

33. Carbon Disclosure Project, "CDP Overview 2007," www.escinst.org/pdf/CDP.pdf.

34. Ylan Q. Mui, "Walmart Aims to Enlist Suppliers in Green Mission," *Washington Post*, September 25, 2007.

35. Davidson, "Walmart Meeting Focused on Sustainability."

36. John Addison, "Wal-Mart to Save $300 Million with Hybrids," Clean Fleet Report, www.cleanfleetreport.com/fleets/wal-mart-to-save-300-million-with-hybrids.

37. Charles Fishman, "How Many Lightbulbs Does It Take to Change the World? One. And You're Looking at It," *Fast Company*, September 2006, p. 74.

38. Andy Ruben (Walmart vice president of corporate strategy and sustainability), personal communication, October 29, 2006.

39. Ann Monroe, "Wal-Mart: Jolly 'Green' Giant?," MSN Money, http://articles.moneycentral.msn.com/Investing/StockInvestingTrading/Wal-MartJollyGreenGiant.aspx.

40. H. Lee Scott, Jr. (CEO and president of Walmart Stores), "Sustainability 360: Doing Good, Better, Together," lecture to the Prince of Wales's Business and the Environment Programme, February 1, 2007, http://walmartstores.com/pressroom/news/6238.aspx.

41. Jonathan Lash and Fred Wellington, "Competitive Advantage on a Warming Planet," *Harvard Business Review*, March 2007.

42. Amy Gillintine, "Walmart Pulls Suppliers onto Sustainability Train," *Colorado Springs Business Journal*, April 13, 2007.

43. Scott, "Sustainability 360."

44. Andrew Winston, November 19, 2009, www.andrewwinston.com/blog/2008/11/the_green_wave_marches_on_walm.php.

45. E. Bruce Harrison, "McDonald's, Walmart: Lessons in Green Lift," February 1, 2009, www.envirocomm.com/comm_lessons_green_lift_020109.php.

46. Nicole Maestri, "Walmart's New CEO Duke Needs to Build on Momentum," Reuters, January 29, 2009.

47. Mui, "Walmart Aims to Enlist Suppliers In Green Mission," *Washington Post*, September 25, 2007, www.washingtonpost.com/wp-dyn/content/article/2007/09/24/AR2007092401435.html.

48. "Walmart Announces Goal to Eliminate 20 Million Metric Tons of Greenhouse Gas Emissions from Global Supply Chain," http://walmartstores.com/FactsNews/NewsRoom/9668.aspx.

49. Mazria quoted in Clayton Sandell, "What Global Warming Looks Like," ABC News, September 14, 2007.

50. Alex Wilson et al., *Green Building: Integrating Ecology and Real Estate* (New York: Wiley, 1999). This book remains one of the best comprehensive guides to the whole field of green building.

51. Heschong Mahone Group, "Skylighting and Retail Sales," report, August 20, 1999.

52. Ibid.; Bill Browning, personal communication, Old Snowmass, Colo., September 1999.

53. Joseph J. Romm and William D. Browning, "Greening the Building and the Bottom Line: Increasing Productivity Through Energy-Efficient Design," Rocky Mountain Institute, Dec. 1994, www.greenbiz.com/sites/default/files/document/O16F8527.pdf.

54. "Zero Interest Rates Punish Savers," October 15, 2010, http://bestmoneymarketratesguide.com.

55. See calculator at http://hes.lbl.gov/consumer.

56. "The Jobs Connection," U.S. Department of Energy, www.localenergy.org/pdfs/Document%20Library/The%20Jobs%20Connection.pdf.

57. Mayors Climate Protection Center, http://usmayors.org/climateprotection/ClimateChange.asp.

58. "US Grassroots Tackle Climate Change," BBC, July 11, 2007.

59. Dr. Randall Pozdena and Dr. Stephen Grover, "Economic Impact Analysis of Energy Trust of Oregon Program Activities," EcoNorthwest, April 2003.

60. Gavin Newsom, "Local Green Jobs Rise as SF Solar and Energy Efficiency Incentive Programs Expand," March 26, 2009, http://cleantechnica.com/.../local-green-jobs-rise-as-sf-solar-and-energy-efficiency-incentive-programs-expand/.

61. Governor's Action Team on Energy and Climate Change, "Florida's Energy and Climate Change Action Plan," October 15, 2008, www.flclimatechange.us/ewebeditpro/items/O12F20028.pdf; see also the executive summary, www.flclimatechange.us/ewebeditpro/items/O12F20028.pdf. It is interesting to note that Republican governors of coastal states have been among the early public officials to recognize the seriousness of climate change: Mark Sanford in South Carolina, Arnold Schwarzenegger in California, and Charlie Crist in Florida. It is probably no accident that the mayors of Seattle and New York have also been leaders.

62. Greg Kats of Capital E, quoted in Steven Mufson, "In Energy Conservation, Calif. Sees Light," *Washington Post*, February 17, 2007.

63. Arthur Rosenfeld, California Energy Commission, personal communication, Berkeley, Calif., April 2009.

64. David Roland-Holst, "Energy Efficiency, Innovation and Job Creation in California," Ceres report, October 20, 2008.

65. Paul Solman, in "Pittsburgh Renews Itself with 'Green' Technologies," *PBS News-Hour*, April 25, 2008, transcript, www.pbs.org/newshour/bb/environment/jan-june08/green_04-25.html.

66. Roger Bezdek, "Renewable Energy and Energy Efficiency: Economic Drivers for the 21st Century," Solar Research Report prepared for the American Solar Energy Society, 2007, download at www.greenforall.org/resources/renewable-energy-and-energy-efficiency-economic.

67. Andrew Burger, "Green Jobs Watch: Solar in Colorado, Small Wind in Michigan," www.globalwarmingisreal.com/blog/2009/04/16/green-jobs-watch-solar-in-colorado-small-wind-in-michigan.

68. Daniel Kammen, Kamal Kapadia, and Matthias Fripp, "Putting Renewables to Work: How Many Jobs Can the Clean Energy Industry Generate?" (Berkeley: University of California–Berkeley, Goldman School of Public Policy, Energy and Resources Group, April 13, 2004, updated January 31, 2006).

69. Center for Climate Strategies, "Climate Change Policy as Economic Stimulus: Evidence and Opportunities from the States," November 2008, http://issuu.com/johnshopkinsaap/docs/jhu-ccs_climate-energy-report/1?zoomed=&zoomPercent=&zoomX=&zoomY=&noteText=&noteX=&noteY=&viewMode=magazine. For other similar studies, see Green Recovery, Center for American Progress, www.americanprogress.org/issues/2008/09/pdf/green_recovery.pdf; www.unep.org/labour_environment/PDFs/Green-Jobs-Background-paper-18-01-08.pdf.

70. CNA Corporation, "National Security and the Threat of Climate Change," n.d., http://securityandclimate.cna.org/report/National%20Security%20and%20the%20Threat%20of%20Climate%20Change.pdf.

71. Global Wind Energy Council, "Global Wind 2008 Report," www.gwec.net/fileadmin/documents/Global%20Wind%202008%20Report.pdf.

72. John Miller, "Idaho Power Gives Up on Coal-Fired Plant," Associated Press, November 7, 2007; Dustin Bleizeffer, "Utility Snuffs Coal Projects," *Casper Star-Tribune*, December 11, 2007.

73. Dr. Mark Cooper, "The Economics of Nuclear Reactors: Renaissance or Relapse?," June 18, 2009, www.vermontlaw.edu/Academics/Environmental_Law_Center/Institutes_and_Initiatives.htm.

74. Jeremy Elton Jacquot, "Largest Solar Farm Ever to Be Built in California," July 9, 2007, www.treehugger.com/files/2007/07/largest_solar_farm_ever.php; Michael Graham Richard, "Turning Big Box Stores into Solar Power Plants in California," March 27, 2008, www.treehugger.com/files/2008/03/big-box-stores-roofs-solar-power-california.php.

75. Vanessa McGrady, Corporate Communications, Southern California Edison, personal communication, Green Innovation Forum, San Francisco, October 19, 2010.

76. Historians place the beginning of the First Industrial Revolution at around 1760. The invention of the cotton gin in 1769 began the era of using water power to produce industrial textiles. The Second Industrial Revolution began around 1850, as the steam engine, invented in 1775, came into widespread use. See www.yale.edu/ynhti/curriculum/units/1981/2/81.02.06.x.html.

77. This concept was first presented in *The Economist*. For a detailed discussion of this thesis refer to K. Hargroves and M. Smith, *The Natural Advantage of Nations: Business Opportunities, Innovation and Governance in the 21st Century* (Earthscan, 2005), developed by the Natural Edge Project, www.naturaledgeproject.net, October 2006.

78. See www.research.hsbc.com/midas/Res/RDV?ao=20&key=wU4BbdyRmz&n=276049.pdf.

79. "HSBC Predicts Low Carbon Energy Market to Triple," September 6, 2010, www.environmentalleader.com/2010/09/06/hsbc-predicts-low-carbon-energy-market-to-triple/#comments; "Low-carbon market to treble by 2020: HSBC," Reuters, September 6, 2010.

80. Keith Bradsher, "Green Power Takes Root in the Chinese Desert," *New York Times*, July 3, 2009.

81. "China's green-tech market could reach $1 trillion by 2013—report," World Business Council for Sustainable Development, September 17, 2009, www.wbcsd.org/plugins/DocSearch/details.asp?type=DocDet&ObjectId=MzU2Njk.

82. Keith Johnson, "Wind Power: China's Massive—and Cheap—Bet on the Wind Farm," *BusinessWeek*, July 6, 2009.

83. Selina Harrison, Cleantech Investment in Asia, *Financier Worldwide*, February 2010.

84. Thomas L. Friedman, "The New Sputnik," *New York Times*, September 26, 2009.

85. Thomas L. Friedman, "Have a Nice Day," *New York Times*, September 15, 2009.

86. Corporate managers are increasingly realizing that value returned to the owners, the real metric of success, derives from more than just attention to next quarter's profits. See L. Hunter Lovins, "Sustainable Executives," *Effective Executive*, May 2006, www.natcapsolutions.org/publications_files/2006/MAY06_India_EffectiveExecutive.pdf.

87. For a description of how the Financial Accounting Standards Board has recently announced that it will revise its definition of "profit" away from this short-term fixation, see David Reilly, "Profit as We Know It Could Be Lost with New Accounting Statements," *Wall Street Journal*, May 12, 2007, p. A1.

88. Goldman Sachs, "Introducing GS Sustain," research report, June 22, 2007, www.unglobalcompact.org/docs/summit2007/gs_esg_embargoed_until030707pdf.pdf.

89. Margo Alderton, "Green Is Gold, According to Goldman Sachs Study," CR—Corporate Responsibility Magazine, www.thecro.com/node/490.

90. Tim Carey, "Sustainability—An Economic Imperative in the Current Economy," Environmental Leader, December 1, 2009, www.environmentalleader.com/2008/12/01/sustainability-an-economic-imperative-in-the-current-economy.

91. Daniel Mahler et al., "Green Winners," prepared for A. T. Kearney, 2009, www .sustaincommworld.com/pdfs/ATKearney_Green_Winners.pdf.

92. Ibid.

93. Pierfrancesco Manenti, Robert Parker, and Georgio Micheletti, "The Business Case for Environmental Excellence Is Real," report prepared for Atos Origin and IDC, 2009, www.atosorigin.com/nr/rdonlyres/56c51085-b33b-4b2d-a2c8-80d5dca74768/ 0/idc_report.pdf.

94. Ram Nidumolu, C. K. Prahalad, and M. R. Rangaswami, "Why Sustainability Is Now the Key Driver of Innovation," *Harvard Business Review*, September 2009.

95. Sir Nicholas Stern, "Stern Review: The Economics of Climate Change," October 2006, executive summary, www.hm-treasury.gov.uk/media/4/3/Executive_Summary .pdf. Sir Nicholas Stern, who served as the chief economist and senior vice president of the World Bank from 2000 to 2003, released a report commissioned by the UK government stating that inaction on climate change will result in a depressed economy worse than the Great Depression of the 1930s, with financial costs higher than those incurred by the Depression and the two world wars. The report concluded that in human terms, the resulting drought and flooding will displace 200 million people from their homes, creating the largest refugee migration in history. Up to 40 percent of the world's known species are likely to go extinct. To avert this tragedy, the report states, the world will need to spend 1 percent of global GDP each year to mitigate climate change, equal to the worldwide advertising budget. Failure to mitigate the crisis, the report stated, would commit the world to spending up to 20 percent of world GDP each year to deal with the consequences.

2. Energy Efficiency

1. Point Carbon estimates that the global carbon market was worth €92bn ($125bn) in late 2009; see www.pointcarbon.com, www.businessgreen.com/bg/news/1801047/ analyst-world-carbon-market-doubles-2008. Bloomberg's New Carbon Finance put the size of the market at $118 billion; see http://carbon.newenergyfinance.com.

2. "2009 Review; 2010 Forecast; Understanding Green ETFs," *Progressive Investor* 68 (January 2010), www.sustainablebusiness.com/index.cfm/go/progressiveinvestor .sample/id/92/sectionid/427.

3. "Greener Business Practices Save KKR Companies $160M," GreenBiz.com, June 3, 2010, www.greenbiz.com/news/2010/06/03/greener-business-practices-save-8-kkr -companies-160m.

4. World Resources Institute and A. T. Kearney, "Rattling Supply Chains: The Effect of Environmental Trends on Input Costs for the Fast-Moving Consumer Goods Industry," November 2008, http://pdf.wri.org/rattling_supply_chains.pdf.

5. Johnson Controls, "2009 Energy Efficiency Indicator," www.johnsoncontrols.com.

6. Marilyn A. Brown et al., "Engineering Economic Studies of Energy Technologies to Reduce Greenhouse Gas Emissions: Opportunities and Challenges," *Annual Review*

of Energy and the Environment 23 (November 1998): 287–385, http://arjournals
.annualreviews.org/doi/abs/10.1146/annurev.energy.23.1.287;jsessionid=
oG8-m21d8Po-dHtuiH?cookieSet=1&journalCode=energy.

7. Per-Anders Enkvist, Thomas Naucler, and Jerker Rosander, "A Cost-Curve for
Greenhouse Gas Reduction," *McKinsey Quarterly*, no. 1, 2007, www.epa.gov/oar/
caaac/coaltech/2007_05_mckinsey.pdf.

8. Amory B. Lovins and L. Hunter Lovins, "Climate: Making Sense and Making
Money," 1997, www.natcapsolutions.org/articles/1997/HLovins-ALovins_Climate
-MakingSenseandMakingMoney_NOV1997.pdf.

9. Ibid.

10. Jon Creyts et al., "How Much at What Cost? U.S. Greenhouse Gas Abatement
Mapping Initiative," study, December 2007, identified 27 gigatons per year of abate-
ment that could be captured by implementing measures that cost under forty euros
per ton (considered "low cost"). See http://gei.newscorp.com/resources/files/
mckinsey—howmuchatwhatcost.pdf. See also Hannah Choi Granade et al.,
"Unlocking Energy Efficiency in the U.S. Economy," McKinsey Global Energy and
Materials report, July 2009, www.mckinsey.com/clientservice/electricpowernaturalgas/
US_energy_efficiency.

11. "This Plan maps out strategies for cost-effectively achieving the contract objectives
with a target yield of 46.08 MWh per $10,000 of spending and a levelized utility
cost of $0.028 per kilowatt-hour" (Vermont Public Service Board, "Efficiency Ver-
mont Annual Plan 2009–2011," December 16, 2008, www.efficiencyvermont.org/
stella/filelib/EVT%20Annual%20Plan%202009-2011.pdf, p. 7). See also GDS Associates, Inc., "Vermont Electric Energy Efficiency Potential Study, Final Report.
Rep. Jan. 2007," report prepared for the Vermont Department of Public Service
(http://publicservice.vermont.gov/energy/vteefinalreportjan07v3andappendices
.pdf), shows ten residential energy efficiency measures having a cost of conserved
energy less than $.02 per kWh saved. In general, commercial savings are even
cheaper than residential. See www.efficiencyvermont.org/stella/filelib/EVT%20
Annual%20Plan%202009-2011.pdf.

12. "Going Green at Google: Step 2: Efficient Data Centers," www.google.com/
corporate/green/datacenters/step2.html.

13. Andrew Nusca, "HP Opens First Wind-Cooled Green Data Center; Most Efficient
to Date," February 11, 2010, www.smartplanet.com/business/blog/smart-takes/
hp-opens-first-wind-cooled-green-data-center-most-efficient-to-date/4191/?tag=
content.

14. Tarmo Virki, "Cloud Computing Goes Green Underground in Finland," Planet
Ark, December 1, 2009, http://planetark.org/enviro-news/item/55720.

15. Mark Peters, "Google Cleared on Power Bid," *Wall Street Journal*, February 18,
2010.

16. Katie Fehrenbacher, " 'Google Energy' Subsidiary: What's Google Up To?" GigaOM
(blog), January 7, 2010.

17. In 2010, The U.S. Department of Energy's Save Now and Federal Energy Manage-

ment Programs, U.S. Environmental Protection Agency's Energy Star Program, the European Union Code of Conduct, Japan's Ministry of Economy, Trade and Industry's Green IT Initiative, and Japan's Green IT Promotion Council have partnered to create the Green Grid Consortium to set guiding principles for globally accepted data center energy-efficiency metrics with the Green Grid's power usage effectiveness rating at the center of the industry's new preferred energy-efficiency metric.

18. Elizabeth Souder, "Will Wal-Mart Sell Electricity One Day?" *Dallas Morning News*, January 29, 2007.

19. Philips EcoVision 4 program, www.philips.com/about/sustainability/environmental responsibility/ecovision4program/index.page.

20. "T.K. Chemical Complex Ltd.: Increase of Condensate Recovery from Boiler," Energy Efficiency Guide for Industry in Asia, 2006, www.energyefficiencyasia.org/docs/casestudies/bangla/TKIC/TKCCL%20-%20Increase%20of%20condensate%20recovery.pdf.

21. "ITC Limited—Paperboards and Specialty Paper Division," Energy Efficiency Guide for Industry in Asia, 2006, www.energyefficiencyasia.org/tools/companycasestudies/india/itc.html.

22. Ibid.

23. Small Business Administration, "Frequently Asked Questions," www.sba.gov/advo/stats/sbfaq.pdf.

24. "When Going Green Isn't About Marketing," *Bloomberg BusinessWeek*, http://images.businessweek.com/ss/09/08/0807_going_green/31.htm.

25. The phantom loads of older VCR and DVD players can be significant. Energy Star DVD players consume a quarter of the energy of a standard DVD model when turned off (Energy Star, "DVD and Blu-ray for Consumers," 2008, www.energystar.gov/index.cfm?fuseaction=find_a_product.showProductGroup&pgw_code=DP).

26. Home Energy Saver, http://hes.lbl.gov/hes/profitable_dat.html.

27. Energy Star, "2006 Small Businesses and Congregations Award Winners," August 13, 2007, www.energystar.gov/index.cfm?c=sb_success.sb_2006winners#basil.

28. New York State Energy Research and Development Authority, "New York State Energy Research and Development Authority (NYSERDA) Sets the Pace for New York Energy $mart Offices," www.nyserda.org/programs/offices/case_studies/nyserda.pdf.

29. Anna Clark, "Practical Advice for Greening the SME [Small- and Medium-sized Enterprise]," www.greenerbuildings.com/news_detail.cfm?NewsID=34996.

30. Michael Burnham, "Energy Policy: Kerry, Snowe Slam Agencies for Work on Small Businesses," *Environment & Energy Daily*, March 9, 2007.

31. Joe Santana (COO Mi Rancho Tortillas), personal communication, San Leandro Chamber of Commerce Sustainability and Innovation Symposium, October 25, 2010.

32. Home Energy Saver, http://hes.lbl.gov/hes/profitable_dat.html.

33. Robert Kropp, "U.S. Corporate Support for Climate Laws Tops 6,000 Firms," May 24, 2010, SocialFunds.com, www.socialfunds.com/news/article.cgi/2954.htm.

The USCAP (www.us-cap.org) has thirty-one members, including such manufacturers as Alcoa, Siemens, GE, Caterpillar, Johnson & Johnson, DuPont, and Dow; utilities including PG&E, AES, Duke Energy, and Exelon; auto makers Ford and GM; and oil companies Shell, BP, and ConocoPhillips.

34. Jonathan Lash and Fred Wellington, "Competitive Advantage on a Warming Planet," *Harvard Business Review*, March 2007.

35. Gil Friend, "New Bottom Line Volume 14.7—Avoiding the Next Train Wreck," September 1, 2005, www.natlogic.com/resources/publications/new-bottom-line/vol14/7-avoiding-the-next-train-wreck.

36. "EU Businesses Lead Move to a Low Carbon Economy—Conclusions of the High Level Group on Competitiveness, Energy and Environment," EU press release, November 30, 2007, http://europa.eu/rapid/pressReleasesAction.do?reference=IP/07/1823.

37. James Murray, "UN Confirms 55 Nations Met Copenhagen Accord Deadline," *BusinessGreen*, February 2, 2010, www.businessgreen.com/business-green/news/2257137/un-confirms-55-nations-met.

38. "Carbon in Waste Declared Solid Waste," The Babylon Project, June 22, 2009, www.thebabylonproject.org/blog/2009/6/22/carbon-in-waste-declared-solid-waste.html.

39. Debra Kahn, "State Regulators Approve the Nation's Biggest Cap-and-Trade Plan," *New York Times*, December 17, 2010.

40. Western Area Power Administration, "Integrated Resource Planning Guidelines," November 30, 2006, www.wapa.gov/powerm/pmirp.htm.

41. U.S. Department of Energy, "The Jobs Connection: Energy Use and Local Economic Development," November 1996, www.cpfund.ca/pdf/the-jobs-connection.pdf.

42. Health and Energy Company (a Nebraska energy testing company), "Osage Municipal Utilities Energy Efficiency Program," February 2005, http://healthandenergy.com/osage_energy_efficiency.htm.

43. U.S. Department of Energy, "The Jobs Connection: Energy Use and Local Economic Development."

44. Ed Smeloff (general manager SMUD), personal communication, Taipei, Taiwan, October 2000.

45. See http://newsroom.cisco.com/dlls/global/canada/news/2010/pr_03-18.html; Gary Holden, personal communication, Calgary, October 2010.

46. Paul Hawken, Amory Lovins, and Hunter Lovins, *Natural Capitalism: Creating the Next Industrial Revolution* (New York: Little, Brown, 1999), pp. 273–74.

47. Lovins, Amory, "Negawatts, 12 Transitions," 1996, www.rmi.org/rmi/Library/U96-11_NegawattsTwelveTransitions.

48. Vice President Dick Cheney, in prepared remarks to the annual meeting of the Associated Press, Toronto, Canada, stated, "Conservation may be a sign of personal virtue, but it is not a sufficient basis for a sound, comprehensive energy policy." He called for dramatic increases in building power plants and offshore drilling. See transcript, www.pbs.org/newshour/bb/environment/energy/cheney_4-30.html.

49. Susan Chang, "The Rise of the Energy Efficiency Utility," Institute of Electronics

and Electronics Engineers, May 7, 2008. http://spectrum.ieee.org/green-tech/conservation/the-rise-of-the-energy-efficiency-utility.

50. Fred Wellington et al., "Scaling Up: Global Technology Deployment to Stabilize Emissions," World Resources Institute, April 13, 2007, www.wri.org/publication/scaling-up, p. 14.

51. Thomas Content, "Power Plant Cost to Top $1 Billion," *Milwaukee Journal-Sentinel*, June 14, 2008.

52. Paul Sheldon, "Coal Plants in Transition," Natural Capitalism Solutions, www.natcapsolutions.org.

53. www.energy-aware.com.

54. Blue Innovations, "Results of Two-Year Study Demonstrate Residential Electricity Monitors Help Homeowners Conserve Electricity in a Big Way," www.bluelineinnovations.com/documents/pr-ceati.pdf.

55. "Smart Grid Innovation to Electrify West Coast Green 2010," Business Wire, September 22, 2010. The keynote speakers at the conference were Hunter Lovins and Gregory Miller; for an interview with Lovins and Miller, see www.treehugger.com/files/2010/10/west-coast-green-2010-michelle-kaufmann-interviews-hunter-lovins.php; http://greenagenda.info/madrone-league-open-source-sustainability-education.

56. Sandra Kwak, Kendell Laine, and Liz Stuart (the Powerzoa team), personal communications with Hunter Lovins at West Coast Green, October 3, 2010.

57. Claire C. Miller, "Efficient Power Use Attracts Investors from the Green Side," *New York Times*, May 10, 2009.

58. Bob Willard, *The Next Sustainability Wave* (Gabriola Island, British Columbia: New Society Publishers, 2007).

59. Tom Bergin, "BP Says Oil Spill Compensation Payout Rate Soars," Reuters, September 20, 2010, www.reuters.com/article/idUSTRE68J0OT20100920.

60. Bob Willard, *The Sustainability Advantage* (Gabriola Island, British Columbia: New Society Publishers, 2002), chapter 2; see also www.sustainabilityadvantage.com.

61. Sir Nicholas Stern, *The Stern Review on the Economics of Climate Change*, http://webarchive.nationalarchives.gov.uk/+/http://www.hm-treasury.gov.uk/sternreview_index.htm. Similar findings are available in the Climate Group's "In the Black: The Growth of the Low Carbon Economy" executive summary report, May 24, 2007, p. 16, www.theclimategroup.org/publications.

62. Jeffrey Immelt and Jonathan Lash, "The Courage to Develop Clean Energy," *Washington Post*, May 21, 2005.

3: Both Are Better

1. International Energy Agency, World Energy Outlook, 2009.

2. "EU Nations Confident on Renewable Energy Goals," January 25, 2010, www.euractiv.com/en/energy/eu-nations-confident-renewable-energy-goals/article-189170.

3. Ibid.

4. Intelligent Energy–Europe (IEE) is the EU Community's support program for nontechnological actions in the field of energy, particularly in the field of energy efficiency and renewable-energy sources. The program was adopted by the European Parliament and the Council on June 26, 2003. It was published in the *Official Journal of the European Union*, July 15, 2003, pp. 29–36, and entered into force on August 4, 2003.

5. "EU 20% Renewable Energy Target Can Deliver 2.8 Million Jobs," Environmental Leader, June 8, 2009, www.environmentalleader.com/2009/06/08/eu-20-renewable-energy-target-can-deliver-28-million-jobs.

6. Michael Northrop, "The Clean Energy Gold Rush," *Huffington Post*, February 16, 2010, www.huffingtonpost.com/michael-northrop/the-clean-energy-gold-rush_b_463888.html.

7. George Sterzinger and Jerry Stevens, "Renewable Energy Demand: A Study of California," October 2006, www.repp.org/articles/static/1/binaries/Final_California_GSEXECSUMMARY2_Long3.pdf, p. 4.

8. David Roland-Holst and Fredrich Kahrl, "Clean Energy and Climate Policies Lead to Economic Growth in the United States," University of California–Berkeley, Department of Agriculture and Resource Economies, http://are.berkeley.edu/~dwrh/Ceres_Web/Docs/EAGLE%20Fact%20Sheet%20on%20ACES.pdf.

9. Tom Peterson (Center for Climate Strategies), personal communication, March 9, 2010.

10. Kiran Stacey, "Clean Energy Funding Slumps," *Financial Times*, November 25, 2010.

11. Sue Grist Sturgis, "Growth in Renewable Energy Outpaces Nuclear, Fossil Fuels," *Grist Magazine*, September 30, 2009.

12. U.S. Energy Information Administration, *Electric Power Monthly*, June 2010, www.eia.doe.gov/cneaf/electricity/epm/table1_1.html.

13. Ryan Wiser and Edward Kahn, "Alternative Windpower Ownership Structures: Financing Terms and Project Costs," Lawrence Berkeley Laboratory's Energy and Environment Division, May 1996 (http://eetd.lbl.gov/ea/emp/reports/38921.pdf). Wiser and Kahn estimate that a typical 50-megawatt wind plant, which would deliver power at just under 5 cents/kWh if financed by a wind developer, could generate power for 3.5 cents/kWh—a nearly 30 percent cost reduction—if an investor-owned utility owned and financed the facility instead. See also www.awea.org/faq/cost.html.

14. Craig A. Severance, "Business Risks and Costs of New Nuclear Power," http://climateprogress.org/wp-content/uploads/2009/01/nuclear-costs-2009.pdf.

15. Lester Brown, "Dousing the Coal-Fired Plant," CBS Moneywatch.com, September 2008, http://findarticles.com/p/articles/mi_m1272/is_2760_137/ai_n28571856/.

16. "China's Green-Tech Market Could Reach $1 Trillion by 2013," Environmental Finance, www.wbcsd.org/plugins/DocSearch/details.asp?type=DocDet&ObjectId=MzU2Njk.

17. "China to Invest $14.6 Billion in Wind Power by 2010," *Bloomberg News*, June 2, 2009.
18. Duane Sharp, "Global Wind Power Projections for 2010," January 4, 2010, http://energy-conservation.suite101.com/article.cfm/global_wind_power_projections_for_2010.
19. Selina Harrison, "Cleantech Investment in Asia," *Financier Worldwide*, February 2010.
20. Keith Bradsher, "Green Power Takes Root in the Chinese Desert," *New York Times*, July 3, 2009.
21. Knight, Robin, "China Will Take Over U.S. as No. 1 Consumer: WPP CEO," CNBC, June 2009, www.cnbc.com/id/31204762.
22. Joseph Kahn and Jim Yardley, "As China Roars, Pollution Reaches Deadly Extremes," *New York Times*, August 26, 2007, www.nytimes.com/2007/08/26/world/asia/26china.html?_r=1&oref=slogin.
23. Jonathan Watts, "China Blames Growing Social Unrest on Anger over Pollution," *Guardian*, July 6, 2007, http://www.guardian.co.uk/environment/2007/jul/06/china.pollution.
24. Richard McGregor, "750,000 a Year Killed by Chinese Pollution," *Financial Times*, July 2, 2007.
25. Peter Ford, "How Baoding, China, Becomes World's First 'Carbon Positive' City," *Christian Science Monitor*, August 16, 2009.
26. Taro Aso, "Japan's Future Development Strategy and Growth Initiative Towards Doubling the Size of Asia's Economy," April 9, 2009, www.kantei.go.jp/foreign/asospeech/2009/04/09speech_e.html.
27. Tomoko Hosaka, "Japan Wants to Sell Energy-Efficient 'Smart' Cities to the World: Ceatec 2010," *Huffington Post*, October 7, 2010, www.huffingtonpost.com/2010/10/08/japan-wants-to-sell-energ_n_755451.html.
28. The Climate Group, "In the Black: The Growth of the Low-Carbon Economy," www.theclimategroup.org/_assets/files/In_the_Black_full_report_May-06.pdf, p. 11.
29. Richard K. Wallace, "India Details Solar Plans," *EE Times*, June 15, 2009.
30. Cho Meeyoung, "South Korea to Spend $85 Billion on Green Industries," Reuters, July 6, 2009.
31. "'Green New Deal' for South Korea $38.1 Billion," *Huffington Post*, January 6, 2009, www.huffingtonpost.com/2009/01/06/green-new-deal-for-south-_n_155504.html.
32. "Defining, Estimating and Forecasting the Renewable Energy and Energy Efficiency Industries in the U.S. and Colorado," GreenBiz.com, January 15, 2009.
33. Brandon MacGillis, "Pew Finds Clean Energy Economy Generates Significant Job Growth," June 10, 2009, www.pewtrusts.org/news_room_detail.aspx?id=53254.
34. White House, "Vice President Biden, CEA Chair Romer Release New Analysis on Job and Economic Impact of the Recovery Act," press release, July 14, 2010.
35. "Senate Adds Key Clean Energy Program to Tax Bill," Climate Progress, December 13, 2010.

36. Wendy Patton, "The Impact of Impact: Creating Jobs in Ohio," Public Economy Research Institute, February 2010, www.policymattersohio.org/pdf/IMPACT2010 .pdf.

37. Ibid.

38. Teryn Norris, "Will America Lose the Clean Energy Race?" *Huffington Post*, July 27, 2009, www.huffingtonpost.com/teryn-norris/will-america-lose-the-cle_b_245163 .html.

39. See "Fast Solar Energy Facts: German PV Market," www.solarbuzz.com/fastfacts germany.htm. To learn more about Hermann Scheer, who died tragically on October 15, 2010, see Amy Goodman of Democracy Now, "Hermann Scheer (1944–2010): German Lawmaker, Leading Advocate for Solar Energy and 'Hero for the Green Century,'" www.democracynow.org/seo/2010/10/15/hermann_scheer _1944_2010_german_lawmaker.

40. "German Town Will Soon Use 100% Renewable Power," April 29, 2007, Metaeffi- cient (blog), www.metaefficient.com/renewable-power/german-town-will-soon -use-100-renewable-power.html; "Despite Downturn German Solar Market Will Grow 25% This Year," Techpulse 360, August 31, 2009; Federal Ministry of Eco- nomics and Technology.

41. Jane Burgermeister, "Germany: The World's First Major Renewable Energy Econ- omy," *Renewable Energy World*, April 3, 2009.

42. Paul Gipe, "Dardesheim: Germany's Renewable Energy Town," January 25, 2007, Wind-Works.org, www.wind-works.org/articles/DardesheimGermanysRenewable EnergyCity.html.

43. DONG company announcement at the Copenhagen Conference of the Parties (COP 15), December 15, 2009.

44. Melissa McNamara, "Danish Island is Energy Self-Sufficient," *CBS Evening News*, March 8, 2007, www.cbsnews.com/stories/2007/03/08/eveningnews/main2549273 .shtml.

45. "New Report Projects $50 Billion in Renewable Energy Investment by 2011," RenewableEnergyAccess.com, November 20, 2007, www.renewableenergyaccess .com/rea/news/story?id=50622.

46. Terry Macalister, "Renewable Revolution Is Here, Says UN Report," *Guardian*, June 21, 2007; Global Trends in Sustainable Development Annual Review, www .commondreams.org/archive/2007/06/21/2016/.

47. "Renewables Can Meet 50 Per Cent of Energy Needs by 2040, Claims Report," *Times Higher Education*, June 1, 2004, www.timeshighereducation.co.uk/story.asp ?storyCode=189068&sectioncode=26.

48. California Solar Center, "The History of Solar Energy," www.californiasolarcenter .org/history_solarthermal.html. See also Ken Butti and John Perlin, *A Golden Thread: 2,500 Years of Solar Architecture and Technology* (New York: Van Nostrand Reinhold, 1981).

49. David Pierson, "China, Green? In the Case of Solar Water Heating, Yes," *Los Angeles Times*, September 6, 2009.

50. Ibid.

51. See ESTIF, "Solar Thermal Action Plan for Europe" (summary), www.estif.org/policies/st_action_plan; complete text: www.estif.org/fileadmin/estif/content/policies/STAP/Solar_Thermal_Action_Plan_2007_A3.pdf.

52. Ibid.

53. Gregory Miller, "Investing in a Cleaner Energy Revolution," Google.org blog, November 27, 2007, http://blog.google.org/2007/11/investing-in-cleaner-energy-revolution.html.

54. Ira Flatow, "Deal Suggests Bright Solar Future in China," NPR, *Science Friday*, January 15, 2010, www.npr.org/templates/story/story.php?storyId=122620060.

55. eSolar, brochure, 2009.

56. "eSolar Ushers in New Era of Solar Energy with Unveiling of Sierra Power Plant," press release, August 5, 2009, www.eSolar.com/news/press/2009_08_05.

57. "Coney Island Gets Solar Thermal Project," Environmental Leader, June 7, 2010, www.environmentalleader.com/2010/06/07/coney-island-gets-solar-thermal-project.

58. Sarah McBride, "World's Largest Solar Plant Wins Key Approval," Reuters, September 16, 2010.

59. "Global Wind Capacity Grew 31% in 2009, Adding 37.5 GW: GWEC," Clean Edge News, February 4, 2010, www.cleanedge.com/news/story.php?nID=6673.

60. Ibid.

61. European Wind Energy Association, "IEA Issues Climate Change 'Wake Up Call,' Touts Wind as Major Solution," press release, November 12, 2008.

62. Roddy Scheer, "Wind Power Beats Predictions," *E Magazine*, November 12, 2007.

63. "IIIS CERA, Power Plant Construction Costs Falling for All Types of New Plants," press release, June 23, 2009, http://press.ihs.com/article_display.cfm?article_id=4051.

64. Keith Johnson, "Wind Power: China's Massive—and Cheap—Bet on Wind Farms," *BusinessWeek*, July 6, 2009.

65. "Siemens and DONG Energy Have Further Expanded Their Cooperation in Offshore Wind Power," *Power Industry News*, January 17, 2010.

66. Sharp, "Global Wind Power Projections for 2010."

67. "Iberdrola Renewables Signs Its Largest PPA Ever with TVA, Power to Come from Illinois's Largest Wind Farm," January 14, 2010, www.iberdrolarenewables.us/rel_10.01.14.html.

68. David Roman et al., "Spain to Cut Solar and Wind Power Subsidies in December," *Wall Street Journal*, November 24, 2010.

69. Sharp, "Global Wind Power Projections for 2010."

70. Radnor Township, "Energy," www.radnor.com/department/division.asp?fDD=26-269.

71. See www.bergey.com/Products/Excel.html.

72. See www.aerotecture.com/projects_hornblower.html; www.aerotecture.com/our vision.html.

73. Rindi White, "More Alaskans Harness Renewable Energy," *Anchorage Daily News*, November 28, 2009.
74. J. Matthew Roney, "Solar Cell Production Climbs to Another Record in 2009," Earth Policy Institute, September 24, 2010, www.renewableenergyworld.com/rea/news/article/2010/09/solar-cell-production-climbs-to-another-record-in-2009.
75. Larry Flynn, "Driven to Be Green," *Building Design and Construction*, November 1, 2003.
76. "Eric Schmidt on Strategies and Solutions for Energy Security," www.youtube.com/watch?v=LRJlO5gdsfk.
77. CEO of JEA, personal communication, Jacksonville, Fla., October 2010.
78. Energy Empowers, "Vet's Company Installing Solar Across Massachusetts," February 25, 2010, www.eereblogs.energy.gov/energyempowers/post/Veterane28099s-company-installing-solar-across-Massachusetts.aspx.
79. Dr. Peter B. deNeufville, chairman of Voltaix, personal communication; Voltaix newsletter, p. 6, www.voltaix.com/images/news/newsletter_02_10.pdf.
80. Christopher Mims, "Iceland's Geothermal Bailout," *Popular Science*, June 19, 2009, www.popsci.com/environment/article/2009-06/icelands-power-down-below#.
81. Ibid.
82. Robert P. Wright, "Development of Geothermal Resources: The Heat Is On," University of Texas School of Law, www.utcle.org/eLibrary/preview.php?asset_file_id=23397.
83. Energy Efficiency and Renewable Energy, Geothermal Technologies Program, "The Future of Geothermal Energy," www.eere.energy.gov/geothermal/future_geothermal.html.
84. John Guerrerio, "AltaRock Project Abandoned, Geothermal Potential Still Untapped," Energy Examiner (blog), December 13, 2009.
85. Gregory Miller, personal communication, November 26, 2010.
86. Adam Gabbatt, "Swiss Geothermal Power Plan Abandoned After Quakes Hit Basel," *Guardian*, December 15, 2009.
87. Guerreo, "AltaRock Project Abandoned."
88. Geothermal Map of North America, American Association of Petroleum Geologists, http://smu.edu/geothermal/2004NAMap/2004NAmap.htm.
89. "West Virginia—Country Roads to Geothermal Power," Google.org blog, November 4, 2010, http://blog.google.org/2010/10/west-virginia-country-roads-to.html.
90. Alex Salmond, first minister of Scotland, personal communication, World Renewable Energy Congress, Glasgow, July 2008.
91. "Scotland's First Minister Launches Oyster," *Green Jobs*, November 20, 2009.
92. "Scotland Takes Euro Lead in Renewable Energy," news release by Scottish government, May 5, 2009.
93. ScottishPower Renewables, "Pioneering Tidal Power Device to Be Tested in Scotland," press release, February 2, 2010.
94. Mara Hvistendahl, "China's Three Gorges Dam: An Environmental Catastrophe?" *Scientific American*, March 25, 2008.

95. Energy Alternatives, "MicroHydro" (www.energyalternatives.ca/content/Categories/MicroHydroInfo.asp), enables you to calculate whether you have a microhydro site worth developing.

96. Lucid Energy Technologies, "Riverside's Gage Canal Is Part of a First-Ever Hydro-electric Power Test," February 24, 2010, www.lucidenergy.com/press/2010/25.

97. Tim Braun (a student of Hunter Lovins's), personal communication, August 18, 2010.

98. Ibid.

99. "Mayors and Climate Protection Best Practices," United States Conference of Mayors, June 2009, www.usmayors.org/pressreleases/uploads/ClimateBest Practices061209.pdf.

100. "Raba-Kistner Agrees to Go 'Green' by Buying Renewable Energy," *San Antonio Business Journal*, May 15, 2008.

101. "Windtricity Continues to Generate Partners," Environmental Leader, May 18, 2008.

102. Nils Moe (sustainability director, city of Berkeley), personal communication, November 2008.

103. Loralee Stevens, "Half Dozen Solar Companies Flock to Sonoma County," *North Bay Business Journal*, December 14, 2009.

104. "Green Jobs Created Through $100 Million Sonoma County Energy Independence Program," MarketWire, November 23, 2009, www.marketwire.com/press-release/Green-Jobs-Created-Through-100-Million-Sonoma-County-Energy-Independence-Program-1080905.htm. J. V. Loceff, "Study: Energy Program Could Be Jobs Booster," *North Bay Business Journal*, December 14, 2009.

105. Gwen Hallsmith (city planner, Montpelier, Vermont), personal communication, August 10, 2010.

106. Lawrence Ragonese, "Morris County Solar Energy Project Will Save About 35 Percent on Energy Bills," *Star Ledger*, February 11, 2010.

107. John Farrell, "Energy Self-Reliant States: Second and Expanded Edition," October 2009, www.newrules.org/energy/publications/energy-selfreliant-states-second-and-expanded-edition.

108. Severance, "Business Risks and Costs of New Nuclear Power." American Progress, January 2, 2009.

109. Jerome R. Stockfish, "New Nuclear Plant Would Boost Electric Bills for a Decade," *Tampa Tribune*, March 12, 2008.

110. It was proved back in 1980 that reactor-grade plutonium is quite sufficient for the construction of a nuclear bomb. See L. Hunter Lovins and Amory B. Lovins, *Energy War: Breaking the Nuclear Link* (New York: Friends of the Earth, 1981).

111. "Gambling on Nuclear Power: How Public Money Fuels the Industry," Global Subsidies Initiative, www.globalsubsidies.org/en/subsidy-watch/commentary/gambling-nuclear-power-how-public-money-fuels-industry.

112. Gary Hirshberg, speaking at "Global Warming and Energy Solutions," conference organized by Clean Air, Cool Planet, 2009, www.cleanair-coolplanet.org/conference_GWS07/finalsummary.php.

113. CleanTech, "Clean technology venture investment totaled $5.6 billion in 2009 despite non-binding climate change accord in Copenhagen, finds the Cleantech Group and Deloitte," press release, January 6, 2010, http://cleantech.com/about/pressreleases/20090106.cfm.

114. See www.carbonwarroom.com.

115. "Portland Selected for Low-Carbon Economic Development Program," April 30, 2010, www.sustainablebusinessoregon.com/articles/2010/04/portland_selected_for_low-carbon_economic_development_program.html.

116. Joel Kirkland, "Business: Branson's 'Carbon War Room' Puts Industry on Front Line of U.S. Climate Debate," April 22, 2010, www.eenews.net/public/climatewire/2010/04/22/1

117. Ibid. In December 2010 Hunter Lovins agreed to chair the War Room's Small Island Nation Initiative.

118. Martin Lagod and the Eos team, personal communication, April 24, 2008; see also www.firelakecapital.com/team.html#martin.

119. Environmental Technologies Fund, www.etf.eu.com.

120. J. Matthew Roney, "Solar Cell Production Climbs to Another Record in 2009," Earth Policy Institute, September 24, 2010, www.renewableenergyworld.com/rea/news/article/2010/09/solar-cell-production-climbs-to-another-record-in-2009.

121. Alan Simpson, "Not the Great Green Rip-off, by George," *Guardian*, March 5, 2010.

122. Deutsche Bank, "Paying for Renewable Energy: TLC at the Right Price—Achieving Scale Through Efficient Policy Design," December 2009, www.dbcca.com/dbcca/EN/investment-research/investment_research_2144.jsp.

123. EPA, "Renewable Portfolio Standards Fact Sheet," April 2009, www.epa.gov/chp/state-policy/renewable_fs.html.

124. Jeff Siegel, "Colorado's New Renewable Energy Mandate," Examiner.com, Baltimore, April 6, 2010.

125. Deutsche Bank, "Paying for Renewable Energy."

126. GRU, "Leading the Nation: GRU's Solar Feed-in-Tariff," February 6, 2009, www.gru.com/AboutGRU/NewsReleases/Archives/Articles/news-2009-02-06.jsp.

127. Ibid.

128. Paul Gipe, "Britain Abandons Renewable Power Mandates, Embraces Feed-in Tariffs," *Grist*, December 21, 2010, www.grist.org/people/Paul+Gipe.

129. "New 1BOG Solar Campaigns Prepare for Takeoff," 1BOG blog, June 7, 2010.

130. Robert Sanders, "Investment in Renewable Energy Better for Jobs as Well as Environment," University of California–Berkeley, news release, April 13, 2004.

131. Stated in a speech to the U.S. Conference of Mayors Climate Protection Summit, November 2, 2007.

132. Siemens vice president, personal communication with Hunter Lovins, October 2009.

133. Michael Weinhold, "Talking Tomorrow's Energy System," April 2, 2010, www.energy.siemens.com/mx/pool/hq/energy-topics/living-energy/issue-2/LivingEnergy_Issue2_Energys_Future.pdf.

134. "Intelligent Intel Metre Project Gets $100M in Fed Gov't Funding," Smarthouse, October 10, 2010, http://smarthouse.com.au/Automation/Industry/B8G4P4K6.

4: Green Buildings, Green Neighborhoods

1. U.S. Energy Information Administration, "Emissions of Greenhouse Gases Report," 2006, www.eia.doe.gov/oiaf/1605/ggrpt/carbon.html.

2. World Green Building Council, "The Business Case for GBCs," www.worldgbc .org/green-building-councils/the-business-case-for-gbcs; Architecture 2030, "Problem: The Building Sector," www.architecture2030.org/current_situation/building _sector.html; U.S. Energy Information Administration, "EIA Annual Energy Outlook," 2008, www.eia.doe.gov/oiaf/aeo/consumption.html.

3. Carbon footprint study conducted by the University of the South, Sewanee, Tennessee.

4. U.S. Green Building Council, "USGBC Research Program," www.usgbc.org/ DisplayPage.aspx?CMSPageID=1718; Environmental Protection Agency, in "Estimating 2003 Building-Related Construction and Demolition Materials Amounts," 2009 (www.epa.gov/osw/conserve/rrr/imr/cdm/pubs/cd-meas.pdf), calculates that 170 million tons of building-related construction and demolition debris were generated in the United States in 2003, with 61 percent coming from nonresidential and 39 percent from residential sources.

5. Personal communication, David Johnston, president of What's Working, www .whatsworking.com, Hygeine, Colorado, August 29, 2010.

6. Commission for Environmental Cooperation, "Green Building in North America," 2008, www.cec.org/files/PDF//GB_Report_EN.pdf.

7. McGraw-Hill Construction, "Green Building," SmartMarket Report, 2006.

8. Norm Miller, Jay Spivey, and Andy Florance, "Does Green Pay Off?" 2007, www .sandiego.edu/business/documents/USDEconofBeingGreen.pdf.

9. David W. Orr, Design on the Edge: The Making of a High-Performance Building (Cambridge, Mass.: MIT Press, 2006).

10. Ann Underwood, "American Campuses Get Greener Than Ever," Newsweek, August 15, 2007.

11. Environmental Protection Agency, "Why Build Green?" www.epa.gov/green building/pubs/whybuild.htm.

12. Lisa Fay Matthiessen and Peter Morris, "Costing Green: A Comprehensive Database," Davis Langdon Research, July 2004, www.davislangdon.com/USA/Research/ ResearchFinder/2004-Costing-Green-A-Comprehensive-Cost-Database-and -Budgeting-Methodology; Greg Kats, "The Costs and Financial Benefits of Green Buildings: A Report to California's Sustainable Building Task Force," 2003, www .usgbc.org/ShowFile.aspx?DocumentID=1992.

13. L. A. Wallace, "The Total Exposure Assessment Methodology (TEAM) Study: Summary and Analysis," volume 1 (Washington, D.C.: Environmental Protection

Agency, Office of Research and Development, 1987), www.exposurescience.org/Wallace87.

14. Environmental Protection Agency, "An Introduction to Indoor Air Quality," 2008, www.epa.gov/iaq/voc.html.

15. Environmental Protection Agency, "Indoor Air Facts No. 4 (revised) Sick Building Syndrome," April 26, 2010, www.epa.gov/iedweb00/pubs/sbs.html.

16. U.S. Green Building Council, Colorado chapter, "Greening Colorado Schools," 2007, www.usgbccolorado.com/resources/green-schools.html.

17. Heschong Mahone Group, "Daylighting in Schools: An Investigation into the Relationship Between Daylighting and Human Performance," 1999.

18. Joseph J. Romm and William D. Browning, "Greening the Building and the Bottom Line: Increasing Production Through Energy-Efficient Design," Rocky Mountain Institute, Dec. 1994, www.greenbiz.com/sites/default/files/document/O16F8527.pdf.

19. Ibid.

20. William J. Fisk, "How IEQ Affects Health, Productivity," *ASHRAE Journal*, May 2002.

21. William J. Fisk, "Health and Productivity Gains from Better Indoor Environments," in *The Role of Emerging Energy-Efficient Technology in Promoting Workplace Productivity and Health*, edited by Satish Kumar and William J. Fisk (Berkeley, Calif.: Lawrence Berkeley National Laboratory, February 2002).

22. McGraw-Hill Construction, "Greening of Corporate America," SmartMarket Report, 2007, http://construction.ecnext.com/coms2/summary_0249-238822_ITM_analytics.

23. A. Aaras et al., "Musculoskeletal, Visual and Psychosocial Stress in VDU Operators Before and After Multidisciplinary Ergonomic Interventions," *Applied Ergonomics*, 1998: 335–54.

24. "Corporate Citizenship: Profiting from a Sustainable Business," Economist Intelligence Unit, 2008, http://sdmdev.mit.edu/img/murray.jpg.

25. Heschong Mahone Group, "Skylighting and Retail Sales: An Investigation into the Relationship Between Daylighting and Human Performance," report prepared for Pacific Gas and Electric Co. and the California Board for Third Party Efficiency Program, 1999, www.pge.com/includes/docs/pdfs/shared/edusafety/training/pec/daylight/RetailCondensed820.pdf.

26. "Michael's Top 10: Things You Can Do in Your Home to Save Lighting Energy," California Lighting Technology Center, http://cltc.ucdavis.edu/images/images/Downloads/michael_topten.pdf.

27. LED City program, www.ledcity.org/about_led_city.htm.

28. Ibid.

29. LED City program, Anchorage, Alaska, www.ledcity.org/Anchorage.htm.

30. U.S. Department of Energy, reported at www.ledcity.org/about_led_city.htm.

31. Ronald Utt, "The Subprime Mortgage Market Collapse: A Primer on the Causes and Possible Solutions," April 22, 2008, www.heritage.org/Research/Reports/2008/04/The-Subprime-Mortgage-Market-Collapse-A-Primer-on-the-Causes-and-Possible-Solutions.

32. "Housing Starts Mixed in March, Calculated Risk," April 16, 2010, www.calculated riskblog.com/2010/04/housing-starts-mixed-in-march.html.

33. McGraw-Hill Construction, "2009 Green Outlook: Trends Driving Change," report, 2009, see http://construction.ecnext.com/coms2/summary_0249-294642 _ITM_analytics.

34. U.S. Department of Commerce, U.S. Census Bureau News, "September 2010 Construction at $801.7 Billion Annual Rate," press release, November 1, 2010, www .census.gov/const/C30/release.pdf.

35. McGraw-Hill Construction, "2009 Green Outlook: Trends Driving Change."

36. Ibid.

37. U.S. Green Building Council, "Green Jobs Study," prepared by Booz Allen Hamilton, 2009, www.usgbc.org/ShowFile.aspx?DocumentID=6435.

38. Sari Kreiger, "Half of Non-Residential Buildings Will Be Green by 2015—Study," *Wall Street Journal*, January 6, 2010; Jerry Yudelson, *Green Building Revolution* (Washington, D.C.: Island Press, 2007); Luis Perez-Lombard, Jose Ortiz, and Christine Pout, "A Review on Buildings Energy Consumption Information," *Energy and Buildings* 40, no. 3 (2008): 394–98.

39. Doug Cogan et al. (Risk Metrics Group), "Corporate Governance and Climate Change: Consumer and Technologies," a Ceres report, December 2008, www.ceres .org/Document.Doc?id=397.

40. "Tesco Opens U.K.'s Most Energy-Efficient Store," press release, January 12, 2009, www.tescoplc.com/plc/media/pr/pr2009/2009-01-13b.

41. Joyanna Laughlin, "Founding Father," *Natural Home Magazine*, September–October 2003, p. 86.

42. David Johnston, personal communication, May 2010, Boulder, Colorado.

43. U.S. Green Building Council, "Green Jobs Study," www.usgbc.org/ShowFile.aspx? DocumentID=6435, p. 6.

44. To hear Mark Ginsberg describe the early years of USGBC, see "USGBC— 15 Years—Chapter 4 of 8," www.youtube.com/watch?v=2RDah5H0soc&feature =channel; hear S. Richard Fedrizzi speak in "Sustainability Conference 2007, Part 7," 2007,www.youtube.com/watch?v=3iyDxbhOmnY,SustainabilityConference2007— Part 7.

45. See "USGBC Press Kit," "About USGBC" link, at www.usgbc.org/DisplayPage .aspx?CMSPageID=97.

46. U.S. Green Building Council, "Green Jobs Study."

47. "New Studies Confirm Energy Savings in Green Buildings," HGTVPro.com, April 3, 2008, www.hgtvpro.com/hpro/nws_ind_nws_trends/article/0,,HPRO_26519 _5840891,00.html.

48. GSA Public Buildings Service, Office of Applied Science, "Assessing Green Building Performance: A Post Occupancy Evaluation of 12 GSA Buildings," 2008, www.capitalmarketspartnership.com/UserFiles/Admin GSA June 2008 - Assessing Green Building Performance.pdf. These numbers will no doubt be central to helping the USGBC win a malicious lawsuit filed against the organization, alleg-

ing that claims that green buildings saved energy and money were false advertising. See "USGBC Sued over False Advertising, Fraud," Environmental Leader, October 15, 2010, www.environmentalleader.com/2010/10/15/usgbc-sued-over -false-advertising-fraud.

49. Gary Christensen, personal communication, April 30, 2009. See also "2007 Excellence in Design Awards—Excellence in Commercial Design: The Banner Bank Building," *ED+C*, May 1, 2007, www.edcmag.com/Articles/Cover_Story/BNP _GUID_9-5-2006_A_10000000000000094972.

50. U.S. Department of Energy, "Zero Energy Buildings: Science House at the Science Museum of Minnesota," http://zeb.buildinggreen.com/overview.cfm ?projectid=284.

51. Aldo Leopold Foundation, "Aldo Leopold Legacy Center," www.aldoleopold.org/ legacycenter/index.html.

52. "What is the Difference between LEED and ENERGY STAR?" Green-Buildings .com, www.green-buildings.com/content/78308-leed-vs-energy-star.

53. "New Studies Confirm Energy Savings in Green Buildings," HGTVPro.com, April 3, 2008, www.hgtvpro.com/hpro/nws_ind_nws_trends/article/0,,HPRO_26519 _5840891,00.html.

54. "Success Story: Thomas Mott Homestead Bed & Breakfast," www.energystar.gov/ index.cfm?c=sb_success.sb_successstories_thomasmott.

55. U.S. Department of Energy, "Zero Energy Buildings."

56. City of Vancouver, "Passive Design Toolkit: Best Practices," 2008, http://vancouver .ca/sustainability/documents/PassiveDesignToolKit.pdf.

57. See "Interview: Dr. Wolfgang Feist, Passivhaus Institut (PHI) and Innsbruck University," www.lowcarbonproductions.com/2010/11/interview-dr-wolfgang-feist -passivhaus-institut-phi-and-innsbruck-university-2; see also Jarrod Denton, "Passive House," *Green Scene*, August 2009, www.northbaybiz.com/Special _Features/Green_Scene/Passive_House.php.

58. "The Passive House in Darmstadt—Kranichstein during Spring, Summer, Autumn and Winter," www.passivhaustagung.de/Kran/Passive_House_Spring _Winter.htm.

59. See "Energy Efficiency Reduces Energy Losses—the Energy Demand Approaches Zero," Passivhaus Institute, www.passivhaustagung.de/Passive_House_E/ energyefficiency.html.

60. For the proceedings of the 14th Passive House Conference, see link at www .passivhaustagung.de/vierzehnte/englisch/index_eng.html.

61. Numerous how-to books can help you achieve the high quality of life that comes from living in a passive home: Daniel D. Chiras, *The Solar House: Passive Heating and Cooling* (White River Junction, Vt.: Chelsea Green, 2002), is one of the classics; David Johnston and Scott Gibson, *Green from the Ground Up: Sustainable, Healthy, and Energy-Efficient Home Construction* (Newtown, Conn.: Taunton Press, 2008), and *Toward a Zero Energy Home: A Complete Guide to Energy Self-Sufficiency at Home* (Newtown, Conn.: Taunton Press, 2010), are two others.

62. Lester Brown, "Plan B Updates," Earth Policy Institute, 2008, www.earthpolicy.org/index.php?/plan_b_updates/2008/update80.
63. See "Rated Buildings," NABERS, www.nabers.com.au/frame.aspx?show=buildings&code=BUILDINGS&site=2. It was also rated as a five-star Green Star office (the equivalent of LEED Gold) by the Australian Green Building Council, or AGBC.
64. Jorge Chapa, "30 THE BOND: Sydney's Greenest Building," March 19, 2007, www.inhabitat.com/2007/03/19/30-the-bond-sydneys-greenest-building.
65. Jorge Chapa, "CH2: Australia's Greenest Building," March 13, 2007, http://inhabitat.com/CH2-australias-greenest-building/.
66. Diane Pham, "Melbourne Convention Center Achieves 6 Star Green Certification," Inhabitat, July 15, 2009, http://inhabitat.com/2009/07/15/melbourne-convention-centre-achieves-6-star-green-star-certification.
67. Jennie Organ, "Case Study Detail: Beddington Zero Energy Development (BedZED)," Sustainable Development Commission, www.sd-commission.org.uk/communitiessummit/show_case_study.php/00035.html.
68. ZEDfactory, "Practice Profile," www.zedfactory.com/practice%20profile_090514.pdf, p. 36.
69. Ben Edwards, "China Passes U.S., Leads World in Power Sector Carbon Emissions—CGD," Center for Global Development, August 27, 2008, www.cgdev.org/content/article/detail/16578.
70. This case study is part of a series of WBCSD member company and Regional Network partner good practice examples on energy efficiency. See "Hong Kong BEAM—Green Building Label: Business Environment Council," at the World Business Council for Sustainable Development website.
71. Catherine Hart, "Visitors Wowed by Greensburg's Progress," Greensburg GreenTown, May 4, 2010, www.greensburggreentown.org.
72. "Greensburg Wind Farm," NativeEnergy, November 30, 2009, www.nativeenergy.com/pages/greensburg/517.php.
73. Del Sur, "Leading U.S. Green Residential Development Recognized as One of America's 'Greenest,'" press release, May 11, 2008, Reuters.
74. Paul Solman, "Green Industry Hub Rises from Rust Belt Ruins," broadcast on PBS, May 12, 2008, transcript, www.pbs.org/newshour/bb/business/jan june08/greenjobs_05-12.html.
75. "Fill It Up—Braddock Station Promotes Biofueling," May 2, 2007, Pop City, www.popcitymedia.com/innovationnews/5907fossilfuel.aspx.
76. United Nations Department of Economic and Social Affairs, "World Urbanization Prospects: The 2007 Revision Population Database," http://esa.un.org/unup/index.asp?panel=2.
77. World Bank, "More Than Half the World Is Now Urban," press release, July 11, 2007.
78. International Energy Agency, "Cities Can Take the Lead in Renewable Energy and Show National Governments the Way," press release, December 8, 2009, www.ica.org/press/pressdetail.asp?PRESS_REL_ID=295.

79. Edward Mazria and Kristina Kershner, "Nation Under Siege, Sea Level Rise at Our Doorstep," 2030 Research Center, 2007, www.architecture2030.com/pdfs/nation _under_siege_lr.pdf, p. 10.

80. Ron Dembo, "Re-Skinning Competition—Environmentally Smart Buildings and Cities," *Huffington Post*, January 15, 2010, www.huffingtonpost.com/ron-dembo/ reskinning-competition_b_424831.html.

81. Michael Northrop, "Creating the Next American Economy," *Miami Herald*, October 22, 2008.

82. Pike Research, "Energy Efficiency Retrofits for Commercial and Public Buildings," 2009, www.pikeresearch.com/research/energy-efficiency-retrofits-for-commercial -and-public-buildings.

83. Matthew Wald, "Energy Funds Went Unspent, U.S. Auditor Says," *New York Times*, August 13, 2010.

84. U.S. Department of Energy, Office of Inspector General, Office of Audit Services, "Audit Report," www.ig.energy.gov/documents/OAS-RA-10-16.pdf.

85. Tom Plant (director of the Governor's Energy Office), personal communication, October 14, 2010.

86. "Envirolution's Win-Win Campaign," https://sites.google.com/a/envirolution.org/ win-win/Win-Win-Campaign.

87. Greg Davis (founder, kwhours.com), personal communication, May 2010.

88. This program, invented by Natural Capitalism Solutions' Paul Sheldon, is now being operated by Boulder's Climate Smart Program; see "Save Money, Save Energy" ClimateSmart Loan Program website, www.bouldercounty.org/bocc/cslp.

89. "Dynamic City Foundation: Project Summary," www.dynamiccity.org/summary .php.

90. Roger Wood (Arup), "Dongtan Eco-City Shanghai," presentation, May 4, 2007, www .arup.com/_assets/_download/8CFDEE1A-CC3E-EA1A-25FD80B2315B50FD.pdf.

91. Austin Williams, "Dongtan: The Ecocity That Never Was," Spiked, September 1, 2009, www.spiked-online.com/index.php/site/article/7330.

92. Jesse Fox, "China's Zero-Carbon City Dongtan Delayed, but Not Necessarily Dead, Says Planner," Treehugger.com, January 24, 2010, www.treehugger.com/files/2010/ 01/arup-peter-head-dongtan-interview.php.

93. "Welcome to Masdar City," www.masdarcity.ae/en/index.aspx.

94. Kate Calamusa, "Most Influential: Jason McLennan," www.seattlemag.com/ 0p135a1764/power-09-jason-mclennan.

95. For Berkibile's comments see "USGBC—15 Years—Chapter 4," www.youtube.com/ watch?v=2RDah5H0soc&feature=channel.

96. Personal communication, David Johnston to L. Hunter Lovins.

5: Moving On

1. "OAG Reports 29.6 Million Flights Worldwide," *Breaking Travel News*, December 14, 2007, www.breakingtravelnews.com/news/article/btn20071214104331417.

2. Phillip Gott, "Demand for Cars and Trucks to Quadruple at Current Trends by 2035: Is Mobility as We Know It Sustainable?" June 17, 2008, www.globalinsight .com/sustainablemobility.

3. "350.org's Bill McKibben on the Letterman Show: Put Solar on the White House on 10/10/10," www.youtube.com/watch?v=0JcRj-Yokuw&feature=player_embedded.

4. "Charge! Carmakers Are Shifting Towards Electric Vehicles; Policymakers Must Do Their Part, Too," *The Economist*, September 3, 2009.

5. Environmental Protection Agency, "National Emissions Inventory (NEI) Air Pollutants Emissions Trends Data," 2006 figures (see link for "1970–2008 Average annual emissions, all criteria pollutants in MS Excel"), www.epa.gov/ttn/chief/trends.

6. "Global Transport Sector Meets to Discuss Greenhouse Gas," redOrbit, January 15, 2009, www.redorbit.com/news/science/1623956/global_transport_sector_meets_to _discuss_greenhouse_gas.

7. Rupert Taylor, "Highway Death Toll Keeps Rising," Suite101.com, April 24, 2009, www.suite101.com/content/highway-death-toll-keeps-rising-a112150.

8. Luigi Fraschini, "AAA: Despite Recession, Cost of Driving Remains Static," 2009, www.drivingtoday.com/wjz/features/archive/cost_of_driving_sideways/index .htm.

9. "AAA Reports That Cost of Owning & Operating a New Vehicle Is Now 54.1 Cents per Mile," AAA, press release, April 4, 2008, reported by Reuters; "What Is the Average Car Insurance for Males and Females from Ages 18–25 Married and Single?" CarInsurance.com, www.carinsurance.com/kb/content17532.aspx. See also Scott Bernstein and Carrie Makarewicz, "Rethinking Affordability, the Inherent Value of TOD," www.community-wealth.org/_pdfs/articles-publications/tod/ article-bernstein-mak.pdf, p. 1 (Consumer Expenditure Survey figures), citing U.S. Bureau of Labor Statistics' Consumer Expenditure Survey, 1998, also www.reuters .com/article/pressRelease/idUS70206+04-Apr-2008+MW20080404.

10. "Transportation and Economic Prosperity," Surface Transportation Policy Project, www.transact.org/library/factsheets/prosperity.asp.

11. David Dickson, "Oil Woes Mask Improvement in Deficit, Demand for Imported Goods Slows; Exports Have Increased," *Washington Times*, August 17, 2008.

12. Environmental Law Institute, "Estimating U.S. Government Subsidies to Energy Sources: 2002–2008," www.elistore.org/Data/products/d19_07.pdf.

13. Jane Holtz Kay, *Asphalt Nation: How the Automobile Took Over America and How We Can Take It Back* (Berkeley: University of California Press, 1998), p. 129.

14. See www.smartgrowthamerica.org/narsgareport2007.htm.

15. "What Is the Average Car Insurance for Males and Females from Ages 18–25 Married and Single?"

16. "America's Other Auto Industry," *Wall Street Journal*, December 1, 2008.

17. Peter Gorrie, "China's Green Leap Forward," *Toronto Star*, March 25, 2008.

18. Bryan Usre, "Toyoda: Toyota Sacrificed Safety for Growth," *Automotive News Examiner*, February 23, 2010.

19. Dan Shipley, "The Most Fuel-Efficient 2010 Cars and SUVs," *Daily Green*, April 3,

2010, www.thedailygreen.com/environmental-news/latest/fuel-efficient-cars
-47102201.

20. "CSI/40MPG.ORG: 'Fuel-Efficient Car Gap' Growing as U.S. Falls to Two 40mpg+
Vehicles, While Number of Gas-Sipping Cars Unavailable in U.S. Rises to Well over
100" February 14, 2007, www.civilsocietyinstitute.org/media/pdfs/021407_CSI
_40mpg_fuel_efficiency_news_release.pdf.

21. "EPA: Honda Has the Most Fuel-Efficient Lineup," *US News and World Report*,
November 24, 2009.

22. Tim Plouff, "On The Road Review: A Shift in Small Car Thinking," *Fence Viewer*,
March 1, 2010.

23. Chrissie Thompson, "GM's IPO Day Buzzes with Success, Volt Triumph," *Detroit
Free Press*, November 19, 2010, www.toolsofthetrade.net/industry-news.asp?section
ID=1516&articleID=1449882.

24. Clayton Cornell, "The World's Most Fuel Efficient Car: 285 MPG, Not a Hybrid,"
Gas 2.0, March 12, 2008, http://gas2.org/2008/03/12/the-worlds-most-fuel-efficient
-car-285-mpg-not-a-hybrid.

25. VanDyne SuperTurbo Inc., "SuperTurbocharger," VanDyneSuperTurbo.com.

26. Beveridge & Diamond, P.C., "California Approves Low-Carbon Fuel Standard,"
January 15, 2010, www.bdlaw.com/news-773.html.

27. Environmental Protection Agency, "DOT, EPA Set Aggressive National Standards
for Fuel Economy and First Ever Greenhouse Gas Emission Levels for Passenger
Cars and Light Trucks," news release, April 1, 2010.

28. "US: AIAM to Support EPA in California Emissions Lawsuit," February 6, 2008,
www.automotiveworld.com/news/environment/66191-us-aiam-to-support-epa
-in-california-emissions-lawsuit.

29. Wade Watson, "Low Carbon Fuel Standard Lawsuit," Weaver (public accountants)
website, December 20, 2009, www.weaverllp.com/industries/energy-oil/energy
-blog/09-12-29/Low_Carbon_Fuel_Standard_Lawsuit.aspx.

30. See www.ogj.com/index/article-display/8289160832/articles/oil-gas-journal/general
-interest-2/hse/2010/02/npra_-others_sue_over.html.

31. Alex Taylor III, "Toyota: The Birth of the Prius," *Fortune*, February 21, 2006.

32. PRNewswire, "Small and Energy Efficient Cars Are the Buzz at the 2010 Detroit
Auto Show," January 13, 2010, http://nadaguides.mediaroom.com/index.php?s=43
&item=154.

33. Jeff Green and Mike Ramsey, "Ford U.S. January Sales Rise 25% as Toyota Pulls
Back (Update 1)," February 2, 2010, *Bloomberg Businessweek*, www.businessweek
.com/news/2010-02-02/ford-u-s-sales-rise-25-nissan-gains-16-as-toyota-pulls
-back.html.

34. CalCars, the California Cars Initiative, "All About Plug-in Hybrids (PHEVs),"
www.calcars.org/vehicles.html.

35. Brian Thompson, "Electric Cars Charge to the Front at NY Auto Show," NBC New
York, April 1, 2010.

36. "The Citroën Ev'ie by The Electric Car Corporation," May 8, 2009, www.youtube.com/watch?v=OHMMlURBh14.

37. Ben Wojdyla, "2010 Ford Transit Connect Officially First Ford Electric Vehicle," February 9, 2009, http://jalopnik.com/5147717/2010-ford-transit-connect-officially-first-ford-electric-vehicle.

38. Nick Chambers, "Prototype Ford Escape Plug-in Hybrid: 88 MPG on 85% Ethanol," June 13, 2008, http://gas2.org/2008/06/13/prototype-ford-escape-plug-in-hybrid-88-mpg-on-85-ethanol.

39. Justin Hyde, "Ford Intends to Use Microsoft Software to Schedule Charging," *Detroit Free Press*, April 1, 2010.

40. Anthony Mason, "'Karma' for Plug-in Hybrid," November 24, 2008, www.cbsnews.com/video/watch/?id=4631319n?source=mostpop_video.

41. Cliff Kuang, "Object of Desire: Yves Béhar's Mission One Motorcycle," *Fast Company*, April 1, 2010.

42. Jim Motovalli, "California E.V. Corridor Is Open for Business," *New York Times*, September 22, 2009.

43. "UPS Adds 245 CNG Trucks to the Company's Green Fleet," GreenBiz.com, January 19, 2010, www.greenbiz.com/news/2010/01/19/ups-adds-245-cng-trucks-green-fleet.

44. "UPS to Expand U.S. Green Fleet by 30%," Sustainable Life Media, May 14, 2008, www.sustainablelifemedia.com/products/story/ups_to_expand_us_green_fleet_by_30_percent.

45. Leslie Berliant, "FedEx Introduces All-Electric Delivery Trucks in the U.S.," EnergyBoom Transportation (blog), April 1, 2010, www.energyboom.com/transportation/fedex-introduces-all-electric-delivery-trucks-us-1.

46. Grist, "Extra-Special Delivery," May 20, 2003, http://www.grist.org/article/extra.

47. Jeremy Korzenlewski, "FedEx Puts 2 Million Miles on Hybrid Trucks, Adds 75 More," Autobloggreen, April 28, 2008, http://green.autoblog.com/2008/04/28/fedex-puts-2-million-miles-on-hybrid-trucks-adds-75-more.

48. Lee Scott, personal communication to Hunter Lovins, March 15, 2006, Sustainable Business Milestone Meeting, Bentonville, Arkansas.

49. "Wal-Mart Improves Fleet Fuel Efficiency 15%," July 16, 2007, Environmental Leader, www.environmentalleader.com/2007/07/18/wal-mart-improves-fleet-fuel-efficiency-15.

50. "Wal-Mart Tests New Trucks, Surpasses Fuel Efficiency Goals," Environmental Leader, February 3, 2009, www.environmentalleader.com/2009/02/03/wal-mart-tests-new-trucks-surpasses-fuel-efficiency-goals.

51. Jonathan Katz, "Paccar Supplies Hybrid Truck to Honda," *IndustryWeek*, March 4, 2009, www.industryweek.com/articles/paccar_supplies_hybrid_truck_to_honda_18609.aspx?SectionID=2.

52. Based on SAE Type II testing; see ATDynamics information and video on the TrailerTail at their website, www.atdynamics.com/trailertail.htm.

53. Jeff Crissey, "ATDynamics Partners with Navistar for SuperTruck Project," *Commercial Carrier Journal*, February 9, 2010, www.ccjdigital.com/atdynamics -partners-with-navistar-for-supertruck-project.

54. Michael Ehard, "Call of the Truck-Stop: Gentlemen, Stop Your Engines," *New York Times*, March 7, 2007.

55. "Wal-Mart to Save $300 Million with Hybrids," Clean Fleet Report, March 20, 2007, www.cleanfleetreport.com/fleets/wal-mart-to-save-300-million-with-hybrids.

56. "Freight Companies Work to Limit Idling," Environmental Leader, March 9, 2007, www.environmentalleader.com/2007/03/09/freight-companies-work-to-limit -idling.

57. Arlyn Tobias Gajilan, "Smog Killer: A New Green Truck-Stop Service Helps Drivers Rest—and the Rest of Us Breathe," February 1, 2005, http://money.cnn.com/ magazines/fsb/fsb_archive/2005/02/01/8250634/index.htm.

58. Jill Dunn, "IdleAire Shuts Down," January 29, 2008, etrucker.com, www.etrucker .com/apps/news/article.asp?id=84551.

59. Gajilan, "Smog Killer."

60. United Nations Environmental Programme, "Aviation and the Global Atmosphere," report, section 8.3.2., "Ambient Factors," www.grida.no/publications/ other/ipcc%5Fsr/?src=/climate/ipcc/aviation/125.htm.

61. Bryan Walsh, "Does Flying Harm the Planet?" *Time*, August 20, 2007.

62. Juliet Eliperin, "Cutting the Global Carbon Footprint of Planes and Ships," *Washington Post*, January 4, 2010.

63. Boeing, "Boeing 787 Dreamliner Will Provide New Solutions for Airlines, Passengers," www.boeing.com/commercial/787family/background.html.

64. See www.airlines.org/Environment/Pages/Environment.aspx.

65. Federal Aviation Administration, "Fact Sheet—Getting the Green Light for Aviation," press release, "How FAA Initiatives Are Reducing Environmental Impacts," December 6, 2007, www.faa.gov/news/fact_sheets/news_story.cfm?newsId= 9433.

66. Carbon Trust, "Carbon Trust Reveals Uncertain Impact of EU Emissions Trading Scheme on Airline Industry," December 8, 2009, www.carbontrust.co.uk/news/ news/press-centre/2009/Pages/carbon-trust-reveals-uncertain-impact.aspx.

67. David Suzuki, "Air Travel and Climate Change," www.davidsuzuki.org/search/ index.php?q=Air+Travel&x=12&y=10.

68. Stanley Hart and Alvin Spivak, *The Elephant in the Bedroom: Automobile Dependence and Denial* (Pasadena: Hope Publishing, 1993), p. 111.

69. "Shinjuku Station," www.japaneselifestyle.com.au/tokyo/shinjuku_station.htm.

70. Oliver Keating, "The Shinkansen (Bullet Train)," www.o-keating.com/hsr/bullet .htm.

71. Oliver Keating, "Countries Operating Trains @ 300 km/h or 186 mph," www .o-keating.com/hsr/hstlist.htm.

72. TriMet (Portland, Oregon), "Dirty Words," http://trimet.org/sustainable/dirty -words.htm#greenhousegas.

73. Chris Cooper, "World's High Speed Train Makers Set Sights on U.S.," *New York Times*, March 19, 2010.

74. Keith Bradsher, "China Is Eager to Bring High-Speed Rail Expertise to the U.S.," *New York Times*, April 7, 2010.

75. Eliperin, "Cutting the Global Carbon Footprint of Planes and Ships."

76. JCNewswire, "NYK and MHI Begin Experiments on Air-Lubrication System; 10% CO_2 Reduction Expected by Lowering Seawater Resistance," Japan Corporate News Network, February 24, 2010, www.japancorp.net/Article.Asp?Art_ID=22544.

77. See www.reuters.com/article/idUS70206+04-Apr-2008+MW20080404; www.carinsurance.com/kb/content17532.aspx.

78. Nancy Trejos, "Recession Lesson: Share and Swap Replaces Grab and Buy," *Washington Post*, July 17, 2009.

79. I-GO Car Sharing, "Save Money," at www.igocars.org/member-benefits/save-money/.

80. Jim Morris and Ted Selker, San Francisco Bay Area ride-share advocates, in "Fighting the Single-Occupancy Vehicle" (www.stanford.edu/group/peec/cgi-bin/docs/events/2008/becc/presentations/19-6E-03 Fighting the Single-Occupancy Vehicle .pdf), list eight programs from around the world that have failed and a dozen that are still operating, along with advice on how to manage such programs.

81. Jim Morris, "SafeRide: Reducing Single Occupancy Vehicles," www.cs.cmu.edu/~jhm/SafeRide.pdf.

82. Morris and Selker, "Fighting the Single-Occupancy Vehicle."

83. City of Seattle, "Way to Go, Seattle!" at www.cityofseattle.net/waytogo.

84. Surface Transportation Policy Project, "Transportation and Economic Prosperity," www.transact.org/library/factsheets/prosperity.asp.

6: World Without Oil

1. "World Economy Runs—and Stalls—on Oil," Energy Policy Information Center, November 5, 2009, http://energypolicyinfo.com/2009/11/world-economy-runs-and-stalls-on-oil.

2. Henry A. Kissinger and Martin Feldstein, "The Rising Danger of High Oil Prices," *New York Times*, September 15, 2008.

3. Mark Smith, "Crude Oil Price Hits Two-Year High amid Concerns over Demand," *The Herald* (Scotland), December 28, 2010.

4. "World Economy Runs—and Stalls—on Oil."

5. Michael Rothman, "Prosperity of the World Hinges on Oil," *Financial Times*, November 4, 2009.

6. Tim Plouff, "On the Road Review: A Shift in Small Car Thinking," *Fenceviewer*, March 1, 2010.

7. Ibid.

8. Paul A. Eisenstein, "Ford, Rivals Betting Small is Beautiful," MSNBC.com, January 22, 2010.

9. Amory Lovins and Hunter Lovins, *Brittle Power* (St. Charles, Mo.: Brickhouse, 1981), downloadable from www.natcapsolutions.org.

10. Frank Sesno and CNN Special Investigations Unit, "We Were Warned: Out of Gas," CNN, May 18, 2007 (available on YouTube; part 1: www.youtube.com/watch?v=1vPi7SEzzWg; links to other parts listed at right of screen).

11. "Location Efficiency and Mortgage Default," Natural Resources Defense Council, January 27, 2010, www.nrdc.org/media/2010/100127.asp.

12. Sam Hopkins, "In the Thick of China's Energy Crisis," www.energyandcapital.com/articles/china-fuel-riots/545.

13. K. S. Deffeyes, *Hubbert's Peak: The Impending World Oil Shortage* (Princeton, N.J.: Princeton University Press, 2003); K. S. Deffeyes, *When Oil Peaked* (New York: Hill and Wang, 2010).

14. Carola Hoyos, "Mexico's Pemex Wrestles with Oil Decline," *Financial Times*, March 29, 2010.

15. James Cordahi and Andy Critchlow, "Kuwait Oil Field, World's Second-Largest, 'Exhausted,'" *Bloomberg News*, November 9, 2005, www.energybulletin.net/node/10878.

16. Merlin Flower, "International Energy Agency: Capitulation to Peak Oil?" OilPrice.net, November 28, 2009, www.oil-price.net/en/articles/international-energy-agency.php.

17. James Moore, "Energy Watchdog Warns of Supply Crunch Within Five Years," *Independent*, July 10, 2007, http://news.independent.co.uk/business/news/article2750517.ece.

18. Terry Macalister, "Key Oil Figures Were Distorted by US Pressure, Says Whistleblower; Exclusive: Watchdog's Estimates of Reserves Inflated Says Top Official," *Guardian*, November 9, 2009, www.guardian.co.uk/environment/2009/nov/09/peak-oil-international-energy-agency.

19. George Monbiot, "When Will the Oil Run Out?" *Guardian*, December 15, 2008.

20. "The Peak-Oil Debate 2020 Vision: The IEA Puts a Date on Peak Oil Production," *Economist*, December 10, 2009.

21. Ibid.

22. "Energy Minister Will Hold Summit to Calm Rising Fears over Peak Oil," *Guardian*, March 21, 2010.

23. "The Oil Crunch: Securing the UK's Energy Future," http://peakoiltaskforce.net/wp-content/uploads/2008/10/oil-report-final.pdf, p. 4.

24. Ibid., p. 6.

25. Ibid. See also IEA World Energy Outlook 2010, www.worldenergyoutlook.org.

26. Stefan Schultz, "Military Study Warns of a Potentially Drastic Oil Crisis," September 1, 2010, www.spiegel.de/international/germany/0,1518,715138,00.html.

27. Joseph Romm, "German Military Study Warns of Peak Oil Crisis," September 8, 2010, http://climateprogress.org/2010/09/08/peak-oil-german-military-study.

28. Monbiot, "When Will the Oil Run Out?"

29. http://transitionus.org/sites/default/files/TransitionUS_2009-AYearInReview
    _web.pdf.

30. See www.postcarboncities.net/guidebook; http://transitionculture.org/shop/the
    -transition-handbook; www.natcapsolutions.org/index.php?option=com_content
    &view=article&id=287&Itemid=72; www.natcapsolutions.org/ClimateProtection
    Manual.htm.

31. Sesno, "We Were Warned."

32. Lester Brown, "Wartime Mobilization to Save the Environment and Civilization,"
    April 8, 2006, www.earthpolicy.org/index.php?/book_bytes/2006/pb2ch13_ss3.

33. "Ford Predicts Fuel from Vegetation," *New York Times*, September 20, 1925, p. 24;
    see also "Timeline of Alcohol Fuel," http://en.wikipedia.org/wiki/Timeline_of
    _alcohol_fuel.

34. "Global Biofuels Production Reduces GHGs Dramatically," *Bulk Transporter*,
    December 11, 2009, http://bulktransporter.com/2010-emissions/global-biofuel
    -production-1211.

35. "Global Biofuels Outlook: 2010–2020," Global Biofuels Center, www.globalbio
    fuelscenter.com/Spotlight.aspx?Id=32.

36. Candace Lombard, "World Biofuel Use Expected to Double by 2015," September 30,
    2009, http://news.cnet.com/8301-11128_3-10364139-54.html.

37. Don Hofstrand, "Brazil's Ethanol Industry," *Ag Decision Maker*, January 2009,
    www.extension.iastate.edu/agdm/articles/hof/HofJan09.html.

38. Ibid.

39. Sesno, "We Were Warned."

40. Peter Taylor, "Reducing The Negative Ecological Impacts from Biofuel Produc-
    tion," March 16, 2010, www.conservationmaven.com/frontpage/reducing-the
    -negative-ecological-impacts-from-biofuel-produc.html.

41. Max Ajl, "Sugarcane: the Miracle Biofuel?" Solve Climate, June 8, 2009, http://
    solveclimate.com/blog/20090608/sugarcane-miracle-biofuel.

42. Larry West, "Brazil Pledges to Cut Amazon Deforestation by 70 Percent," About
    .com, http://environment.about.com/od/biodiversityconservation/a/deforestation
    .htm.

43. Lester Brown, "Ethanol Could Leave the World Hungry," *Fortune*, August 21, 2006.

44. Ibid.

45. Stephen Polasky, quoted in "Cellulosic Ethanol Healthier, Better for the Environ-
    ment, than Corn Ethanol," mongabay.com, February 3, 2009, http://news
    .mongabay.com/2009/0202-ethanol.html.

46. Chris Rogers, "Future Fuel: Iogen's Cellulose Ethanol Helps More than Just the
    Environment," *Entrepreneur*, October 2008.

47. Louisa Taylor, "Straw from Area Farmers Helps Fuel Ferrari's F1 Dream Ma-
    chines," *Ottawa Citizen*, March 14, 2010.

48. "Eight Alternative Fuels That Could Replace Oil," www.thedailygreen.com/
    environmental-news/latest/alternative-fuel-cars-460509.

49. Rebecca Kessler, "Talking Turkey About Biofuels," *E-Magazine*, November 2005.

50. Michael Kanellos, "Fast-Food Fat: Future Fuel for Cars," February 8, 2007, CNET News, http://news.cnet.com/Fast-food-fat-future-fuel-for-cars/2100-1008_3 -6157412.html.

51. "Eight Alternative Fuels That Could Replace Oil," *Daily Green*, www.thedailygreen .com/environmental-news/latest/alternative-fuel-cars-460509.

52. Emily Sohn, "Coffee Could Fuel You, and Your Car," Discovery Channel, January 20, 2008, http://dsc.discovery.com/news/2009/01/20/coffee-biofuel.html.

53. Peter Stiff, "It's All Going to Seed for D1 Oil," *The Times* (London), June 5, 2009.

54. Dave Harcourt, "Jatropha's Failure as a Biodiesel Feedstock Opens Opportunities in Rural Electrification," *Ecoworldly*, May 4, 2009.

55. Amy Westervelt, "Algae Emerge as DOE Feedstock of Choice for Biofuel 2.0—Chu Pledges $80 Million for Algae R&D," January 15, 2010, http://solveclimate.com/ blog/20100115/algae-emerges-doe-feedstock-choice-biofuel-2-0.

56. Keith Johnson, "Biofuels Bonanza: Exxon, Venter to Team Up on Algae," *Wall Street Journal*, July 14, 2009.

57. Kanellos, "Fast-Food Fat."

58. Clean Power Development, LLC, project descriptions, www.cleanpowerdevelopment .us/projects.php.

59. Sir Richard Branson, personal communication to Hunter Lovins, Clinton Global Initiative, New York, September 18, 2008.

60. Sesno, "We Were Warned," parts 1 and 3.

61. Virgin Atlantic, "To Sustainability," www.virgin-atlantic.com/en/us/allaboutus/ environment/manifesto1to15.jsp.

62. Greenpeace UK, "Virgin Guilty of 'High Altitude Greenwash,'" February 24, 2008, www.greenpeace.org.uk/media/press-releases/virgin-guilty-of-high-altitude -greenwash-20080224.

63. Virgin Atlantic, "To Sustainability."

64. See www.solixbiofuels.com/content/company.

65. "CSU Study: Turning Algae into Fuel Is Ecofriendly," CBS News Denver, September 27, 2010.

66. David Blume, *Alcohol Can Be a Gas: Fueling an Ethanol Revolution for the 21st Century* (International Institute for Ecological Agriculture, 2007); see also www.permaculture .com/node/277; Portland Peak Oil, "David Blume: Alcohol Can Be a Gas," video, http://video.google.com/videoplay?docid=5182282754145092406#; Viking Services, "Making Biodiesel at Home," June 29, 2009, http://linkbee.com/F2PWW.

67. See www.betterplace.com/solution.

68. "Better Place Secures $350 Million Series B Round Led by HSBC Group," press release, January 25, 2010.

69. "Better Place to Bring Electric Taxi Program to the San Francisco Bay Area," press release, October 27, 2010, www.betterplace.com/the-company-pressroom -pressreleases-detail/index/id/better-place-to-bring-electric-taxi-program-to-the -san-francisco-bay-area.

70. Matthew Shaer, "Skype Traffic Soars, Leaving Old-School Phone Companies in the Dust," *Christian Science Monitor*, January 19, 2010; see also http://about.skype.com.

71. "HP Customer Case Study: Telepresence," http://h20338.www2.hp.com/enterprise/downloads/Enviro_CsStdyUS_5_16_LR.pdf.

72. Ibid.

73. Climate Cooler, "Lightening the Load: The Global Warming Impact of eBay Infrastructure and Transactions," www.ebaygreenteam.com/assets/documents/study/cooler-research.pdf.

74. Ibid.

75. Andres Duany, Elizabeth Plater-Zyberk, and Jeff Speck, *Suburban Nation: The Rise of Sprawl and the Decline of the American Dream* (New York: Farrar, Straus and Giroux, 2000).

76. Ibid., p. 1; "The Automobile Subsidy," available online at www.assmotax.org/Releases/AMCT%20release:%20The%20Automobile%20Subsidy.php.

77. Curitiba is profiled in Paul Hawken, Amory Lovins, and Hunter Lovins, *Natural Capitalism* (New York: Little Brown, 1999), chapter 14; also in Walter Hook, "Bus Rapid Transit: A Cost-Effective Mass Transit Technology," Institute for Transportation and Development Policy, June 2009; Emily Pilloton, "Transportation Tuesday: Curitiba Public Transit," www.inhabitat.com/2007/12/11/transporation-tuesday-curitiba.

78. Lloyd Wright, "The Limits of Technology: Achieving Transport Efficiency in Developing Nations," University College, London, May 2004, http://eprints.ucl.ac.uk/108/1/Lloyd_Wright,_Bonn,_Germany,_Transport_and_climate_change.pdf.

79. Ibid.

80. "America's Ten Most Walkable Cities," *Daily Green*, www.thedailygreen.com/environmental-news/latest/most-walkable-cities-460708.

81. Elisabeth Rosenthal, "In German Suburb, Life Goes On Without Cars," *New York Times*, May 11, 2009.

82. "Nearly Car-Free," www.nytimes.com/slideshow/2009/05/12/science/20090512-SUBURB_9.html.

83. Rosenthal, "In German Suburb, Life Goes On Without Cars."

84. See www.quarryvillage.org.

85. Smart Growth America, "Survey Shows Americans Prefer to Spend More on Mass Transit and Highway Maintenance, Less on New Roads," press release, October 25, 2007, www.smartgrowthamerica.org/narsgareport2007.html.

86. Scott Bernstein, "Using Linked Housing, Banking and Transportation Policy to Bring Home the Benefits of Livable Communities," Statement Before the Senate Committee on Banking, Housing and Urban Affairs, March 26, 2009, www.cnt.org/repository/BernsteinSenBankingSympMar262009.pdf, p. 3.

87. Ibid.

88. Scott Bernstein, "Why Transit Options Help," *Milwaukee Journal-Sentinel*, February 19, 2009.

89. Jonathan Hiskes, "How to Make Smart Growth Affordable," Grist, August 4, 2010,

www.grist.org/article/2010-08-04-location-efficient-mortgages-smart-growth -housing-affordability.

90. Natural Resources Defense Council,"Location, Location, Location Efficiency: Can Smart Growth Help Beat the Mortgage Crisis?" press release, January 27, 2010, www.nrdc.org/media/2010/100127.asp.

91. Hank Dittmar and Gloria Ohland, *The New Transit Town: Best Practices in Transit-Oriented Development* (Washington, D.C.: Island Press, 2004).

92. Leora Broydo Vestel, "Transportation Department Embraces Bikes, and Business Groups Cry Foul," *New York Times*, March 26, 2010.

93. Texas Transportation Institute, "Traffic Congestion and Urban Mobility," http://tti .tamu.edu/infofor/media/topics/congestion_mobility.htm.

94. Albert Koehl, "Shoppers on Bikes Good for Business," *Toronto Star*, May 21, 2009.

95. "Luyuan and the Electric Bicycle Industry in China," http://en.luyuan.cn/about/ history.asp.

96. Kaitlyn Dreyling, "16 Electric Bikes That Help with the Pedaling," *Daily Green*, April 3, 2010, www.thedailygreen.com/green-homes/latest/electric-bikes-460209.

97. Douglas Adams, *The Restaurant at the End of the Universe* (London: Pan Books Ltd., 1980), p. 128.

7: Growing a Better World

1. "Thomas Jefferson on Politics and Government," "Virtues of Agriculture," http:// etext.virginia.edu/jefferson/quotations/jeff1320.htm.

2. "Boulder Valley School District: Ten Reasons to Fix School Lunch and Save Our Children's Future," www.chefann.com/html/tools-links/Boulder.html.

3. Union of Concerned Scientists, "Hidden Costs of Industrial Agriculture," August 24, 2008, www.ucsusa.org/food_and_agriculture/science_and_impacts/impacts _industrial_agriculture/costs-and-benefits-of.html.

4. Peter Ford, "Why Do Lakes in China Turn Green? Report Finds Surprising New Culprit," *Christian Science Monitor*, February 9, 2010.

5. Sara J. Scherr and Sajal Sthapit, "Farming and Land Use to Cool the Planet," in *State of the World 2009: Into a Warming Planet* (New York: Norton, 2009).

6. "Drivers of Deforestation," June 10, 2010, http://rainforests.mongabay.com/ deforestation_drivers.html.

7. Michael Pollan, "Farmer in Chief," *New York Times*, October 9, 2008.

8. Pacific Northwest Direct Seed Association, "Sustainable Farm Systems: Improving the Quality of Life in the Pacific Northwest," www.directseed.org/sustainablefarming .html.

9. Lester Brown, *Plan B 4.0: Mobilizing to Save Civilization* (New York: Norton, 2009), e-book at www.earth-policy.org/images/uploads/book_files/pb4book.pdf.

10. Lester Brown, "Rising Temperatures Raise Food Prices: Heat, Drought and a Failed Harvest in Russia," Earth Policy Institute, www.earthpolicy.org/index.php?/plan _b_updates/2010/update89.

11. "Climate Change Casts Shadow over World Agriculture," Reuters, May 11, 2007.
12. Gordon Conway, "The Science of Climate Change in Africa," Discussion Paper No. 1, Grantham Institute for Climate Change, Imperial College, London, October 2009, http://workspace.imperial.ac.uk/climatechange/public/pdfs/discussion_papers/Grantham_Institute_-_The_science_of_climate_change_in_Africa.pdf.
13. U.S. Department of Agriculture, "Agriculture Secretary Vilsack Departs for G8 Agricultural Ministerial; Plans to Meet with Counterparts from Key Trade Partners," news release, April 16, 2009, www.usda.gov/wps/portal/!ut/p/_s.7_0_A/7_0_1OB?contentidonly=true&contentid=2009/04/0112.xml.
14. Pollan, "Farmer in Chief."
15. U.S. Department of Agriculture, *U.S. Agriculture and Forestry Greenhouse Gas Inventory, 1990–2005*, "Chapter 5: Energy Use in Agriculture" (www.usda.gov/oce/climate_change/AFGG_Inventory/5_AgriculturalEnergyUse.pdf, p. 1) states that "almost one quadrillion btu of direct energy was used for agriculture in 2005, resulting in about 69 Tg of CO_2 emissions. The same year, total energy consumption for all sectors in the U.S., including agriculture, was approximately 96 quadrillion btu, resulting in 5943 Tg of CO_2 emissions (EPA 2007). Production agriculture's contribution to this total was very small at a little more than 1%. Within agriculture, diesel fuel accounted for about 43% and electricity for about 33% of CO_2 emissions from energy use. Gasoline consumption accounted for about 13% of CO_2 emissions, while LP gas and natural gas accounted for about 7% and 4%, respectively."
16. Danielle Murray, "Oil and Food: A Rising Security Challenge," Earth Policy Institute, May 9, 2005, www.earth-policy.org/Updates/2005/Update48.htm.
17. Ibid.
18. Andrew Martin, "How Green Is My Orange," *New York Times*, January 21, 2009.
19. John Laumer, "Organic Agriculture Could Significantly Reduce the Carbon Footprint of Orange Juice," Treehugger.com, January 22, 2009, www.treehugger.com/files/2009/01/organic-agriculture-could-significantly-reduce-carbon-footprint-orange-juice.php.
20. Murray, "Oil and Food."
21. Jessica Bellarby et al., "Cool Farming: Climate Impacts of Agriculture and Mitigation Potential," report prepared for Greenpeace (Amsterdam: Greenpeace International, 2008), www.greenpeace.org/international/Global/international/planet-2/report/2008/1/cool-farming-full-report.pdf.
22. Christopher L. Weber and H. Scott Matthews, "Food-Miles and the Relative Climate Impacts of Food Choices in the United States," *Environmental Science and Technology* 42 (2008): 3508–13; Food and Agriculture Organization of the United Nations, "Livestock a Major Threat to Environment," November 29, 2006, www.fao.org/newsroom/en/news/2006/1000448; Cool Foods Campaign, "Global Warming & Your Food," http://coolfoodscampaign.org/uploads/MeatandDairyFactSheet.pdf.
23. Food and Agriculture Organization of the United Nations, "Livestock a Major Threat to Environment."

24. Richard Black, "UN Body to Look at Meat and Climate Link," BBC News, March 24, 2010, http://news.bbc.co.uk/2/hi/science/nature/8583308.stm.

25. Bellarby et al., "Cool Farming."

26. Suzanne Nelson, "Beef and Dairy Can Be Good for the Planet: Making a Case for Cows," March 5, 2008, www.indyweek.com/gyrobase/Content?oid=oid%3A194735.

27. Jonathan White (CowsOutside.com), personal communication, December 16, 2008.

28. U.S. Department of Agriculture, Economic Research Service, Data Sets, "Feed Grains Database: Yearbook Tables," www.ers.usda.gov/Data/FeedGrains/FeedYear book.aspx.

29. Will Allen, "Agriculture Is One of the Most Polluting and Dangerous Industries," May 11, 2009, www.alternet.org/water/139962/agriculture_is_one_of_the_most _polluting_and_dangerous_industries/?page=entire.

30. Pollan, "Farmer in Chief."

31. Eatwild ("The #1 Site for Grass-Fed Food and Facts"), "Health Benefits of Grass-Fed Products," www.eatwild.com/healthbenefits.htm.

32. "Health Attribute Literature," All Things Grass-Fed, www.csuchico.edu/agr/ grassfedbeef/research/health-lit.shtml.

33. S. L. Baggott et al., "Greenhouse Gas Inventories for England, Scotland, Wales and Northern Ireland: 1990–2004," report for the Division Research Programme of the Department for Environment, Food and Rural Affairs, November 2006, www .airquality.co.uk/reports/cat07/0611081428-419_Reghg_report_2004_Main_Text _Issue_2.pdf.

34. "The Nitrogen Cycle," http://users.rcn.com/jkimball.ma.ultranet/BiologyPages/N/ NitrogenCycle.html.

35. John A. Harrison, "The Nitrogen Cycle: Of Microbes and Men," Vision Learning, www.visionlearning.com/library/module_viewer.php?mid=98.

36. J. T. Houghton et al., eds., Climate Change 1995: The Science of Climate Change (New York: Cambridge University Press and Intergovernmental Panel on Climate Change, 1996).

37. A. R. Ravishankara et al., "Nitrous Oxide (N_2O): The Dominant Ozone-Depleting Substance Emitted in the 21st Century," Science, August 28, 2009.

38. U.S. Environmental Protection Agency, Agriculture and Food Supply, www.epa .gov/climatechange/effects/agriculture.html.

39. M. L. Parry et al., Contribution of Working Group II to the Fourth Assessment Report of the Intergovernmental Panel on Climate Change, 2007 (New York: Cambridge University Press, 2007), chapter 3, 3.4.1: Surface Waters, www.ipcc.ch/publications_ and_data/ar4/wg2/en/ch3s3-4.html.

40. Jim Tankersley, "California Farms, Vineyards in Peril from Warming, U.S. Energy Secretary Warns," Los Angeles Times, February 4, 2009.

41. Melissa Lamberton, "Southwest Faces Diminished Stream Flows, New Water Poli-cies," University of Arizona, CLIMAS (Climate Assessment for the Southwest), June 23, 2009, www.climas.arizona.edu/feature-articles/june-2009.

42. Henry Fountain, "West Is Told to Expect Water Shortfalls," *New York Times*, April 20, 2010.

43. Arnold J. Bloom, "As Carbon Dioxide Rises, Food Quality Will Decline Without Careful Nitrogen Management," *California Agriculture* 63, no. 2 (2009).

44. R. K. Heitschmidt, L. T. Vermeire, and E. E. Grings, "Is Rangeland Agriculture Sustainable?" *American Society of Animal Science* 82 (E.Suppl; 2004): E138–E146.

45. Hugh Warwick, "Cuba's Organic Revolution," Forum for Applied Research and Public Policy, Summer 2001, www.twnside.org.sg/title/twr118h.htm.

46. Peter Rosset, "Organic Farming in Cuba," WowCuba website, 1994, www.wowcuba .com/discovery/ag-rosset.html.

47. Ibid.

48. Paul Mader et al., "Soil Fertility and Biodiversity in Organic Farming," *Science*, May 31, 2002.

49. Flex Your Power, Agriculture Section, www.fypower.org/agri/.

50. Mark Shepard et al., "An Assessment of the Environmental Impacts of Organic Farming," www.defra.gov.uk/foodfarm/growing/organic/policy/research/pdf/env -impacts2.pdf.

51. Brian Halweil, "Can Organic Farming Feed Us All?" World Watch Institute, April 15, 2006, www.worldwatch.org/node/4060.

52. D. W. Lotter, R. Seidel, and W. Liebhardt, "The Performance of Organic and Conventional Cropping Systems in an Extreme Climate Year," *American Journal of Alternative Agriculture* 18, no. 3 (2003).

53. Catherine Brahic, "Organic Farming Could Feed the World," *New Scientist*, July 2007, www.newscientist.com/article/dn12245-organic-farming-could-feed-the-world .html (quoting Ivette Perfecto of the University of Michigan).

54. Nadia El-Hage Scialabba, "Organic Agriculture and Food Security," conference report, International Conference on Organic Agriculture, Food and Agriculture Organization of the United Nations, May 3–5, 2007, Italy, www.chs.ubc.ca/archives/ files/International Conference on Organic Agriculture and Food Security.pdf.

55. Charles Francis et al., "Science-Based Organic Farming 2008: Toward Local and Secure Food Systems," University of Nebraska–Lincoln, Extension Division, Center for Applied Rural Innovation, http://cropwatch.unl.edu/c/document_library/ get_file?folderId=716529&name=DLFE-11938.pdf.

56. J. Hanson, E. Lichtenberg, and S. Peters, "Organic Versus Conventional Grain Production in the Mid-Atlantic: An Economic Overview and Farming System Overview," *American Journal of Alternative Agriculture* 12, no. 1 (1997): 2–9; J. Hanson et al., "The Profitability of Sustainable Agriculture on a Representative Grain Farm in the Mid-Atlantic Region, 1981–89," *Northeastern Journal of Agricultural and Resource Economics* 19, no. 2 (1990): 90–98; J. C. Hansen and W. N. Musser, "An Economic Evaluation of an Organic Grain Rotation with Regards to Profit and Risk," Working Paper 03-10, University of Maryland, Department of Agricultural and Resource Economics, September 2003.

57. "The Polyface Story," www.polyfacefarms.com/story.aspx.

58. Wendy Dudley, "Holistic Cow: Why Ranchers Are Going Green," *Alberta Views*, July–August 2003, p. 30.

59. Allan Savory, "A Global Strategy for Addressing Global Climate Change," www .savoryinstitute.com/ending-global-climate-change.

60. Ibid.

61. Nora Goldstein, "Historical Perspective: Farm Digesters," *BioCycle* 50, no. 2 (February 2009): 30, www.jgpress.com/archives/_free/001820.html.

62. Climate Trust, "Farm Power," www.climatetrust.org/farm_power.html.

63. Richard Waybright, "Farmer Spotlight: From Robotic Milkers to Hybrids, Technology Is Key for Pennsylvania Farmer," www.dairyfarmingtoday.org/Life-On -The-Farm/Farmer-Spotlight/Pages/RichardWaybright.aspx.

64. Jim Motavalli, "Cow Power," *E-Magazine*, January–February 2007, www.emagazine .com/view/?3510&src=.

65. L. Drinkwater et al., "Legume-Based Cropping Systems Have Reduced Carbon and Nitrogen Losses," *Nature* 396 (1998): 262–65; D. Pimentel, "Environmental, Energetic and Economic Comparisons of Organic and Conventional Farming Systems," *BioScience* 55 (2005): 573–82, 2005; E. E. Marriott and M. M. Wander, "Total and Labile Soil Organic Matter in Organic and Conventional Farming Systems," *Soil Society of America Journal* 70 (2006): 950–59.

66. Doreen Gabriel et al., "Beta Diversity at Different Special Scales: Plant Communities in Organic and Conventional Agriculture," *Ecological Applications* 16 (2006): 2011–21, 2006.

67. Union of Concerned Scientists, "Agricultural Practices and Carbon Sequestration," fact sheet, October 1, 2009, www.ucsusa.org/assets/documents/food_and _agriculture/ag-carbon-sequest-fact-sheet.pdf.

68. Paul R. Hepperly, "The Impact of Agriculture and Food Systems on Greenhouse Gas, Energy Use, Economics and the Environment," Rodale Institute, 2007, download file at http://agwaterstewards.org/txp/file_download/23/Rodale_No-Till.pdf.

69. David Pimentel, "Impacts of Organic Farming on the Efficiency of Energy Use in Agriculture: An Organic Center State of Science Review" (Boulder: The Organic Center, August 2006), www.organic-center.org/reportfiles//ENERGY_SSR.pdf, p. 40; David Pimentel et al., "Environmental, Energetic, and Economic Comparisons of Organic and Conventional Farming Systems," *Bioscience* 55, no. 7 (2005): 573–82.

70. Hepperly, "Impact of Agriculture and Food Systems."

71. D. Lotter, R. Seidel, and W. Liebhardt, "The Performance of Organic and Conventional Cropping Systems in an Extreme Climate Year," *American Journal of Alternative Agriculture* 18, no. 2 (2003): 1–9.

72. T. Huntington, "Available Water Capacity and Soil Organic Matter," in *Encyclopedia of Soil Science*, 2nd ed. (Boca Raton, Fla.: Taylor and Francis, 2006).

73. P. Hepperly et al., "Organic Farming Enhances Soil Carbon and Its Benefits," in *Soil Carbon Management Economic, Environmental, and Societal Benefits*, edited by John Kimble et al. (Boca Raton, Fla.: CRC Press, 2007), p. 268; Rattan Lal, "Global

Potential of Soil Carbon Sequestration to Mitigate the Greenhouse Effect," *Critical Reviews in Plant Sciences* 22, no. 2 (2003): 151–84.

74. This calculation assumes 2006 U.S. carbon dioxide emissions from burning fossil fuels of 6.5 billion tons, and U.S. EPA standards for vehicle mileage. See Timothy LaSalle, "Greenhouse Gases Could Be Used to Grow Organic Food," July 1, 2008, www.treehugger.com/files/2008/07/stop-global-warming-organic.php.

75. Enzo Faviono and Dominic Hogg, "The Potential Role of Compost in Reducing Greenhouse Gases," abstract, February 28, 2008, http://wmr.sagepub.com/content/26/1/61.abstract.

76. Organic Trade Association, "U.S. Organic Sales Grow by a Whopping 17.1 Percent in 2008," press release, May 4, 2009, www.organicnewsroom.com/2009/05/us_organic_sales_grow_by_a_who.html.

77. "2009: A Tough Year for Organic," *Nutrition Business Journal*, March 1, 2010.

78. "Market Report, 'Organic Food: Global Industry Guide,' Published," PRLog, press release, May 1, 2010, www.prlog.org/10652447-market-report-organic-food-global-industry-guide-published.html.

79. International Federation of Organic Agriculture Movements, and Research Institute of Organic Agriculture, *The World of Organic Agriculture: Statistics and Emerging Trends, 2006* (Bonn, Germany, and Frick, Switzerland: 2009), www.soel.de/fachthemen/downloads/s_74_08.pdf.

80. Helga Willer and Lucas Kilcher, eds., *The World of Organic Agriculture 2010* (Bonn, Germany, and Frick, Switzerland: International Federation of Organic Agriculture Movements and Research Institute of Organic Agriculture, Switzerland, 2009), Organic-world.net, "Key Facts," www.organic-world.net/470.html.

81. Pacific Northwest Direct Seed Association, "Sustainable Farm Systems: Improving the Quality of Life in the Pacific Northwest."

82. Chicago Climate Exchange, "CCX Offsets Program," www.chicagoclimatex.com/content.jsf?id=23.

83. For more background on biochar, see James Bruges, *The Biochar Debate* (White River Junction, Vt.: Chelsea Green, 2009).

84. Berkeley Institute of the Environment, "BIE Faculty Roundtable: Improved Cookstoves in Developing Countries—Mission Statement," http://bie.berkeley.edu/cookstoves.

85. International Biochar Initiative, "What Is Biochar? Biochar Is a Valuable Soil Amendment," www.biochar-international.org/biochar.

86. "Biochar Provides Another Market for Rural Landowners in New Energy Future," 25x'25 REsource, August 14, 2009.

87. International Biochar Initiative, "What Is Biochar?"

88. International Biochar Initiative, "Tim Flannery: An Open Letter on Biochar," www.biochar-international.org/timflannery.

89. Scott Bilby, "Flannery Talks Biochar and Why We Need to Move into the Renewable Age," Beyond Zero Emissions blog, January 11, 2008, transcript, http://beyondzero

emissions.org/media/radio/tim-flannery-talks-bio-char-and-why-we-need-move
-renewable-age-080111.

90. George Monbiot, "Woodchips with Everything: It's the Atkins Plan of the Low-Carbon World," *Guardian*, March 24, 2009.

91. Dynamotive, "BlueLeaf Inc. and Dynamotive Announce Biochar Test Results: CQuest Biochar Enriched Plots Yield Crop Increase Ranging From 6–17 Percent vs. Control Plots," news release, May 12, 2009.

92. See www.re-char.com.

93. Office of the Special Envoy for Haiti, "Celebrating Earth Day, April 22, 2010 . . . High-Efficiency Clean-Burning Cookstoves," www.haitispecialenvoy.org/press/celebrating-earth-day. See also www.worldstove.com.

94. From www.ecotechnologies.com and personal communications, Jeff Wallin to Hunter Lovins, at Biochar 2010, U.S. Biochar Initiative Annual Conference, Ames, Iowa, June 27, 2010.

95. Union of Concerned Scientists, "Hidden Costs of Industrial Agriculture."

96. Allen, "Agriculture Is One of the Most Polluting and Dangerous Industries."

97. World Health Organization, "World Cancer Report 2008, Summary," 2009, http://apps.who.int/bookorders/anglais/detart1.jsp?sesslan=1&codlan=1&codcol=76&codcch=26.

98. Pollan, "Farmer in Chief."

99. Ibid.

100. Lisa Belkin, "The School Lunch Test," *New York Times*, August 20, 2006.

101. Ann Cooper, personal communication, July 22, 2009.

102. Belkin, "School Lunch Test."

103. Ibid.

104. Michael Useem, "America's Best Leaders: Indra Nooyi, PepsiCo CEO," November 19, 2008, www.usnews.com/articles/news/best-leaders/2008/11/19/americas-best-leaders-indra-nooyi-pepsico-ceo.html.

105. Rob Schasel, " Why PepsiCo Is Changing Its Renewable Energy Strategy," April 9, 2010, Greenbiz.com, www.greenbiz.com/blog/2010/04/09/why-pepsico-changing-renewable-strategy.

106. Ibid.

107. Carol Ness, "Is Organic Better? It Depends," *San Francisco Chronicle*, November 28, 2007.

108. Alyson E. Mitchell et al., "Ten-Year Comparison of the Influence of Organic and Conventional Crop Management Practices on the Content of Flavonoids in Tomatoes," *Journal of Agriculture and Food Chemistry* 55 (2007): 6154–59.

109. Brian Halweil, "Home Grown: The Case for Local Food in a Global Market," Worldwatch Paper 163 (Washington, D.C.: Worldwatch Institute, November 1, 2002).

110. Pollan, "Farmer in Chief."

111. Ron Sims, King County executive, personal communication, October 18, 2006; staff in the Boulder County Open Space department, personal communications, July 8, 2010.

112. Eric Applebaum, "Organic Farms as Subdivision Amenities," *New York Times*, June 30, 2009.

113. Steve McFadden, "Community Farms in the 21st Century: Poised for Another Wave of Growth?" Rodale Institute, http://newfarm.rodaleinstitute.org/features/0104/csa -history/part1.shtml.

114. Yue-man Yeung, "Examples of Urban Agriculture in Asia," www.unu.edu/unupress/ food/8F092e/8F092E05.htm.

115. Cayce Hill and Hiroko Kubota, "Thirty-five Years of Japanese Teikei," in *Sharing the Harvest: A Citizen's Guide to Community Supported Agriculture*, eds. Elizabeth Henderson and Robyn Van En (White River Junction, Vt.: Chelsea Green, 2007), p. 267.

116. Shelley Crispin and Ron Strochilic, "Community Supported Agriculture in California, Oregon and Washington: Challenges and Opportunities," California Institute for Rural Studies, June 9, 2010, www.cirsinc.org/Documents/Pub0504.1.pdf.

117. For more information see Biodynamic Farming and Gardening Association CSA listings, www.biodynamics.com/csa.html; Local Harvest, www.localharvest.org/ csa/; Farm Locator, www.rodaleinstitute.org/new_farm; Wilson College, Robyn Van En Center CSA Farm Database, www.wilson.edu/wilson/asp/content.asp?id=1567; The Eat Well Guide, www.eatwellguide.org; ATTRA: The National Sustainable Agriculture Information Service, http://attra.ncat.org/attra-pub/localfood_dir.php; www.agcensus.usda.gov/Publications/2007/Full_Report/Volume_1,_Chapter_2_ US_State_Level/st99_2_044_044.pdf.

118. Personal communication with Hunter Lovins, Kyoto, Japan, December 1997.

119. "Locally Grown at Walmart," Walmart fact sheet, November 2008, http://walmart stores.com/download/2999.pdf.

120. Katty Kay, "Planting Detroit," BBC News, August 5, 2010, http://news.bbc.co.uk/2/ hi/programmes/world_news_america/8890510.stm.

121. David Whitford, "Can Farming Save Detroit?" *Fortune*, December 29, 2009.

122. Ariel Schwartz, "At Cleveland Mall Green Market, Sustainability Is the New Hot Topic," March 9, 2010, www.fastcompany.com/1576976/cleveland-galleria-mall -greenhouse-gardens-under-glass?partner=homepage_newsletter.

123. Http://openlibrary.org/books/OL16509991M/village_as_solar_ecology.

124. Pollan, "Farmer in Chief."

125. "Farm Output Efficiency Climbed 158% Since 1948," *Environmental Leader*, July 2, 2010, www.environmentalleader.com/2010/07/02/farm-output-efficiency-climbed -158-since-1948.

126. Pollan, "Farmer in Chief."

127. Allen, "Agriculture Is One of the Most Polluting and Dangerous Industries."

128. International Fund for Agricultural Development, "The Adoption of Organic Agriculture Among Small Farmers in Latin America and the Caribbean—Executive Summary," www.ifad.org/evaluation/public_html/eksyst/doc/thematic/pl/organic .htm.

129. "Organic Agriculture, A Way Out of Poverty for Small Farmers, According to New Research," *Organic News*, February 2005, p. 7.

130. Steven Hoffman (Compass Natural), personal communication, July 2010, Boulder, Colorado.

131. For an account of the term "Green Revolution," coined by William Gaud, the first director of USAID, see http://en.wikipedia.org/wiki/Green_Revolution.

132. Daniel Zwerdling, "India's Farming 'Revolution' Heading for Collapse," National Public Radio, April 13, 2009.

133. "India to Import Food Amid Drought," BBC, August 21, 2009.

134. See Somini Sengupta, "On India's Farms, a Plague of Suicide," *New York Times*, September 19, 2006; Shatrughan Sahu, "1,500 Farmers Commit Mass Suicide in India," *Belfast Telegraph*, April 15, 2009.

135. Report on the International Conference on Organic Agriculture and Food Security, May 2007, ftp://ftp.fao.org/docrep/fao/meeting/012/j9918e.pdf.

136. Hilary Byerly, "India: Organic Farming Saves Lives and Land," Green Grants, July 27, 2009, www.greengrants.org/grantstories.php?news_id=131.

137. Janet Cotter and Reyes Tirado, "Food Security and Climate Change: The Answer Is Biodiversity," report prepared for Greenpeace, June 2008.

138. Wes Jackson, "The 50-Year Farm Bill," *Solutions* 1, no. 3 (July 7, 2010), http://the solutionsjournal.com/node/649.

139. Ibid.

140. Dan Daggett, *Gardeners of Eden: Rediscovering Our Importance to Nature* (Santa Barbara: Thatcher Charitable Trust and EcoResults, 2005).

141. Wendell Berry, personal communication, Swannanoa, North Carolina, April 1985.

8: Carbon Markets

1. Business for Social Responsibility, "Who's Going 'Carbon Neutral'?" www.bsr.org/reports/BSR_Carbon-Neutral-Chart.pdf.

2. For an example of such scoffing, see www.cheatneutral.com.

3. Ricardo Bayon, Amanda Hawn, and Katherine Hamilton, *Voluntary Carbon Markets: An International Business Guide to What They Are and How They Work* (London: Earthscan Publications, 2007). Amazon.com lists more than six thousand books that reference the Kyoto Protocol.

4. "Kyoto Protocol 'Loophole' Has Cost $6 Billion," *New Scientist*, February 9, 2007.

5. Point Carbon, "Carbon Project Manager," www.pointcarbon.com/aboutus/product sandprices/tradinganalytics/1.260542.

6. Per-Otto Wold, personal communication to Boyd Cohen, December 2009.

7. Ken Silverstein, "Corporations Cutting Carbon Emissions," *EnergyBiz Insider*, November 11, 2008, www.renewableenergyworld.com/rea/news/article/2008/11/corporations-cutting-carbon-emissions-54048.

8. John Davies, "Green Powers the Pepsi Generation," *Forbes*, June 11, 2007.

9. "PepsiCo Drops RECs in Favor of $30M in On-site Generation," Environmental Leader, April 12, 2010, www.environmentalleader.com/2010/04/12/pepsico-drops-recs-in-favor-of-30m-in-on-site-generation.

10. See Russell Gold, "Club Pigou: James Hansen and Carbon Tax Aficionados," *Wall Street Journal*, June 23, 2009.

11. Environment for Europeans, "Emissions Trading: Cheap Carbon Only Temporary in the EU ETS," report, http://ec.europa.eu/environment/news/efe/climate/20090820_carbonets_en.htm.

12. "Analysts Credit EU ETS with Helping Cut Emissions," *Carbon Finance*, February 18, 2009, www.carbon-financeonline.com/index.cfm?section=europe&action=view&id=11857.

13. Environmental Defense Fund, "The Cap and Trade Success Story," www.edf.org/page.cfm?tagID=1085.

14. Environment for Europeans, "Emissions Trading: Cheap Carbon Only Temporary in the EU ETS."

15. Gretchen Mahan, "Polluters Are Buying Their Way Out of Carbon Cuts in the EU," *Huffington Post*, March 11, 2010, www.huffingtonpost.com/2010/03/12/polluters-are-buying-thei_n_496386.html.

16. "2008 U.S. Fossil Fuel CO2 Emissions See Biggest Drop in Nearly 30 Years," ClimateBiz, May 20, 2009, www.greenbiz.com/news/2009/05/20/2008-us-fossil-fuel-co2-emissions-see-biggest-drop-nearly-30-years.

17. "Farmers Enter World of Carbon Trading Through Biogas Use," *Thaiindian News*, May 13, 2008, www.thaiindian.com/newsportal/environment/farmers-enter-world-of-carbon-trading-through-biogas-use_10048440.html.

18. Ibid.

19. "ICE Cuts Staff at Chicago Climate Exchange—Sources," Reuters, August 12, 2010.

20. Timothy Gardner, "Regional U.S. Cap-Trade Proceeds Fund Efficiency," Reuters, March 24, 2010.

21. "Arizona Nixes Trade in Western Climate Market," Reuters, February 12, 2010.

22. "Vote No on Proposition 23," *SFGate*, September 20, 2010.

23. "Japan Emissions Trading Scheme Prepares for 2013 Launch," BusinessGreen.com, August 31, 2010, www.businessgreen.com/business-green/news/2268932/japan-emissions-trading-scheme.

24. For the Voluntary Carbon Standard, see www.v-c-s.org/about.html. For the Gold Standard, see www.cdmgoldstandard.org. For the International Organization for Standardization's ISO 14064 standard, see www.iso.org/iso/catalogue_detail?csnumber=38381. For the EPA's Climate Leaders, see www.epa.gov/climateleaders. For the Department of Energy's 1605(b) program, see www.eia.doe.gov/oiaf/1605. For the Carbon Disclosure Project, see www.cdproject.net/en-US/Pages/HomePage.aspx.

25. Jaymi Heimbuch, "Readers' Choice Winners for Treehugger's Best of Green Awards—Travel and Nature," April 8, 2010, http://planetgreen.discovery.com/travel-outdoors/readerschoice-winners-bestofgreen-travelnature.html.

26. Carbon Offset Watch, "The Rankings," www.carbonoffsetwatch.org.au/the-rankings.

27. Personal communication with Boyd Cohen.

28. World Wildlife Fund, "Gold Standard," www.panda.org/what_we_do/how_we_work/businesses/climate/offsetting/gold_standard.

29. Business for Social Responsibility, "Who's Going 'Carbon Neutral'?" www.bsr.org/reports/BSR_Carbon-Neutral-Chart.pdf.

30. See information on offsets for tourists at Sustainable Travel International, "Our Programs—Carbon Offsets," www.sustainabletravelinternational.org/documents/carbonneutraltraveltourism.html.

31. "NFL Plants Trees, Buys RECs & Feels Heat," Environmental Leader, January 31, 2007, www.environmentalleader.com/2007/01/31/nfl-plants-trees-buys-recs-feels-heat.

32. Silverstein, "Corporations Cutting Carbon Emissions."

33. Conor Greene, "Solar Energy Powers Contractor's Building," Hunterdon County Democrat, October 12, 2006, www.ferreiraconstruction.com/news/Hunterdon Democrat_10_12_2006_.html.

34. Tom Abate, "Silicon Valley Firm Turns Parking Lot into Solar Power Plant," San Francisco Chronicle, September 19, 2008.

35. Allison Pruitt, "Intel Increases Renewable Energy Credit Purchase by Ten Percent," Emerging Energy, February 10, 2010, www.energyboom.com/emerging/intel-increases-renewable-energy-credit-purchase-ten-percent.

36. Elisabeth Rosenthal, "Vatican Seeks to be Carbon Neutral," New York Times, September 3, 2007. Pope Benedict, like many of the world's religious leaders, has taken a strong stand for environmental protection and climate action, stating in a speech in early 2010 that he shared "the growing concern caused by economic and political resistance to combating the degradation of the environment" ("Vatican Messages: Concerned About Copenhagen, Pope Benedict XVI Urges New Agreement," Catholic Climate Covenant, http://catholicclimatecovenant.org/catholic-teachings/vatican-messages).

37. Daniel Howden, "Deforestation: The Hidden Cause of Global Warming," Independent, May 14, 2007.

38. Andrew Mitchell, "Big Business Leaves Big Forest Footprint," BBC, February 16, 2010, http://news.bbc.co.uk/2/hi/science/nature/8516931.stm.

39. Ibid.; see also "Global Forest Footprints," report, www.forestdisclosure.com/docs/FFD-Global-Forest-Footprints-Report.pdf.

40. "UNEP Unveils the Climate Neutral Network to Catalyze a Transition to a Low Carbon World," Climate Neutral Network, February 21, 2008, www.unep.org/climateneutral/News/UNEPNews/UNEPunveilstheClimateNeutralNetwork/tabid/195/Default.aspx.

41. UN-REDD Programme, www.un-redd.org/AboutREDD/tabid/582/language/en-US/Default.aspx. See also Avoided Deforestation Partners, www.adpartners.org.

42. Ibid.

43. Michael Szabo and Paul Sandle, "JPMorgan to Buy EcoSecurities for $204 Million," Reuters, September 14, 2009.

44. Adrian Fernando, personal communication with Boyd Cohen, December 14, 2009.

45. Global ozone-depleting substances (ODS) banks (gases not yet emitted into the

atmosphere) represent the equivalent of 18 billion tons of CO_2 equivalent. Intergovernmental Panel on Climate Change–Technology and Economic Assessment Panel, "IPCC/TEAP Special Report on Safeguarding the Ozone Layer and the Global Climate System," May 19, 2005, projected that by 2015, more than 6 billion tons of CO_2eq will be emitted as CFC and HCFC refrigerants leak from older equipment. See www.ipcc.ch/pdf/presentations/briefing-bonn-2005-05/safeguarding -ozone-layer.pdf.

46. ERA Carbon Offsets, Ltd., "ERA Executes Term Sheet with the Forest Carbon Group AG for the Sale of 1,800,000 Tonnes of VERs over 3 Years," news release, September 24, 2010, www.eraecosystems.com/investors/news_release/index.php ?&content_id=144.

47. See www.nexus-c4d.org.

9: Adapting to Climate Chaos

1. Sharon Begley, "Learning to Love Climate Change," *Newsweek*, December 22, 2007.

2. Annie Jia, "Businesses Stand to Profit from Adapting to Climate Change—Report," *New York Times*, September 15, 2009.

3. State of California, "2009 California Climate Adaptation Strategy Discussion Draft—Frequently Asked Questions," www.climatechange.ca.gov/adaptation/ documents/2009-07-31_Discussion_Draft-Adaptation_FAQs.pdf.

4. Ellen Lockyer, "Construction of Seawall Underway to Protect Shishmareff," *Alaska Public Radio Network*, May 1, 2009, http://aprn.org/2009/05/01/construction-of -sea-wall-underway-to-protect-shishmareff.

5. Rajesh Chhabara, "Climate Change Refugees Seek a New International Deal," Climate Change Corp, December 2008, www.climatechangecorp.com/content .asp?ContentID=5871.

6. "U.S. Climate Change Adaptation Industry," *Climate Change Business Journal* 2, no. 11 (November 2009), www.climatechangebusiness.com/US_Climate_Change _Adaptation_Industry.

7. Justin Gillis, "In Weather Chaos, a Case for Global Warming," *New York Times*, August 14, 2010.

8. "World Bank Raises Pakistan Flood Aid To $1 Billion," RTT News, August 2, 2010, www.rttnews.com/Content/GeneralNews.aspx?Node=B1&Id=1408511.

9. Mila Sanina, "Pakistan Crisis a 'Slow-Motion Tsunami,' UN Chief Says," CNN, August 2010; David Batty and Saeed Shah, "Impact of Pakistan Floods as Bad as 1947 Partition, Says Prime Minister," *Guardian*, August 14, 2010.

10. "Floods Leave 2M Indians Homeless," *Daily Times*, September 22, 2010.

11. "Katrina May Cost as Much as Four Years of War," MSNBC.com, September 19, 2005.

12. B. Ekwurzel, "Hurricanes and Climate Change," Union of Concerned Scientists, 2006, www.ucsusa.org/global_warming/science_and_impacts/science/hurricanes -and-climate-change.html.

13. Evan Mills, "From Risk to Opportunity: Insurer Responses to Climate Change," Ceres report, 2009, p. 9.
14. "Insurance Regulators Adopt Climate Change Risk Disclosure," March 27, 2009, www.naic.org/Releases/2009_docs/climate_change_risk_disclosure_adopted .htm.
15. Evan Mills, "From Risk to Opportunity."
16. Ibid.
17. Ibid.
18. Koko Warner et al., "Solutions for Vulnerable Countries and People: Designing and Implementing Disaster Risk Reduction and Insurance for Adaptation," United Nations University and Munich Climate Insurance Initiative. August 2010.
19. "RBAP-MABS Shares Philippine Experiences at the Microinsurance Asia Summit 2010 in Singapore," August 24, 2010, www.microinsurancenetwork.org/ microinsurancenews-2010-8.php.
20. Frank Ackerman and Elizabeth Stanton, "The Cost of Climate Change: What We'll Pay if Global Warming Continues Unchecked," Natural Resources Defense Council, May 2008.
21. "Nuclear Power Can't Stand the Heat," Public Citizen, www.citizen.org/documents/ HotNukesFactsheet.pdf.
22. Robin Pagnamenta, "France Imports UK Electricity as Plants Shut," Times (London), July 3, 2009.
23. "Venezuela—The Power Sector," All Business, November 9, 2009, www.allbusiness .com/energy-utilities/utilities-industry-electric-power/13413704-1.html.
24. M. Parraga, "Venezuela Plans Blackouts in Caracas, Oil Town," Reuters, January 2010.
25. "Van Jones on Clean Energy Jobs from 'Humble Hard-Working Energy Efficiency,' " Climate Progress, May 31, 2009.
26. Evan Mills, "Synergisms Between Climate Change Mitigation and Adaptation: An Insurance Perspective," Mitigation and Adaptation Solutions for Global Change 12 (2007): 809–42, http://evanmills.lbl.gov/pubs/pdf/miti-mills-2007.pdf.
27. Frank Ackerman and Elizabeth Stanton, "Cost of Climate Change."
28. Hurricane Katrina News Alert, PWC, September 2005, www.pwc.com/en_US/us/ consumer-finance/publications/assets/0905mipok.pdf.
29. http://morphopedia.com/projects/float-house.
30. A, Kroeger, "Dutch Pioneer Floating Eco-Homes", BBC News, March 2007, http:// news.bbc.co.uk/2/hi/europe/6405359.stm.
31. "Dutch Homes Will Float with the Climate," Marketplace, January 2008, http:// marketplace.publicradio.org/display/web/2008/01/29/planb_am2_floatinghouses/.
32. "Tourism Is NOT the World's Largest Industry—So Stop Saying That It Is," http:// tourismplace.blogspot.com/2008/04/tourism-is-not-worlds-largest-industry.html, United Nations World Tourism Organization, Tourism Highlights, 2009 edition.
33. M. Henderson, "Maldives President Mohammed Nasheed Demands Action on

Climate Change," *Times* (London), July 6, 2009. www.timesonline.co.uk/tol/news/environment/article6643750.ece.

34. Randeep Ramesh, Paradise "Almost Lost: Maldives Seek to Buy a New Homeland," *Guardian*, November 10, 2008, www.guardian.co.uk/environment/2008/nov/10/maldives-climate-change.

35. UNFCCC, "Climate Change, Small Island Developing States," 2006, p. 24.

36. Ibid.

37. P. Whoriskey and Spencer Hsu, "Levee Repair Costs Triple," *Washington Post*, March 31, 2006.

38. Ivor van Heerden, *The Storm: What Went Wrong and Why During Hurricane Katrina: The Inside Story from One Louisiana Scientist* (New York: Viking, 2006).

39. "Climate Change and Tourism, Proceedings of the 1st International Conference on Climate Change and Tourism," WTO, April 2003.

40. See www.jis.gov.jm/ggpages/html/20060725t110000-0500_9526_jis_governor_general_commends_work_on_dolphin_head_trust.asp.

41. See www.jpat-jm.com/virtour/dolphinhead/dolphinhead.html.

42. See www.ecotourism.org/site/c.orLQKXPCLmF/b.4835303/k.BEB9/What_is_Ecotourism_The_International_Ecotourism_Society.htm.

43. International Ecotourism Society, "Fact Sheet: Global Ecotourism," 2006, www.mekongtourism.org/site/uploads/media/IETS_Ecotourism_Fact_Sheet_Global_1__01.pdf.

44. See http://water.org/learn-about-the-water-crisis/billion/.

45. "Water Crisis to Be the Biggest World Risk," *Telegraph*, June 5, 2008, www.telegraph.co.uk/finance/newsbysector/utilities/2791116/Water-crisis-to-be-biggest-world-risk.html.

46. Ambrose Evans-Pritchard, "Water Crisis to Be Biggest World Risk," *Guardian*, January 5, 2008, www.infiniteunknown.net/2008/06/06/water-crisis-to-be-biggest-world-risk/.

47. Eric Young, "Report: More than One Out of Three U.S. Counties Face Water Shortages Due to Climate Change," Natural Resources Defense Council, www.nrdc.org/media/2010/100720.asp.

48. Ackerman and Stanton, "Cost of Climate Change."

49. Oxfam, "The New Adaptation Marketplace Climate Change and Opportunities for Green Economic Growth," 2009, www.oxfamamerica.org/files/the-new-adaptation-marketplace.pdf-1.

50. Barclays, "Barclays Announces Recommended Cash Offer for Carbon Developer Tricorona AB (publ)," press release, June 2, 2010.

51. Stephanie Schomer, "Meet the Creators of Sunspring, a Portable, Solar, Water-Purification System," *Fast Company*, July 1, 2010.

52. Water for People, "How PlayPumps Works," www.waterforpeople.org/extras/playpumps/how-playpumps-works.html.

53. Andrew Chambers, "Africa's Not-So-Magic Roundabout," *Guardian*, November 24,

2009, www.guardian.co.uk/commentisfree/2009/nov/24/africa-charity-water-pumps-roundabouts.

54. FogQuest project: "Yemen—Hajja/Mabijan 2003–2005," www.fogquest.org/projectinformation/yemen1.html.

55. World Wildlife Fund, "Turkey Floods Highlight Need for Climate Change Adaptation," September 11, 2009.

56. S. Lovgren, "Climate Change Creating Millions of Eco Refugees, UN Warns," *National Geographic*, November 2005.

57. Rajesh Chabara, "Climate Change Refugees Seek a New International Deal," Climate Change Corp., December 27, 2008.

58. Bureau of Meteorology Bushfire Cooperative Research Centre and CSIRO, "Bushfire Weather in Southeast Australia: Recent Trends and Projected Climate Change Impacts," 2007.

59. Lucian Kim and Maria Levitov, "Russia Heat Wave May Kill 15,000, Shave $15 Billion of GDP," August 10, 2010, www.bloomberg.com/news/2010-08-10/russia-may-lose-15-000-lives-15-billion-of-economic-output-in-heat-wave.html.

60. Michael Tobis, "Moscow Doesn't Believe in This," In It for the Gold (blog), http://initforthegold.blogspot.com/2010/08/moscow-doesnt-believe-in-this.html.

61. Alister Doyle, "Russian Heat Wave Dents Hopes of Climate 'Winners,'" Reuters, August 2010.

62. Alfonso Do, Mighel Bugalho, and Luis Silva, "Forest Fires and Climate Change," report, World Wildlife Fund, June 2009.

63. Dave Hughell and Rebecca Butterfield, "Impact of FSC Certification on Deforestation and the Incidence of Wildfires," Rainforest Alliance, 2008.

64. "New Study Finds FSC Provides Better Forest Protection," Forest Stewardship Council, April 2008, www.fscus.org/news/archive.php?article=515&.

65. "Policy Implications of Greenhouse Warming: Mitigation, Adaptation, and the Science Base," Committee on Science, Engineering, and Public Policy (COSEPUP), 1992.

66. Dan Collyns, "Can Painting a Mountain Restore a Glacier?" BBC, June 17, 2010.

67. Katherine L. Ricke, M. Granger Morgan, and Myles R. Allen, "Regional Climate Response to Solar-Radiation Management," *Nature Geoscience* 3 (2010): 537–41.

68. Toni Johnson, "Deforestation and Greenhouse-Gas Emissions," Council on Foreign Relations, December 2009.

69. Tobis, "Moscow Doesn't Believe in This."

10: A Future That Works

1. U.S. Global Change Research Program, "Global Climate Change Impacts in United States," report, June 15, 2010. The administration has set up a website with a page that will "introduce and lead you through the content of the most comprehensive and authoritative report of its kind" (www.globalchange.gov/publications/reports/scientific-assessments/us-impacts).

2. As described in Donella Meadows, Dennis L. Meadows, and Jorgen Randers, *Beyond the Limits: Confronting Global Collapse, Envisioning a Sustainable Future* (White River Junction, Vt.: Chelsea Green, 1993), the converging crises now facing the globe are not caused by any one event. They reflect a systemic breakdown that can only be understood and responded to in a whole-systems way. See also Donella Meadows, *Thinking in Systems* (White River Junction, Vt.: Chelsea Green, 2008).

3. "Global Biodiversity Outlook 3," United Nations Environment Programme and Convention on Biological Diversity, www.cbd.int/doc/publications/gbo/gbo3 -final-en.pdf.

4. Martin Parry et al., "Assessing the Costs of Adaptation to Climate Change: A Review of the UNFCCC and Other Recent Estimates," August 2009, www.iied.org/ pubs/pdfs/11501IIED.pdf.

5. Dr. Pachauri quoted in Geoffrey Lean, "Global Warming Approaching Point of No Return, Warns Leading Climate Expert," *Independent on Sunday*, January 23, 2005; Alex Kirby, "Aid Agencies' Warning on Climate," BBC News, October 2004, http:// news.bbc.co.uk/1/hi/sci/tech/3756642.stm. What makes Pachauri's comment noteworthy is that he was put into his position by the Bush administration as a chairman who would not make climate an issue. "A memorandum from Exxon to the White House in early 2001 specifically asked it to get the previous chairman, Dr. Robert Watson, the chief scientist of the World Bank, 'replaced at the request of the U.S.' The Bush administration then lobbied other countries in favor of Dr. Pachauri— whom the former vice president Al Gore called the 'let's drag our feet' candidate— and got him elected to replace Dr. Watson, who had repeatedly called for urgent action."

6. Steven Connor, "'The State of the World? It Is on the Brink of Disaster," *Independent*, March 30, 2005.

7. Peter N. Spotts, "Little Time to Avoid Big Thaw, Scientists Warn," *Christian Science Monitor*, March 24, 2006; David Biello, "How Fast Are Himalayan Glaciers Melting?" *Scientific American*, January 21, 2010.

8. "The Anatomy of a Silent Crisis," from the Global Humanitarian Forum report "Human Impact Report—of Climate Change," May 29, 2009, www.appinsys.com/ GlobalWarming/Deforestation.htm.

9. Scott Baldauf, "Africans Are Already Facing Climate Change: Is Darfur the First Climate-Change Conflict?" *Christian Science Monitor*, November 6, 2006.

10. United Nations Development Programme, "Climate Change Threatens Unprecedented Human Development Reversals," UNDP Human Development Report 2008, November 27, 2007.

11. "The Anatomy of a Silent Crisis," report by the Global Humanitarian Forum, May 29, 2009.

12. Alex Kirby, "Aid Agencies' Warning on Climate." See also Oxfam America, Africa Action, OneWorld US, OneClimate.net, Environmental Defense, Greenpeace International, World Wildlife Fund, "Climate Disasters Threaten to Overwhelm Aid Systems," April 22, 2009.

13. For abstracts for all of the scientific presentations made, see IOP Conference Series: Earth and Environmental Science, vol. 6, 2009, "Climate Change: Global Risks, Challenges and Decisions, 10–12 March 2009, Copenhagen, Denmark," www.iop .org/EJ/volume/1755-1315/6. For a transcript of the closing plenary session, see Talking Points, Dan Kammen, "Climate Scientists Debate with Prime Minister," Environmental Research Web, http://environmentalresearchweb.org/cws/article/ opinion/39126.

14. Copenhagen Synthesis Report, International Alliance for Research Universities, June 2009, http://climatecongress.ku.dk/pdf/synthesisreport, p. 1 (Executive Summary).

15. James Hansen, "Dear Barack and Michelle," Grist, January 2, 2009.

16. "350.org's Bill McKibben on the Letterman Show: Put Solar on the White House on 10/10/10," www.youtube.com/watch?v=0JcRj-Yokuw&feature=player_embedded.

17. Weatherdem's Weblog (where science meets politics), "Record Atmospheric CO2 Concentration in 2010: 392.94ppm," http://weatherdem.wordpress.com/2010/09/ 01/record-atmospheric-co2-concentration-in-2010-392-94ppm.

18. J. M. Barnola et al., "Historical Carbon Dioxide Record from the Vostok Ice Core," Carbon Dioxide Information Analysis Center, 2003, http://cdiac.ornl.gov/trends/ co2/vostok.html.

19. Environmental Protection Agency, "Inventory of U.S. Greenhouse Gas Emissions and Sinks: 1990–2006," www.epa.gov/climatechange/emissions/downloads10/US -GHG-Inventory-2010_Report.pdf.

20. James Kirkup and Louise Gray, "Copenhagen Climate Conference: Leaked UN Document Shows Deal Could Still Lead to Catastrophic Global Warming," Telegraph (UK), December 17, 2009.

21. "Last Days on Earth," 20/20, August 31, 2006, http://abcnews.go.com/2020/story ?id=2319986.

22. Elisabeth Rosenthal, "U.N. Report Describes Risks of Inaction on Climate Change," New York Times, November 17, 2007.

23. Lester Brown, Eco-Economy: Building an Economy for the Earth (New York: Norton, 2001).

24. Joseph Stiglitz and Nicholas Stern, "Obama's Chance to Lead the Green Recovery," Financial Times, March 2, 2009.

25. New York Times Magazine, September 13, 1970; Jim Heskett, "Are Elite Business Schools Fostering the Deprofessionalization of Management?" Harvard Business Review 7 (September 2007).

26. Rick Heede, "A Preliminary Assessment of Federal Energy Subsidies," 1984, www .rmi.org. A more conservative analysis, done by the U.S. Energy Information Administration, estimated the total impact of all federal energy subsidies in 2007 at $16.6 billion, but appears only to count direct payments, not the multiplicity of indirect support mechanisms. See also Adenike Adeyeye et al., "Estimating U.S. Government Subsidies to Energy Sources: 2002–2008," Environmental Law Institute, www.elistore.org/reports_detail.asp?ID=11358.

27. Kevin Bullis, "Fossil Fuel Subsidies Dwarf Support for Renewables," *Technology Review*, July 29, 2010; Riverbend Advisors, "Tax Breaks and Subsidies for Energy," July 19, 2010, www.riverbendadvisors.com/blog/2010/07/tax-breaks-and-subsidies -for-energy.

28. Adeyeye et al., "Estimating U.S. Government Subsidies." This conclusion is supported by Lawrence Berkeley National Lab, Environmental Energies Technologies Division, "Using the Federal Production Tax Credit to Build a Durable Market for Wind Power in the United States," November 2007 (http://eetd.lbl.gov/ea/emp/reports/63583.pdf). The report concluded that the erratic history of the credit has slowed the development of wind energy in the United States, increased our reliance on wind turbine components manufactured overseas, and increased the price of wind energy.

29. Alex Morales, "Fossil Fuel Subsidies Are 12 Times Support for Renewables, Study Shows," *Bloomberg News*, July 29, 2010.

30. "Obama Pledges Government Will Cut Greenhouse Emissions," CNN, January 29, 2010.

31. International Energy Agency, "Energy Subsidies: Getting the Prices Right," 2010, www.iea.org/files/energy_subsidies.pdf.

32. Javier Blas, "IEA Counts $550bn Energy Support Bill," *Financial Times*, June 6, 2010. The G-20 has embraced a proposal by President Obama to phase out international fossil energy subsidies. However, the G-20 only committed to do this in the midterm (rather than quickly) and details remain vague. It appears its commitment applies only to consumer, not producer, subsidies. At that point, global fossil subsidies were estimated at $300 billion annually. The IEA reevaluated subsidies shortly after, concluding they are actually in the range of $550 billion annually. Again, that covers only consumer subsidies.

33. Sourcewatch, "Global Climate Coalition," www.sourcewatch.org/index.php?title =Global_Climate_Coalition.

34. In one such briefing sponsored by the U.S. Chamber of Commerce in Denver, Colorado, on November 12, 2008, a man from the Heartland Institute stated that there was no scientific evidence of climate change. Representatives from the coal industry, specifically Peabody Coal, stated that the only way to meet our energy needs was to burn coal and that clean coal was available today, even though no commercial carbon capture and storage facility has yet been built. A representative of the U.S. Chamber of Commerce stated that any attempt to regulate the use of fossil fuels would bankrupt the economy. These types of positions in part prompted GE, Apple, Nike, and the utilities Pacific Gas and Electric, Public Service of New Mexico, and Exelon to resign from the U.S. Chamber of Commerce in the fall of 2009.

35. Koch Industries, titled the "kingpin of climate science denial," significantly outspent ExxonMobil from 2005 to 2008 in fighting legislation related to climate change, underwriting a massive network of foundations, think tanks, and political front groups. In summer 2010, the Koch brothers, owners of Koch Industries, a hundred-billion-dollar-a-year oil and products empire, estimated to be the

second-largest privately owned enterprise in the United States, spent a million dollars to sponsor a California amendment to overturn the climate protection legislation introduced by the Republican governor. The provision, Proposition 23, received over $10 million in funding, more than 80 percent from out-of-state companies, according to the California Secretary of State; approximately 79 percent from oil companies with Valero and Tesoro leading the way. Valero and Tesoro are considered the #12 and #32 worst polluters in the nation in the "Toxic 100 Air Polluters" report, issued by the University of Massachusetts Amherst Political Economy Research Institute. A Koch spokesperson stated that the state's global warming law "sets a bad precedent for future regulation by other states and the federal government." In a recent *New Yorker* article on the Koches' efforts to foster climate denial, Charles Lewis, the founder of the Center for Public Integrity, a nonpartisan watchdog group, stated, "The Koches are on a whole different level. There's no one else who has spent this much money. The sheer dimension of it is what sets them apart. They have a pattern of lawbreaking, political manipulation, and obfuscation. I've been in Washington since Watergate, and I've never seen anything like it. They are the Standard Oil of our times." See PERI, "The Toxic 100 Air Polluters," www.peri.umass.edu/toxic100; Margo Roosevelt, "Bid to Suspend California Global-Warming Law Gets $1 Million from Billionaire Brothers' Firm," *Los Angeles Times*, September 4, 2010; Jane Mayer, "Covert Operations," *The New Yorker*, August 2010.

36. Johnson Keith, "Out the Door: Exelon Leaves Chamber of Commerce over Climate Policy," *Wall Street Journal*, September 28, 2009; see also Sourcewatch, "U.S. Chamber of Commerce," www.sourcewatch.org/index.php?title=U.S._Chamber _of_Commerce#cite_note-7.

37. "Ford's Energy Efficiency Efforts Earn EPA Award," Media.Ford.com, press release, March 31, 2009, http://media.ford.com/article_display.cfm?article_id=30103.

38. J. S. Maxwell, F. Briscoe, and A. Marcus, "Green Schemes: Comparing Environmental Strategies and Their Implementation," *California Management Review* 3 (1997):39, 118–34.

39. "Best Practices in Sustainability: Supply Chain," Kanal Consulting, www.kanal consulting.com/Sustainability_SupplyChain_KanalConsulting.pdf.

40. "The 100 Most Sustainable Corporations in the World," Globe-net, January 29, 2010.

41. Kathleen Gilligan, "Sustainability Trends of the Oughts," EcoStrategy Group, January 12, 2010.

42. Alan D. Smith, "Growth of Corporate Social Responsibility as a Sustainable Business Strategy in Difficult Financial Times," *International Journal of Sustainable Economy*, December 4, 2009.

43. Chrystia Freeland, "What's BP's Social Responsibility?" *Washington Post*, July 18, 2010.

44. "The 2009 Ernst & Young Business Risk Report: The Top 10 Risks for Global Business"; "'Radical Greening' Seen as Top 10 Business Risk," Environmental Leader, August 4, 2010.

45. Ram Nidumolu, C. K. Prahalad, and M. R. Rangaswami, "Why Sustainability Is Now the Key Driver of Innovation," *Harvard Business Review*, September 2009.

46. Michael E. Porter and Mark R. Kramer, "The Link Between Competitive Advantage and Corporate Social Responsibility," *Harvard Business Review*, December 2006.

47. David M. Dickson, "Oil Woes Mask Improvement in Deficit; Demand for Imported Goods Slows; Exports Have Increased," *Washington Times*, August 17, 2008.

48. Jonathan Porritt, "Perfect Storm of Environmental and Economic Collapse Closer Than You Think," *Guardian*, March 23, 2009.

49. Thomas L. Friedman, "The Inflection Is Near?" *New York Times*, March 7, 2009.

50. Many books profile the necessary transformation: Rob Hopkins, *Transition Handbook* (White River Junction, Vt.: Chelsea Green, 2008); David Korton's *The Great Turning: From Empire to Earth Community* (San Francisco: Berrett-Koehler, 2007); and the brilliant and timeless writings of Wendell Berry, including "The Idea of a Local Community," *Orion*, Winter 2001. All of Wendell Berry's writings on community advocate a grassroots, bottom-up approach to living in ways that solve the climate crisis and deliver a higher quality of life.

51. See the Carbon Disclosure Project website: www.cdproject.net/en-US/Pages/HomePage.aspx.

52. "GE to Invest $10B More in Ecomagination R&D by 2015," GreenBiz.com, June 24, 2010.

53. The terms "cradle-to-cradle" and "circular economy" were coined by Walter Stahel of the Product Life Institute (see www.product-life.org/en/cradle-to-cradle; www.product-life.org/en/node). For more information on China's adoption of Stahel's concept see www.indigodev.com/Circular1.html.

54. See Janine M. Benyus, *Biomimicry: Innovation Inspired by Nature* (New York: William Morrow, 1997); www.biomimicryinstitute.org.

55. See the Calera company's website at http://calera.com/index.php/home.

56. Nonnie de la Pena, "Sifting the Garbage for a Green Polymer," *New York Times*, June 19, 2007.

57. This concept was pioneered by Gifford Pinchot and Ron Pellman in the landmark book *Intrepreneuring in Action: A Handbook for Business Innovation* (San Francisco: Berrett-Koehler, 2000).

58. Dr. Zhu Dajian, "Circular Economy and China's New Industrialization," Science Publication Company, 2007, www.socialinnovationexchange.org/files/event/attachments/Circular%20Economy%20and%20China's%20New%20Industrialization.pdf.

59. At a minimum, a wise civilization ensures that its activities leave a safety margin to keep all critical ecological services undamaged. This is the precautionary principle: if the risk from a particular activity is sufficiently high, a proponent will be required to prove that it is safe before being allowed to go forward; the burden of proof that it is *not* harmful falls on those wishing to take the action. The precautionary principle is now being written into European Union legislation. See Commission of the European Communities, "Communication from the Commission on the Precautionary Principle," http://ec.europa.eu/environment/docum/20001_en.htm. A few Ameri-

can cities have followed suit, with San Francisco formalizing the precautionary principle in its governance. In general, however, American business has persuaded legislatures that an activity should be allowed until it has been proved harmful.

60. Ray Anderson, personal communication, Wingspread Conference, June 2008.

61. Hunter Lovins addressed an ICAEW symposium on this in London in November 2009.

62. "Paul Krugman: King of Pain," *Economists View,* http://economistsview.typepad .com/economistsview/2006/09/paul_krugman_ki.html.

63. Paul Wiseman, "TARP Report: Good for Wall Street, Not Main Street," *USA Today,* December 11, 2009, www.usatoday.com/money/economy/2009-12-09-tarp-report _N.htm.

64. See "Simon Kuznets," Wikipedia, http://en.wikipedia.org/wiki/Simon_Kuznets.

65. "Remarks of Robert F. Kennedy at the University of Kansas, March 18, 1968," John F. Kennedy Presidential Library and Museum.

66. The commission published a report: www.stiglitz-sen-fitoussi.fr/documents/ rapport_anglais.pdf.

67. Jon Gertner, "The Rise and Fall of the G.D.P.," *New York Times,* May 30, 2010.

68. "Nic Marks: The Happy Planet," lecture, TED: Ideas Worth Spreading, www.ted .com/talks/nic_marks_the_happy_planet_index.html.

69. See www.grossnationalhappiness.com.

70. E. F. Schumacher, *Small is Beautiful: Economics as if People Mattered* (Reprint, New York: HarperPerennial, 1989).

71. Don Duncan, "Economists Appraise Bhutan's Happiness Model," *San Francisco Chronicle,* December 4, 2008.

72. Ibid.

73. Ibid.

74. Johan Rockström, Katrin Vohland, et al., "Making Progress Within and Beyond Borders," in H. J. Schellnhuber, M. Molina, et al., eds., *Global Sustainability: A Nobel Cause* (New York: Cambridge University Press, 2010), www.nobel-cause.de/ book/NobelCauseBook_chapter4.pdf.; comments made at World Energy Conference, September 1, 2009.

75. Global Footprint Network, info@footprintnetwork.org; World Wildlife Fund, "2010 Living Planet Report," www.panda.org/about_our_earth/all_publications/ living_planet_report.

76. Buckminster Fuller, *Operating Manual for Spaceship Earth* (Baden, Switzerland: Lars Müller, 2008), free download at http://free-ebook-download.org/Operating -Manual-for-Spaceship-Earth.html.

77. See Herman Daly and Joshua Farley, *Ecological Economics* (Washington, D.C.: Island Press, 2004).

78. Donella H. Meadows et al., *Limits to Growth: The 30-Year Update,* 3rd ed. (White River Junction, Vt.: Chelsea Green, 2004). See also "Beyond the Limits—Executive Summary" (downloadable Word document; type into search engine).

79. Meadows et al., *Beyond the Limits* (Executive Summary), www.sustainability.ufl.edu/forum/ . . . /Beyond%20the%20Limits.doc.

80. Ibid., p. 1.

81. Justin Lahart, Patrick Barta, and Andrew Batson, "New Limits to Growth Revive Malthusian Fears," *Wall Street Journal*, March 24, 2008.

82. Johan Rockström et al., "Planetary Boundaries: Exploring the Safe Operating Space for Humanity," *Ecology and Society* 14, no. 2: 32; see also Stockholm Resilience Centre, "Tipping Towards the Unknown."

83. Stiglitz and Stern, "Obama's Chance to Lead the Green Recovery."

84. "Nic Marks: The Happy Planet."

85. Keith Bradisher, "China Fears Consumer Impact on Global Warming," *New York Times*, July 4, 2010.

86. David Leonhardt, "In China, Cultivating the Urge to Spend," *New York Times*, November 24, 2010, www.nytimes.com/2010/11/28/magazine/28China-t.html?_r=1&nl=todaysheadlines&emc=a210.

87. Joseph Kahn and Jim Yardley, "As China Roars, Pollution Reaches Deadly Extremes," *New York Times*, August 26, 2007.

88. Candace Lombardi, "China, South Korea Lead in Green Tech Funding," CNET News, Green Tech, May 6, 2010, http://news.cnet.com/8301-11128_3-20004323-54.html.

89. Elisabeth Rosenthal, "Nations That Debate Coal Use Export It to Feed China's Need," *New York Times*, November 22, 2010, www.nytimes.com/2010/11/22/science/earth/22fossil.html?_r=1&pagewanted=2&ref=world.

90. Ibid.

91. Edward B. Barbier, *A Global Green New Deal* (New York: Cambridge University Press and UN Environment Programme, 2009).

92. Ibid., p. 4.

93. Porritt, "Perfect Storm of Environmental and Economic Collapse Closer Than You Think."

94. United Nations Environment Programme, "'Global Green New Deal'—Environmentally-Focused Investment Historic Opportunity for 21st Century Prosperity and Job Generation; UNEP Launches Green Economy Initiative to Get the Global Markets Back to Work," press release, October 22, 2008. In May 2010 Hunter Lovins spent an hour with Achim Steiner, advising him on how such a summit might be configured. She was also an invited facilitator at the Prep Comm held in November 2010 in San Francisco.

95. Randy Hayes, personal communication, San Francisco, October 2006. Randy is also the founder of Rainforest Action Network.

96. Donella Meadows, *Thinking in Systems: A Primer* (White River Junction, Vt.: Chelsea Green, 2008).

97. See also the work of Scott Spann, www.inatestrategies.com.

98. Download the LASER guide here: www.natcapsolutions.org/index.php?option

=com_content&view=article&id=287&Itemid=72. Download the *Climate Protection Manual for Cities* here: www.climatemanual.org/Cities/index.htm.

99. Joseph E. Stiglitz, "Reversal of Fortune," *Vanity Fair*, October 2008; see also Joseph E. Stiglitz, *Freefall: America, Free Markets, and the Sinking of the World Economy* (New York: Norton, 2009).

100. "Number of Lobbyists per Congressman," #NumberOf.net, www.numberof.net/number-of-lobbyists-per-congressman.

101. "Dirty Money: Big Oil and Corporate Polluters Spent Over $500 Million to Kill Climate Bill, Push Offshore Drilling," *Climate Progress* (blog), September 27, 2010.

102. www.natcap.org/sitepages/pid20.php.

103. See *Natural Capitalism*, chapter 12, "Climate: Making Sense and Making Money."

104. Adam Smith, *Theory of Moral Sentiments (The Glasgow Edition of the Works of Adam Smith)* (Indianapolis: Liberty Fund, 2009), pp. 27, 56.

105. Ibid., p. 211.

106. Mishko Hansen, "Note on Adam Smith as Theorist of Sustainability," personal communication, Cambridge University, October 2007.

107. Thomas L. Friedman, "Superbroke, Superfrugal, Superpower?" *New York Times*, September 4, 2010.

108. Lester Brown, "New Energy Economy Emerging in the United States," Earth Policy Institute, October 15, 2008, www.earthpolicy.org/Updates/2008/Update77.htm.

109. Thomas L. Friedman, *Hot, Flat, and Crowded: Why We Need a Green Revolution— and How It Can Renew America* (New York: Farrar, Straus and Giroux, 2008), pp. 5, 6.

110. 350.org's Bill McKibben, *The Late Show with David Leterman*, August 31, 2010.

111. Dr. Martin Luther King, "Beyond Vietnam," sermon given at Riverside Church on April 4, 1967, in New York City.

112. The countries surveyed included Australia, Brazil, Canada, China, France, Germany, Hong Kong, India, Japan, Malaysia, Mexico, Singapore, the United Kingdom, the United States, and Vietnam. Japan, Singapore, and Vietnam were included in the survey for the first time this year.

113. HSBC, "Climate Confidence Monitor 2010," report, www.hsbc.com/1/PA_1_1_S5/content/assets/sustainability/101026_hsbc_climate_confidence_monitor_2010.pdf.

114. For McCain's speech see Bryan Montopoli, "McCain Ad Pushes 'Energy Security,'" CBS News website, June 23, 2008.

115. Meadows et al., *Beyond the Limits*, pp. 234–36.

116. J.R.R. Tolkien, *The Return of the King* (New York: Ballantine Books, 1965), p. 33.

Acknowledgments

Hunter:

Bringing a book into the world is no trivial task, and this one is no exception.

It owes its existence to Boyd Cohen, who approached me several years ago and proposed to partner with me to write the sequel to *Natural Capitalism*. I chuckled politely.

Boyd went on to find us an agent, who turned out to be my old friend Bill Gladstone, without whom this book would not now be in your hands and to whom we owe a great debt of gratitude.

Through Bill's good offices we were introduced to what is clearly one of the best publishing houses in the business, Farrar, Straus and Giroux, and to our magnificent editor at its Hill and Wang imprint, Thomas LeBien. I'm no easy author with whom to work, and Thomas has made this whole process a great deal of fun. His gentle, cajoling hand astutely strengthened this manuscript. My deep thanks to Dan Crissman and the great production team at FSG. You guys rock. Again, we are deeply grateful.

So many colleagues lent generously of their time to offer research and guidance of every sort. They read drafts, chased facts, pointed out when we'd gone astray, and became the council of advisers any author would welcome.

The book would not have been possible without the dedicated work of our staff at Natural Capitalism, starting with our able CEO, Toby Russell, Chief of Staff Robert Noiles, Director of Research Nick Sterling, Intern Coordinator Lily Thaiz, my exec Nancy Johnston, Business Development Director Kara Seeley, our implementation team, Jeff Hohensee, Paul Sheldon, Steve Wilton, Bill Becker, and Margo Boteilho, and our outstanding interns: Emily Basham, Lauren Baum, Jessica Bonsall, Max Carlson, Garrett Collier, Edmon Garibyan, Steven Hirshhorn, Joshua Kruger, Brett Levin, Miles Livermore, Jennifer Lukas, Bryant Mason, Justine Meihsner, Kaitlyn Minich, Andy Neville, Fred Oelsner, Hanna Schum, Sylvia Stone, Matthew Trujillo, Matthew Tucker, and Francesca Wahl.

A small army of dedicated business minds, policy experts, activists, and friends gave generously of their time to make this book possible. While there are far too many to thank here (you know who you are, and I hope know my deepest gratitude), *Climate Capitalism* could not have come into being without the work of Dr. Tariq Banuri, Janine Benyus, Bob Berkibile, Dr. Eric Berlow, Scott Bernstein, Wendell Berry, David Blume, Tim Braun, Clark Brockman, Alison Burchell, Antuan Cannon, Eric Carlson, Norm Clasen, Dr. Jeff Cohen, Kelly Cookson, Greg Davis, Dr. Tom Dean, Dr. Peter deNeufville, Nancy Clanton, Bob Dunham, Jay Eikenhorst, Dr. Richard Grey, Rick Fedrizzi, Ryan Fix, George Gay, Dr. Eban Goodstein, Leslie Glustrom, Catherine Greener, Gil Friend, Linaya Hahn, Gwen Hallsmith, Randy Hayes, Elliot Hoffman, Steve Hoffman, Dr. John Holdren, Gail Horvath, Marion Hunt, Dr. Dune Ives, Dr. Wes Jackson, Audrey James, David Johnston, Alan Joyce, Dr. Dan Kammen, Rick Levine, Marty Lagod, Craig Lewis, Ernest Lowe, Joe Madden, Tony Manwaring, Clare Mendelsohn, Dr. Ron Nahser, Michael Northrup, Dr. Jay Ogilvy, Dr. David Orr, Jacob Park, John Petersen, Ryan Renner, Tom Rivett-Carnac, Dr. Joe Romm, Sheila Samuelson, Dr. Richard Sandor, Dorothy Segel, Floyd Segel, Will Semmes, Frank Sesno, Shripal Shah, Steve Shueth, Nathan Shedroff, David Shearer, Bill Shutkin, Scott Spann, Brooke Sprague, Achim Steiner, Philip Sutton, Dr. Jim Thompson, Edward West, Dr. Bryan Willson, R. James Woolsey, and Jamie Workman.

My co-professor Gregory Miller, the finest partner an insurgent could wish for, has been a sounding board, cocreator, and friend. My students have been great colleagues with whom to wrestle over ideas, and most understanding of the demands on my time.

To my family: thank you. Thank you, especially, Robbie, for having suggested even before Boyd approached me that it was time to write another book, for bearing with a year of my being unavailable, and for all of the love and support that you give to me. Thanks, Pig, Peter, Tigger, Stalker, and Wrangler for filling my life with joy.

Boyd:

It is surreal to be coauthor of the sequel to *Natural Capitalism* with Hunter. In 2001, just as I was finishing my Ph.D. at the University of Colorado, my adviser, Dr. Tom Dean, gave me *Natural Capitalism* to read. Like the millions of others who read that seminal work, I was inspired to focus my professional career on the intersection of commerce and the planet. When I first approached Hunter and surprisingly managed to convince her to write this book with me, I honestly thought, given how busy she is, that I would carry the load but get the benefit of her editing and, I hoped, her voice in the book. Hunter has instead proven herself to be a work horse as well as a visionary, making the writing of this book, my first, a delightful experience. It has been an honor working with her on this project and, I hope, the start of a lifelong collaboration.

The team at CO2IMPACT, starting with my cofounder and life partner, Elizabeth

Obediente, was also instrumental to the support and feedback required to move the project forward. Senior Carbon Analyst Pedro Camanho, as well as Javier Guerrero and Ivonne San Miguel, key members of our Colombian operation, all provided guidance and feedback. CO2IMPACT's NGO partner in Colombia, Corciencias, also gave great advice.

I owe my gratitude to the global business leaders who provided insight from the front lines of the low-carbon economy: Per Otto Wold, CEO, Point Carbon; Freddy Sharpe, CEO, Climate Friendly; Rob Safrata, CEO, Novex Couriers; Adrian Fernando, COO, Ecosecurities; Marc Barasch, Executive Director, Green World Campaign; and David Rokoss and Robert Falls, ERA (Ecosystem Restoration Associates).

Finally, my gratitude for the support of my parents, Stuart and Judy, and to Mateo, my son, who is my inspiration to contribute to the climate solution.

These and many other people have contributed to the book you now hold in your hands in ways too many to enumerate. Any errors, omissions, or plain old stupidity remain the responsibility of the authors. We'd be grateful if you'd point any out so that the next edition, and the Web version, can continue to improve.

Thanks most of all to you. It is your desire to read this that made it all possible. You are our partner in making it happen.

Index

Abu Dhabi, 120–21
Access, 164
accounting, 286
Acela Express, 142
acid rain, 227, 298
Adam Lewis Center for Environmental Studies, 98, 101
Adams, Douglas, 176–77
Adobe Systems, 110
Aerotecture, 71
Afghanistan, 71, 289, 297
Africa, 93, 117, 179, 181, 196, 255, 274, 289, 297
Africa Centre for Holistic Management, 191–92
Agassi, Shai, 168, 169
Agatston, Arthur, 206
agriculture, 154, 178–219, 298; biochar in, 199–203; climate change and, 178–81, 186–87, 257; conventional, cutting carbon loss and enhancing profitability with, 196–99; conventional, problems with, 181–87; in developing world, 213–16; fertilizers in, 179, 182, 185, 186, 188, 189, 194, 195, 200, 208, 212–15, 270; greenhouse gas emissions from, 179, 181, 182–83; Green Revolution and, 213–14; health problems and, 178, 203–208; industrial, 211–12, 214; meat and dairy production, 182–85, 191, 204, 205; no-till and direct seeding, 194–99; organic, 187–91, 194–96, 213, 215, 257; perennials in, 217–18; pesticides in, 178, 179, 187, 188, 194, 204, 212, 213, 214; soil carbon and, 180, 191, 194–96, 196–99; urban and localized, 208–11, 270
Agriculture, U.S. Department of (USDA), 45–46, 181, 210
Aguçadoura wave farm, 77
air-conditioning, 40, 100, 110, 256

air pollution: in China, 23, 24, 60, 61;
    indoor, 99–100, 102; transportation
    and, 124
Airports Council International, 139
air travel, 123, 139–41
Alaska, 72, 232, 251
Aldo Leopold Legacy Center, 108
algae, as biofuel, 165–66, 167, 257
algae blooms, 179, 197–98
Allen, Will, 212–13, 216
ALL Power Labs, 165
Altarock, 76–77
Alter Eco, 241
Amader, 164
AMEC, 163
American Clean Energy and Security
    bill, 63
American Council for an Energy-
    Efficient Economy, 8
American Electric Power (AEP), 28–29
American Institute of Architects, 98, 106,
    117, 121, 211
American Recovery and Reinvestment
    Act (2009), 63
American Trucking Association, 129
Amsterdam, Netherlands, 175
Amtrak, 142, 143
Anchorage, Alas., 102
Anderson, Ray, 286, 302
AngloAmerican, 35–36
Annan, Kofi, 274
Anthony, Chris, 133
Anthyodaya, 231
appliances, 46
Applied Materials, 24, 238
Aptera Motors, 133
Aquamarine Power, 78
Aquascan, 266
Aquaspy, 261
Aramburu, Jason, 202
Arbenz, Markua, 213
Architecture 2030, 4, 15, 117–18
Arizona, 232

Arkansas, 206
Army, U.S., 128
Arthur D. Little, 280
Arup, 120
Asia, 8, 64, 117, 179, 255, 273; building
    in, 113–15
Association of International Automobile
    Manufacturers, 129
AT&T, 132
ATDynamics (Advanced Transit
    Dynamics), 137–38
A. T. Kearney, 26, 29; Green Winners, 26
Atos Consulting, 26
Australia, 94, 168, 233, 240, 267, 274, 290
Austria, 66
automobile industry, 43, 126–31, 298;
    conservatism in, 128; Ford, 7, 43, 126,
    127, 130–31, 132, 149, 229, 280;
    General Motors, see General Motors;
    oil and, see oil; opposition to
    regulation in, 129–30; start-up
    companies in, 133–34; Toyota, 5, 43,
    72, 126, 127, 130; Volkswagen, 5,
    127–28; World War II and, 158–59
automobiles, 123; car and ride sharing,
    144–46; commuting and, 124, 125–26,
    173; congestion pricing and, 172; costs
    of ownership, 124; culture of, 171;
    electric, see electric vehicles; flex-fuel,
    160, 162; number of, 123
AutoPacific, Inc., 149
Avego, 145

Babylon, N.Y., 44
Badgett, Tom, 139
Bangladesh, India, 36, 251–52
Ban Ki-moon, 253
Banner Bank Building, 107
Banuri, Tariq, 290
Baoding, China, 60–61
Barclays, 263
Barker, Jack, 264

Basil Bandwagon Natural Market, 40
Batinovich, Robert, 48
BC Hydro, 46, 47
beach resorts, 261
BEAM (Building Environmental
    Assessment Method), 114–15
Becker, Bill, 304–305
Beddington, John, 282
Beddington Zero Energy Development
    (BedZED), 112–13
Begley, Sharon, 250
Benyus, Janine, 218, 285
Bergey Windpower, 71
Bering Straits Native Corporation, 72
Berkebile, Bob, 121–22
Berkeley, Calif., 81–82
Berkeley First, 82
Bernstein, Scott, 173–74
Berry, Wendell, 219
Better Place, 93, 167–69
Beyond the Limits (Meadows, Meadows,
    and Randers), 291–92, 306
Bhattacharya, Jit, 134
Bhutan, 289–90
Bi Bangquan, 66
bicycles, 175–76
Bicycle Transportation Systems, 176
biochar, 199–203
biofuels, 46, 59, 159–61, 257; algae,
    165–66, 167, 257; biodiesel, 159,
    163–64, 166; second-generation,
    161–65; subsidies given to, 278; Virgin
    Airlines and, 166–67
biogas, 193, 231
biomass, 59, 61, 64, 94
Biomimicry Institute, 218, 285
Birdsall, Wes, 45, 47, 50
Birol, Fatih, 153, 154, 155, 279, 293
Black Mountain Ranch, 116
*Black Swan, The: The Impact of the Highly
    Improbable* (Taleb), 272
Bloomberg, Michael, 118
Bloomberg Businessweek, 40, 281

Blue Spruce, 193–94
BNM Architects, 121
Boeing, 139–40
Bogota, Colombia, 171–72
Bolivia, 262
Booz Allen Hamilton, 103
Boston, Mass., 142
Boulder, Colo., 44, 96, 120
BP (British Petroleum), 53, 164, 273
Braddock, Pa., 18, 116
Braine, Bruce, 29
Branson, Richard, 86–87, 166–67
Braun, Tim, 79, 80
Brazil, 160–61, 239, 240, 243, 290
Brinley, Stephanie, 149
Brower, David, 304
Brown, Lester, 158, 161, 276–77, 302
British Columbia, Canada, 44, 46, 51, 232
Buckminster Fuller Challenge Award,
    191–92
Building Research Establishment
    Environmental Assessment Method
    (BREEAM), 105
buildings, 15–16, 32, 95–122, 268;
    climate change and, 252–53, 258–59;
    construction industry attitudes and,
    103; energy audits and, 119–20;
    Energy Star, 108; greenhouse gas
    emissions from, 95–96; greening
    preexisting structures, 108–109; heating
    and cooling systems in, 40, 100, 110,
    256; housing market collapse and,
    102–103; LEED and, 96, 105–108, 112,
    114, 115, 116, 121; lighting in, *see*
    lighting; passive design in, 109–10;
    schools, 100; sick building syndrome,
    99–100, 102; stores, 101; workplaces,
    100–101; zero-energy, 112
Bundeswehr Transformation Center,
    155–57
buses, 74, 174; bus rapid transit, 171–72
Bush, George W., 153, 286–87
Bush, Laura, 264

Business Environment Council, 114, 115
BusinessWeek, 40, 281
Butti, Ken, 104

Calera, 285
Calgary, Canada, 46–47
California, 17–18, 21, 48, 66, 68, 72, 79,
  80, 82, 91, 143, 168, 232, 233, 256, 262,
  273, 274; agriculture in, 186, 189, 208;
  cars and, 128–29, 134
California Air Resources Board, 128
California Climate Adaptation Strategy
  Discussion Draft, 251
California Climate Protection Act, 233
California Energy Commission, 68
California Lighting Technology
  Center, 101
California State University–Chico, 185
Cambridge Energy Research Associates
  (CERA), 153–54
Cameron, Murray, 91
Canada, 168, 232, 267, 290
Canadian Green Building Council
  (CaGBC), 105
cancer, 178, 204, 205, 214
Cancun Accord, 223
cap and trade, 221, 225–26, 228, 298
capitalism, 5
capital markets, 85–92
carbon, 187; biochar and, 199–203; in
  soil and trees, 179, 180, 187, 191,
  194–96, 196–99
carbon-based fuels, taxation of, 226–27
carbon credits, 198, 222, 225, 242
carbon dioxide, 44, 231
Carbon Disclosure Project (CDP), 10–11,
  13, 14, 29, 234, 280, 284
carbon (CO_2) emissions, 8, 29, 35, 84,
  274, 276, 279; aviation and, 139;
  buildings and, 97; calculating, 309; in
  California, 18; cap and trade and, 221,
  225–26; in China, 293; DuPont and,

6–7; Kyoto Protocol and, *see* Kyoto
  Protocol; Sarbanes-Oxley Act and, 10;
  STMicroelectronics and, 7; targets for
  reducing, 236–38; transportation and,
  124, 128–29; Walmart and, 13, 14
Carbon Fund, 234, 309
carbon markets, 220–48, 298–99;
  business opportunities in, 242–47; in
  European Union, 228–29; prices in,
  227; regional, 232–33; in U.S., 229–31;
  voluntary, 233–36
Carbon Mercantile Exchange, *see* Google
carbon neutrality, 7, 237, 242
carbon offsets, 141, 197, 220–22, 224–26,
  234, 242, 309; additionality and, 222,
  235; forest, 238–42; scams and, 222;
  social/charismatic, 246–47; voluntary
  standards for, 233
Carbon Offset Watch, 234–35
carbon responsibility, four steps to,
  222–23
Carbonscape, 201
Carbon Trade Watch, 221
Carbon Trust, 78
Carbon War Room, 87, 143
Carmanah Technologies, 74
Carrera, Jose Roman, 268
car sharing, 144–46
Cascadia Green Building Council, 121
cattle, 183–84, 185, 192, 193, 204
Ceatec (Combined Exhibition of
  Advanced Technologies), 61
Celebre, Alice, 40
cellulosic ethanol, 162
Center for Climate Strategies, 58
Center for Neighborhood Technologies,
  173
Centers for Disease Control, 204, 205
Ceres, 104, 254
Ceres Principles, 280
Chacko, K. V., 231
Changing World Technologies, 163
charcoal, 199–200; biochar, 199–203

Charles, Prince, 240, 282
Chase, Robin, 145
Chevrolet 149, 162; Volt, 127, 132, 134
Chez Panisse Foundation, 206
Chicago, Ill., 71, 119
Chicago Climate Exchange (CCX), 197,
    198, 199, 229–31, 299
chickens, 184
Chile, 233
China, 23, 62, 84, 93, 150, 233, 239, 240,
    242, 253, 274, 277, 293–95, 297, 304;
    agriculture in, 179, 208–209, 213, 262;
    bicycles in, 175–76; building in,
    113–14, 115; building of cities in, 120;
    carbon credit scam in, 222; cars in,
    123–24, 126; Circular Economy
    Initiative in, 285; consumerism in,
    293–94; Green Building Council of,
    105; oil market and, 124–25, 152;
    pollution in, 23, 24, 60, 61, 179;
    renewable energy in, 23–24, 59–61;
    solar energy in, 66, 67, 294; Three
    Gorges Dam in, 79, 256; trains in, 143;
    Walmart suppliers in, 11, 13; wind
    power in, 69, 294
China Greentech Initiative, 23
chlorofluorocarbons, 244–45
Christensen, Gary, 107
Christian Science Monitor, 61
Chrysler, 127, 131, 134–35
Chu, Stephen, 186
Cisco, 47
cities, 16–17, 44, 80–84, 115–21;
    agriculture in, 208–11, 270;
    alternatives to cars in, 172–76;
    building of, 120–21; car-free, 172–73;
    lighting in, 101–102
Cities and the Wealth of Nations
    (Jacobs), 117
Citroën, 131–32
Civil Society Institute, 149
Clanton, Nancy, 101
Clean Air, Cool Planet, 86

Clean Power, 166
"Climate: Making Sense and Making
    Money," 32, 300
Climate, Community & Biodiversity
    Alliance, 233
Climate, Community and Biodiversity
    Standards (CCBS), 235
Climate Action Registry, 232
Climate Action Reserve, 245
ClimateBiz, 237
Climate Capitalism, principles of, 283–86
climate change, 5; agriculture and,
    178–81, 186–87, 257; mitigation
    of, 249–51, 270–71; overwhelming
    evidence for, 275–76; skeptics of,
    6, 276
climate change, adaptation to, 249–71,
    274; construction industry and,
    252–53, 258–59; disaster preparedness
    and response, 265–69; energy
    companies and, 252–53, 256–58;
    insurance industry and, 252–56;
    tourism and, 252–53, 259–62; water
    supplies and, 252, 262–65, 274
"Climate Confidence Monitor," 304
Climate Cooler, 170
Climate Friendly, 235
Climate Group, 167
Climate Neutral Network, 240
Climate Progress, 299–300
Climate Protection Manual for Cities,
    158, 298
Climate Registry, 224
Climate Trust, 141
Clinton, Bill, 93, 106
CO2IMPACT Social Carbon, 245–47
coal, 35–36, 47, 57, 60, 69, 153; U.S.
    production of, 18
coal mines and plants, 21, 45, 46, 59,
    63, 77
Coates, Geoff, 285
Coca-Cola, 224
coffee, 164

Cogbooks, 41

Cohen, Boyd, 245–46

Collins, Jim, 7

Colombia, 233, 245, 246–47

Colorado, 18, 82, 90, 119, 208

Colorado River, 187

Colorado State University Engines and Energy Conversion Lab, 128

Commercial Real Estate Information Company (CoStar), 107

Commission on the Measurement of Economic Performance and Social Progress, 288

communities, 16–17; see also cities

community-supported agriculture (CSA), 209

compost, 195, 208, 210, 213

computers, turning off, 7, 39

ConAgra, 163

concentrated animal-feeding operations (CAFOs); 184–85

construction industry, 103, 252–53, 258–59; see also buildings

Consumer Reports, 184

Conway, Gordon, 180–81

cooling systems, 40, 100, 104, 110, 256

Cooper, Ann, 206

Copenhagen, Denmark, 175

Copenhagen Accord, 44, 241

Copenhagen Summit, see United Nations

Corciencias, 246

Cornell University, 195

corn ethanol, 160, 161, 162, 257

Corporate Knights, 280

Costa Rica, 240, 293

"Cost of Climate Change, The," 256, 258

Council House2, 111–12

"Courage to Develop Clean Energy, The" (Immelt and Lash), 55

courier companies, 136

cows, 183–84, 185, 192, 193, 204

CPS Energy, 81

Crist, Charlie, 17

Cuba, 187–88

Cummins Diesel, 136

Curitiba, Brazil, 171

D-1 Oils PLC, 164

Daggett, Dan, 218–19

Dahle, Øystein, 276–77

dairy and meat production, 182–85, 191, 204, 205

Danish Research Centre for Food and Farming, 190

Dardesheim, Germany, 64–65

Darrieus, Georges Jean Marie, 79

Davis, Doug, 51

Deffeyes, Kenneth, 161

Dehen, Wolfgang, 69

Delaware, 49–50

Deloitte, 4, 75

Del Sur, Calif., 116

Deng Xiaoping, 60

Denmark, 44, 65, 93, 168

Denver Homebuilders, 96

Desertec, 93

Detroit, Mich., 210–11

Deutsche Bank, 89, 90–91

diapers, 163

diesel, 165, 166, 182; biodiesel, 159, 163–64, 166

Diesel, Rudolf, 159

diseases, 178, 203–208; diabetes, 178, 205

Diversey, 8

Doerr, John, 42, 52

Dolphin Head Trust, 261

DONG Energy, 65, 69, 93, 168, 169

Dongtan, China, 120

Dow Jones Industrial Average, 273

Dow Jones Sustainability Index, 26, 281

droughts, 250, 257, 262, 267, 274, 275

Duany, Andres, 171

Duke, Mike, 14

DuPont, 6–7, 22, 25, 229, 237

Dura Vermeer, 258–59

Dutton, John, 9
Dynamotive Energy Systems, 201–202

E+Co, 88
Earth Policy Institute, 181–82
East Timor, 71
eBay, 170
Eberhard, Martin, 133
Eco-Economy: Building an Economy for the Earth (Brown), 276–77
Ecology and Society, 292
Ecomagination, 140, 142, 284, 285
economic crisis of 2008–2009, 3–4, 5, 27, 150, 272, 287, 291
Economics Foundation, 298
Economist, 153–54
Economist Intelligence Unit, 26
EcoSecurities, 237, 242–43
Ecosystem Restoration Associates (ERA), 247
EcoTechnologies Group, 202–203
ecotourism, 261–62
Edmunds, Kevin, 115
E. F. Schumacher Society, 216
Egypt, 216
electricity, 37, 41, 42, 57, 256; average price of, 59; Google and, 33–34; grid parity and, 21, 89; phantom load and, 39–40; from renewable energy sources, 47, 57, 59; smart grids and, 52, 63, 93, 94, 169; smart meters and, 34, 51–53; utilities and, *see* utilities; Walmart and, 34
electric vehicles, 94, 131–32, 134–35, 169; Better Place and, 167–69; charging of, 134–35, 168; hybrid, 62, 94, 131, 132, 133, 135–37
electronics manufacturers, 43
Elite Worldwide, 136
Empire State Building, 101
employment, 17, 18–19, 39, 58, 62–63, 90, 92, 125

Endesa, 229
endocrine disrupters, 204
energy, 298; renewable, *see* renewable energy; waste of, 7–8, 29, 40
Energy, U.S. Department of, 31, 52, 71–72, 76–77, 80, 90, 96, 102, 135, 138, 157, 165, 234
Energy Australia, 94
EnergyAustralia Consortium, 94
Energy Aware, 51
energy companies, 252–53, 256–58
Energy Detective, The (T.E.D.), 34
energy efficiency, 28–56, 57–58; combining renewable energy with, 31, 57, 58; vs. cost of providing new energy, 31; market barriers to, 32; regulation and, 42–44; small businesses and, 39–42; utilities and, 44–51
Energy Efficiency Indicator, 30
Energy Inc., 34
Energy Information Administration (EIA), 50, 95, 151
Energy Intelligent Europe Initiative, 57–58
Energy Policy Information Center, 148
Energy Star, 40, 41, 72, 108
Energy Trust, 16–17, 50
Enernoc, 53
Enhanced Geothermal System (EGS), 76–77
ENMAX, 46–47
Entergy, 197
Envirolution, 119
Environmental Defense Fund, 29, 198
Environmental Law Institute, 278
Environmental Protection Agency (EPA), 44, 99–100, 127, 129, 207, 224, 280; Energy Star program of, 40, 41, 72, 108
Environmental Technologies Fund (ETF), 89
EOS Climate, 88, 244–45
Ernst & Young, 281

eSolar, 67–68
ethanol, 159–62, 257
Europe, 8, 43, 93; agriculture in, 195–96; solar thermal in, 66–67; wind energy in, 69–70
European Climate Exchange, 230
European Commission, 66
European Marine Energy Centre (EMEC), 78
European Renewable Energy Council, 65
European Solar Thermal Industry Federation, 66–67
European Union (EU), 44, 57–58, 140–41, 207, 220, 227, 228–29, 288
European Union Emissions Trading System (EU ETS), 226, 228–29, 242
Exxon, 62, 165, 276

FACT Foundation, 164
Fambro, Steve, 133
farming, see agriculture
Farming Systems Trial, 194
fat, waste, 163–64
Federal Aviation Administration, 140
Federal Energy Regulatory Commission (FERC), 33–34
FedEx, 135–36
Fedrizzi, Rick, 105
feed-in tariffs, 19, 89–92
Feist, Wolfgang, 110
Fernando, Adrian, 242, 243–44
Ferreira Construction, 237–38
fertilizers, 179, 182, 185, 186, 189, 194, 200, 208, 212–15, 270; biofertilizers, 188, 195
Fetterman, John, 116
FIFA World Cup, 236
Figir, Isaac V., 260
Financial Times, 11, 60, 148, 280
Financial Times 500, 10
Finland, 33, 44

Firelake Capital, 88, 244
fires, 267–69, 270, 274
First Light Ventures, 246
Fiskar Automotive, 134
FiT Coalition, 91
Fitoussi, Jean-Paul, 288
Fix, Ryan, 241
Flannery, Tim, 201, 283
Flex Your Power, 189
floods, 9, 250, 253, 259, 265–66, 270, 273, 274–75
Florida, 17, 143, 206, 254
Florida Power and Light (FPL Group), 70, 71
FogQuest, 264–65
food: health problems linked to, 178, 203–208; in restaurants, 209–10; see also agriculture
Food and Agriculture Organization (FAO), 189–90
Food and Drug Administration (FDA), 184–85
Food Policy Research Institute, 190
Ford, Bill, 130
Ford, Henry, 159
Ford, Peter, 61
Ford Motor Company, 7, 43, 126, 127, 130–31, 132, 149, 229, 280
Forest Carbon Group, 247
forest fires, 267–69, 270, 274
forest offsets, 238–42
Forest Stewardship Council (FSC), 268
Forum for the Future, 296
Fossil Free Fuel, 116
fossil fuel sector, 63; jobs in, 18; subsidies given to, 19, 278–79
fossil fuels, 30, 59; agriculture and, 181; see also coal; oil
Foundation Capital, 52, 53
France, 142, 169, 256, 290, 304
Friedman, Milton, 277, 283
Friedman, Thomas, 23–24, 60, 282, 302–303

FTSE Index, 8
fuel-efficient vehicles, 5, 43
Fuller, Buckminster, 290
Futurama, 304
"Future We Want, The," 305

Gainesville Regional Utilities, 91
Galleria Mall, 211
Garalo, 164
garbage, 165
*Gardeners of Eden: Rediscovering
    Our Importance to Nature* (Daggett),
    218
Garrett-Peltier, Heidi, 63
gas, natural, 57, 63, 153
gasoline, 150, 159, 160, 162, 163, 165,
    166, 168, 182; ethanol blended with,
    160; prices of, 148, 149, 297
Gates, Bill, 86
General Electric (GE), 140, 142–43, 277,
    280, 283, 284, 285
General Motors (GM), 5, 62, 126, 127,
    136, 159, 160; Chevrolet, 127, 132,
    134, 149, 162
geoengineering, 252, 269–70
geothermal energy, 59, 75–77
Germany, 19, 23, 64–65, 72, 89–90, 91,
    93, 94, 142; passive houses in, 110
Gingrich, Newt, 305
Give Something Back Office Products, 42
glaciers, 251, 252, 262, 263, 269, 274
Global Canopy Programme, 239
Global Climate Coalition, 279, 280
"Global Green New Deal," 295
Global Humanitarian Forum, 275
Global Insight Automotive Group, 123
Global Reporting Initiative, 280
global warming, *see* climate change
GNH (Gross National Happiness), 289–90
GNP (gross national product),
    287–88, 291
Gold, Eduardo, 269

*Golden Thread, A: 2,500 Years of Solar
    Architecture and Technology* (Butti and
    Perlin), 104
Goldman Sachs, 4, 26, 262
Gold Standard, 233–36, 245, 247
golf courses, 261
GoLoco, 145
Google, 33, 67, 72–73, 77, 133, 238;
    Carbon Mercantile Exchange, 33; in
    electricity business, 33–34; Green
    Carbon Bank, 33; RE<C, 67; 2030
    project of, 73
Gore, Al, 5, 52, 106
Gorlov, Alexander, 79–80
Gorlov Helical Turbine (GHT), 79–80
Gottfried, David, 105
Great Britain, 44, 142, 172, 189, 228, 304
Greece, 273, 274
Greenbuild, 106
Green Building Council Italia, 105
Green Carbon Bank, *see* Google
Greenhouse Friendly, 234
greenhouse gases (GHG), 5, 10, 30, 31,
    33, 36, 37; agriculture and, 179,
    181, 182–83; biofuels and, 159;
    buildings and, 95–96; cap-and-trade
    and, 221, 225–26, 228, 298; carbon
    dioxide, *see* carbon emissions;
    chlorofluorocarbons, 244–45; forest
    fires and, 270; Kyoto Protocol and,
    see Kyoto Protocol; methane, 183,
    192, 231; nitrous oxide, 185, 186;
    transportation and, 124, 129, 135;
    tropical forests and, 239; Walmart
    and, 13, 14
Greenhouse Gas Protocol, 224
Greenland, 274
Green Mountain College, 194
Green New Deal, 62
Greenpeace, 182
Green Revolution, 213–14
Greensburg, Kans., 115–16
"Green Winners," 26

grid parity, 21, 89
grocers, 210
Gross, Bill, 67–68
Gross National Happiness (GNH), 289–90
gross national product (GNP), 287–88, 291
Guardian, 60, 152–53, 264
Guatemala, 268

Haiti, 202, 264, 266, 290
Halo Telepresence, 169–70
Hammerfest Strom AS, 78
Hansen, James, 84, 226, 275–76
Hansen, Mishko, 300–301
Han Seung-soo, 62
Hantz, John, 210–11
Hantz Farms, 210
happiness, 289–90, 293, 301, 302
Happy Planet Index, 289
Hara Software, 224
Harris, Sydney, 279
Harvard Business Review, 27, 281
Harvard University, 106
Hawaii, 169, 203
Hawaiian Mahogany Project, 203
Hay, Lewis, III, 70
Hayes, Randy, 277, 296–97
Head, Peter, 120
health problems, 178, 203–208
heating systems, 100, 110
heat waves, 273, 274
helical turbine, 79–80
Heritage Foundation, 102
Herman-Miller, 101
Hero Arts, 42
Hewlett Packard (HP), 33, 169–70
High Level Group on Competitiveness, Energy and Environment, 43
high-speed rail, 141–43
Himalayas, 274
Hirsch, Robert L., 157

Hirshberg, Gary, 86
Holden, Gary, 47
Holdren, John, 250
Honda, 127
Hong Kong, 114–15, 304
Hornblower Hybrid, 71
Hosaka, Tomoko, 61
Hot, Flat, and Crowded (Friedman), 302–303
housing market, 102–103
Houston, Tex., 81
Howard, Steve, 167
Howe, Dan, 102
HSBC, 60, 168, 220, 304
Hubbert, M. King, 151
Huffington Post, 61
Hu Jintao, 294
hurricanes, 251, 252, 275; Katrina, 253, 258, 260
hydrocarbons, 124
hydropower, 256–58; electric, 59, 78–80; wave, 77–78
Hyundai, 127

Iberdrola, 70, 71, 78
IBM, 94
Iceland, 75–76
Idaho, 48
IdeaLab, 133
IdleAire, 138–39
I-GO, 144
I'm In Control, 52
Immelt, Jeffrey, 42, 55, 283, 284
IMPACT (Investment for Manufacturing Progress and Clean Technology), 63
Inconvenient Truth, An, 5
India, 36–37, 62, 152, 230, 231, 266, 274, 277, 290, 304; agriculture in, 213–16; flooding in, 253; vehicles in, 124
Indian Green Building Council, 105
Indonesia, 239, 240

Industry Taskforce on Peak Oil and
    Energy Security, 154–55
Industry Week, 280
innovation, 3, 7, 8, 21–24, 25, 27, 30, 39,
    301–302; waves of, 21–22, 301
Innovative Water Technologies, 264
insurance, 9, 252–56
Intel, 51, 94, 238
Integrated Bottom Line, 25–26, 54, 286
Integrated Resource Planning, 44
Intelligent Energy–Europe, 66
Intercontinental Exchange, 231
Interface, 220
Intergovernmental Panel on Climate
    Change (IPCC), 266, 275
International Alliance of Research
    Universities, 275
International Biochar Initiative, 200–201
International Energy Agency (IEA), 81,
    152–53, 154, 155, 278–79, 293
International Federation of Organic
    Agriculture Movements, 213
International Federation of Red Cross
    and Red Crescent Societies, 9
International Fund for Agricultural
    Development, 213
International Institute for Environment
    and Development, 274
International Organization for
    Standardization (ISO), 224, 233–34
Intuit, 224
investment, return on, 15–16, 40, 97
Investor Network on Climate Risk, 10, 25
Iogen, 162
Iowa Farm Bureau, 199
Iran, 152
Ireland, 273
"Is Mobility as We Know It
    Sustainable?," 123
Israel, 168
Istanbul, 265
i-Stop, 74
Italiano, Mike, 105

Italy, 142, 273
ITC Limited, 36–39

Jackson, Wes, 217, 218
Jacksonville, Fla., 73–74
Jacobs, Jane, 117
Jacobson, John, 109
Jamaica, 260, 261
Japan, 61–62, 168, 233, 304; subscription
    farming in, 209
jatropha, 164
JEA, 73–74
Jefferson, Thomas, 104, 178
John Deere, 128
Johnson, Christine, 84
Johnson Controls, 30
Johnston, David, 96, 122
Joint Implementation (JI), 226, 236
Jones, Van, 257
Journal of Sustainable Real Estate, 174
JP Morgan, 243
Juwi Solar GmbH, 73–74

Kansas, 217
Kennedy, Robert, 287–88
Kenya, 263
Kerby, Chuck, 12
Kettering, Charles, 159
Khosla, Vinod, 86, 285
Kia, 127
Kimbara, Yoshiro, 130
King, Martin Luther, Jr., 303–304
King County, Wash., 208
Kleiner Perkins Caufield and Byers,
    52, 86
Koch Enterprises, 232
Kohlberg Kravis Roberts & Co. (KKR), 29
Krick, Dave, 209–10
Krugman, Paul, 287
Kuwait, 152
Kuznets, Simon, 287

KwhOURS, Inc., 119–20
Kyoto Protocol, 6, 8, 16, 61, 81, 198, 220, 223, 225–26, 228, 229, 236, 237, 243, 244, 251

Lagod, Martin, 88
LaHood, Ray, 142, 174–75
Land Institute, 217–18
LASER (Local Action for Sustainable Economic Renewal), 158, 298
Lash, Jonathan, 55
Latin America, 179, 213, 275
Lawrence Berkeley National Laboratory, 31
League of American Bicyclists, 175
"Learning to Love Climate Change" (Begley), 250
Leary, Dan, 74
Lecomte, Tristan, 241
LEED (Leadership in Energy and Environmental Design), 96, 105–108, 112, 114, 115, 116, 121
Leinberger, Christopher, 174
Lend Lease, 110–11
Liberty Mutual, 255
lightbulbs, compact fluorescent, 34, 46, 102; replacing incandescent bulbs with, 12, 15, 33, 39; unions and, 32
lighting, 7, 12, 39, 40, 42; in cities, 101–102; leaving lights on, 7; light-emitting diodes (LEDs), 12–13, 101–102, 285; in workplaces, 101
Limits to Growth (Meadows et al.), 291, 292
Living Building Challenge, 121
"Living Planet Report, The," 290
Lloyd, Douglas, 58–59
lobbyists, 299–300
"Location Efficiency and Mortgage Default" (report), 174
Logan, Andrew, 9
Lord of the Rings, The (Tolkien), 306–307

Lovins, Hunter, 79, 111, 244
Low Carbon Accelerator, 88–89
LuciaStoves, 202
Lucid Energy Technologies, 79–80
Lula da Silva, Luiz Inacio, 161, 240
Lunch Lessons: Changing the Way We Feed Our Children (Cooper), 206
Luyuan, 176

Maas, Fred, 116
Maersk, 87
Make It Right Foundation, 258
Maldives, 259–60
Mali, 164
Malthus, Thomas, 291
manufacturing sector, 58, 63–64, 95
Marks, Nic, 289
Masdar City, 120–21
Mason Dixon Farm, 192–93
Massachusetts, 74
Massachusetts Institute of Technology, 268
Mazria, Ed, 15
McCain, John, 305
McDonald's, 163
McGraw-Hill Construction, 103, 105
McGray, Heather, 251
McKibben, Bill, 303
McKinsey & Company, 31–33
McLennan, Jason, 121
McMillion, Charles, 124
Meadows, Donella H., 291, 297
meat and dairy production, 182–85, 191, 204, 205
Melbourne, Australia, 111–12
Mercedes Benz, 131
methane, 183, 192, 231
Mexico, 151–52, 233, 255
MicroEnsure, 255
Micronesia, 260
Microsoft, 132
Middle East, 125, 297

Miller, Gregory, 67, 73
Mi Rancho Tortilla Factory, 42, 284
Mission Motors, 134
MissionPoint Capital Partners, 75
Mitchell, Alyson, 207–208
Mitchell, Andrew, 239
Mitsubishi, 131
Mitsubishi Heavy Industries, 143–44
Monbiot, George, 201
Montana, 21, 232
Montreal Protocol on Substances
  That Deplete the Ozone Layer,
  186, 244
Morphosis Architects, 258
Morris, Jim, 145
motorcycles, 134
Motorola, 229
MSCI, 26
Mubadala, 121
Mulcahy, Nathaniel, 202
Murray, Paul, 101
Musk, Elon, 133

NABERS (National Australian Built
  Environment Rating System), 111
Nasheed, Mohammed, 259, 260
National Academy of Sciences, 31,
  186–87, 269
National Advanced Biofuels
  Consortium, 165
National Alliance for Advanced Biofuels
  and Bioproducts, 165
National Association of Home Builders,
  103, 116
National Association of Insurance
  Commissioners (NAIC), 9, 253
National Association of
  Manufacturers, 175
National Association of Realtors, 125
National Football League, 236
National Petrochemical and Refiners
  Association, 129

National Renewable Energy
  Laboratory, 165
National Research Council, 278
National Resource Conservation Service
  Districts, 198
national security, 19–20, 74
"National Security and the Threat of
  Climate Change," 19–20
"Nation Under Seige, Sea Level Rise at
  Our Doorstep," 117–18
Natural Capitalism (Hawken, Lovins, and
  Lovins), 283, 300
Natural Capitalism, Inc. (NCI),
  41–42, 284
Natural Capitalism Solutions (NCS), 7,
  41, 107, 158, 221, 230, 261, 286
natural disasters, 8–9; insurance and,
  252–56; preparedness and response
  to, 265–69
natural gas, 57, 63, 153
Natural Resources Agency, 251
Natural Resources Defense Council
  (NRDC), 256, 258
Natural Systems Agriculture, 217
Navistar, 137–38
Neighborhood Electric Vehicle (NEV),
  135
Netherlands, 251
New Alchemy Institute, 211
New Buildings Institute (NBI), 106
New Economics Foundation, 289
New Jersey, 83–84, 208
New Mexico, 232
Newsweek, 250, 281
New York, N.Y., 32, 142, 208; buildings
  in, 118; Coney Island, 68; stimulus
  money and, 119
New York State Energy Research and
  Development Authority, 40
New York Times, 23, 282, 288–89, 294
New Zealand, 44, 233
Nexamp, 74
Nextera, 70

Next Sustainability Wave, The (Willard),
    53–55
Nexus, 247
Nickels, Greg, 81
Nike, 220, 280
Nippon Yusen Kaisha, 143–44
Nissan, 127, 131
nitrogen, 185–86
nitrogen oxides, 124
nitrous oxide, 185, 186
Nooyi, Indra, 207
Northrop, Michael, 118
North Sea, 152
Northwest Pipe Company, 80
Norway, 240
Novex Couriers, 136
nuclear power, 46, 59, 60, 84–85, 278
nuclear power plants, 21, 59, 84; closure
    of, 256
Nuride, 145

Oak Investment Partners, 67
Oak Ridge National Laboratory, 31
Obaid, Thoraya Ahmed, 117
Obama, Barack, 179, 204–205, 231, 250,
    292–93
Obama, Michelle, 209
Oberlin College, 98, 101
Obediente, Elizabeth, 245–46
O'Brian, Robyn, 203–204
ocean iron fertilization, 269
Office of Technology Assessment, 31
oil, 57, 59, 60, 63, 124–25, 147–58,
    279, 297; discovery in U.S., 22;
    peak, 150–59, 161, 167; prices of,
    147–52, 160
oil industry subsidies, 125
Omnivore's Dilemma, The (Pollan), 181,
    190
One Block Off the Grid (1BOG), 92
"100 Ideas to Save the Planet," 269
Operation Hope, 191–92

Option of Urbanism, The (Leinberger),
    174
Oregon, 16–17, 50, 232
organic agriculture, 187–91, 194–96, 213,
    215, 257
organic food: benefits of, 207–208;
    market for, 196
Organization for Economic Cooperation
    and Development, 288
Orr, David, 98, 283
Osage Iowa Municipal Utility, 45–46, 47
Oxfam International, 8–9, 263
Oyster, 78
ozone layer, 186, 244–45

PACE (Property Assessed Clean Energy),
    82–83
Pachauri, Rajendra, 274
Pacific Gas and Electric, 15, 48–49
Pacific Northwest Direct Seed
    Association (PNDSA), 197–99
Pacific Northwest National
    Laboratory, 165
packaging, 13, 14, 42
Pakistan, 253, 273, 274
Palm Desert, Calif., 82–83
Palo Alto, Calif., 224
paper and pulp mills, 35–39
paper use, 29
parking, employee, 146
Parr, Doug, 167
Passive Solar Industries Council, 96
Passivhaus, 110
Pawar, Sharad, 214
Peabody Coal, 285
peanut allergy, 204
Pelamis Wave Power, 77
Pemex, 151–52
Pennsylvania, 70–71
People's Grocery, 210
PepsiCo, 182, 207, 224–25, 236
Perlin, John, 104

Persians, 104
pesticides, 178, 179, 187, 194, 204, 212, 213, 214; biopesticides, 188
Peterbilt, 136, 137
Peter G. Peterson Institute for International Economics, 293
Petrobras, 160
Pew Charitable Trust, 62–63
Philips, 34
Piebalgs, Andris, 58
Pike Research, 118
Plan B 4.0 (Brown), 158
"Planetary Boundaries: Exploring the Safe Operating Space for Humanity," 292
Plan Viro, 235
Plater-Zyberk, Elizabeth, 171
PlayPumps International, 264
Point Carbon, 223
Pollan, Michael, 179–80, 181, 184–85, 190, 204–205, 208, 212, 216
polycarbonates, 285
Polyface Farm, 190
Porsche, 130, 131
Porrit, Jonathan, 282, 296
Porter, Michael, 281
Portland, Ore., 16, 142
Portugal, 77, 93, 273
Post Carbon Institute, 157, 298
Powerzoa, 51–52
Press, Jim, 130
PricewaterhouseCoopers, 173
Progressive Investor, 28
Proven Energy, 88–89
PSEG Solar Source, 74
Public Economy Research Institute (PERI), 63
Public Utility Commission, 47
Pure Planet, 241

Qatar, 134
Quality of Life Commission, 288

Quarry Village, Calif., 173
Quebec, Canada, 44, 232

Rabobank America, 134
rail, 141–43, 171, 173, 174
Rainforest Alliance, 268
Raleigh, N.C., 102
"Rattling Supply Chains," 29–30
Readysetgoose, 145
Reagan, Ronald, 96, 299
RE<C, *see* Google
Re:char, 202
REDD (Reducing Emissions from Deforestation and Forest Degradation), 223, 240–41
Red Feather, 209–10
refrigerators, 12–13
Regan, Ed, 91
Regional Greenhouse Gas Initiative (RGGI), 44, 230, 232
regulation, 19, 42–44; stages from resistance to, to innovating, 53–55
ReMax, 40
renewable energy, 11, 22–23, 46, 57–58, 257; biofuels, *see* biofuels; biomass, 59, 61, 64, 94; capital markets for, 85–92; in cities, 80–84; combining energy efficiency with, 31, 57, 58; electricity generation from, 47, 57, 59; geothermal, 59, 75–77; hydropower, 59, 78–80, 256–58; solar power, *see* solar power; subsidies given to, 278; wave power, 77–78; wind power, *see* wind power; worldwide examples of, 59–65
renewable energy credits (RECs), 91, 224–25, 238
"Renewable Energy Demand: A Study of California," 58
Renewable Fuels Association, 129
Renewable Portfolio Standards (RPS), 90–91, 92

Restaurant at the End of the Universe,
   The (Adams), 176–77
restaurants, 209–10
return on investment (ROI), 15–16,
   40, 97
Ricke, Katherine L., 269
Right Livelihood Award, 216
Rio Earth Summit, 225
Ripe, 39–40
risk management, 8–9
Rizhao, China, 66
Robins, Nick, 22
Rodale Institute, 194–95, 216
Romm, Joseph, 283
Roosevelt, Franklin D., 158
Rothman, Michael, 148
Russia, 142, 180, 267, 273, 274

Sacramento, Calif., 46, 47
SafeRide, 145
Salatin family, 190
Salmond, Alex, 77, 78
Samsø Island, 65
Sandalow, David, 23–24
Sandor, Richard, 229
S&P 500, 26
San Francisco, Calif., 17, 44, 142
San Francisco Bay, 71
San Jose, Calif., 224
Sarbanes-Oxley Act, 10, 11
Sarkozy, Nicholas, 288
Saudi Arabia, 151
Savory, Allan, 191–92
Savory Institute, 191
Sawin, Janet, 266
Schallert, Patrick, 109
Scheer, Hermann, 64
Schmidt, Eric, 72–73
schools: food in, 206; sick building
   syndrome in, 100
Schumacher, E. F., 289

Schwarzenegger, Arnold, 68, 251
Scotland, 77–78, 93
Scott, Lee, 12, 13
ScottishPower Renewables, 78
sea levels, 251, 259, 260, 266, 270, 274
Seattle, Wash., 146
Sebastopol, Calif., 16
Securities and Exchange Commission
   (SEC), 10, 44
SEKEM, 216
Sen, Amartya, 288
Sesno, Frank, 150, 151, 157
Severance, Craig, 84
SF Energy Watch, 17
SGS, 242–43
Shah, Jigar, 87
Shandong Penglai Electric Power
   Equipment Manufacturing, 67
Shapiro, Mary, 10
Sharpe, Freddy, 235
Shi Lishan, 60
shipping: UPS and FedEx, 135–36; by
   water, 143–44
"sick building syndrome," 99–100, 102
Siemens, 69, 71, 93, 94, 169
Silver Spring, 52–53
Simmons, Matthew, 151
Sipila, Juha, 33
"Sizing the Climate Economy"
   (Robins), 22
ski industries, 260–61
Skype, 169
skysails, 143
small businesses, 39–42
Small Is Beautiful (Schumacher), 289
smart grids, 52, 63, 93, 94, 169
smart meters, 34, 51–53
Smith, Adam, 300–301
Smith, Alan, 280–81
Smith, Andrew, 138
Smith, Kevin, 221
Smith, Rafael, 266

SMU Geothermal Laboratory, 77
Social Carbon, 233
Socrates, 104
soil, 185–86; biochar and, 199–203; carbon in, 180, 187, 191, 194–96, 196–99
Soil Association, 216
SolarCity, 134
solar power, 21, 23, 46, 59, 61, 91, 92, 93, 257; in China, 60, 66, 294; electric, 71–75; in Germany, 64; in India, 62; leaky buildings and, 96; in New Jersey, 83–84; panel fabrication, 24; passive, 104, 109–10; subsidies given to, 278; thermal, 66–68
solar radiation management, 269–70
Solid Applied Technologies, 265–66
Solix Biofuels, Inc., 167
"Solutions at the Speed of Business," 41–42, 284
Solvatten, 263
Sonoma County, Calif., 82
Sony Electronics, 229
South Africa, 35–36
Southern California Edison (SCE), 21
South Korea, 23, 62, 295
Southwest, Native Americans in, 66, 104
Spain, 70, 142, 273, 274
Speck, Jeff, 171
Spellman, James, 180
Speth, James Gustave, 283
Spratt, David, 283
states, 17–20, 44
Steiner, Achim, 296
Stern, Nicholas, 55, 263, 292–93, 296
Stern Review on the Economics of Climate Change, The, 55, 263
Stiglitz, Joseph, 277, 288–89, 292–93, 298
stimulus money, 118–19
STMicroelectronics, 7, 25, 220, 229
Stockholm Resilience Center, 292
stock values, 4, 6, 14

stores, 101
strawberries, 204
Styrofoam, 285
Subaru, 127
Suburban Nation: The Rise of Sprawl and the Decline of the American Dream (Duany, Plater-Zyberk, and Speck), 171
sugarcane, 160–61
sulfur emissions, 227–28, 298
SunEdison, 87
Sunspring Water Purification System, 264
SuperTruck, 138
sustainability imperative, 4, 273
Sustainable Facilities Management Conference, 110
Sutton, Philip, 283
Sweden, 44
Swiss Re, 9
Switzerland, 189

Taleb, Nessim, 272
Tanaka, Nobuo, 81
Tarpennin, Marc, 133
taxes, 226–27
Tellus Institute, 31
Tennessee Valley Authority (TVA), 256
terrorism and national security, 19–20, 74
Tesco, 104
Tesla Motors, 133–34, 134
Tesoro Corporation, 232
Texas, 81
Texas Transportation Institute, 124, 175
Theory of Moral Sentiments, The (Smith), 300–301
Thettayil, Peter, 231
Thinking in Systems: A Primer (Meadows), 297
Thinley, Jigme, 290

30 The Bond, 110–11
Thomas Mott Homestead Bed and
    Breakfast, 108–109
Tianjin, China, 230
Time, 281
Times World Forum on Enterprise and
    the Environment, 259
T. K. Chemical Complex Ltd., 36
TK Ranch, 190–91
Tobis, Michael, 267, 271
Todd, John, 211
Todd, Nancy Jack, 211
Tokyo, Japan, 141–42
Tolkien, J.R.R., 306–307
tourism, 252–53, 259–62; ecotourism,
    261–62
Toyoda, Akio, 126
Toyoda, Eiji, 130
Toyota, 5, 43, 72, 126, 127, 130
Transition Towns, 157–58, 298
transportation, 95, 123–46, 155, 170–77;
    air travel, 123, 139–41; automobiles,
    see automobiles; bicycles, 175–76;
    buses, 74, 171–72, 174; electric cars,
    94, 131–32, 134–35; fuel efficiency
    and, 5, 126, 129, 135, 149, 158;
    greenhouse gas emissions from, 124,
    129, 135; hybrid vehicles, 62, 94, 131,
    132, 133, 135–37; oil and, *see* oil;
    public, 125, 142, 155, 174; ships,
    143–44; rail, 141–43, 171, 173, 174;
    trucks, *see* trucks; virtual, 169–70
Transportation Department, 175
TreeHugger, 234
Tricorona, 263
Tropicana, 182
trucks, 12, 127, 135–39, 149; hybrid,
    135–37; IdleAire and, 138–39;
    long-haul, 136, 138; number of, 123
Turkey, 265
turkeys, 163
Twilight in the Desert (Simmons), 151
Tyson Foods, 163

Uber Shelter, 266–67
*Unhealthy Truth, The: How Our Food Is
    Making Us Sick and What We Can Do
    About It* (O'Brian), 203–204
Union of Concerned Scientists, 179
unions, 32
United Kingdom, 23
United Nations, 5, 65, 71, 117, 183, 202,
    233; Clean Development Mechanism
    (CDM), 222, 226, 234, 235, 236, 241,
    242, 243; Climate Change Conference
    (Copenhagen Summit), 65, 80, 162,
    223, 240–41, 242, 276, 299, 303;
    Development Programme, 275;
    Earth Summit, 35; Environment
    Programme, 240, 295, 296; Food and
    Agriculture Organization (FAO), 215,
    240; Framework Convention on
    Climate Change, 241–42, 276; Global
    Compact, 41; Green Economy summit
    scheduled by, 296; Intergovernmental
    Panel on Climate Change (IPCC), 182,
    274; Third Global Biodiversity
    Outlook, 286
United Nations Foundation, 180
United Nations University, 255
United Parcel Service (UPS), 135
University of California–Berkeley,
    58, 92
University of California–Davis, 189,
    194, 207, 216
University of California Cooperative
    Extension, 185
University of Maryland, 190
University of Michigan, 189
University of Minnesota,
    161–62
Unreasonable Institute, 266
Ura, Dasho Karma, 290
Urban Land Institute, 173, 208
Urgent Couriers, 136
U.S. Biochar Initiative, 200–201
U.S. Chamber of Commerce, 279, 280

U.S. Climate Change Adaptation Industry, 252
U.S. Conference of Mayors Climate Protection Agreement, 81
U.S. Green Building Council (USGBC), 100, 105–107, 121–22
U.S. National Research Council, 212
Utah, 232
utilities, 44–51, 59, 63, 256; auctions and, 49; decoupling and, 48; feed-in tariffs and, 19, 89–91, 92; inverted rates and, 48; smart meters and, 34, 51–53

Valero Energy Corporation, 232
Van Dyne, Ed, 128
Vatican, 238
Vauban, Germany, 172–73, 176
Venezuela, 256–58
Venter, Craig, 165
venture capital funds, 86–89
Vermont, 193
Vietnam, 304
Village as Solar Ecology (Todd and Todd), 211
Vilsack, Tom, 181
Virgin Airlines, 166–67
Volkswagen, 5, 127–28
Voltaix, 75, 237–38
Voltree Power, 268
Voluntary Carbon Standard (VCS), 233, 234, 242, 245

Wallach, Daniel, 115
Wallin, Jeff, 203
Wall Street Journal, 9, 45, 103, 292
Walmart, 4–5, 12–14, 29, 30, 62, 102, 210, 225, 234, 283, 284, 285; green building and, 15; suppliers of, 11, 13, 14, 15; Texas Retail Energy created by, 34; trucks of, 136–37, 138

Walton, Rob, 283
Wang Jinnan, 60
Washington (state), 232
Washington, D.C., 142
Washington, George, 178
Washington Post, 9
water power, 256–58; electric, 49, 78–80; wave, 77–78
Waters, Alice, 206
water supplies, 252, 262–65, 274, 298
wave power, 77–78
Waybright, Richard, 192, 193
Way to Go Seattle, 146
Wealth of Nations, The (Smith), 300, 302
weatherization, 40, 119
Weathermakers, The (Flannery), 201
Webster, Jeff, 163
Weinhold, Michael, 93–94
Welch, Jack, 277, 283
West Coast Green, 51
Western Climate Initiative, 232
West Virginia, 77
"We Were Warned: Out of Gas," 150
White, Bill, 81
White, Jonathan, 183–84
Whole Foods, 220
wildfires, 267–69, 270, 274
Willard, Bob, 53–55
Willson, Bryan, 167
wind power, 20–21, 23, 29, 46, 59, 65, 68–71, 84, 90, 93–94, 257; in China, 60, 294; in Germany, 64–65; subsidies given to, 278
Winter Olympics, 260
W. K. Kellogg Foundation, 185
Wolcott Eco Office, 109
Wold, Per-Otto, 223
Woodward Governor Company, 128
woody waste, 165
Woolsey, R. James, 19
workplaces, 100–101
World Agricultural Forum, 180
World Bank, 60, 114, 221, 269

World Business Council for Sustainable Development (WBCSD), 35–36, 41, 114, 224
World Carfree Network, 173
World Economic Forum, 168, 280
World Future Council, 277
World Health Organization, 99, 204
World Renewable Energy Congress, 77
World Resources Institute, 29, 50, 224, 230, 251
WorldStove, 202
World War II, 158–59, 165, 212
Worldwide Shelters, 266

World Wildlife Fund (WWF), 236, 265, 267

Yemen, 265
Yokohama, Japan, 61
Yu Quin, 61

ZEDfactory, 112–13
Zimride, 145
Zipcar, 144, 145
Zurich, 255